Seeing Wittgenstein Anew

Edited by

WILLIAM DAY
Le Moyne College

VICTOR J. KREBS
Pontificia Universidad Católica del Perú

CAMBRIDGE
UNIVERSITY PRESS

CAMBRIDGE UNIVERSITY PRESS
Cambridge, New York, Melbourne, Madrid, Cape Town, Singapore,
São Paulo, Delhi, Dubai, Tokyo

Cambridge University Press
32 Avenue of the Americas, New York, NY 10013–2473, USA

www.cambridge.org
Information on this title: www.cambridge.org/9780521547321

First published 2010

Printed in the United States of America

A catalog record for this publication is available from the British Library.

Library of Congress Cataloging in Publication data
   Seeing Wittgenstein anew / edited by William Day, Victor J. Krebs.
     p.   cm.
   Includes bibliographical references (p.) and index.
   ISBN 978-0-521-83843-6 (hardback) – ISBN 978-0-521-54732-1 (pbk.)
   1. Wittgenstein, Ludwig, 1889–1951. Philosophische
   Untersuchungen.   2. Perception (Philosophy)   I. Day, William,
   1954–   II. Krebs, Victor J., 1957–   III. Title.
   B3376.W563P53274 2009
   192–dc22   2009016985

ISBN 978-0-521-83843-6 Hardback
ISBN 978-0-521-54732-1 Paperback

Contents

List of Contributors   *page* vii

Acknowledgments   xiii

Abbreviations of Wittgenstein's Works   xv

Introduction: Seeing Aspects in Wittgenstein   1
   William Day and Victor J. Krebs

I ASPECTS OF "SEEING-AS"

1   **Aesthetic Analogies**   23
    Norton Batkin

2   **Aspects, Sense, and Perception**   40
    Sandra Laugier

3   **An Allegory of Affinities: On Seeing a World of Aspects
    in a Universe of Things**   61
    Timothy Gould

4   **The Touch of Words**   81
    Stanley Cavell

II ASPECTS AND THE SELF

II.1 Self-Knowledge

5   **In a New Light: Wittgenstein, Aspect-Perception, and
    Retrospective Change in Self-Understanding**   101
    Garry L. Hagberg

6   **The Bodily Root: Seeing Aspects and Inner Experience**   120
    Victor J. Krebs

II.2 Problems of Mind

7   (Ef)facing the Soul: Wittgenstein and Materialism   143
    David R. Cerbone

8   Wittgenstein on Aspect-Seeing, the Nature of Discursive
    Consciousness, and the Experience of Agency   162
    Richard Eldridge

III ASPECTS AND LANGUAGE

9   The Philosophical Significance of Meaning-Blindness   183
    Edward Minar

10 Wanting to Say Something: Aspect-Blindness
    and Language   204
    William Day

IV ASPECTS AND METHOD

IV.1 Therapy

11 On Learning from Wittgenstein, or What Does It Take
    to *See* the Grammar of Seeing Aspects?   227
    Avner Baz

12 The Work of Wittgenstein's Words: A Reply to Baz   249
    Stephen Mulhall

13 On the Difficulty of Seeing Aspects and the "Therapeutic"
    Reading of Wittgenstein   268
    Steven G. Affeldt

IV.2 Seeing Connections

14 Overviews: What Are They of and What Are They For?   291
    Frank Cioffi

15 On Being Surprised: Wittgenstein on Aspect-Perception,
    Logic, and Mathematics   314
    Juliet Floyd

16 The Enormous Danger   338
    Gordon C. F. Bearn

Appendix: A Page Concordance for Unnumbered Remarks in
    Philosophical Investigations   357
    William Day

List of Works Cited   373
Index   385

Contributors

Steven G. Affeldt is Assistant Professor in the Program of Liberal Studies at the University of Notre Dame. He works in moral and political philosophy, American philosophy, nineteenth- and twentieth-century Continental philosophy, and Wittgenstein. His publications include "The Ground of Mutuality: Criteria, Judgment, and Intelligibility in Stephen Mulhall and Stanley Cavell" (*European Journal of Philosophy*); "Captivating Pictures and Liberating Language: Freedom as the Achievement of Speech in Wittgenstein's *Philosophical Investigations*" (*Philosophical Topics*); and (forthcoming) "The Normativity of the Natural" (*Skepticism in Context*, ed. James Conant and Andrea Kern).

Norton Batkin is Dean of Graduate Studies and Associate Professor of Philosophy and Art History at Bard College. He was the first director of Bard's Center for Curatorial Studies and Art in Contemporary Culture, and he directed its graduate program in curatorial studies from 1994 until 2008. He has written on photography, aesthetics, and Wittgenstein and is the author of *Photography and Philosophy* (1990).

Avner Baz is Assistant Professor of Philosophy at Tufts University. He has written on ethics, aesthetics, epistemology (perception), Kant, and Wittgenstein. His publications include "What's the Point of Seeing Aspects?" (*Philosophical Investigations*); "The Reaches of Words" (*International Journal of Philosophical Studies*);

and (forthcoming) "Seeing Aspects and Philosophical Difficulty" (*The Oxford Handbook of Wittgenstein*, ed. Marie McGinn and Oskari Kuusela). His forthcoming book from Harvard University Press is titled *When Words Are Called For.*

Gordon C. F. Bearn is Professor of Philosophy at Lehigh University. He has written articles on Nietzsche, Wittgenstein, Cavell, Derrida, and Deleuze. He is the author of *Waking to Wonder: Wittgenstein's Existential Investigations* (1997). He is currently revising the manuscript of a book to be called *Life Drawing: An Aesthetics of Existence.*

Stanley Cavell is Walter M. Cabot Professor of Aesthetics and the General Theory of Value, Emeritus, at Harvard University. He has published widely on topics and crosscurrents in Wittgenstein and Austin, Emerson and Thoreau, music and opera, Shakespeare, film, psychoanalysis, and autobiography. His writings on Wittgenstein are included in *Must We Mean What We Say?* (1969, updated edition 2002), *The Claim of Reason* (1979), *This New Yet Unapproachable America* (1989), *Conditions Handsome and Unhandsome* (1990), *Philosophical Passages* (1995), and *Philosophy the Day After Tomorrow* (2005). He is a recipient of a MacArthur Fellowship and is Past President of the American Philosophical Association.

David R. Cerbone is Professor of Philosophy at West Virginia University. He is the author of *Understanding Phenomenology* (2006) and *Heidegger: A Guide for the Perplexed* (2008). His other publications include "How to Do Things with Wood: Wittgenstein, Frege, and the Problem of Illogical Thought" (*The New Wittgenstein*, ed. Alice Crary and Rupert Read); "The Limits of Conservatism: Wittgenstein on 'Our Life' and 'Our Concepts'" (*The Grammar of Politics: Wittgenstein and Political Philosophy*, ed. Cressida Heyes); and (forthcoming) "Wittgenstein and Idealism" (*The Oxford Handbook of Wittgenstein*, ed. Marie McGinn and Oskari Kuusela).

Frank Cioffi is Research Professor of Philosophy at the University of Kent. He began academic life as a social psychologist and has taught at the Universities of Singapore, Berkeley, and Essex. His papers are collected in *Freud and the Question of Pseudoscience* (1998) and *Wittgenstein on Freud and Frazer* (1998). His recently published papers include "The Evasiveness of Freudian Apologetic" (*Who Owns Psychoanalysis?*, ed. Ann Casement); "Wittgenstein and the

Riddle of Life" (*The Third Wittgenstein*, ed. Danièle Moyal-Sharrock); and "Wittgenstein on 'the Sort of Explanation One Longs for'" (*Perspicuous Presentations*, ed. Danièle Moyal- Sharrock).

William Day is Associate Professor of Philosophy at Le Moyne College. He writes on aesthetics and moral perfectionist thought, with a particular focus on the work of Wittgenstein, Cavell, Emerson, and Confucian thinkers. His publications include "*Moonstruck*, or How to Ruin Everything" (*Ordinary Language Criticism: Literary Thinking after Cavell after Wittgenstein*, ed. Walter Jost and Kenneth Dauber); "Knowing as Instancing: Jazz Improvisation and Moral Perfectionism" (*Journal of Aesthetics and Art Criticism*); and "Jazz Improvisation, the Body, and the Ordinary" (*Tidskrift för kulturstudier/Journal of Cultural Studies*).

Richard Eldridge is Charles and Harriett Cox McDowell Professor of Philosophy at Swarthmore College. He has held visiting appointments at Stanford University, Universität Bremen, and the University of Essex. He is the author of *On Moral Personhood: Philosophy, Literature, Criticism, and Self-Understanding* (1989); *Leading a Human Life: Wittgenstein, Intentionality, and Romanticism* (1997); *The Persistence of Romanticism* (2001); *An Introduction to the Philosophy of Art* (2003); and *Literature, Life, and Modernity* (2008).

Juliet Floyd is Professor of Philosophy at Boston University. She has received fellowships from the American Council of Learned Societies, the Dibner Institute for the History of Science and Technology, M.I.T., the American Philosophical Society, and the American Academy in Berlin. Her areas of research focus on the history of analytic philosophy and the philosophies of logic, language, and mathematics. She has written extensively on Wittgenstein, Kant, Gödel, and Quine. She is co-editor (with Sanford Shieh) of *Future Pasts: The Analytic Tradition in Twentieth-Century Philosophy* (2001).

Timothy Gould is Professor of Philosophy at Metropolitan State College of Denver. He has written numerous articles on Kant's aesthetics, Emerson, Thoreau, Nietzsche, Romanticism, and Wittgenstein; and he is the author of *Hearing Things: Voice and Method in the Writing of Stanley Cavell* (1998). He is completing a manuscript entitled *The Names of Action: In Austin, Wittgenstein, Cavell, Emerson,*

Marx and Nietzsche. He has also been writing a series of essays, tentatively titled *Saving the Story*, on narrative in comedy, history, movies, trauma, and autobiography.

Garry L. Hagberg holds a Chair in the School of Philosophy at the University of East Anglia and is the James H. Ottaway Professor of Philosophy and Aesthetics at Bard College. He has written extensively at the intersection of aesthetics and the philosophy of language. He is the author of *Meaning and Interpretation: Wittgenstein, Henry James, and Literary Knowledge* (1994); *Art as Language: Wittgenstein, Meaning, and Aesthetic Theory* (1995); and *Describing Ourselves: Wittgenstein and Autobiographical Consciousness* (2008).

Victor J. Krebs is Associate Professor of Philosophy at the Pontificia Universidad Católica del Perú. He works on Wittgenstein, Cavell, language, aesthetics, and depth psychology. He is the author of *Del Alma y el Arte: Reflexiones en torno a la cultura, la imagen y la memoria* (1997); *La recuperación del sentido: Wittgenstein, la filosofía y lo trascendente* (2008); and *El impulso pigmaliónico: ensayos en torno a un complejo filosófico* (forthcoming). Publications in English include "The Subtle Body of Language and the Lost Sense of Philosophy" (*Philosophical Investigations*) and "'Around the Axis of Our Real Need': The Ethical Point of Wittgenstein's Philosophy" (*European Journal of Philosophy*).

Sandra Laugier is Professor of Philosophy at the Université de Picardie Jules Verne (Amiens) and a member of the Institut Universitaire de France. She specializes in ordinary language philosophy, contemporary American philosophy, and moral philosophy. Her books include *L'anthropologie logique de Quine* (1992); *Recommencer la philosophie* (1999); *Du réel à l'ordinaire* (1999); *Wittgenstein, Métaphysique et jeu de langage* (2001); *Une autre pensée politique américaine* (2004); and *Ethique, littérature, vie humaine* (2006).

Edward Minar is Associate Professor of Philosophy at the University of Arkansas. He has written extensively on Wittgenstein and Heidegger, and he is currently working on Wittgensteinian responses to different forms of skepticism and on animal minds. His publications include "Wittgenstein's Response to Skepticism in *On Certainty*" (*Readings of Wittgenstein's* On Certainty, ed. William Brenner and Danièle Moyal-Sharrock); "Living with the Problem of the Other" (*Wittgenstein and Scepticism*, ed. Denis McManus); and "Heidegger's Response to Skepticism in *Being and Time*" (*Future Pasts*, ed. Juliet Floyd and Sanford Shieh).

Stephen Mulhall is Fellow and Tutor in Philosophy, New College, Oxford. He is the author of *On Being in the World: Wittgenstein and Heidegger on Seeing Aspects* (1990); *Stanley Cavell: Philosophy's Recounting of the Ordinary* (1994); *Heidegger and* Being and Time (1996); *Inheritance and Originality: Wittgenstein, Heidegger, Kierkegaard* (2001); *Wittgenstein's Private Language: Grammar, Nonsense, and Imagination in* Philosophical Investigations, §§*243–315* (2006); *The Conversation of Humanity* (2007); *On Film: Second Edition* (2008); and *The Wounded Animal: J. M. Coetzee and the Difficulty of Reality in Literature and Philosophy* (2009).

Acknowledgments

The editors wish to thank the Research and Development Committee at Le Moyne College for its generous support of this project; Wiley-Blackwell for permission to quote extensively from *Philosophical Investigations*; the British Film Institute for allowing us to reproduce a still from Derek Jarman's 1993 film *Wittgenstein* as our cover image; and Hopeton Smalling for capturing this image from an old video-tape cassette.

We are grateful for the sustained and supportive advice of our editor at Cambridge University Press, Ms. Beatrice Rehl.

Most especially, our thanks go to the contributors to this volume for their patience during and beyond the editing process and for the privilege of making available for the first time their original work on what is still a conspicuous blind spot in Wittgensteinian studies.

Abbreviations of Wittgenstein's Works

BB	*The Blue and Brown Books*
BT	*The Big Typescript*
CM	*The Collected Manuscripts of Ludwig Wittgenstein on Facsimile CD-ROM*
CV	*Culture and Value*
CVR	*Culture and Value: Revised Edition*
DB	*Denkbewegungen: Tagebücher 1930–1932, 1936–1937*
L3032	*Wittgenstein's Lectures, Cambridge, 1930–1932*
L3235	*Wittgenstein's Lectures, Cambridge, 1932–1935*
LC	*Lectures and Conversations on Aesthetics, Psychology and Religious Belief*
LFM	*Wittgenstein's Lectures on the Foundations of Mathematics, Cambridge, 1939*
*LW*I	*Last Writings on the Philosophy of Psychology*, vol. 1
*LW*II	*Last Writings on the Philosophy of Psychology*, vol. 2. References to remarks are given by page number followed by a letter indicating the position of the remark on that page – for example, "12c" for the third remark on page 12, "12d" for the fourth remark, etc.
NB	*Notebooks 1914–1916*
OC	*On Certainty*
PG	*Philosophical Grammar*

PI   *Philosophical Investigations,* 2d ed. References to remarks in Part II are given by page number followed by a letter indicating the position of the remark on that page – for example, "193a" for the first remark on page 193, "193b" for the second remark, etc. References to whole sections within Part II are indicated by Roman numerals – for example, "II.xi" for Part II, Section 11, etc.

PO   *Philosophical Occasions*

PR   *Philosophical Remarks*

RC   *Remarks on Colour*

RFM   *Remarks on the Foundations of Mathematics*

*RPP*I   *Remarks on the Philosophy of Psychology,* vol. 1

*RPP*II *Remarks on the Philosophy of Psychology,* vol. 2

TLP   *Tractatus Logico-Philosophicus*

WWK   *Wittgenstein and the Vienna Circle*

Z   *Zettel*

Seeing Wittgenstein Anew

Introduction

Seeing Aspects in Wittgenstein

William Day and Victor J. Krebs

To see and describe aspects in Wittgenstein (aspects of insight, of perspicuity, of profundity, etc.) is what any discussion of his writings, and in particular of the enigmatic *Philosophical Investigations*, attempts to do. It would be a cute pun, but a sad excuse for a book, if this volume of new essays offered simply the promise of "seeing" and describing "aspects" in Wittgenstein's discussion of aspect-seeing. Having invited and then discussed the essays in the present volume with our contributors over a handful of years, we find that they offer more than that simple promise. At a minimum, they bring out a range of connections between Parts I and II of the *Investigations* that should interest Wittgensteinian scholars whose central concerns would otherwise seem untouched by the discussions of aspect-seeing in the *Investigations* and elsewhere. More than occasionally these essays open up novel paths across familiar fields of thought to anyone for whom, for example, the objectivity of interpretation, the fixity of the past, the acquisition of language, or the nature of human consciousness remain live issues. But a recurring discovery in the chapters that follow is that there is something to be found in his remarks on aspect-seeing that is crucial to, yet all but overlooked in, the reception of the later Wittgenstein. And since the fate of the reception of the later Wittgenstein remains tied to one's reading of the *Investigations*, however broadened by the publication of subsequent volumes of his later writings, it matters that these essays also have something to contribute to that perennial, and perhaps most pressing, question in understanding the later Wittgenstein: What does it mean to *read* the text called *Philosophical Investigations?*

1. WHY SEEING ASPECTS NOW?

In 1989, in an essay entitled "Declining Decline: Wittgenstein as a Philosopher of Culture," Stanley Cavell wrote: "Even when the acceptance of Wittgenstein as one of the major philosophical voices in the West since Kant may be taken for granted, it is apt to be controversial to find that his reception by professional philosophy is insufficient, that the spiritual fervor or seriousness of his writing is internal to his teaching, say the manner (or method) to the substance, and that something in the very professionalization of philosophy debars professional philosophers from taking his seriousness seriously."[1] He thus recorded his sense of the general situation in the secondary literature on Wittgenstein at the end of the 1980s, and it proved to be a fateful pronouncement.

The following decade marked a noticeable change in the spirit of Wittgenstein's reception, which started to open up a series of issues previously excised from the familiar focus of attention. A telling instance of this is the volume of scattered remarks from Wittgenstein's personal journals that appeared as *Culture and Value*. First published as *Vermischte Bemerkungen* in 1977, it was revised against the editor's original judgment that they "do not belong directly with his philosophical works" (*CV* Preface), because, as the editor admitted reticently seventeen years later, that judgment "might appear controversial to some" (*CVR* xiie). It is in this changing spirit that the 1990s witnessed a significant proliferation of books and a renewed vitality in Wittgenstein scholarship.

Ray Monk's biography of Wittgenstein,[2] published in 1990, was the first in a line of books from that decade that set a new tone in the literature surrounding his work. It took on the task of bringing together the philosopher's life with his philosophical concerns, and thus broke with an implicit (and sometimes not so implicit) resistance

[1] Stanley Cavell, "Declining Decline: Wittgenstein as a Philosopher of Culture," in *This New Yet Unapproachable America: Lectures after Emerson after Wittgenstein* (Albuquerque, N.M.: Living Batch Press, 1989), 30.
[2] Ray Monk, *Ludwig Wittgenstein: The Duty of Genius* (New York: Free Press, 1990).

to addressing the kinds of issues Wittgenstein's own texts seem to demand. The consequence of this decision was that many of the central philosophical themes in the literature came under reassessment. Language-games, family resemblances, the possibility of a private language, and other loci in the text that until then had been considered discrete topics were supplemented in Monk's work by the significance of such features as "seeing connections" (*PI*§122), "the morphological method" inherited from Goethe, and the battle of "soul and heart" against the speculative mind of science. Monk's account made possible a reshuffling of priorities in assessments of the Wittgensteinian corpus that found echo in many books published during the years that followed. Stephen Mulhall's *On Being in the World*,[3] published that same year, established significant connections between Wittgenstein and the Continental tradition that were explored further in books that appeared during the next several years. Gordon Bearn's *Waking to Wonder* (1997)[4] examined the connections between Wittgenstein and Nietzsche, and Richard Eldridge's *Leading a Human Life* (1997)[5] developed the continuities between Wittgensteinian and Romantic themes. Other authors contributed to this change of tide by exploring new areas of Wittgenstein's thought: Frank Cioffi and Louis Sass explored connections with psychoanalytical issues,[6] Garry Hagberg with issues in art and aesthetics,[7] and Paul Johnston with issues in morality.[8] A propitious space was thus opened during the 1990s for a reevaluation of Wittgenstein's thought and of his conception of philosophy.

The first decade of the twenty-first century has seen a proliferation of edited volumes advancing this reevaluation of Wittgenstein's concerns and methods in the face of the growing availability of, and attention to, his *Nachlass*. And so it can seem that "the spiritual fervor

---

[3] Stephen Mulhall, *On Being in the World: Wittgenstein and Heidegger on Seeing Aspects* (London: Routledge, 1990).
[4] Gordon C. F. Bearn, *Waking to Wonder: Wittgenstein's Existential Investigations* (Albany, N.Y.: State University of New York Press, 1997).
[5] Richard Eldridge, *Leading a Human Life: Wittgenstein, Intentionality, and Romanticism* (Chicago: University of Chicago Press, 1997).
[6] See Frank Cioffi, *Wittgenstein on Freud and Frazer* (Cambridge: Cambridge University Press, 1998) and Louis A. Sass, *The Paradoxes of Delusion: Wittgenstein, Schreber, and the Schizophrenic Mind* (Ithaca, N.Y.: Cornell University Press, 1994).
[7] See Garry Hagberg, *Art As Language: Wittgenstein, Meaning, and Aesthetic Theory* (Ithaca, N.Y.: Cornell University Press, 1995).
[8] See Paul Johnston, *Wittgenstein: Rethinking the Inner* (London: Routledge, 1993).

or seriousness of his writing" has begun to find a critical mass of interpreters. The contributors to *Wittgenstein: Biography and Philosophy* (2001)[9] argue for the unusual, if not singular, significance of this philosopher's life (and way of life) to his philosophy. *Wittgenstein, Aesthetics and Philosophy* (2004)[10] and *The Literary Wittgenstein* (2004)[11] focus on Wittgenstein's writings and lectures on aesthetic matters, and develop readings of their significance for his philosophical outlook and writerly concerns. And *The Third Wittgenstein* (2004)[12] devotes itself to Wittgenstein's last writings – those contemporaneous with Part II of the *Investigations* – in which concepts like "experiencing meaning" and "patterns of life" take on the importance that "following a rule" and "family resemblance" had in earlier remarks.

The present volume takes this changed understanding of Wittgenstein's work as its starting point and seeks to draw renewed attention to what is, in its sustained development and wealth of instances, already a central notion for Wittgenstein in the later texts, a notion which should contribute to a more coherent picture of his thinking than it has been credited with doing. The cumulative claim of the essays assembled here is that awareness of the importance of seeing aspects to Wittgenstein's thought clarifies, and in many respects transfigures, our understanding of that thought.

2. THE IMPORTANCE OF SEEING ASPECTS

While the *locus classicus* for Wittgenstein's aspect-seeing remarks is the longest section (Section 11) of Part II of the *Investigations*, other (and mostly earlier) remarks on aspect-seeing appear in *Zettel*,[13] in the two volumes published as *Remarks on the Philosophy of Psychology*,[14] and in the two volumes published as *Last Writings*.[15] Related

---

9   *Wittgenstein: Biography and Philosophy*, ed. James C. Klagge (Cambridge: Cambridge University Press, 2001).
10 *Wittgenstein, Aesthetics and Philosophy*, ed. Peter B. Lewis (Aldershot: Ashgate, 2004).
11 *The Literary Wittgenstein*, ed. John Gibson and Wolfgang Huemer (New York: Routledge, 2004).
12 *The Third Wittgenstein: The Post-Investigations Works*, ed. Danièle Moyal-Sharrock (Aldershot: Ashgate, 2004).
13 See, for instance, Z §§155–225.
14 See, for instance, *RPP* I §§411–436, 505–546, 860–890, 952–1137; *RPP* II §§355–391, 435–497, 506–557.
15 See, for instance, *LW* I §§146–180, 429–613, 622–812; *LW* II 12c–19e.

remarks can also be found in *The Blue and Brown Books, Remarks on the Foundations of Mathematics, Remarks on Colour, On Certainty,* and *Culture and Value.* One could argue further that the role of the concept of a picture in the early Wittgenstein – what came to be known as his Picture Theory of Meaning – anticipates his later concern with seeing aspects. If this is right, then the circle of relevant remarks expands to encompass nearly all of his writings. Indeed, according to the so-called "New Reading" of the *Tractatus,*[16] the attempt to bring the impulse to philosophize into vision-altering reflection on its own tendencies – a clear goal of the later method – is already present in this early work. The implication is that Wittgenstein's later attention to the "hugely many interrelated phenomena and possible concepts" (*PI* 199d) of seeing aspects is merely the explicit articulation of one of his central and persistent philosophical concerns. In any case, it is a mistake to imagine that the remarks on aspect-seeing are a mere diversion, a sidestreet detour in the "long and involved journeyings" (*PI* Preface) of the *Investigations.* They are, rather, the expression of a theme whose figures and turns we might have been hearing, however faintly, all along.

One way to hear this more clearly is to take note of a common feature of Wittgenstein's method of exposition: he introduces what one might think of as his "theoretical position" only *after* the reader has had to work through exercises that give her the relevant practical experience to ground his theoretical claims. This is nowhere more true than with the *Investigations,* where we are told nothing about his conception of the nature of philosophy until we are well into the first fifty pages. Saul Kripke may have been observing an instance of this approach when he claimed that the so-called "private language argument" articulated in *PI* §243 had already been introduced and elaborated in the previous several dozen sections of the book.[17] The same strategy determines the placement of the discussion of aspect-seeing: Wittgenstein introduces it explicitly only in the later set of remarks that was to become Part II of the *Investigations,* where it takes

---

[16] For a summary of the relevant actors in and features of the New Reading, see Victor J. Krebs, "'Around the Axis of our Real Need': On the Ethical Point of Wittgenstein's Philosophy," *European Journal of Philosophy* 9, no. 3 (December 2001): 344–74.

[17] See Saul Kripke, *Wittgenstein on Rules and Private Language: An Elementary Exposition* (Cambridge: Harvard University Press, 1982), 2–3.

on the role of providing theoretical articulation to what the book has, in practice, been dedicated to from the very beginning.[18] Just as we begin to see how to read the *Tractatus Logico-Philosophicus* when we arrive at its closing sentences, we will be in a better position to grasp what is at stake in Wittgenstein's later thought as a whole if we read the *Investigations* in light of its closing preoccupation with aspect-seeing.

Consider in this regard the following moments early on in the *Investigations* where the trick, or the stumbling block, of Wittgenstein's new method lies precisely in the appeal to look at (or weigh or consider), not a new *x*, but a given *x* in a new way:

1. After introducing a language "meant to serve for communication between a builder A and an assistant B" consisting in the four words "block," "pillar," "slab," and "beam," Wittgenstein issues the instruction, "Conceive this as [cf. "See this as"] a complete primitive language" (*PI* §2).

2. The reader is asked to imagine someone falsely interpreting a script in which letters are employed not only phonetically but to indicate emphasis and punctuation; the interpreter reads "as if there were simply a correspondence of letters to sounds and as if the letters had not also completely different functions" (*PI* §4).

3. We are brought to consider that a foreigner "who did not understand our language" but who frequently heard the order "Bring me a slab!" might take "this whole series of sounds" as *one* word corresponding to his word for "building-stone"; and that, on hearing him pronounce the command oddly, we might surmise that "he takes it for a *single* word" (*PI* §20).

4. We are told to imagine a picture of a boxer in a particular stance, and are then invited to notice that "this picture can be used to tell someone how he should stand, should hold himself; or how he should not hold himself; or how a particular man did stand in such-and-such a place; and so on"; here the point is to

---

[18] As we know from the "Editors' Note" to the *Investigations*, the decision to place the aspect-seeing remarks in one of the later sections of Part II – let alone in a separate "Part II" – was not Wittgenstein's. But noting this is no excuse for overlooking his evident intention that these remarks should follow (as they frequently assume and occasionally echo and extend) the bulk of what we have as Part I of the *Investigations*.

see in this an emblem for Frege's thought that "every assertion contains an assumption" (*PI* p. 11, bottom; §22).

5. Wittgenstein observes that the necessity of our adding the word "number" to an ostensive definition of, for example, "two," "depends on whether without it the other person takes the definition otherwise than I wish" (takes it, for example, as the name for "*this* group of nuts") (*PI* §§28–29).

6. The reader is instructed to "point to a piece of paper," is invited next to point "to its shape," "to its color," "to its number," … and is then asked to consider, if she imagines that she did something *different* each time, what that difference consists in (*PI* §33).

7. An interlocutor who suggests that a chessboard is "obviously, and absolutely, composite" – presumably by imagining it as composed of alternating black and white squares – is asked to consider whether we couldn't say as well that it was "composed of the colors black and white and the schema of squares," and so to reconsider whether she is still tempted to call it absolutely "composite" "if there are quite different ways of looking at it" (*PI* §47).

If these moments are not everywhere clear cases of *seeing* (#1 and #6 might be called cases of imagining; #3 is about a way of hearing; #5 is an illustration of someone making a wrong connection), it is also clear that the aspect-seeing remarks of Part II, Section 11 frequently wind their way through similar, non-seeing cases.[19] And if you recognize these moments in the opening pages of the *Investigations* as broaching the central concerns of those pages – the relation of "grammar" to human forms of life; philosophy's idealized picture of language; the notion that something "inner" must correspond to the way we utter a sentence; the multiplicity of kinds of sentence; when and how we can give ostensive definitions; what "pointing to an object" consists in; the idea that names signify simples – then you will have begun to see the ubiquity of the concept of "seeing an aspect" in Wittgenstein's *Philosophical Investigations*.

This is not to deny that what the aspect-seeing remarks are about, in the most straightforward sense, is seeing (or noticing) aspects.

---

[19] Cf., for example, *PI* 201a, 202h, 206i–207a, 208c, 209c, 209e–g, 210b, 213c–e, and, of course, 214d and following (where the discussion turns to "the connection between the concepts of 'seeing an aspect' and 'experiencing the meaning of a word'").

Although Wittgenstein's use of "aspect-seeing" and its cognates shows it to be a kind of grab-bag category, he is firm in identifying "noticing an aspect" as an experience with, one might say, a double aspect. It is an experience in which, first, something changes – as it were before our eyes or ears – but in which, second, we know that nothing has changed, that is, we know that the change is not (so to speak) in the world, but (so to speak) in us. Because such an experience is, at the very least, like the experience of discovery that is characteristic of our interactions with works of art, it is not surprising that philosophers of art were among the first readers of the *Investigations* to take an interest in the aspect-seeing remarks. Thus it may have seemed until recently that the reception of these remarks had their heyday in the mid-1950s and 1960s, when Virgil Aldrich, Richard Wollheim, and others sought to "apply" the aspect-seeing material to aesthetics, as well as to the theory of mind.[20]

It was perhaps only after Mulhall's *On Being in the World* that the remarks on aspect-seeing began to be viewed widely as significant for more than their merely local exegetical interest. And yet Mulhall's work bears the imprint of Cavell's far-ranging exploration, in Part IV of *The Claim of Reason* (1979), of the significance of aspect-seeing to the problem of other minds and of philosophical self-knowledge.[21] One might conclude from this that Cavell's longest and most important book planted the seed for a reappraisal of Wittgenstein's remarks on aspect-seeing. If so, one should add that this reappraisal is not divorced from an interest in ways in which aspect-seeing bears specifically on aesthetics. Indeed, Cavell's development of the significance of aspect-seeing in *The Claim of Reason* is the product, in part, of his essays from the 1960s on Wittgenstein and aesthetics collected in *Must We Mean What We Say?* (1969).[22] There is certainly no denying that Wittgenstein's discussion of aspect-seeing helps to clarify what we do, or try to do, in our

---

[20] See Virgil C. Aldrich, *Philosophy of Art* (Englewood Cliffs, N.J.: Prentice-Hall, 1963) and "An Aspect Theory of Mind," *Philosophy and Phenomenological Research* 26 (March 1966): 313–26; Richard Wollheim, *Art and Its Objects: An Introduction to Aesthetics* (New York: Harper & Row, 1968).

[21] See Cavell, *The Claim of Reason: Wittgenstein, Skepticism, Morality, and Tragedy* (Oxford: Oxford University Press, 1979), 354ff.

[22] See "Aesthetic Problems of Modern Philosophy" and "Music Discomposed" in Cavell, *Must We Mean What We Say? A Book of Essays* (Cambridge: Cambridge University Press, 1969), 73–96, 180–212.

critical appraisals of works of art. But such considerations, rather than "ghetto-izing" aesthetics, ought to help underscore the importance of aesthetic reflection to what Wittgenstein conceives as philosophy's task. One could say – to preview a claim defended in several of the essays to follow – that Wittgenstein's aspect-seeing remarks shed light on the mode of attention that his writing demands from his reader, and so help to clarify the intrinsic relation between his writing and the problem of philosophical self-knowledge. Or, put another way: these discussions of aspect-seeing reveal that Wittgenstein's conception of philosophy demands, not just a way of seeing, but – as Steven Affeldt argues below – a way of attending to, and a willingness to discover, the aspects of things that are most important for us (for us humans) but that, for some reason, we are driven to repudiate.

To indicate more generally what the aspect-seeing remarks are for, we might summarize three kinds of response that are offered in what follows, offered for the most part not in opposition to one another but as reflective of "the wide field of thought" *(PI* Preface) traversed by Wittgenstein's investigations of the concept of aspect-seeing. First, as was apparent in the early reception of the *Investigations,* aspect-seeing is pertinent to describing and thinking through the central conundrum of aesthetic judgment – namely, how can an aesthetic experience that is not only prompted by, but (we feel) *attached to,* a publicly available object be had in full recognition that others may not, or will not, have it? (Hamlet: Do you see nothing there? Gertrude: Nothing at all, yet all there is, I see.) This is the puzzle that sets the goal of criticism; as Cavell words it, "The work of ... criticism is to reveal its object as having yet to achieve its due effect. Something there, despite being fully opened to the senses, has been missed."[23]

Later in their reception, the aspect-seeing remarks came to be read by some as a figure for how philosophy has made Gertrudes of us all. According to this second way of reading the aspect-seeing remarks, what "has been missed" systematically by philosophy – namely, the ordinary conditions of our words meaning what they do and as they do – is the central topic of the *Investigations* as a whole. An

[23] Cavell, "Something Out of the Ordinary," in *Philosophy the Day After Tomorrow* (Cambridge: Harvard University Press, 2005), 11.

early remark (alluded to above) from the *Investigations* brings out the connection: "Imagine a script in which the letters were used to stand for sounds, and also as signs of emphasis and punctuation. ... Now imagine someone interpreting that script as if there were simply a correspondence of letters to sounds and as if the letters had not also completely different functions. Augustine's conception of language is like such an over-simple conception of the script" (*PI* §4). The first of these scenarios represents our normal relation to the words we speak, while the latter represents traditional philosophy's reading of that relation. In Cavell's formulation, "the ordinary is discovered not as what is perceptually missable but as what is intellectually dismissable, ... what must be set aside if philosophy's aspirations to knowledge are to be satisfied."[24] What Augustine's description – and, by implication, traditional philosophy – lacks is a recognition of our life with words; it fails to see aspects of the work of words in the human form of life. Philosophy's Augustinian failure is an explicit target of Wittgenstein's discussion of aspect-seeing in *PI* II.xi. Late in that discussion Wittgenstein comes to suggest that the way we pick out and insist upon particular words is evidence of our ability to see (and feel) "the familiar physiognomy of a word," and that this manifestation of our "attachment" to words is what would be missing from the meaning-blind, that is, from human beings who failed to see (and feel) a word as a "likeness of its meaning" (*PI* 218g). Something sensible or affective, something almost bodily, so to speak, is entwined in our conception of language, despite philosophy's best efforts to deaden itself to it.

A third way to characterize these remarks, tied to the relevant particulars of Wittgenstein's biography and to the stringent demands not only of what he wrote, but of how he lived, is that his extended consideration of aspect-seeing is Wittgenstein's indirect meditation on the difficulties of receiving his (later) philosophical methods. His sense of these difficulties is expressed directly in other places, from the Preface to the *Investigations* ("It is not impossible that it should fall to the lot of this work, in its poverty and in the darkness of this time, to bring light into one brain or another—but, of course, it is not likely") to a remark he made to Maurice Drury ("It is impossible for me to say in my book one word about all that music has meant in my life. How then can I hope to be understood?"). In another conversation with Drury, Wittgenstein confesses that he conceived philosophical problems always "from a religious point of view" – this at a time when much of Anglo-American philosophy would have been hostile to the religious.[25] Receiving the *Investigations* in light of these hints seems to rely on sources of interpretive acumen not required or accessed by most texts, even most philosophical texts. (As we will see, this produces stark disagreements over what the "therapeutic" aspiration of Wittgenstein's writing amounts to.) To be told, as we are by Wittgenstein, "don't think, but look" at the "complicated network" of the conditions of our utterances (*PI* §66) is not enough, it seems, to bring about the needed change in seeing. The aspect-seeing remarks in the *Investigations* offer, from this standpoint, both an extended allegory of how to appropriate or receive the text of the *Investigations*, and a detailed working-out of the vicissitudes that, invariably or constitutionally, one finds along the way.

3. THE ESSAYS

The present volume is organized around four "aspects" of Wittgenstein's aspect-seeing remarks that are significant both to Wittgensteinian studies and to the goals and methods of philosophy generally.

The essays of the first section, "Aspects of 'Seeing-As'," together make the case for a revision of philosophy's idealized conception of "seeing" – seeing as seeing to the essence of things (or necessarily failing to), where seeing the result of an empirical experiment is the paradigm of seeing – in favor of a conception which includes our *responsiveness* to what is seen. But just as elsewhere in Wittgenstein's thought, this feature is not to be understood as something added on to philosophy's idealized conception – *viz.*, seeing *plus* responsiveness to what is seen – but as revelatory of the everyday grammar of seeing that, in the grips of philosophy, we are wont to overlook, not least in our suspicions about the claims of aesthetics.

---

[25] M. O'C. Drury, "Some Notes on Conversations with Wittgenstein," *Recollections of Wittgenstein*, ed. Rush Rhees (Oxford and New York: Oxford University Press, 1984), 79.

Norton Batkin's "Aesthetic Analogies" (Chapter 1) is guided by the thought that, while the aspect-seeing remarks "are not in the first place about matters in aesthetics," features of Wittgenstein's discussion bear upon aesthetics "by analogy." One such instance is the parallel Batkin observes between Wittgenstein's view, in his rejection of the "inner object" explanation of the experience of an aspect dawning (which I express when I say that my "visual impression" has "a quite particular 'organization'" [*PI* 196b]), and the traditional view of "form" in painting, which is not a visual concept but one more often tied to linguistic notions or, more broadly, to the entire scope of my responsiveness to the work before me. This proves to be revelatory of how Wittgenstein's visual examples – in contrast to their employment by psychologists – "draw our attention back to the everyday circumstances of our life with objects and with others." Sandra Laugier's contribution, "Aspects, Sense, and Perception" (Chapter 2), argues, from a careful assessment of J. L. Austin's writing on the philosophical ambiguities surrounding the notion of "sense," that seeing is not an act of giving a sense to the world, but of perceiving a sense. Our agreement and disagreement on how we describe things involves the reciprocal relation between language and perception that Laugier calls "linguistic phenomenology." The differences we perceive are within language, not as a set of utterances, but as a "space of agreement about what we say when," and seeing-as illustrates, in fact, that a sharpened awareness of words sharpens our perception of phenomena.

Timothy Gould's "An Allegory of Affinities: On Seeing a World of Aspects in a Universe of Things" (Chapter 3), carries the discussion of aspects beyond issues in the psychology of perception, with which it is generally linked, to issues of interpretation. Gould questions the point of trying to find an underlying unity to the project of the *Investigations*, and he suggests, rather, that we should see it from an allegorical stance. Wittgenstein's text asks from us a certain intensification of our relation to our words that enables us to relate one region of significance of the things we do to different, apparently unrelated ones: "there is nothing to prevent us from considering the world as a realm of familiarities, analogies, likenesses and affinities." In particular, the properties of things or substances don't have "priority" over the aspects of things: there is no "basic constitution of the world," and hence no need for metaphysics. In "The Touch of Words" (Chapter 4), Stanley Cavell responds to Cora

Diamond's reflections on J. M. Coetzee's novel *Elizabeth Costello,* which raise for Cavell the question of what it is to see non-human animals, on the one hand, as companions, and, on the other, as subject to systematic and mechanized slaughter for food. Wittgenstein's seeing-as discussion serves Cavell as an instrument to explore the ways in which our affective attachment to our words accounts for one way of seeing, or of failing to see, aspects of the world and our relationship to others. More precisely, he considers how, in a world one sees as brandishing reason against itself (by making unmistakably systematic killing appear benign), it might be possible to discover in oneself "the tortured perception … that words are cursed" and to still want, or need, to live with that perception. Thus, as becomes apparent in this first set of essays, the discussion of seeing aspects involves Wittgenstein in the recovery of the responsive and interpretive in our conceptions of seeing and of language-meaning.

The essays of the second section, "Aspects and the Self," turn the lesson of the experience of aspect-seeing the other way around, as it were, and consider how the phenomenon of a change in aspect can direct us to a new understanding of the self as the source and sufferer of alterations and transformations of "what is seen".

Within this section, the pair of essays under the heading "Self-Knowledge" suggest that the ancient goal of philosophy – coming to know oneself, or to reflect on one's being what one is – is fruitfully rendered intelligible through the conception of the self as having aspects. Self-knowledge, one could say, waits on one's growing to learn how to see oneself (in some sense) again, or anew, through the particular ways that humans are wont to present themselves to themselves (retrospective thinking) or to others (the gestural possibilities of the body). Garry L. Hagberg's "In a New Light: Wittgenstein, Aspect-Perception, and Retrospective Change in Self-Understanding" (Chapter 5) brings out a range of connections between Wittgenstein's discussion of the concept of aspect-seeing and the effort to reflect on and reengage with one's memories that is the source of one's conception of oneself. Through a close reading of several of Wittgenstein's remarks, Hagberg argues against the picture of this process as either a necessarily delusional projection of one's present self-understanding onto past events, or a simple recollection of objective events viewed "accurately and non-prismatically." What counts as "genuine seeing" of the significance of the events of one's past is found, rather, in the "capacious grasp of the life of which the event in question is one significant part," a life that is consequently viewed, in Iris Murdoch's phrase, as "unfrozen." According to Victor J. Krebs' "The Bodily Root: Seeing Aspects and Inner Experience" (Chapter 6), Wittgenstein's critique of the intellectualist search for essences relies on and helps to articulate the concept of "seeing-as." Following Merleau-Ponty, Krebs claims that aspect-seeing flows from an awareness of the constitutive role of the bodily in perception and language meaning, hence a sensitivity to the expressiveness of words. The intellectualist's meaning-blindness results precisely from a lack of "attachment" to our words, a disconnection from the sensible. Wittgenstein thus redefines the goals of philosophy, turning it towards an inquiry into what is meaningful rather than a search for the attainment of truth – an inquiry that demands, moreover, a revision of what is involved in first-person awareness in light of what Krebs calls "the bodily root of language."

The pair of essays in the next subsection ("Problems of Mind") show how work in the philosophy of mind might more faithfully render what it is to be a (conscious, living) person who is not reducible to material or mental stuff, as is required by those conceptions of mind that are concerned to explain how the "parts" of mental life "fit together." For David R. Cerbone in "(Ef)facing the Soul: Wittgenstein and Materialism" (Chapter 7), the expressive character of the human face, which is a recurring topic in the aspect-seeing remarks, is taken as evidence of the soul as a philosophical category for Wittgenstein, measurable against the notion of mind shared by both materialists and "mysterians." While the former want to eliminate the concepts and categories describing subjective experience altogether, the latter make subjective experience into "an elusive, mysterious, wholly inner phenomenon." But the concept of the soul, as it appears in Wittgenstein's remarks about reading gestures, reveals rather that psychological concepts are embedded in the weave of our life, a fact missed by the thought-experiments of the materialist interpretation of the mental. Insofar as the materialist and mysterian pictures of the mind overlook the contextuality that make their own thought-experiments intelligible and guides their application, both conceptions of the mind can be characterized as forms of "blindness to the outer," of blindness to the transparency of human expressiveness. Richard Eldridge's "Wittgenstein on Aspect-Seeing, the Nature of Discursive Consciousness, and the Experience of Agency" (Chapter 8) argues that Wittgenstein's discussion of seeing-as helps to defeat the attempt to naturalize "discursive consciousness," the human capacity to recognize one's own role in the way one takes things in. Noticing an aspect is an experience in which our perception is placed, through an act of seeing, in a field of comparisons that involves shared ways of seeing that Eldridge calls "intersubjectively shared perspectival construals." It is the mastery of a technique of seeing connections in language, and not a causal mechanism, that makes discursive consciousness possible. The issue for Eldridge is how concepts become fixed and how our senses become discursively structured; the notion of seeing aspects helps to explain the development of imagination as a condition for learning a language and hence for discursively structuring experience. Seeing aspects makes clear that discursive consciousness is a practical rather than a theoretical matter, and that it is irreducible to material processes. Both Cerbone's and Eldridge's essays find in Wittgenstein's remarks an invitation to see human-mindedness as a matter of noticing aspects.

The essays of the third section, "Aspects and Language," focus on the second half of Wittgenstein's aspect-seeing remarks (*PI* 213c and following) and on their suggestion that the concept of aspect-seeing – as well as the concept of its absence, aspect-blindness – provides a key to understanding our life with words and the absence of "life" in our words. These essays offer a conception of language in which what we mean when we speak is not given by the supposed fixity of rule-governed meanings of our words, any more than what we see or hear when we attend to the world is given by the supposed fixity of the physiognomy of the (of our) world. Rather, one should read even the Wittgensteinian dictum "meaning is use" as a directive to "look and see" the uses of "use," to notice how the life of our words rests on our inhabiting human practices – just as our coming to speak a first word, and so our beginning to inhabit human practices, rests on our interest in aspects of the world.

Edward Minar's "The Philosophical Significance of Meaning-Blindness" (Chapter 9) develops a reading of Wittgenstein's remarks on the imagined possibility of humans who lack "an attachment to their words." He takes his cue from Rush Rhees' contention that the aspect-seeing remarks are concerned with "'the principal theme of the *Investigations*' which is 'the relation between language and logic' (and in particular the tendency – wellspring of philosophical confusion – to think that uncovering the underlying logic of language shows what makes language possible)." Minar argues that our uses of language rely on, and are constituted by, an agreement in judgment (evidenced in "the way we choose and value words") that cannot be character-ized from outside an inhabiting of our practices. The philosophical search for a ground to our linguistic practices arises from a "posture of meaning-blindness," a resistance to allowing the objectivity of mean-ing to rest on something as fragile as our contingent attunement in judgments. In "Wanting to Say Something: Aspect-Blindness and Language" (Chapter 10), William Day argues against those readers of the aspect-seeing remarks who claim that the ability to be struck by an aspect presupposes the ability to see non-aspectually or continuously. He asks how we ever come to speak a first word, and he finds that this proves to be inconceivable as an act of attaching a label to a thing con-tinuously seen. This leads to Day's claim that "a word's meaning begins for [the child] necessarily as the experience of its meaning, as finding a new home in its utterance." The child's interest in his experience, and the adult's loss of that interest, are in the background of Wittgenstein's remarks on aspect-blindness, which are prompted by the false model of language as proceeding without our interest, a model expressive of the human propensity to relinquish one's will. A task of Wittgenstein's writ-ing thus becomes not only to expose the temptations to this model of language, but to model in his writing an interest in one's experience.

While the first three sections of the volume speak to the famil-iar (if broadly conceived) philosophical topics of perception, self-knowledge, philosophy of mind, and language – revealing novel approaches to these topics through the application of Wittgenstein's later methods – the last section, "Aspects and Method," presents essays that take Wittgenstein's innovations in philosophical method as their topic. Their claim to our interest lies in their proposing that this method can be elucidated through considerations of the con-cepts of aspect-seeing and aspect-blindness.

The essays under the heading "Therapy" address various (and in some cases, conflicting) ways of taking seriously Wittgenstein's having remarked, "The philosopher's treatment of a question is like the treatment of an illness" (*PI* §255). Together they sharpen and deepen the growing interest in the alleged "therapeutic" aims of Wittgenstein's writing. They ask whether the mark of understanding his writing is not the ability to paraphrase his teaching, but the recognition of hitherto overlooked drives to philosophical emptiness, and whether that understanding requires the transformation of our relation to the words we speak no less than to those Wittgenstein wrote.

Avner Baz's "On Learning from Wittgenstein, or What Does It Take to *See* the Grammar of Seeing Aspects?" (Chapter 11) is concerned with how Wittgenstein's teaching in his remarks on seeing aspects is meant to work, and with how easy it is to fall back precisely on the kinds of confusions Wittgenstein's text is supposed to counter. Wittgenstein's remarks on aspects are meant as reminders, to project us into situations of speech that help us see "things [about the meaning of the words we utter] that we cannot have failed to know, and yet things that were, *are*, for some reason, hard to *see*." The teaching is inseparable from this practical effect, *viz.*, a reconfiguration of our life with words. For Baz, Stephen Mulhall's "therapeutic dissolution" of what he calls "the paradox of aspect-dawning" is an example of the kind of explanation Wittgenstein is attempting to preclude with his remarks, an explanation whose consequence is that the most important feature of aspects is missed. Responding to Baz's claims that he is unfaithful to the spirit of Wittgenstein's purpose, Stephen Mulhall casts doubt in "The Work of Wittgenstein's Words: A Reply to Baz" (Chapter 12) on whether we can take the style of Part II of the *Investigations* as an indicator of that spirit, considering that the text is in a state that Wittgenstein would have considered neither satisfactory nor final. And regarding Baz's assertion that Mulhall obviates the centrality of the distinction between two categories of objects of sight, with which Wittgenstein's discussion of aspects begins, he argues that Baz overlooks important details of his account and that he has been misguided by the order of presentation, which does not reflect the importance of the issues discussed. Mulhall claims that his strategy in his writings on seeing aspects is to reduce our sense of puzzlement about aspect-dawning by relocating it in the broader context of our lives with pictures. The central aim of Steven G. Affeldt's "On the Difficulty of Seeing Aspects and the 'Therapeutic' Reading of Wittgenstein" (Chapter 13) is to reconsider in what sense Wittgenstein's work is rightfully said to be "therapeutic," and to derive a deeper understanding of this therapeutic dimension through a consideration of the aspect-seeing remarks in the *Investigations*. While Affeldt is in sympathy with the core spirit of what is now commonly known as the therapeutic reading of Wittgenstein – a reading which helps to undercut the idea that Wittgenstein's work unfolds substantive philosophical positions on meaning, states of consciousness, rule-following, and the like – he wants to argue that Wittgenstein's work is directed not just at enabling us to recognize when we are speaking nonsense, but toward showing us that we are possessed of drives toward emptiness, unearthing the shapes of these drives, and treating them.

The last three essays of the book, under the heading "Seeing Connections," marry the notion of "the dawning of an aspect" to Wittgenstein's claim that his method aims at a "perspicuous representation" that effects or enables the "seeing" of "connections" (*PI* §122). What makes his method desirable and even necessary, Wittgenstein believes, is that such seeing "makes me capable of stopping doing philosophy when I want to" and so "gives philosophy peace" (*PI* §133). The essays address, in turn: how to characterize the discovery that follows "putting into order what we already know"; how to reckon the apparently antagonistic epistemic concepts of coming to understand and being surprised or struck; and whether aspect-seeing might reveal an unavoidable instability in Wittgenstein's announced goal of peace.

Frank Cioffi's contribution to this volume, "Overviews: What Are They of and What Are They For?" (Chapter 14), explores why we seek overviews, or to "order what we already know without adding anything." He distinguishes three different cases (all of which he finds in Wittgenstein) where overviews may be used and useful: (1) when we are faced with problems of understanding that resist rational explanation; (2) when we are disconcerted by the impression that something has caused in us; and (3) when we are resistant to accepting the contingency of experience. Cioffi examines the "therapeutic" effects that are involved in the use of overviews in each of these cases, and he provides a reflection on the third kind of overviews, which are offered to assuage an attitude of resignation before the unresolvable complexity of our being human. Cioffi's remarks suggest the thought that these overviews – and, in particular, the third kind – enable us to fashion a life wherein differing, and even contrary, aspects can be seen as irreducibly constitutive of our experience. Juliet Floyd's "On Being Surprised: Wittgenstein on Aspect-Perception, Logic, and Mathematics" (Chapter 15) traces the origin of the notion of seeing aspects to Wittgenstein's reflections on how logic and mathematics structure our perception and understanding. Floyd finds in the aspect-seeing remarks echoes of Wittgenstein's earlier idea that "in logic and mathematics there are no surprises – no discovery of facts or of possibilities construed on the model of properties or facts – but instead activities, trains of thought and arrangements of grammar that strike us." Thus the limits of empiricism lie "not in *a priori* assumptions guaranteed, but in the ways in which we make comparisons and in which we act." The idea of accuracy of representation is replaced by an idea of interest and relevance, of our being struck by the complexity in our uses of pictures in everyday settings. In the volume's final essay – and the only essay that situates itself in opposition to aspects of Wittgenstein's project – Gordon C. F. Bearn's "The Enormous Danger" (Chapter 16) highlights Wittgenstein's warning against "the danger of making fine distinctions" and asks, What is this enormous danger? If the aim of philosophy is, as Wittgenstein affirms, the attainment of peace, then perhaps fine distinctions are what we need to avoid. But don't we need to make fine distinctions to clarify what is involved in seeing aspects? Wittgenstein says that fine distinctions either leave things open-ended or lead us into dead ends; does he thereby make the unanswerability of a question a sign of its dispensability? If so, philosophical peace seems purchased at the expense of attention to fine distinctions in our experience. For Bearn, this suggests that Wittgenstein is trying to avoid expressing the singularity of experiences because of language's inability to find closure to it. It is as if one were to gain peace at the expense of excitement, since representational simplicity "floats atop an untamed world of barely nameable sensuality." The point of philosophy, as Bearn sees it, should be not to shy away from labyrinthine sensuality but, quite to the contrary, to sink into it.

As this summary of their contents suggests, the present essays are not everywhere in agreement – and in a couple of places they are in explicit disagreement – but each is motivated by the recognition of the fecundity (for Wittgensteinian studies, for diverse research areas in philosophy, for sorting out philosophy's aim) of the concept of aspect-seeing, and by Wittgenstein's clear-sighted, nuanced, never simplified, self-reflective account of it. When a concept manages to open doors to such fruitful philosophical pathways as are represented by the essays in this volume, it invites, at the very least, a second look.

I ASPECTS OF "SEEING-AS"

1

Aesthetic Analogies

Norton Batkin

Wittgenstein's remarks about "seeing-as" in Part II, Section 11 of *Philosophical Investigations* are not in the first place about matters of aesthetics.[1] He begins his discussion in that section by noting a distinction (a "difference of category") between what he calls "two 'objects' of sight." The distinction is between what you can be said to see when you say, simply, "I see *this*" and give a description or draw or point to something, and what you can be said to see when you declare "a likeness" between two objects. He calls the last sort of seeing "noticing an aspect."

Wittgenstein says that he is interested in "the concept [of noticing an aspect] and its place among the concepts of experience" (*PI* 193e). He notes this by way of explaining how his interest in this sort of seeing is different from that of psychologists ("Its *causes* are of interest to psychologists"). He then introduces an example of a geometric figure that we can see first as one thing and then as another ("here a glass cube, there an inverted open box, there a wire frame of that shape," and so on) when we encounter it in different places in a "textbook," accompanied in each place by a different interpretation. The

---

[1] An earlier draft of this chapter was presented at a panel discussion entitled "A Double Take on Wittgenstein's Aspect-Seeing Remarks," organized by William Day and Victor J. Krebs for the annual meeting of the American Society for Aesthetics in October 2001. Bill Day's invitation to participate on the panel, and in the present book of essays, noted his and Victor's interest in (among other topics) the "implication" of the remarks on aspect-seeing "for an understanding of the aesthetic dimension of [Wittgenstein's] thought."

particular example (a simple line drawing) with its particular range of interpretations ("glass cube, … inverted open box, … wire frame …") is something, I suppose, that we might find in a textbook in psychology (perhaps with "picture objects" and Jastrow's "duck-rabbit"). Of course, we also find it in *Philosophical Investigations*, which is not obviously a textbook. Wittgenstein's example again suggests a question about the difference between philosophy and psychology, between the examples that are offered in each, and why.

In the ensuing discussions in *PI* II.xi of these and similar examples of visual experience, Wittgenstein remains preoccupied with differences among our concepts of "seeing" (see *PI* 200a) and with philosophy's difference from psychology. Yet questions about our capacity of "noticing [seeing] an aspect" – and topics of experience and of interpretation – are central concerns of aesthetics and criticism. Couldn't Wittgenstein have such concerns in view as well? His pictorial examples – his figures of a rectangular solid, joined planes, or a triangle; his "picture objects," such as his simple drawing of a smiling face; and the duck-rabbit – are not instances or examples of art, but sketched or schematized, as if deliberately to show their difference from art. Nonetheless, the very deliberation here may invite comparison with Hume's offering, as a lesson about taste generally, a story about a tasting of a cask of wine, or Kant's offering a rose as an example of beauty. Neither a cask of wine nor a rose is an example of art, but each is entered in consideration of the nature of critical or aesthetic judgment, which addresses (part of) our interest in art.[2] Are Wittgenstein's reflections on how we might see the pictures he offers any less aptly taken as lessons about our judgments about, or interests in, art? On the other hand, when Wittgenstein brings up the question of aesthetics in *PI* II.xi, he does so as an aside ("Here it occurs to me that in conversation on aesthetic matters we use the words: 'You have to see it like *this*, this is how it is meant'" [*PI* 202h]).[3]

[2] The term "critical or aesthetic judgment," which I use to describe the central concern of Hume's and Kant's examples, is our term, not Hume's or Kant's. Hume speaks of "taste," Kant of "the judgment of beauty." While Kant finds the judgment of beauty to discover a part of our interest in the fine arts ("*Schöne Kunst*"), it does not discover or define every essential element or interest of the work of art. See note 13.
[3] The suggestion in the aside that art is incidental to Wittgenstein's concerns, something that comes up by the way, may find confirmation, and specification, in the way that he offers paintings (*PI* 201d), a photograph (*PI* 205e–f), a tune (*PI* 210b)

If we find significance for aesthetics in Wittgenstein's remarks in *PI* II.xi, we find it by analogy. The questions there about experience or interpretation or noticing an aspect can be found to be like questions that we encounter in aesthetics. Does this show us something about how Wittgenstein thinks the problems of aesthetics arise for us? Are they problems somehow aside from or outside philosophy, as Wittgenstein, in his earlier "Lectures on Aesthetics," finds them to be outside psychology?[4]

I return to the opening of Section 11, to the example of the geometric figure that appears in different places in a textbook, in each case

as examples. Nothing depends on the specific art of the examples – that is, their individual achievements as art – but only their being paintings, a photograph, or a tune, something made to be regarded by us, noticed by us.

4 See "Lectures on Aesthetics" (*LC* 1–40). Wittgenstein's specific animus in the "Lectures" against psychological interpretations of aesthetic judgment is that "An aesthetic explanation is not a causal explanation" (*LC* 18) ("Aesthetic questions have nothing to do with psychological experiments, but are answered in an entirely different way" [*LC* 17]).

Briefly, on Wittgenstein's philosophical or grammatical analysis in the "Lectures," aesthetic judgment is not in every instance simply an expression of approval or disapproval ("A person who has a judgment doesn't mean a person who says 'Marvelous!' at certain things" [*LC* 6]; "Buffon ... [makes] ever so many distinctions which I only understand vaguely but which he didn't mean vaguely – all kinds of nuances like 'grand', 'charming', 'nice'" [*LC* 8]). Aesthetic judgments importantly have objects, not just occasions ("We have here a kind of discomfort which you may call 'directed'. ... There is a 'Why?' to aesthetic discomfort not a 'cause' to it. The expression of discomfort takes the form of a criticism and not 'My mind is not at rest' or something. It might take the form of looking at a picture and saying: 'What's wrong with it?'" [*LC* 14–15]). In making an aesthetic judgment ("This is slightly too dark. This is slightly too loud" [*LC* 7]), I am not assigning the cause of my judgment, but stating what stands out for me or is aesthetically significant. I am saying what I find "right" or "correct" (*LC* 3). In making an aesthetic judgment like "That is grand," Buffon does not simply express approval, but is "giving ... a character" to a passage of writing (*LC* 3). This undermines the belief that an aesthetic judgment is simply a kind of psychological (causal) explanation ("You could say: 'An aesthetic explanation is not a causal explanation'" [*LC* 18]).

To understand an aesthetic judgment – to see or to hear what it finds significant; that is, to *appreciate* its object as it does – you need to understand what it discovers in the object. For Wittgenstein, this means understanding a culture (the culture of dress at a particular moment, the culture of music in a given period [*LC* 8]).

I will add that if the last sort of understanding is not something that psychology (what Wittgenstein calls "psychology") can provide, it is not something that philosophy provides either ("The work of the philosopher consists in assembling reminders for a particular purpose" [*PI* §127]).

For Wittgenstein's use of the term "appreciation," see *LC* 7.

differently interpreted. Wittgenstein observes: "But we can also *see* the illustration [as it appears in different places] now as one thing now as another. —So we interpret it, and *see* it as we *interpret* it" (*PI* 193f). Indeed, we might observe this much in our own case, as we look at the figure on the page of *Philosophical Investigations* and try out the series of interpretations that Wittgenstein offers. (The surprise that Wittgenstein expresses at the fact that we "*see* it [the figure] as we *interpret* it" is something that we might also feel and is allied to the surprise we experience in other cases of a "change in aspect.")[5]

In the paragraphs following, Wittgenstein goes on to consider what we might say, and what we would not, when presented with pictures of various kinds, among them pictures of a specific object ("picture-rabbit," "picture-face") and pictures that can be seen first one way and then another (the "duck-rabbit," a "double cross"). He notes that if I am shown a picture-rabbit – a simple picture of a rabbit – and asked what I see, I might say "It's a rabbit," but I would not say "Now it's a rabbit." To say "Now it's a rabbit" or "Now I see it as a rabbit" would imply that the figure has somehow changed for me, yet nothing about this figure indicates or suggests how it could change ("If you say 'Now it's a face for me', we can ask: 'What change are you alluding to?'" [*PI* 195d]).

Wittgenstein also considers general statements about perception or visual experience that we might derive from what we say and do in such cases. For instance, comparing what we say when shown a picture-rabbit ("It's a rabbit") with what we might say when presented with a duck-rabbit, he concludes that "It's a duck-rabbit" or "It's a rabbit" may be reports of perception when I am shown a duck-rabbit, but "Now it's a rabbit," said of the same figure, would not report a perception. Why not? I can say, looking at the figure of the duck-rabbit, "Now it's a rabbit," but what that would report, if it reported anything, would not be a perception (what "It's a rabbit" reports) but a change of perception. Yet that is precisely what I don't see or perceive.[6]

Wittgenstein considers such generalizations and other things that we might say about the experience of seeing-as, but not, mostly, to accept or

---

[5] See note 23.

[6] "The expression of a change of aspect is the expression of a *new* perception and at the same time of the perception's being unchanged" (*PI* 196a). That is, "Now it's a rabbit" says that I now see a rabbit and that "it" (what I am looking at, the figure of the duck-rabbit) is still what it was.

to reject them definitively (although he may reject a claim once and for all; for example, the suggestion that the expression "see ... as ..." is "an indirect description" of my visual experience [*PI* 193g] or that in seeing a picture, I see "a quite particular 'organization'" as well as shapes and colors [*PI* 196b]). He is not prepared to say either that seeing-as is a visual experience ("'Seeing as. ...' is not part of perception" [*PI* 197a]) or that it is "half visual experience, half thought" (*PI* 197d). What he wants us to see are the circumstances – and the way that we miss the circumstances – of what we say and do with the figures that he presents ("It's a rabbit," "Now it's a rabbit") and the ways that what we say and do, in particular circumstances, may justify us or fail to justify us in saying, for example, that seeing-as is a matter of "perception" or "visual experience," or that "I see it as a rabbit" expresses the fact that I am having "a special impression" (see *PI* 201g). But then isn't Wittgenstein denying something here? Isn't he saying that our *experience* cannot justify us or fail to justify us in saying these things about seeing-as? —The experience in each instance is there, such as it is. His question is why we *call* it a "perception" or "visual experience" or "special impression."[7]

I said that if we find significance for aesthetics in Wittgenstein's remarks in *PI* II.xi, it is by analogy. I will give an example. The following passage initiates a discussion of the visual impression as what Wittgenstein calls an "inner object": "I suddenly see the solution of a puzzle-picture. Before, there were branches there; now there is a human shape. My visual impression has changed and now I recognize that it has not only shape and color but also a quite particular 'organization'. —My visual impression has changed; —what was it like before and what is it like now? —If I represent it by means of an exact copy — and isn't that a good representation of it? — no change is shown" (*PI* 196b). The idea of the "organization" of the impression – something that changes with a change in aspect – cannot be given sense by representing my visual impression by an exact copy, that is, another picture that I can present to you. Indeed, the very puzzle-picture that I am looking at, which appears first *this* way, then *that*, is the best picture ("representation,"

---

7 "What we have rather to do is to *accept* the everyday language-game, and to note *false* accounts of the matter *as* false" (*PI* 200b). And again: "Here it is *difficult* to see that what is at issue is the fixing of concepts" (*PI* 204h).

"copy") of my visual impression in both cases. Wittgenstein goes on to remark that the notion that my visual impression has "a quite particular 'organization'" is informed by a particular idea that I have of my visual impression, an idea of it as an "inner picture" or "inner object" (what the picture looks like to me). The topic of the "inner picture" or "inner object" has bearing on Wittgenstein's preoccupations with the conceptual confusions of psychology and on other matters addressed in Part I of *Philosophical Investigations*.[8]

The question that I would like to raise here is whether, and how, the remarks that I have quoted, which appear to deny coherence to a particular idea of the "organization" of a visual impression, bear on the aesthetic notion of form.[9] We might speak of the form of a picture (I will speak here only of visual works of art) in very much the terms that Wittgenstein speaks of the "organization" of a visual impression; that is, we might define "form" by specifying that a picture has "not only shape and color but also a quite particular 'organization'." This is more or less the notion that Richard Wollheim, in *On Formalism and Its Kinds*, attributes to "Manifest Formalists" (he offers Roger Fry and Leo Steinberg as examples). For reasons that I will not elaborate here, Wollheim finds our understanding of "manifest form" to be "in doubt."[10] Elsewhere I suggest that the

---

[8] The importance of the idea of an "inner object" for Wittgenstein's discussion of mental life and of our knowledge of others is a central topic of Stanley Cavell, *The Claim of Reason: Wittgenstein, Skepticism, Morality, and Tragedy* (Oxford: Oxford University Press, 1979). See, in particular, Chapter V, "Natural and Conventional," 86–111 ("The *Investigations* takes many ways of approaching ideas which construe the inner life as composed of objects (and if objects then for sure *private* ones). To combat such ideas is an obsession of the book as a whole" [91]); and Chapter XIII, "Between Acknowledgment and Avoidance," 329–54 ("I would be glad to have suggested that the correct relation between inner and outer, between the soul and its society, is the theme of the *Investigations* as a whole" [329]).

[9] Wittgenstein's discussion at *PI* 196b of the idea that a visual impression has "a quite particular 'organization'" touches upon other topics taken up in the present paper. I mention one: in our preoccupation with the idea of an impression, prompted by Wittgenstein's discussion, we fail to notice what changes, or how much changes, in Wittgenstein's experience of the puzzle-figure; that he is no longer looking at a branch, but at a "human shape" (a description itself formulated under the idea of impression), something toward which Wittgenstein has what he calls a wholly different "attitude" or "regard."

[10] See Richard Wollheim, *On Formalism and its Kinds* (Barcelona: Fundació Antoni Tàpies, 1995). Wollheim distinguishes between Manifest Formalism (in which

notion has motivations in psychological conceptions of perception of the sort that preoccupied early analytic philosophy. (So the notion of "manifest form" and the idea of the "organization" of a visual impression may be similarly motivated, may depend upon similar ideas or the same idea of what constitutes a (visual, pictorial) image.) I also argue that the notion of "manifest form" as Wollheim characterizes it – roughly, a work's composition as distinct from its subject or content – is different from traditional notions of form in painting and the other visual arts.[11]

Unlike Wittgenstein's notion of "organization" and Wollheim's notion of "manifest form," the conceptions of organization or composition that enter traditional notions of form are not, in the first place, visual, but are more likely to be based in rhetorical, literary, or (broadly) linguistic notions. For example, Michael Baxandall has traced Alberti's notion of *compositio* and related critical terms – variety (*varietas*), abundance (*copia*), restraint (*gravis*), modesty (*moderata*), dignity (*dignitas*), disconnectedness (*dissolutus*) – to contemporary humanist rhetorical conceptions of the organization or structure of prose.[12] Kant's notions of "form" and the "aesthetical idea," in his accounts of beauty and of art, are both defined in terms drawn from his general conception of language, specifically, his conception of the relationship of the imagination and the understanding in judgment. When I judge the beauty of a work (its "form") or when I judge its content ("aesthetical ideas"), I allow my imagination and understanding to play not only over its lines and shapes, but over the entire field of its conception, including the relations of emotion, human relationship, and more, that I discover in its content. Or, as I might put it, I allow my imagination and understanding to play over

---

form is "observable") and Latent Formalism (in which form is a matter of "underlying" – for example, "syntactic" – relations) (see ibid., 14, 26). The remark about our understanding of manifest form being "in doubt" is at ibid., 21.

[11] See Norton Batkin, "Formalism in Analytic Aesthetics," in *Encyclopedia of Aesthetics*, ed. Michael Kelly, 4 vols. (New York: Oxford University Press, 1998), 2:217–21.

[12] For Baxandall's discussion of Alberti, see Michael Baxandall, *Giotto and the Orators: Humanist Observers of Painting in Italy and the Discovery of Pictorial Composition 1350–1450* (Oxford: Oxford University Press, 1971) and Batkin, "Formalism in Analytic Aesthetics," 2:219. The rhetorical notion of *compositio* is a notion that applies to the sentence; the other critical terms listed in the text (*varietas, copia*, and so on) apply to prose style.

the entire field that judgment discovers in the work, the field of all
that I might think or say about my experience of it. This free play
constitutes what Kant calls "form" and the "aesthetical idea."[13]

[13] For Kant's notions of "form" and "aesthetical idea," see Immanuel Kant, *Critique
of Judgment*, trans. J. H. Bernard (New York: Hafner Press, 1951), §§11–14, 56–62,
and §49, 156–63. (As here, references to this work are given by section number, followed by page number.) Kant explains the judgment of form (in beautiful objects)
in terms of "the mere formal purposiveness in the play of the subject's cognitive
powers" (ibid., §11, 58) – what he earlier describes as a "free play of the representative powers [imagination and understanding] in a given representation with reference to a cognition in general" (ibid., §9, 52). He defines the "aesthetical idea" (a
notion of the content of a work of art) in similar terms, as "that representation of the
imagination which occasions much thought, without however any definite thought,
i.e., any *concept*, being capable of being adequate to it" (ibid., §49, 157; see also 158).
As I note in "Formalism in Analytic Aesthetics" (2:219–20), Kant's notion of the
aesthetical idea has affinities with Romantic conceptions of poetic metaphor.
     I understand Kant to be arguing that the free play of imagination and under-
standing that is prompted by delineation or composition *constitutes* the possibilities
of form. The pleasure that we discover in allowing our imagination and understanding to play over the features of an object or a work of art marks out the object's or
work's significant formal attributes. For this reason, "form" is not a simple notion of
composition, a pattern merely of line or shape. The possibilities and limits of form
in Kant's sense are dictated not just by geometry, but by the full play of imagination
and the understanding; that is, by the pleasure I find in the free play of these faculties as I reflect on an object. The beauty of an object may depend as much on how
it puts my thought to work as on how it puts my eye to work. Since works of art may
represent relations of objects, persons, and actions, the beauty of a work of art may
involve a play of identity or cause or possibility as much as a play of line or shape.
     In a similar fashion, the free play of imagination and conception prompted by
the content of a work of art constitutes its aesthetical idea(s) ("ideas of invisible
beings, the kingdom of the blessed, hell, eternity, creation, etc.; or ... death, envy
and all vices, also love, fame, and the like ... [presented] to sense with a completeness of which there is no example in nature" [*Critique of Judgment*, §49, 157–58]).
     On Kant's account of form, natural and artificial objects, including works of art,
may be judged to be beautiful (to have beauty of form). His account of aesthetical ideas
pertains to what he calls "beautiful art," what we call the fine arts. The beautiful arts
require aesthetical ideas, which Kant argues are the products of genius. When Kant
speaks of our judging works of art, he speaks only of our judging their form. But I will
allow, here and in the text, that we can speak of a judgment or criticism of aesthetical
ideas as well. That judgment or criticism, like the judgment of form, also calls on a
free play of our faculties of imagination and understanding, but what it judges is the
content of the work of art – specifically, the originality and idealism of its aesthetical
ideas (for "originality" and "idealism" see ibid., §46, 150–51, and §58, 196). (On Kant's
account, in judging the beauty of a work of art, I must consider "the form of the presentation of [the] concept" (ibid., §48, 155); that is, I must judge how beautifully the work
presents its concept or – what seems to come to the same – its aesthetical ideas. But that
is not yet a judgment of the significance of those ideas. Once genius has produced and
presented an aesthetical idea, I can judge both its beauty and its significance.)

But now we might say: Traditional conceptions of form in the visual arts, at least those that appeal to rhetorical or linguistic notions, are perfectly analogous to Wittgenstein's examples of seeing-as. On those conceptions of form, a picture is seen under an "interpretation"; namely, the interpretation given by the rhetorical or linguistic notions (*compositio*, "free play of imagination and understanding"). These notions interpret paintings in the way that a description or text accompanying one of Wittgenstein's pictures – for example, his figure of a rectangular solid – interprets the picture. In both cases, we are brought to see an aspect: in one case, the form (composition) of a painting; in the other, a glass cube (see *PI* 193f).

On the other hand, in Wittgenstein's examples, there are competing interpretations. The figure of the rectangular solid can be seen as an inverted box and a glass cube; the duck-rabbit as a duck and as a rabbit. What is the alternative or competing possibility in the case of traditional notions of form in the visual arts? Kant's notion of form, I have noted, enters his explanation of where I find the beauty in a thing; namely, in a free play of imagination and understanding that constitutes form. But then, if Kant's notion of form is analogous to Wittgenstein's examples of seeing-as, is the beauty of an object only one of its aspects? What is another? Can we say: If you do not see the beauty in an object, then you just see it as ordinary? And if I am struck by the beauty of an object, does this alternate for me with its ordinary aspect or appearance? Of course, an extraordinary prospect that I have on an object or scene may alternate with other, ordinary prospects on the world. But can the same object strike me at one time as beautiful, at another as ordinary, and alternate between these?

What does Wittgenstein mean by an "aspect" of an object?

I claimed earlier that it is a lesson of Wittgenstein's remarks about seeing-as that in considering the examples he gives – his figure of a rectangular solid or the duck-rabbit – we may look for changes in our visual impressions or experience when we should be considering the circumstances of what we say and do. A simple instance of Wittgenstein's appeal to such circumstances can be found in the following remarks:

If I saw the duck-rabbit as a rabbit, then I saw: these shapes and colors (I give them in detail) —and I saw besides something like this: and here I point to a number of different pictures of rabbits. —This shows the difference between the concepts.

"Seeing as.... " is not part of perception. And for that reason it is like seeing and again not like. (*PI* 196h–197a)

I can draw or paint the shapes and colors of the duck-rabbit to show someone what shapes and colors I see. But drawing or painting the figure will not show which aspect I see. To show that I am now see-ing the figure as a rabbit, I must point to or draw *other* pictures of rabbits. This shows, Wittgenstein says, "the difference between the concepts" – namely, the concepts of "seeing the picture (the shapes and colors)" and "seeing the picture as a rabbit." The difference in concepts is shown in what I *do* in the two instances to show what I see (I draw what I see; I point to something that is not what I see, but resembles it). If drawing the figure indicates what I perceive (what in this instance I understand or count as "perception"), then pointing to other shapes indicates something that I must say I do not perceive. The drawing and pointing show that, and they show how, "'Seeing as. ...' is not part of perception."

A more complicated instance of Wittgenstein's appeal to the cir-cumstances of what I say and do is the following: "'To me it is an animal pierced by an arrow'. That is what I treat it as; this is my *atti-tude* to the figure. This is one meaning in calling it a case of 'seeing'" (*PI* 205a). My saying "I see it as an animal pierced by an arrow" is an expression of how I treat the figure. Saying this is *part* of my treating it (acting toward it) as an animal pierced by an arrow (there may be more that I do). When I say that I see the picture this way, I express my attitude, my stance, toward it.[14]

Wittgenstein also speaks of my *regarding* a picture as something:

I say: "We regard a portrait as a human being," —but when do we do so, and for how long? *Always*, if we see it at all (and do not, say, see it as something else)?

I might say yes to this, and that would determine the concept of regarding-as. —The question is whether yet another concept, related to this one, is also of importance to us: that, namely, of a seeing-as which only takes place while I am actually concerning myself with the picture as the object depicted. (*PI* 205g)

---

[14] For "stance," see also *PI* 194c: "In some respects I stand towards it as I do towards a human face."

In answer to the last question he remarks:

I might say: a picture does not always *live* for me while I am seeing it.

"Her picture smiles down on me from the wall." It need not always do so, whenever my glance lights on it. (*PI* 205h)

To speak of my "attitude" toward something or how I "regard" it, is to describe how it is with me, my stance toward it. The stance can have, as Wittgenstein puts it, a life, in this case a life with what is depicted. (This is not my only life with the picture. I also treat it as an object: dust it, straighten it on the wall.)[15]

Shortly after the remarks quoted above and immediately after remarks characterizing the "tone of voice [that] expresses the dawning of an aspect" (*PI* 206i), Wittgenstein notes the phrase " 'Fine shades of behavior' " (*PI* 207a), a phrase he had used earlier in *PI* II.xi to describe "certain gestures" (indicating "a certain kind of 'knowing one's way about' ") by which someone shows that he sees a drawing three-dimensionally (*PI* 203b). The suggestion in the phrase, beyond its directing attention to behavioral evidence for what someone sees, rather than psychological or "inner" evidence (an "impression" or "experience"), is that knowing what aspect someone is seeing may call for a refined appreciation of behavior, of what he does in the particular circumstances. Not only his gestures, but also what he says – which is part of what he does – may be finely shaded or gauged.

When someone says that she sees a picture under a particular aspect ("I see the face as smiling"), she not only says what she sees, but expresses her response to the picture, her attitude toward it. Her remark draws our attention to her circumstances, those in which she now finds herself speaking (and so acting, responding), and gives

---

[15] My saying "To me it is an animal pierced by an arrow" or "She smiles down on me" not only describes what I see but expresses an attitude, a stance, a response, to the figure before me. Wittgenstein remarks: "This is one meaning in calling [my experience] a case of seeing" (*PI* 205a). His examples here and his remarks about our attitude toward pictures, or the way we regard them, exemplify what Stanley Cavell calls "the dependence of reference upon expression in naming our states of consciousness" (*The Claim of Reason*, 343). Cavell's reading in *The Claim of Reason* of Wittgenstein's *Philosophical Investigations* has informed my understanding of Part II, Section 11 in many ways, but especially here.

Not all pictures elicit the same range of attitude or regard. My attitude toward a photograph is not my attitude toward a painting or an animation. I discuss some differences in the ways that we respond to photographs, paintings, and animations in *Photography and Philosophy* (New York: Garland Publishing, 1990).

salience to particular features of those circumstances (features of her position and of the picture). Her saying, before another picture, "The woman in the corner is beguiling," expresses a different response or attitude to the picture than her saying, "She is smiling."

It is difficult, considering only her words, to see the fact of her circumstances and how far they extend. Why is she called upon to respond as she does? In part, the picture calls forth her response. For her, the picture is not only a face. The woman she sees is smiling, or she is beguiling. But then, why is she looking at these pictures? And to whom do we suppose she is saying what she says?

Wittgenstein's examples of the rectangular solid, picture-rabbit, and duck-rabbit are at first presented as a psychologist might present them: "I am shown a picture-rabbit and asked what it is" (*PI* 195h). Little is said about the fact that in saying "I see this as ...," I am speaking to someone, that in the ordinary circumstances in which I might say this, I enter my remark into my life with others. Those circumstances of what I say are easily missed if we imagine a psychologist asking what we see, in part because the psychologist stages our encounter with the figure he presents as if we are responding only to him, or to no one in particular. In the setting of a psychological test or experiment, we are turned to our experience ("impression"). By contrast, Wittgenstein's examples of a rabbit running across the landscape (*PI* 197b) or a portrait photograph on our wall (*PI* 205e–h) draw our attention back to everyday circumstances of our life with objects and with others, the ordinary circumstances in which we say "I see ..." ("I see a rabbit," "I see her face as smiling") when something comes into sight or when an aspect of an object or a picture dawns or changes before us. His remarks about these examples, and others, also draw our attention to the ways in which my *saying* "I see ..." is doing something (exclaiming a dawning or change of aspect, expressing my attitude to what I see) and, more, to how my learning to say such things (like my learning to say anything, on Wittgenstein's general teaching about "language-games") requires a mastery of concepts and techniques together ("You only 'see the duck and rabbit aspects' if you are already conversant with the shapes of those two animals" [*PI* 207g]).[16]

---

[16] See also *PI* 208e:

In the triangle I can see now *this* as apex, *that* as base—now *this* as apex, *that* as base.—Clearly the words "Now I am seeing *this* as the apex" cannot so far mean

Wittgenstein's examples can strike us at moments as calling upon a refined awareness of circumstance and act that borders on a literary sensibility. His phrase, "fine shades of behavior," registers the feature of his examples that strikes us this way. The ability to mark such nuances in our own case ("I see the face as smiling," "The woman is beguiling") or the ability of another to mark them ("She sees the face as smiling," "She is beguiled by the woman") can seem extraordinary. We may find this even with the simplest pictures that Wittgenstein discusses ("To me it is an animal pierced by an arrow"), although other examples may put us in mind of the fact that more sophisticated pictures – paintings and photographs – can call for even more sophisticated responses ("I '*see the sphere floating in the air*' " [*PI* 201e], "I see the picture of a galloping horse" [*PI* 202e]).[17] In all these instances, our ordinary mastery of language can strike us as extraordinary. That lesson is not confined to the examples in this section of *Philosophical Investigations*. The appreciation of circumstance that is called upon in Wittgenstein's examples of seeing-as – and in understanding those examples philosophically – instances aspects of his philosophical observation and writing generally, an attention to "fine shades of behavior" (in what we say, in what we do) that he demands generally of philosophy.

For Kant, to judge an object to be beautiful is not to describe a feature of the object, certainly not something seen or perceived ("The judgment of taste is ... not a judgment of cognition"),[18] but, rather, to express pleasure in a discovery of form. Kant says that our pleasure or satisfaction in the beautiful is "related ... to *favor*,"[19] which I take to mean that, in saying "This is beautiful," I declare my pleasure as

anything to a learner who has only just met the concepts of apex, base, and so on.—But I do not mean this as an empirical proposition.

"Now he's seeing it like *this*," "now like *that*" would only be said of someone *capable* of making certain applications of the figure quite freely.

The substratum of this experience is the mastery of a technique.

[17] "I see the picture of a galloping horse" may allude to the dispute that arose around Eadweard Muybridge's famous photographs of horses running and the paintings that those photographs were thought to call into question.

Psychologists, given the company of the examples they keep, may miss the subtlety of the responses that pictures call upon, even in the simplest cases. Perhaps Wittgenstein mostly keeps to such examples for this very reason, to show that the sophistication that they call upon, and that is being missed, is ordinary.

[18] Kant, *Critique of Judgment*, §1, 37.

[19] Ibid., §5, 44.

an attitude or stance toward the object, an appreciation of it. What is more, Kant maintains that, in speaking as I do, I declare or claim ("demand") the agreement of others in my judgment and "[speak] of beauty as if it were a property of things."[20] My judgment, "This object is beautiful," declares my pleasure or appreciation and yours together.[21] This is unlike other expressions of feeling. In the judgment of beauty, what makes it possible to declare my pleasure or appreciation and yours together is that the conditions of the judgment ("the ... play of the imagination and the understanding")[22] are just the conditions of judgment or thought in general. In all these respects, the structure of what we call the aesthetic – what Kant calls "the beautiful" – has analogies to the structure of seeing-as. "'Seeing as'.... [like "the beautiful"] is not part of perception" (*PI* 197a). Yet "the flashing of an aspect on us [like the appearance of "the beautiful"] seems half visual experience, half thought" (*PI* 197d).[23]

---

[20] Ibid., §7, 47.

[21] The specific importance of Kant's terms here (a person judges "as if [beauty] were a property of things"; he "*demands* [the agreement of others]" [ibid., §7, 47]) is discussed in the section "Aesthetic Judgment and a Philosophical Claim" in Stanley Cavell's essay, "Aesthetic Problems of Modern Philosophy," in *Must We Mean What We Say? A Book of Essays* (Cambridge: Cambridge University Press, 1969), 86–96. Cavell argues that Kant, in speaking as he does, is characterizing what Wittgenstein would call the "grammar" of judgments of taste.

Kant's expression "the agreement of others" can also be understood in terms similar to those in which Cavell, in *The Claim of Reason*, explains Wittgenstein's appeal to our "agreement ... in judgments" (*PI* §242). For Kant, my judgments of beauty and the judgments of others must be, as Cavell puts it, "in harmony" (*The Claim of Reason*, 32). Our judgments must be in agreement, harmonize. Kant grounds this claim about our judgments of beauty in the very necessity to which Wittgenstein appeals in accounting for our agreement in concepts generally: namely, the fact that "language is ... a means of communication" (*PI* §242; and compare *Critique of Judgment*, §9, 51–2: "Hence it is the universal capability of communication of the mental state ... which ... must be fundamental").

[22] Kant, *Critique of Judgment*, §9, 52.

[23] Wittgenstein suggests, in the particular case (our seeing a rabbit run across our view, at which we exclaim "A rabbit!"), that our surprise is what inclines us to say that what we experience "seems half visual experience, half thought." He goes on to question this way of describing such experiences. The difference between Kant's and Wittgenstein's examples, as I understand them, is as follows: in Kant's example, there is something that we can call "thinking" – namely, our reflection on the object ("the play of the imagination and the understanding"), which may be elaborated in criticism. In Wittgenstein's example, we have only our exclamation ("A rabbit!"), which expresses our surprise and tells whoever is listening what we have seen ("The very expression which is also a report of what is seen, is here a cry

Kant's account of the judgment of the beautiful provides a partial account of what we call aesthetic or critical judgment, or, more generally, criticism.[24] It describes possibilities and necessities of criticism: for example, the possibility of arriving at a judgment of a work through the discovery of significant possibilities of form, and the necessity of declaring, in your judgment, your appreciation and others' together. As in Wittgenstein's examples of seeing-as, what brings out the salience of certain features of the object is "interpretation": the critic's application of a particular word ("*compositio*," "delineation," "composition") or, more generally, the way he or she writes about the object. And again, as in Wittgenstein's examples, the critic does not just describe something he or she sees but expresses an attitude or stance – an appreciation of the object.

But is the analogy of criticism with seeing-as perfect? Must the critic allow that there is another interpretation of the work, another as good as the one given? Again, will it do here to speak of the work's "ordinary aspect" or "ordinary appearance" as against its aspect under interpretation (the critic's interpretation)? If the conditions of criticism are the conditions of the judgment of the beautiful as Kant describes them, there cannot be a perfect analogy here. In judging an object to be beautiful, I don't speak of it *as* beautiful. I say that it *is* beautiful, demanding your agreement. The ordinary is not another possibility in the circumstances, not another as good as this one.

I offer another word, or parable, about taking a stance in criticism. Early in *Painting as an Art*, Richard Wollheim offers, as a representation of the account of pictorial meaning that he will give in his book, the image of a painter standing before his work:

Inside each artist is a spectator upon whom the artist, the artist as agent, is dependent. And this dependence is enshrined in what is one of the few

---

of recognition" [*PI* 198a]). Wittgenstein asks whether, and why, we want to call the experience of recognition "thinking" ("half thought") ("The question is: *why* does one want to say this?" [*PI* 197h]). But he doesn't deny that we can speak of the cry of recognition, our wording of what we see, as "thinking" ("the expression of thought" [*PI* 197c]).

[24] Kant's account of the judgment of the beautiful does not offer a characterization of everything that a critic does. Aesthetical ideas, realized by the artist (Kant's "genius"), are also subject to criticism. See note 13.

constancies in the history of pictorial art: that is, the artist's posture, or that, in the act of painting, he positions himself in front of the support, on the side of it that he is about to mark, facing it, with his eyes open and fixed upon it.[25]

The artist standing before his painting, looking at it, represents the way that pictorial meaning, for Wollheim, depends on certain of our perceptual capacities. On Wollheim's account, the painter paints "*with* the eyes … [and] *for* the eyes."[26] The painter discovers significance in the shapes and figures that he paints in the very way that we will discover significance in them, by looking at what is before our eyes.

Against this picture or image of the painter, I place another image, that of the painter drawing or making a mark with his brush.[27] Until the artist's hand touches his work, draws a line or makes a mark, he has not yet taken a position or stance toward it. Drawing the line, making the mark, places him before the painting, and it cuts into the world that he is painting, creates a significant division or foregrounding, singles something out. If this reveals something about the artist's position that is missed in Wollheim's image, does it reveal anything

Criticism, if it is to give an account or appreciation of the artist's aesthetical ideas (which "approximate to a presentation of concepts of reason (intellectual ideas)" [*Critique of Judgment*, §49, 157]), requires what Kant calls "culture" (see ibid., §29, 105); that is, education in "rational ideas," for example, the ideas of freedom, the soul, God, "invisible beings, the kingdom of the blessed, hell, eternity, creation, etc." (ibid., §49, 157). Presumably, for Kant, this "culture" (education in rational or intellectual ideas), calling only upon our possession of reason, can be acquired by anyone. So the critic offering an appreciation of aesthetical ideas can still be said to speak with a "universal voice" (ibid., §8, 50).

[25] Richard Wollheim, *Painting as an Art* (Princeton: Princeton University Press, 1987), 43.

[26] Ibid., 44.

[27] As it turns out, the paintings that Wollheim reproduces to illustrate his picture or image of the painter can also be used to illustrate my image. The painters in those illustrations are in the act of drawing or painting, or are about to paint (see figures 11, 12, 13, 15, and 16 in Wollheim, *Painting as an Art*, pages 38, 39, 40, and 42).

The image that I offer is based on the Abbé Du Bos's conception of drawing. In an unpublished essay, "Single Moments: Philosophical Reflections on Painting and Photography," I contrast Du Bos's conception of drawing with Lessing's conception of the "means or signs" of painting. For Lessing here, see Gotthold Ephraim Lessing, *Laocoön: An Essay on the Limits of Painting and Poetry*, trans. Edward Allen McCormick (Baltimore: Johns Hopkins University Press, 1962, 1984), 78.

about our position? What is there for us to do, after the artist's drawing or marking, except to look? But we don't just stand and look, or that is not all that we do. We respond to what we see, we speak or write, inscribing ourselves into the artist's work. His gesture, his attitude of inscribing, must be met by ours. His drawing or marking must be met by our judgment, our criticism, our acts of bringing out the salience and significance of his delineations of shape, relation, and idea. Without our acts of judgment and criticism, without declaring our position or stance, his work will remain ordinary for us, will fail to yield its significance as *art*.

2

Aspects, Sense, and Perception

Sandra Laugier

Contemporary interpretations of phenomenology, as well as current theories of perception, define perception (and seeing) in terms of *sense*: for example, in terms of a conceptualization set over against a brute perceptual given, which is a notion John McDowell has defined and criticized in *Mind and World* as the "Myth of the Given".[1] This idea is founded on the related idea of a sense immanent to perception, called a "noema." This employment of the term "sense" has its roots, paradoxically, in a psychologizing reading of Frege; it also infects how we understand seeing-as in Wittgenstein. The question I want to ask, then, can be put simply: Is seeing (giving) a sense? Naturally I cannot pretend here to resolve the crucial question, central to much current philosophical discussion, of the connection of language to perception. My aim here is simply to bring out certain difficulties for the idea of perceptual sense, difficulties raised by Wittgenstein (and, along parallel lines, by Austin). These difficulties come from the specific point of view of ordinary language philosophy. Bringing out these difficulties will be the aim of my first two sections. In a third section, I will try to show how, in opposing the idea of perceptual sense, these criticisms at the same time constitute the emergence of something like a "linguistic phenomenology," which, instead of adding sense to perception, can

---

[1] John McDowell, *Mind and World* (Cambridge: Harvard University Press, 1994); see, for example, 8 ff.

address the perception of the "phenomenon" of language as such, and thereby make possible a reconsideration of the notion of aspect.

1. THE SENSES OF SENSE: SENSE AND PERCEPTION

Talk of perceptual sense takes its start in Frege's notion of sense. This notion was the basis for the so-called Fregean readings of phenomenology,[2] while it was at the same time being taken up in the analytic tradition in various and sometimes incompatible ways. It is not insignificant that analytic philosophy is essentially founded on the English translation of a distinction (Frege's distinction between *Sinn* and *Bedeutung*) that was originally formulated in German, and all the more so since these terms are not without their own ambiguities in German. *Sinn* was from the beginning the victim of a certain indeterminacy of translation: it was sometimes translated as "sense," sometimes as "meaning." As for *Bedeutung*, until the translation "reference" became the most common choice, there was some confusion: it has also been translated as "meaning," as well as by "indication," "denotation," and "significatum." It certainly strikes one as curious that "meaning" could be used indifferently for *Sinn* and for *Bedeutung* even by philosophers (Russell is the most outstanding example) who otherwise took account of, or were familiar with, Frege's distinction. What I will examine here is this initial confusion, and its consequences for the history of analytic philosophy and for analytic philosophy's connection with phenomenology.

A significant example of the ambiguities of these terms is to be found in C. K. Ogden and I. A. Richards' celebrated book *The Meaning of Meaning* (written in stages beginning in 1910 and published in 1923).[3] This book is a bit forgotten today, but it had a considerable influence in its time. While Ogden and Richards stand clearly in the Frege-Wittgenstein tradition, they play on diverse senses of "meaning." In their book, "meaning" stands equally for *Sinn* and for *Bedeutung.*

---

[2] The best example is Dagfinn Føllesdal's famous paper "Husserl's Notion of Noema," *Journal of Philosophy* 66 (1969): 680–87. See also several papers in *Husserl, Intentionality, and Cognitive Science*, ed. Hubert L. Dreyfus and Harrison Hall (Cambridge: MIT Press, 1982).

[3] C. K. Ogden and I. A. Richards, *The Meaning of Meaning* (San Diego: Harcourt Brace Jovanovich, 1989).

By contrast, in the English translation of *Tractatus Logico-Philosophicus* that Ogden had just produced (1922), "meaning" stands for *Bedeutung* and "sense" for *Sinn*. Russell, in his own introduction to the *Tractatus*, takes "meaning" to refer both to the sense of the proposition (*Sinn*) and to the denotation of the sub-propositional sign (*Bedeutung*). It seems, then, that the existence of the term "meaning" in English allowed the development of a hybrid term covering both sense and denotation, and thus, curiously enough, obscuring precisely the distinction Frege meant to draw. Use of the term "meaning" allows the two dimensions to quite naturally run together; its use is one of the things that makes it difficult to mark Frege's distinction clearly in English. But the problem is not one limited to English; there is a real difficulty about marking any such distinction within ordinary language. In Volume I of his *Logical Investigations*, Husserl writes with regard to the Fregean distinction between *Sinn* and *Bedeutung*:

A further consideration is our ingrained tendency to use the two words as synonymous, a circumstance which makes it seem rather a dubious step if their meanings [*Bedeutungen*] are differentiated, and if (as G. Frege has proposed) we use one for meaning in our sense [*die Bedeutung in unserem Sinn*], and the other for the objects expressed. To this we may add that both terms are exposed to the same equivocations which we distinguished above in connection with the term "expression," and to many more besides, and that this is so both in scientific and in ordinary speech.[4]

An important element in natural language can also be found in an ambiguity that is common to English and to German (as well as to French, if less suggestively so), with regard to the "sensorial" sense of "sense." The title of Strawson's *The Bounds of Sense*[5] speaks to this ambiguity; this influential work on Kant's first *Critique* transforms the problem of the limits of knowledge and of sensibility into a semantic question about the limits of sense (of the space in which our questions have a sense). One can also think in this connection of Austin's title *Sense and Sensibilia*,[6] as well as of Putnam's

4 Edmund Husserl, *Logical Investigations*, vol. 1, trans. J. N. Findlay (London: Routledge, 1970), 201.
5 P. F. Strawson, *The Bounds of Sense: An Essay on Kant's Critique of Pure Reason* (London: Methuen, 1966).
6 J. L. Austin, *Sense and Sensibilia*, ed. G. J. Warnock (Oxford: Oxford University Press, 1962).

more recent "Sense, Nonsense, and the Senses."[7] There is Quine's charming expression (in "Five Milestones of Empiricism") of the principle of empiricism, as well: "*Only sense makes sense.*"[8] In "The Meaning of a Word," Austin gave what is certainly the most significant criticism of this unsurprising, but problematic, passage from linguistic to perceptual sense. There Austin first rejects the idea of meaning, and then goes on likewise to reject the idea of reference. Taking up, in succession, Stuart Hampshire and Charles Morris, he says about both that they succeed admirably in avoiding thinking of meaning as an entity, but then that they both unfortunately fall back on talk of denotation and significatum. These latter notions are, from Austin's point of view, equally hollow and artificial: "Now this is quite as fictitious an entity as any 'Platonic idea'; and is due to precisely the same fallacy as looking for 'the meaning (or designatum) of a word'."[9]

If Austin rejects both sense and denotation, it is because, in his view, we have not sufficiently reflected on reasons why, for example, we might give different things the same name, as well as because we are so tempted, as Frege was, to take proper names as our paradigm when thinking about denotation. For Austin, the same mythology underlies talk both of meaning and of denotation as they are defined by philosophers, and those who see through the former ought to look equally closely at the latter. Austin's rejection of the Fregean distinction is thus quite absolute:

Why are we tempted to slip back in this way? Perhaps there are two main reasons. First, there is the curious belief that all words are *names*, i.e., in effect *proper* names, and therefore stand for something or designate it in the way a proper name does. But this view that general names "have denotation" in the same way that proper names do, is quite as odd as the view that proper names "have connotation" in the same way that general names do, which is commonly recognized to lead to error.[10]

---

[7] Hilary Putnam, "Sense, Nonsense, and the Senses: An Inquiry into the Powers of the Human Mind," in *The Threefold Cord: Mind, Body, and World* (New York: Columbia University Press, 1999), 3–70.

[8] W. V. Quine, "Five Milestones of Empiricism," *Theories and Things* (Cambridge: Harvard University Press, 1981), 68.

[9] Austin, "The Meaning of a Word," in *Philosophical Papers*, Third Edition, ed. J. O. Urmson and G. J. Warnock (Oxford: Oxford University Press, 1979), 61.

[10] Ibid.

This whole tendency, as Austin sees it, bespeaks a more general malady, namely that of demanding too much analysis: "When we have given an analysis of a certain sentence, containing a word or phrase '*x*', we often feel inclined to ask, of our analysis, 'What *in it, is* "*x*"?'" Austin thus denounces our (philosophical) tendency to seek out entities for our utterances to be about, entities that are not the objects about which we ordinarily speak, but intermediate entities like meanings or denotations. This sort of thing happens particularly when we talk about perception: "Or again, when we have analyzed the statement 'trees can exist unperceived' into statements about sensing sensa, we still tend to feel uneasy unless we can say *something* '*really does*' 'exist unperceived': hence theories about 'sensibilia' and what not."[11]

This, then, is the breadth of Austin's criticism: it rejects not only a certain form of logical analysis as found, for instance, in Russell, but also the other sense of "sense," namely, perceptual sense. In effect, Austin is rejecting the idea that seeing or sensing themselves already involve seeing with a *sense*. Not that he proposes the opposite, offering an account of perception as direct – some have spoken in this connection of his "direct realism" – instead of an account of perception as sense-mediated. The idea of such an account itself makes no sense. For what would an indirect realism be? And could we say that we see *either* directly or indirectly? There is a passage in "Truth" that clearly calls the dichotomy into question. Austin passes here again from the level of language to the level of perception in asking about the object of a definition, for example, of an elephant. He compares the question "Do we define the word or the thing?" with the question "Do we see the object or an image of the object?": "it is nonsense to ask 'Do we *define* the word or the animal?' For defining an elephant (supposing we ever do this) is a compendious description of an operation involving both word and animal (do we focus the image or the battleship?). ..."[12] We have here an elegant and radical formulation of the question of seeing, one that can specify, as Cavell says in *Pursuits of Happiness*, "the internality of words and world,"[13] but which also, in the context of our discussion

[11] Ibid.
[12] Austin, "Truth," in *Philosophical Papers*, 124.
[13] Stanley Cavell, *Pursuits of Happiness: The Hollywood Comedy of Remarriage* (Cambridge: Harvard University Press, 1981), 204.

of aspects, allows us to reconsider seeing-as. (Note that – and this is a point I will return to in what follows – the issue here is one not of seeing but of looking, of *focus*.) We must come to see that the question as to whether what I "see" is an image or a battleship is one that does not itself have a sense.

At this point I would like to make a few precautionary remarks in order to make clear exactly what view it is that Austin is criticizing. A superficial reading of *Sense and Sensibilia* could leave the impression that he is there defending a linguistic theory of perception. In fact it is just the opposite. Austin rejects the idea that our perceiving *depends* on language. But for all that, he does not say that our perception is *independent* of language: in fact these two opposed ideas share the fault of being metaphysical – that is to say, of not only neglecting ordinary language but of perverting it. This is why it is false to say, as is said in certain contemporary discussions of Austin and, though with less distortion, in recent writings by Putnam, that Austin defends a naïve or direct realism; for by Austin's own lights, it makes no sense to speak of *realism*. The doctrine explicitly attacked by Austin in *Sense and Sensibilia* was that "we never see or otherwise perceive (or 'sense'), or anyhow we never *directly* perceive or sense, material objects (or material things), but only sense-data (or our own ideas, impressions, sensa, sense-perceptions, percepts, &c.)."[14] Austin's critique of this doctrine is equally damaging to the idea of perceptual sense: "I am *not*, then ... going to maintain that we ought to be 'realists', to embrace, that is, the doctrine that we *do* perceive material things (or objects). This doctrine would be no less scholastic and erroneous than its antithesis. The question, do we perceive material things or sense-data, no doubt looks very simple – *too* simple – but is entirely misleading. ... One of the most important points to grasp is that these two terms, 'sense-data' and 'material things', live by taking in each other's washing – what is spurious is not one term of the pair, but the antithesis itself."[15] It is of course true that since the time Austin made his criticism, the problems about perception have been greatly modified and refined: one no longer contrasts sense-data with material objects, rather one talks of sense and

[14] Austin, *Sense and Sensibilia*, 1962.
[15] Ibid., 3–4.

intentionality on one side, and of the world or of nature on the other. But this makes no difference with regard to the objections raised by Austin. The criticisms in *Sense and Sensibilia*, though leveled directly at traditional empiricism, are perhaps even more useful today, now that a whole analysis of perception has been worked out in terms of sense. Austin has the merit of having shown that the majority of questions about perception are unanswerable simply because they are posed in a particular way: in terms, dichotomies, and problematics imposed by philosophy. So we are *not* to look for an answer to the question "What kind of thing do we perceive?" – a question which is indeed empty, but which has continued to be posed in the greater part of recent analytic writing.

One can ask then, starting from Austin, whether current discussions of perception (for instance, as to whether there is a preconceptualization or "prestructuration" of the perceptual given, or if there is a meaning contained already in perception, or as to what the relation is between perception and the object perceived) do not begin with a mistaken question, which distorts the ordinary use of "see," "perceive," and "real." *Sense and Sensibilia* develops arguments already formulated in "Other Minds": the philosopher demands "how I know" that there is a real object there, even though this question – how do you know – cannot be posed (in ordinary language) except in certain contexts, where there is a question of setting aside a doubt:

If the context doesn't make it clear, then I am entitled to ask "How do you mean? Do you mean it may be stuffed or what? *What are you suggesting?*" The wile of the metaphysician consists in asking "Is it a real table?" (a kind of object which has no obvious way of being phoney) and not specifying or limiting what may be wrong with it, so that I feel at a loss "how to prove" it *is* a real one.[16]

Considering these things leads Austin to deny the existence of a proper object of perception, the sort of thing that could be common, for instance, to both veridical and delusional experience.

Like Quine, Austin took as one of his targets the introduction in philosophy of artificial or dubious entities like meanings. But he has a further point, as well: the philosopher arbitrarily attributes belief in these entities to the ordinary man, only to reject or amend the belief

[16] Austin, "Other Minds," in *Philosophical Papers*, 87.

thus fabricated. This procedure is still widely practiced today, and is typical of much current work in analytic philosophy. "These entities, which of course don't really figure at all in the plain man's language or among his beliefs, are brought in with the implication that whenever we 'perceive' there is an *intermediate* entity *always* present and *informing* us about something *else*."[17] Austin's argument is directed against theories of perception founded on illusion or fiction, that is, those which make a representation itself the object of perception. Austin doubts whether it even makes sense to suppose, with the classical hypothesis (found, for example, in Cartesian skepticism), that everything we see might be illusion. Certainly the plain man may ask himself whether he is "deceived," but "talk of deception only *makes sense* against a background of general non-deception."[18] Further, even when one is deceived (by a magic trick, or by one's gas gauge) this is not a matter of "perceiving something unreal":

Looking at the Müller-Lyer diagram (in which, of two lines of equal length, one looks longer than the other), or at a distant village on a very clear day across a valley, is a very different kettle of fish from seeing a ghost or from having D.T.s and seeing pink rats. And when the plain man sees on the stage the Headless Woman, what he sees (and this *is* what he sees, whether he knows it or not) is not something "unreal" or "immaterial", but a woman against a dark background with her head in a black bag.[19]

In sum, seeing is what it is and not another thing (not even having perceptions, deceptive or veridical – this supposition helps nothing).[20] If I am looking through a telescope, to take up another of Austin's examples, and you ask me what I see, I can respond, in each case quite correctly: 1) a brilliant spot; 2) a star; 3) Sirius; or 4) the image that is in the fourteenth mirror of the telescope. "I can say, quite correctly and with no ambiguity whatever, that I see any of these."[21] "Seeing" does not have different senses in these different cases. That these various answers can be given does not mean that we ought to distinguish, in these various cases, different "senses" of seeing, or different entities to be the objects of perception (the real object, an intermediate entity, a purely subjective

---

[17] Austin, *Sense and Sensibilia*, 11.
[18] Ibid.
[19] Ibid., 14.
[20] Cf. Hilary Putnam's remarks on this topic in *The Threefold Cord*, 1999, 152.
[21] Austin, *Sense and Sensibilia*, 99.

representation). For Austin, there is only *one* sense of seeing. This sums up what Putnam is now calling the "disjunctive theory of perception," that is, the denial that there is an element in common (internal state or quale) between the experience of seeing an object, and the experience of an hallucination or an entirely deceptive seeing of an object.[22]

Despite this persistent criticism, the idea of such a common element is fundamental to much contemporary work on the content of perception. This is partly due to the influence of Frege (of whose theory of perception Austin's and Putnam's work are a radical, if implicit, criticism). "On *Sinn* and *Bedeutung*" turns on an example similar to the telescope example I quoted from Austin; in light of it, Frege, contrary to Austin as well as to Wittgenstein, posits a difference between seeing as having a subjective representation, seeing as seeing an objective image, and seeing the object itself. He thereby also posits an entity that is in common between different representations, without being for all that the object of perception. It is this example that has inspired perceptual interpretations of sense and Fregean theories of perception. Frege writes:

Somebody observes the Moon through a telescope. I compare the Moon itself to the *Bedeutung*; it is the object of the observation, mediated by the real image projected by the object glass in the interior of the telescope, and by the retinal image of the observer. The former I compare to the sense, the latter is like the idea or intuition [*Anschauung*]. The optical image in the telescope is indeed one-sided and dependent upon the standpoint of observation; but it is still objective, inasmuch as it can be used by several observers.[23]

Frege goes on to note that one could, by use of a display device, see one's own retinal image, and that, therefore, such an image can itself be taken as an object of perception – but this image does not figure in seeing in the same way when one is seeing it, and when it is one's seeing. It is well known that Frege chose not to pursue the question of what we see, on the grounds that it would take him too far afield. Certainly he was aware of the difficulties in thinking that what we see is in general a representation. But the same difficulties hold for thinking that what we see is a "real image" (as opposed to the moon), or that seeing such an image is seeing *something other* than seeing the moon, seeing an intermediate entity or internal representation.

---

[22] See, for example, Putnam, *The Threefold Cord*, 129 ff.
[23] Gottlob Frege, "On *Sinn* and *Bedeutung*," in *The Frege Reader*, ed. Michael Beaney (Oxford: Blackwell, 1997), 155.

This brings us back to Austin. Seeing is not giving a sense to a content: seeing is seeing. As he says in one of his most striking passages: " 'I saw an insignificant-looking man in black trousers.' 'I saw Hitler.' Two different senses of 'saw'? Of course not."[24] Austin rejects any intermediary such as a perceptual *Sinn*, without, for all that, yielding to a mythology of "seeing directly": there is, for him, no reason to say that we perceive things directly, any more than that we perceive things indirectly (and the same goes for an appeal to "direct realism," or for saying that intentionality puts us in touch with the world "directly," etc.). Like "real," "direct" is for Austin a "trouser-word," that is, a word whose negative form "wears the trousers," in the sense that the function of the positive form can be characterized entirely in terms of the function of the negative. At the same time, there is from his point of view no reason to think that our perceiving or seeing is conceptualized (or structured, as some now prefer to say). And again, Austin's point is not that our perceiving is therefore *not* structured or conceptualized. He does not therefore fall into the Myth of the Given as criticized by McDowell, either by positing a given that is subject to our concepts, or by positing a pure, non-conceptual given. Charles Travis has recently emphasized the influence of Austin on McDowell,[25] and it seems to me that Austin himself has a role to play in current discussions of the given and its interpretation.

At this point, one begins to see the relevance of Austin's thinking to questions about aspects. That things look to us like this or that is, for Austin, an *ordinary* fact, and to account for it we do not need to invoke a perceptual sense or a conceptualization of the given. The same goes for the classic examples of illusion, faced with which we all know how to correct ourselves, and which have nothing to do with hallucinations. The stick in the water does *not* look like a bent stick; it would have to have quite another aspect in order for us to believe it bent. For Austin this is nothing but an ordinary case of perception, and is not an occasion to conjure up immateriality, inference, or the imposition of sense. "That a round coin should 'look elliptical' (in one sense) from some points of view is exactly what we expect and what we normally find; indeed, we should be badly put out if we ever found this not to be so."[26] This is not a case of illusion, but one of

---

[24] Austin, *Sense and Sensibilia*, 99.
[25] Charles Travis, "Taking Thought," *Mind* 109 (2000): 533–57.
[26] Austin, *Sense and Sensibilia*, 26.

perspective, a phenomenon with which we have become familiar, as
we have with images in mirrors or at the movies. Here what is *ordinary*
resolves the question of illusion. "It is important to realize here how
familiarity, so to speak, takes the edge off illusion."[27]

To conclude on this point, it is interesting to note that Austin's
arguments also cast in doubt certain classic motivations for skepticism, motivations which now reappear as motivations for cognitivism about perception, particularly the idea that dreams furnish us
with a perceptual content that could equally be present in a case of
perception. Why should we think that it is the same thing – even at
the level of the character of the experience, never mind at the level
of ontology – for the subject to encounter a dream and a reality?
Dreams are, Austin says, *dreams.* As Putnam has recently noted in
reprising this argument of Austin's, there is a difference in the character of the perception itself; the difference is not *only* that in one
case the experience corresponds to a real object and in the other
case not.[28] This is then the upshot of Austin's arguments: a veridical and a deceptive experience are neither directed at the same sort
of object nor constituted by the same sort of entity (e.g., a "representation"). And this objection to mythologizing about perception
is one that Wittgenstein could make as well: as he says, seeing is not
seeing-as (which is not to say that seeing-as is a single thing – a point
that Wittgenstein also makes).

2. SEEING SENSE

Seeing is not a matter of giving a sense: there is, on the contrary, something altogether different which we want to call a perception of sense.
To bring this into focus, we will have to take a perspective quite contrary to the one assumed so far. For Austin, we perceive (in a sense
that is not metaphorical) differences within language. If he anticipated
McDowell in rejecting the Myth of the Given, it was to put in place a
new understanding of what *is* given. The philosophical problem is not
one of arriving at agreement on a question of opinion, but rather one
of arriving at a point of departure, a given. What is thus given is, for

[27] Ibid.
[28] Putnam, *The Threefold Cord*, 25–29.

Austin, our language, not now as a body of utterances, but as a space of agreement about *what we should say when*:

> For me, the essential thing is first of all to arrive at agreement on the question of "what we would say when" ... and on the basis of this agreement, this given, this acquisition, we can begin to reclaim our little patch of garden. Let me add that just this is what all too often goes missing in philosophy: an initial *datum* we can agree on as a point of departure.[29]

In the first instance, this understanding of the given can serve as a response to perplexities about sense-data: this agreement is an "agreement on how to determine what has been given," and thus an agreement "on a certain way, one certain way, of describing and of grasping the facts." There is of course generally more than one way to describe things; but if we can come to "agreement on some one particular way to describe things," this is certainly all that is required for perception.[30] It is in the combined activity of agreement and disagreement (in how we describe things) that the real emerges. It is the perception of (real) differences in language, not a perception of sense, that allows us to perceive things. These reflections may shed light on this enigmatic passage from "A Plea for Excuses":

> When we examine what we should say when, what words we should use in what situations, we are looking again not *merely* at words (or "meanings", whatever they may be), but also at the realities we use the words to talk about: we are using a sharpened awareness of words to sharpen our perception of, though not as the final arbiter of, the phenomena. For this reason I think it might be better to use, for this way of doing philosophy, some less misleading name ... for instance, "linguistic phenomenology", only that is rather a mouthful.[31]

On this understanding, differences and resemblances within language (a theme Austin shares with Wittgenstein) constitute what one can in the end speak of as the "realism" of Austin. These differences make possible our perception of things, not because language gives things a sense, but simply because coming to perceive differences in things is a way of coming to perceive differences in things. By examining our use

[29] J. L. Austin and others, "Discussion générale," in *Cahiers de Royaumont, Philosophie No. 4, La Philosophie Analytique* (Paris: Editions de Minuit, 1962), 334. (In French; my translation.)
[30] Ibid.
[31] Austin, "A Plea for Excuses," in *Philosophical Papers*, 182.

of language and its variations, we can establish clearly for ourselves differences in reality (though language does not fix what differences there can be in reality all on its own). Compare Cavell's description of Austin's purposes in drawing distinctions:

Part of the effort of any philosopher will consist in showing up differences, and one of Austin's most furious perceptions is of the slovenliness, the grotesque crudity and fatuousness, of the usual distinctions philosophers have traditionally thrown up. Consequently, one form his investigations take is that of repudiating the distinctions lying around philosophy – dispossessing them, as it were, by showing better ones. And better not merely because finer, but because more solid, having, so to speak, a greater natural weight.[32]

If one takes this perspective on language as given (as *datum*), then a number of questions will arise that will be useful in drawing out more of what is meant by "linguistic phenomenology." How does the notion of a sign figure in it, a notion which, as we have seen in our discussion of Ogden and Richards, constitutes a natural place to effect the transfer from linguistic to perceptual *Sinn*? It is clear, in accordance with our analysis of "see," that signs are not what we perceive of language, and that there is no hope of "reducing" what is given to mere signs (or, in the Wittgensteinian terminology, to "external" symptoms). In "Other Minds," Austin uses the term "inept" (initially coined in this use by John Wisdom and then developed by Austin in "Truth")[33] to characterize talk of "all the signs of bread," as a way of describing what we have when we look into the larder and see it, take it out and taste it, etc. Austin writes:

Doing these things is not finding (some) signs of bread at all: the taste or feel of bread is not a sign or symptom of bread at all. What I might be taken to mean if I announced that I had found signs of bread in the larder seems rather doubtful, since bread is not normally casketed (or if in the bin, leaves no traces), and not being a transient event (impending bread, &c.), does not have any normally accepted "signs".[34]

One has in this passage an allusion to the source of skepticism, namely a passage from "normal" uncertainty as to whether this bread is real (and not plastic) to uncertainty as to whether anything I experience

[32] Cavell, "Austin at Criticism," in *Must We Mean What We Say?: A Book of Essays* (Cambridge: Cambridge University Press, 1969), 103.
[33] Cf. Austin, "Truth," 130.
[34] Austin, "Other Minds," 106–7.

is real, or whether I'm only trafficking in "signs." "If it turns out not to be bread after all, we might say 'It tasted like bread, but actually it was only bread-substitute', or 'It exhibited many of the characteristic features of bread, but differed in important respects: it was only a synthetic imitation.' "[35] What we don't say is: here are all the signs of bread, but there's no bread. In the absence of bread, the signs *aren't* signs of bread.

This argument of Austin's takes on a new significance when we consider how it works against philosophers who want to analyze perception in terms of "signs" of a reality to which we are related. For Austin, such an attempt not only distorts our language, it commits an absurdity: it is equivalent to – and here we come to the heart of the idea of a connection between sense in language and sense in perception – the idea that the senses *speak* or *mean* things. Nothing could be further from Austin's view, or from the tradition in which Putnam (in *The Threefold Cord* and elsewhere) has recently situated Austin's work (James, Wittgenstein, McDowell) than the idea that the senses say something, that the senses make sense, and that what they say gives us access to reality. Austin describes this illusion (and especially how difficult it is to free oneself of it) with striking clarity in "Other Minds." It is, he says, the illusion that sensa, that is things, colors, noises, and the rest, speak or are labeled by nature, so that I can literally *say* what (that which) I *see*: it pipes up, or I read it off. It is as if sensa were *literally* to "announce themselves" or to "identify themselves," in the way we indicate when we say "It presently identified itself as a particularly fine white rhinoceros." But surely this is only a manner of speaking, a reflexive idiom in which the French, for example, indulge more freely than the English: sensa are dumb, and only previous experience enables *us* to identify them. If we choose to say that they "identify themselves" (and certainly "recognizing" is not a highly voluntary activity of ours), then it must be admitted that they share the birthright of all speakers, that of speaking unclearly and untruly.[36]

The same point is made even more forcefully in *Sense and Sensibilia*: "In fact, of course, our senses are dumb ... our senses do not *tell* us anything, true or false."[37] Thinking that there is a language or a

---

[35] Ibid., 107.
[36] Ibid., 97.
[37] Austin, *Sense and Sensibilia*, 11.

meaning in perception is certainly, for Austin, one of the chief illusions
of philosophy: from this point of view, the transfer effected by Fregean
approaches to phenomenology (from linguistic to perceptual sense),
which underlies many theories of aspects, is nothing but an instance
of this perennial philosophical wish to listen to this little voice of the
senses. Austin inverts the phenomenologist's idea that perception itself
has a sense or "says" something: one of the themes running through his
rejection of this idea is that language itself is something we perceive.

Where is Wittgenstein in all this? Our detour by way of Austin has
now allowed us to define the problem: how can we recognize that seeing is "mute" without falling back into thinking of perception as brute,
that is, without making the mistake which is just the mirror image (as
McDowell has urged) of thinking that the senses must speak? The difficulty is that Wittgenstein can seem on a first reading to be advocating a
view of seeing as linguistic or conceptualized (this, as Kuhn points out,
is how he was used by Norwood Russell Hanson).[38] Without elaborat-
ing on how ordinary seeing, in Wittgenstein as in Austin, differs from
seeing-as, I note that the difference is suggested in passages like this
from *Philosophical Investigations*:

> It would have made as little sense for me to say "Now I am seeing it as ..." as to
> say at the sight of a knife and fork "Now I am seeing this as a knife and fork."
> This expression would not be understood. —Any more than: "Now it's a fork"
> or "It can be a fork too". One doesn't "*take*" what one knows as the cutlery at
> a meal *for* cutlery; any more than one ordinarily tries to move one's mouth as
> one eats, or aims at moving it. (*PI* 195b–c)

We can think of this point in connection with Wittgenstein's idea of a
seeing that is *not* an interpretation, but simply a seeing, as opposed to
the illusion that every seeing is a seeing-as, an interpretation or judgment. The case is exactly analogous to the understanding of a rule as it
is discussed in *PI* §201: "What this shows is that there is a way of grasping
a rule which is *not* an *interpretation*, but which is exhibited [äußert] in
what we call 'obeying the rule' and 'going against it' in actual cases."

What is surprising in all this – and here is the crux of the difficulty –
is that for Wittgenstein, unlike for Austin as Putnam and others read

[38] See Thomas S. Kuhn, *The Road Since Structure: Philosophical Essays, 1970–1993,
with an Autobiographical Interview*, ed. James Conant and John Haugeland
(Chicago: University of Chicago Press, 2000), 200; see also 293.

him, the solution to these problems does not lie in a version of direct realism. Here we arrive at the difficult question of whether there is a Wittgensteinian phenomenology, and if so, what it has in common with an Austinian linguistic phenomenology as I outlined it earlier. Certain passages in Wittgenstein, discussed by David Stern in *Wittgenstein on Mind and Language*,[39] can evoke the arguments cited above from *Sense and Sensibilia*. For example: "A phenomenon isn't a symptom of something else: it is the reality. A phenomenon isn't a symptom of something else which alone makes the proposition true or false: it itself is what verifies the proposition" (*PR* §225). A phenomenon is not a symptom or a sign of something else that is real: on this point, Wittgenstein and Austin are in agreement. All the same, it seems to me that to see the problems that Austin was raising in their full depth, we need to confront the question of a linguistic phenomenology as it is posed, though with a difference, in Wittgenstein.

3. PERCEPTION ON HOLIDAY

One thing it is interesting to notice here is how much continuity there is to Wittgenstein's thought on this subject. We can look all the way back to this passage in the *Notebooks*:

Skepticism is *not* irrefutable, but *obvious nonsense* if it tries to doubt where no question can be asked. ...

My method is not to sunder the hard from the soft, but to see the hardness of the soft.

It is one of the chief skills of the philosopher not to occupy himself with questions which do not concern him.

Russell's method in his "Scientific method in philosophy" is simply a retrogression from the method of physics. (*NB* 44, 1.5.15)

Cora Diamond has drawn attention to Wittgenstein's criticism of Russell in this passage.[40] In his discussion of skepticism in *Our Knowledge of the External World*, Russell aimed to separate the hard from the soft, that is, to separate that which could not be doubted (sense-data) from that which could (real objects). Like Austin, Wittgenstein

---

[39] David G. Stern, *Wittgenstein on Mind and Language* (Oxford: Oxford University Press, 1995), see 83–87.
[40] Cora Diamond, "Seeing the Hardness of the Soft," *Skepticism in Context*, ed. James Conant and Andrea Kern (London: Routledge, forthcoming).

takes exception to the idea that, in the first instance, our perception gives us something other than reality: to see the hardness of the soft is to see that certain propositions give us reality by *not* being constructions out of phenomena.

In Wittgenstein's discussions with the Vienna Circle, for example, the issue would arise of the status of hypotheses in physics. Hypotheses do not have sense, because they are not true or false; their sense is *incomplete*: "The equations of physics can neither be true nor false. It is only the findings in the course of a verification, i.e., phenomenological statements, that are true and false. *Physics is not history*. ... The statements of physics are never completed. Nonsense to think of them as completed" (*WWK* 101). An hypothesis is never verified, and just this is what characterizes what Wittgenstein calls hypothetical language – that is, the language of physics and ordinary language, as they both speak of objects and presuppose hypotheses about objects that go beyond phenomenological data. Hypothetical language is about what is sometimes called by Wittgenstein the secondary as opposed to the primary world, that is, the language of ordinary and physical objects, as opposed to the language of the description of experience and aspects. As Wittgenstein says in his 1930 lectures: "The world we live in is the world of sense-data, but the world we talk about is the world of physical objects" (*LWL* 82).

Waismann tries, in his "Theses" (Appendix B to *Wittgenstein and the Vienna Circle*), to convey Wittgenstein's state of mind at this point (in 1929–1930):

The concept of an object involves an hypothesis, for we assume as an hypothesis that the particular aspects we perceive are connected in a law-governed manner. ...

The language of everyday life uses a system of hypotheses. It does so by means of using nouns.

> Aspects are spatially and temporally connected.
> An object is the way aspects are connected.
> An object is a connection of aspects represented by an hypothesis. ...

Here the dispute about whether an object "consists" only of perceived or of possible aspects is ... settled. For an object does not consist of aspects at all. ...

Does the following question make sense? How many aspects is it necessary to have seen before the existence of an object is safely established? No, it does not. No number of aspects can prove that hypothesis. (*WWK* 256, 257, 259).

Waismann means here that, for Wittgenstein, ordinary (or, at this stage, hypothetical) language, and not phenomenological language, "gives" us objects, inasmuch as "an object does not consist of aspects." This distinction of two languages, and of two worlds, is extremely important, as important as the fact that Wittgenstein, early in *Philosophical Remarks*, comes to criticize the distinction: what we actually need is a way to understand that there is only *one* language (one world).

The thesis that objects are appearances or aspects, and the thesis that objects are not reducible to appearances, but exist independently of them, are equivalent theses; they "live by taking in each other's washing." Both are attempts to apply in philosophy a mistaken conception of what propositions are and how they are used. Against this tendency, against Russell, and against a philosophical tradition that is even now back in favor, Wittgenstein redefines the work of philosophy: we are not to separate the hard from the soft, appearance from reality, but to see the hardness of the soft. It is this that we might call (had Wittgenstein himself not shown what would be mistaken in this formulation) the reality of our perceptions.

This is what Waismann tries to recast from Wittgenstein's thought in the perplexing statement that appears in the same passage: "It is striking that the predicate 'real' attaches to the objects and not to the phenomena, which are the only things that are given" (*WWK* 260). (It can be related to the passage from *PR* §225 quoted earlier: the phenomenon is what is real.) So there is a sense in which Wittgenstein did not give up the idea of a phenomenology. Consider, for example, *PR* §47 (cf. The Big Typescript §91):

That it doesn't strike us at all when we look around us, move about in space, feel our own bodies, etc., etc., shows how natural these things are to us. We do not notice that we see space perspectively or that our visual field is in some sense blurred towards the edges. It doesn't strike us and never can strike us because it is *the* way we perceive. We never give it a thought and it's impossible we should, since there is nothing that contrasts with the form of our world.

What I wanted to say is it's strange that those who ascribe reality only to things and not to our ideas move about so unquestioningly in the world as idea and never long to escape from it.

In other words, how much of a matter of course the given is. ...

This which we take as a matter of course, *life*, is supposed to be something accidental, subordinate; while something that normally never comes into my head, reality! ...

Time and again the attempt is made to use language to limit the world and set it in relief – but it can't be done. The self-evidence of the world expresses itself in the very fact that language can and does only refer to it.

As David Stern puts it, it is perhaps here that Wittgenstein "comes as close as he can to simply saying what he wanted to say."[41] Linguistic phenomenology is not a matter of seeing elements of the world jutting into, or lying at the base of, language (bringing the world back in language). Seeing the hardness of the soft is, for Wittgenstein in the thirties, seeing the evidence of the world, that is, that it is evident (*Selbstverständlich*), in our use of language. This is the exact opposite of looking for sense in our perceptions. Rather, sense is itself something perceived, and this itself requires an effort – in the end an effort to see *the face of meaning* in language (in Cora Diamond's phrase).[42] One seems to fall back here into a myth of seeing as an activity (on the model of judgment). But what is interesting in Wittgenstein's position is how he shows that this myth of seeing as an activity is bound up with a myth of seeing as passivity, as in talk of "the world as I found it." Thus one can think of Wittgenstein's concern with seeing-as in terms of the distinction, which appears at a specific moment in his thought, between "seeing" and "looking" (as in: looking for). Paradoxically, it seems that the idea of seeing as passive is as much, if not more, subject to the Myth of the Given (again in its dual aspect), and to the myth of the conceptualization of the given, as is the idea of looking: as if the very idea of seeing were forever linked with the myth of the transcendental subject, to whom the world is given, just as looking is conceived as an activity of description, an active perception of sense, which is nonetheless not a judgment.

Thus, where he discusses seeing things one way rather than another, Wittgenstein aims to envisage a kind of seeing that is neither passive and direct, nor active and indirect (a judgment or an interpretation). We can compare this attempt to Wittgenstein's refusal to conceive of rules either as absolutely rigid (the rails to infinity), or as a matter of sheer interpretation. We must reject these two ways of *seeing* rules, not only because the two come to the same thing, but because they prevent

[41] Stern, *Mind and Language*, 153.
[42] See Cora Diamond, *The Realistic Spirit: Wittgenstein, Philosophy, and the Mind* (Cambridge: MIT Press, 1991), 261.

us from coming to see rules, or what we do in following a rule, against the background of our forms of life. In place of our usual tendency to think of perception as a judgment, Wittgenstein asks us to see judgment as itself a kind of seeing:

> We judge an action according to its background within human life. ... How could human behavior be described? Surely only by showing the actions of a variety of humans, as they are all mixed up together. Not what *one* man is doing *now*, but the whole hurly-burly, is the background against which we see an action. (*RPP* II §§624, 629)

Meaning itself is to be perceived, not understood or determined in terms of rules: "Perhaps what is inexpressible (what I find mysterious and am not able to express) is the background against which whatever I could express has its meaning" (*CV* 16d). The background is not a set of rules or social practices, but is itself the hurly-burly of life (compare, in the passages from *RPP* II, the references to "life itself" to be understood in a quasi-naturalistic sense). The role of this background is not that of a cause; it is what lies behind certain possibilities of description.

To conclude, we can appreciate the particular character of these thoughts if we bring them into connection with the early Wittgenstein. As is well known, Wittgenstein presented in the *Tractatus* a certain theory of vision, associated with a certain theory of the metaphysical subject:

> *Where* in the world is a metaphysical subject to be noted?

> You say that this case is altogether like that of the eye and the field of sight. But you do *not* really see the eye.

> And from nothing *in the field of sight* can it be concluded that it is seen from an eye.

> For the field of sight has not a form like this:

> (5.633–5.6331)

Without addressing the various ways in which Wittgenstein later extends, qualifies, or criticizes this observation (and so raising the now much disputed question of Wittgenstein's Kantianism), I suggest here simply that this moment is a typical instance of what Wittgenstein, in the *Investigations*, calls language "on holiday." He adds: "We can say: when we philosophize it is not only our language that goes on holiday, but also our vision. For when I'm lighting the stove I see it differently from when I'm examining it philosophically; I don't think of a 'visual stove', a sense-datum, etc." Here again one thinks of Austin and of Wittgenstein's critique of the idea that seeing is ordinarily seeing-as. But Wittgenstein goes on to say: "A philosopher, who always keeps one eye closed while philosophizing, could be stricken by different experiences from one who always looked with both eyes."[43]

The theory of the visual field in the *Tractatus* is that of a philosopher who sees with only one eye, as are interpretationist theories of perception, and as are the various forms of the Myth of the Given. What Wittgenstein later recognizes is that even though his position in the *Tractatus* was already a critical one, he there neglected the natural fact that ordinarily we see, we look, with two eyes.[44] What is telling (*bezeichnend*) for Wittgenstein in the thirties is that, in the *Tractatus*, he still saw the subject of language and of perception as transcendental, like many of his contemporary interpreters. To bring language back from its metaphysical to its ordinary use would then be, beyond linguistic therapy, the acknowledgment that in our form of life (in the biological sense) we ordinarily see with two eyes, and that this is bound up with our ability to *see* what we *do*. Seeing-as is thus to be defined in naturalist terms, though the word is to be given a new sense. This reversal of the current thinking on aspects would be a decisive step towards a genuinely ordinary and realist conception of language as *part* of the world.

[43] MS 120, p. 49v, 12 December 1937; cf. Stern, *Mind and Language*, 86.
[44] MS 112, pp. 28r–28v, 14 October 1931.

3

An Allegory of Affinities

On Seeing a World of Aspects in a Universe of Things

Timothy Gould

For many years, there has been a sharp division between two approaches to Wittgenstein's discussion of seeing aspects and the other topics in Part II, Section 11 of *Philosophical Investigations*. However rough my description of this division, we can discern a difference between those commentators who have addressed the question of aspects as primarily concerned with the "psychology" of perception, and those who have tended to think of the topic as involved in larger issues of interpretation or aesthetics.[1]

Useful work has been done under the sway of both approaches. It certainly cannot be denied that Wittgenstein is trying to puzzle out issues about, among other things, the conceptual intersection of seeing and thinking and interpreting (construed here as "seeing something as something"). Taken at face value, these are hardly an intellectually restrictive set of concerns, and they place Wittgenstein in a lineage of investigation that contains such thinkers as Merleau-Ponty and the Gestalt psychologists. But it is equally clear that Wittgenstein makes some bold conceptual jumps from questions of seeing aspects, to questions of "experiencing the meaning of a word," to questions about "primary" and "secondary" senses of words. His way

---

[1] Malcolm Budd's *Wittgenstein's Philosophy of Psychology* (London: Routledge, 1991) is an instance of the former tendency. Budd is also, of course, interested in aesthetics. B. R. Tilghman and Richard Wollheim can serve as two instances of those more exclusively tied up with aesthetic and interpretive concerns.

of drawing connections within this set of problems and interests has little precedent. And it is this set of connections among his interests that has, I believe, drawn philosophers into searching for an underlying scheme or intention that will display the unity of these passages. Such a scheme of concepts and investigations might complement the more austere procedures and results of Part I of the *Investigations*. Thus the nature of Part II, Section 11 seems to lead some philosophers to look for a certain unity in the *Investigations* as a whole.

Stanley Cavell's *The Claim of Reason* has seemed to some philosophers to hold the key to a unification of the *Investigations*.[2] But they tend to omit the combination of caution and allegory that runs through his short discussion of the passages on aspect-seeing. Stephen Mulhall's work (especially *Inheritance and Originality*) seems to display a similar interest in allegory, but he is far less guarded in his effort to produce an approach to seeing aspects that will unify Wittgenstein's insights.[3]

Such a tendency toward unification and toward what I am calling the allegorical seem to go together. I want to emphasize that I am not characterizing some readily identifiable third approach to these topics: I do not think that it is likely that anyone will find such a way, except in allegory. Not only is the *Investigations* likely to remain a fundamentally and deliberately disunified work, but the efforts to see the connection between Parts I and II are likely to remain on the level of allegory. The more one understands the work of Part I as successful, the more Part II displays the freedom from the need for such work. The literal shape the work takes in Part II may well be connected to a broader range of significance – broader than the aesthetic, as well as the psychology of perception narrowly conceived. It presents a world of aspects and the innerness of words, and here philosophy reaches its literal limits. The wish to make an allegory of Wittgenstein's later work speaks to the unappeasable wish to get outside, to see the world as a whole. This wish remains in a human form even when the work of therapy has shown philosophy that this outsideness and wholeness

[2] Stanley Cavell, *The Claim of Reason: Wittgenstein, Skepticism, Morality, and Tragedy* (Oxford: Oxford University Press, 1979).
[3] Stephen Mulhall, *Inheritance and Originality* (Oxford: Clarendon Press, 2001), 154. See also Judith Genova, *Wittgenstein: A Way of Seeing* (New York: Routledge, 1995), chapters 2–3.

cannot be achieved by the means of philosophy. This particular philosophical form of the wish deserves the name of metaphysics.

1. METAPHOR AND ALLEGORY

Even if the connections found in the approach I describe here are not all something that Wittgenstein would have characterized as intentionally allegorical, there are a pair of reasons why I persist in using this word: (1) If you are drawn to find connections between, for instance, issues about the dawning of an aspect and experiencing the meaning of a word, you are likely to be drawn into a kind of heightening or intensifying of the "normal" use of these words; (2) It seems somewhat forced to characterize Wittgenstein's use of words such as "aspect" or "the dawning of an aspect" as technical terms. Yet to describe the duck as an "aspect" of the duck-rabbit (if that is in fact what we are meant to do), or to describe the recognition of a likeness between two faces as "noticing an aspect," is not exactly the ordinary use of those words.

Wittgenstein introduces the topic of aspect-seeing like this:

Two uses of the word "see". The one: "What do you see there?"—"I see *this*" (and then a description, a drawing, a copy). The other: "I see a likeness between these two faces"—let the man I tell this to be seeing the faces as clearly as I do myself. The importance of this is the difference of category between the two "objects" of sight. (*PI* 193a)

Oddly, Mulhall skips over these sentences and makes the following observation: "Section xi begins with the following remark: 'I contemplate a face, and then suddenly notice its likeness to another.' "[4]

By placing these sentences first, Mulhall makes it somewhat easier to characterize the "paradoxical nature" of seeing-as. Whereas Wittgenstein, in beginning by distinguishing two "uses" of "see," seems to have gone out of his way to prevent even the appearance of contradiction, an appearance which is surely one of the criteria of a paradox. Unfortunately for Mulhall, Wittgenstein's use of quasi-technical terms seems designed to avoid direct conflict with our ordinary words

---

[4] Mulhall, *Inheritance and Originality*, 154. Mulhall also uses the term "allegory," but his writing seems to express a wish to transcend the texts of Wittgenstein and Heidegger that Cavell first began to yoke together in the 1960s and 70s. He thus obscures the originality of Cavell's accomplishments and obscures what is useable in Cavell's efforts to explore the rift between the traditions these writers represent.

and acts of speech. Mulhall's emphasis on the paradoxical nature of these experiences seems to lack textual support.

It is not until the third remark of *PI* II.xi that we get this: "I contemplate a face, and then suddenly notice its likeness to another. I see that it has not changed; and yet I see it differently. I call this experiencing 'noticing an aspect'. Its *causes* are of interest to psychologists. We are interested in the concept and its place among the concepts of experience" (*PI* 193c–e). Again, Wittgenstein blatantly signals that his use of "noticing an aspect" (a phrase placed in quotation marks) is a coinage of his own. While it does not seem particularly technical, and while it seems designed to refer to common enough experiences and concepts, there is something hard to grasp about the angle at which Wittgenstein uses these terms to slice into our "concepts of experience."

Later in the discussion (*PI* 216) he introduces the idea of a "primary" and "secondary" sense of a word (again, the quotation marks suggest a quasi-technical use of the terms). He explicitly denies that the secondary sense is metaphorical: "If I say 'For me the vowel *e* is yellow' I do not mean: 'yellow' in a metaphorical sense,—for I could not express what I want to say in any other way than by means of the idea 'yellow' " (*PI* 216g). This suggests that part of the idea of a metaphor is that its sense can be put in another way – in short, a metaphor is something that can, in specific and unforeseen ways, be paraphrased.[5] Indeed, when I move toward the region of the allegorical, I am following the outlines of a contrast that has long been made in literary theory. Coleridge's *The Statesman's Manual* poses the work of allegory in contrast to the function of a symbol (like a flag, a snake, or a cross), which stands for a particular entity or region of meaningfulness.[6] An allegory is a story which relates an entire region of meaningfulness to

---

[5] Cf. Cavell, "Aesthetic Problems of Modern Philosophy," in *Must We Mean What We Say?: A Book of Essays* (Cambridge: Cambridge University Press, 1969), 74–82. Cavell's early discussion of metaphors emphasizes their paraphrasability, in opposition to the New Critical writing that had denied that metaphors *could* be paraphrased. The distinction between myth and metaphor, and the arrival at allegory, came much later in Cavell's thinking. To imagine Cavell's work as a vision timelessly present to him is to freeze his powers of self-education and to cripple our capacity to read him.

[6] Samuel Taylor Coleridge, *The Statesman's Manual*, ed. W. G. T. Shedd (New York, 1875), 437–8, quoted in Angus Fletcher, *Allegory: The Theory of a Symbolic Mode* (Ithaca, N.Y.: Cornell University Press, 1964), 16 n. 29; see 15–18 for a discussion of Coleridge's attitudes toward allegory.

another region of meaningfulness (e.g., the meanings of a journey on earth to the meanings of a journey toward heaven). I am not claiming that this characterization of allegory is explicit in Wittgenstein. It seems clear, however, that he wants to insist on the existence of other fields or objects of significance – as in music and poetry – which cannot simply be paraphrased or used to signify other fields or objects (as, perhaps, in the case of the symbol or the metaphor).

Wittgenstein speaks more often of the mythological than of the allegorical. But "allegory" is a useful way of suggesting a perspective on *PI* II.xi that does not neglect the spate of quasi-technical terms and still allows room for the section's aspirations to a larger field of significance. If its topics are to be stretched toward art or intimacy they will have to be stretched by our capacity for intensifying our utterances and for projecting them into a larger, more vital field of use. Wittgenstein invites us to live within our forms of life as in a humanly more habitable place than the rubble that Part I often seems to be willing to call "peace." "Allegory" is meant to suggest such an intensification of words, an increase in their ability to form affinities with other words and their forms of life.

A final and more immediate reason for using the word "allegory" to characterize this approach is to recapture something of the concepts and argument in Part IV of *The Claim of Reason*. Cavell's actual claims on behalf of "the allegory of words" are somewhat modest, at least in the context of Part IV of that book.[7]

2. ASPECTS AND PICTURES

A question can seem to underlie any approach to seeing aspects: Is there some analogy between "aspects" and "pictures"? Mulhall all but assimilates these two terms; the visual connotation of the term "aspect" predominates in his account. But there is a significant asymmetry between Wittgenstein's treatment of pictures and his treatment of aspects that cannot have gone unnoticed, but that no one, so far as I know, has tried to account for. Whatever else pictures may be, they first attract Wittgenstein's attention by the fact that they work, in various ways, to the detriment of a perspicuous view of our words and

---

[7] See Cavell, *The Claim of Reason*, 354–70.

world. For instance: Pictures hold us captive (*PI* §115); they lie in our language and we cannot get outside them (ibid.); they seem to dictate our application of them, fixating us in relation to them, limiting our freedom of "vision" and hence the perspicuousness of our understanding (cf. *PI* §§352, 422–27). If we are to locate pictures with illuminating or otherwise helpful uses – for instance, in the thought that "the human body is the best picture of the human soul" (*PI* 178g) – such pictures and such uses are to be searched for. Although pictures can lie in our language, as if waiting to ensnare us, the proper use of pictures, however we come to learn it, does *not* apparently lie in our language, waiting to be used in an illuminating way. It is only by doing the work enacted in Part I of the *Investigations* – for instance, by returning words to their ordinary language-games (*PI* §116), or by "seeing connections" (*PI* §122) – that we become free to employ such pictures.

In *PI* II.xi, however, there is no such corresponding work to be done, at least not obviously. One may refer to the idea of aspect-blindness in this context. (Mulhall does so consistently.) But there is to my mind a glaring difference between the affliction of aspect-blindness and the dangers that lie in our misuse of pictures. First of all, if we want to get some sense of the "work" of aspects off the ground, we must ignore the fact that there are at least two opposites of the phenomenon called "the dawning of an aspect": (1) a *particular* aspect fails to dawn on me (e.g., I just cannot see the duck in the duck-rabbit); (2) I suffer from a total inability to see, or apprehend, *any* change of aspects and to "hear" the difference in meaning when *any* word is meant in more than one way (e.g., "bank" as both the bank of a river and the bank with the money, or "till" as both the command "Till the field" and the temporal conjunction "till the cows come home"). Only the latter inability, so far as I know, is ever referred to as "aspect-blindness." There is no specific term for the inability to see the duck in the duck-rabbit or to experience (just) the different "meanings" of "bank" or of "till."

These cases have in common that something of essential importance to Part I of the *Investigations* is apparently missing from the discussion of aspects: namely, the possibility of our doing any philosophical work – or philosophical therapy – to bring about the possibility of "sight" or "perspicuousness." If someone does not see the duck in the duck-rabbit, there is little we can do about it. (Cavell mentions dropping the right hint at the right time – "They can also be ears"[8] – and this might work, with a particular person, on a given occasion. But such remarks seem quite distant from the kind of work that philosophy does in Part I when it assembles reminders for a particular purpose or arranges, in a perspicuous representation, what we say in a given circumstance. What could be more perspicuous than that rabbit? And yet that very perspicuousness is, apparently, blocking our ability to see the duck. Or put from the side of the observer: what could be more intractable than my fixation on the rabbit, my inability to get the duck aspect to dawn on me?) And if the case is generalized to the imagined possibility of a kind of total aspect-blindness, then our situation is worse. For we cannot even say, "This duck-rabbit is like the case of the facing faces which can also be seen as a goblet. Be patient, and perhaps it will happen." For by hypothesis, the person with this affliction has no such other experiences, exceptions to the general blindness, that he or she might build on. The lack of so much as the possibility of a therapy for this blindness is perhaps deliberate on Wittgenstein's part. It stands as a kind of challenge, or as a kind of endpoint to a series whose meaning we have yet to fathom.

Consider in this regard Wittgenstein's analogies to aspect-blindness. They do not seem to take us very far. He mentions "the lack of a 'musical ear'" (*PI* 214c), which might cover a range from the inability to hear a cadence as a cadence to the inability to carry a tune. He also asks whether aspect-blindness would be "comparable to color-blindness or to not having absolute pitch" (*PI* 213f). But the latter absence, presumably widespread, is without much consequence outside of the conservatory. On the other hand, the former absence, presumably less widespread, can possess immediate consequences. At the very least, there are consequences that anyone who lives in a world with traffic lights will have to learn to live with. In both cases, there is a hint of the biological that provides something of an aftertaste to these examples. Moreover, both are the sort of affliction (unlike premature hearing loss, for which more radical measures might be taken) about which one may say: These things happen. So you won't go to Julliard or you won't be happy there. So you need to be more careful, if green and red look like a muddy brown to you.

[8] Ibid., 358.

These examples underscore Wittgenstein's tendency to characterize aspect-blindness as an all-or-nothing affair. It is more like a thought-experiment about the conditions of interpretation than an investigation of an actually existing condition. Wittgenstein never speaks of the *increase* of such a condition, as if its unchecked spread would lead to the further decline of the West. About other matters – like the world-view of progress and science – he is not so reticent. If you share with me a sense of the critical role of examples in Wittgenstein's method and in his writing (cf. *PI* §133), then it can seem perplexing in the extreme that he should be so casual just here in introducing these analogies to aspect-blindness. If this particular inability is *that* important, then why at just this point does Wittgenstein's passionate inventiveness seem so dispassionate?

To highlight Wittgenstein's relative casualness about these examples, I offer some more salient alternatives. Consider the inability to appreciate the various language-games we call "telling jokes." Here I am not imagining someone who is humorless, as that is normally understood, but someone for whom the forms of humor we call telling jokes are alien. Or consider the inability to get the point of winning a game. I don't mean a reluctance to appreciate a particular kind of game (e.g., a person who feels that chess is too complicated to be worth learning, or that boxing and hockey are too violent to be considered sports). Suppose someone finds games *as such* to be pointless and winning to be incomprehensible as a human goal. They could more or less master the rules and moves of the game, including what counts as winning, without ever seeing the point of winning: they don't see how "winning" adds anything to the idea of the end of the game. It is a matter of indifference to them. (Is getting the idea of winning like the dawning of an aspect? Several paths lead off from this question.)

If aspect-blindness is meant to be felt along these lines as a serious obstacle to human flourishing, or worse – if we are meant to find in it a kind of allegory for some even more devastating human condition – then it should seem perplexing that Wittgenstein provides us, apparently, with precisely nothing to be done about this condition, nothing that he sees fit to mention at any rate. If someone cannot see the duck in the duck-rabbit, or experience the difference between saying "till" and meaning it as a verb and meaning it as a conjunction, then that is, pretty much, the end of that.

3. WHERE DO ASPECTS FIT?

At some stage, it is tempting to try to specify the relation of Part II to Part I of the *Investigations*. One especially dangerous temptation is to distinguish a view of "meaning-as-use" in Part I from an account of our acquaintance with aspects that relies on a heightened sense of the imagination or of interpretation. The dawning of an aspect can be as ordinary as solving a puzzle in the Sunday papers. But this does not transform the game of asking whether Wednesday strikes you as "fat" or "lean" (*PI* 216c) into the language-game that is the home of "Wednesday" (or "fat" or "lean"). That is one reason Wittgenstein calls these senses "secondary" (which of course does not make them less interesting). Perhaps philosophers have been drawn to the idea of aspects and the imagination because they sense a danger in leaving the everyday world alone. They sense that Wittgenstein offers us no defense against the idea of the everyday as primarily a scene of alienation, inauthenticity, boredom, mediocrity, and the leveling of all aspiration and achievement, indeed of everything that smacks of the exceptional.

I assert, without directly trying to demonstrate, that *PI* II.xi – and indeed the bulk of Part II of the *Investigations* – presupposes in some sense the philosophical work of Part I. But it does not undertake to adorn the poverty of our everyday world with constructions of the imagination. What unites Parts I and II is the overcoming of what Wittgenstein calls "metaphysics" or sometimes just "philosophy." The struggle of our will to emptiness, our willingness to be lost in thought, with our will to find ourselves once again on rough ground, intermittently at peace, is sufficiently specific to the *Investigations* that Wittgenstein seems content to let the passages characterize themselves. From the point of view of a certain methodological triumph, Part II of the *Investigations* should therefore be read not so much as a further series of "arguments" against the impulse to metaphysics, but as a series of instances of what occurs when we are at least partially free of that impulse. Thus, there need be no single "opposite" to the notion of seeing an aspect, no single means of blockage, because to some extent Wittgenstein takes the real obstacles to his discussion to have already been overcome. (This would account for the relative discursiveness of Part II, as opposed to the dialogues and aphoristic climaxes intrinsic to the writing and method of Part I.) We can discuss certain conceptual problems associated with the dawning of an aspect because the primary metaphysical drive that would tend to dismiss or marginalize this discussion has already been dismantled.

What Wittgenstein means by "metaphysics" relentlessly tends to picture the world as a universe of things and their properties, or facts and their arrangements. If Part I of the *Investigations* has already methodically shown us how to detach this picture from its seemingly inevitable application to the world, then there is nothing to prevent us from considering the world as a realm of familiarities, analogies, likenesses and affinities. The fact that my son resembles my brother when he was a boy is no less a part of the world than the fact that each of them has eyes on either side of his nose, or that each eats with his mouth, and so on. The distinction between the essence of a thing (along with its properties) and an aspect of a thing or a situation is not abolished by Wittgenstein's work. Nonetheless, Wittgenstein dismantles the fixed importance that philosophy has assigned to such distinctions. We can begin to see that the properties of things or substances do not have priority over the aspects of things in the basic constitution of the world. It may be true that if there were no forks then we could not see a fork *as* a dancing figure. But our relation to things (and to words) is wider than our relation to what, on a certain view, *must* be taken as basic.

J. L. Austin once said that how things look or smell or taste is just as much a part of the world as how the world really is. But whereas Austin was content to mock the philosopher's obsession with knowing how things (really, essentially) are, Wittgenstein wanted us to dismantle the very drive to isolate, for example, the absolutely simple parts of a chair (*PI* §47), or to undo the idea that a name has to name an indestructible simple (*PI* §55 ff.) or that logic showed the (sublime) structure of "the nature of all things" (*PI* 89). Against the background of the procedures that are meant to dismantle this wish, Wittgenstein took on these puzzles about seeing something as something and experiencing the meaning of a word. But if Wittgenstein repeatedly shows us how to relinquish the picture of the proposition as a picture of reality, he expends next to no philosophical energy at all in showing us that "aspects" do in fact dawn, that they are there as long as I am engaged with them, and so forth. I take it that the very successes in Part I have freed him to deal with these other issues. It is not that he imagines that we can, once and for all, rid ourselves of a picture of the world as exhaustively made up of things and their properties. It is rather that now we know the way to detach ourselves, methodically, from the captivity of this picture. The metaphysical furniture of the world can now appear as more extensive than was dreamt of in our philosophy.

4. CAVELL AND THE ALLEGORY OF WORDS

In this light, let us look at Cavell's description in *The Claim of Reason* of one world that is opened up by Wittgenstein's discussion of aspect-seeing.

Faced with a labyrinth of issues, Cavell picks out a single thread to follow. He starts with Wittgenstein's noting a "categorical difference" in different objects of sight and his having introduced the notion of the dawning of an aspect and the corresponding notion of an aspect whose physiognomy "passes away" (*PI* 210e). Later, Wittgenstein suggests a connection between "seeing an aspect" and "experiencing the meaning of a word" (*PI* 214d). Cavell develops these connections in ways no one else foresaw and that have proved difficult to make use of. The limits Cavell sets to his discussion are as important as any particular remark within that discussion. Cavell folds his reading of the physiognomy of words into a reading of the physiognomy of human expressiveness. His linking of our attachment to our words, allegorically, to our attachment to ourselves and to others is at once captivating and methodical. It forms one of those cruxes in Cavell's writing that leads some to accept the connections he draws as unassailable, and others to reject them as unsupported. The passage receives much less attention than the famous opening lines of *The Claim of Reason*, but it deserves at least as much attention. Here is Cavell's rapid-fire set of connections, ending with the concluding leap to the allegorical:

Putting together the ideas that [1] noticing an aspect is being struck by a physiognomy; that [2] words present familiar physiognomies; that [3] they can be thought of as pictures of their meaning; that [4] words have a life and can be dead for us; that [5] "experiencing a word" is meant to call attention to our relation to our words; that [6] our relation to pictures is in some respects like our relation to what they are pictures of; – I would like to say that the topic of our attachment to our words is allegorical of our attachments to ourselves and to other persons.[9]

Each of these clauses has a direct reference to a passage in Wittgenstein, the only exception being the close of the sentence following the dash. But it is important to note that once Cavell has drawn the connection between "noticing an aspect" and "experiencing the meaning of a word," he lays out the subsequent steps in a very specific interpretive direction. The reader must check Cavell's sense of this direction into the problem of expressiveness and of "experiencing" the meaning of a word against what I am driven to call his or her experience of these experiences. For instance, Wittgenstein says more than once that (6) our relation to pictures is like our relation to what they are pictures of (cf. *PI* 194c). And he implies that (2) experiencing the meaning of a word can take the form of taking in the "face" of the word and that in turn (3) one might take the "face" of the word as a picture of its meaning (*PI* 218g). But of course the "face" or "physiognomy" of a human being is not a *picture* of that human being – though it is often, even essentially, a crucial part of such a picture. Or we might say that the face is one way of epitomizing a particular human being. To speak of physiognomies of words is already either a kind of metaphor – the unhelpfulness of which I have tried to underscore – or a kind of allegory.

In any event, two of the later steps in Cavell's set of connections leading to his allegory of words are nowhere made explicit in Wittgenstein. In particular, Wittgenstein does not speak of (5) "call[ing] attention to our relation to our words" – which is of course not to deny that Wittgenstein *does* call attention to our relation to our words in just the (allegorical) fashion that Cavell suggests. And the idea that (4) words can go dead for us is not explicit in Wittgenstein – and is not exactly the same region of concern as the one expressed in the remark that the sign by itself seems dead (*PI* §432). A word as such is not a sign (despite the widespread influence of some French thinkers). It can become one, certainly, and in isolation a sign is normally dead. To bring it to life we must restore it to the language-game that is its home. There it lives within the stream of life, the stream of its use. These phenomena are not the same as a word going dead in the midst of its life (and ours), as the word "joy" or "freedom" or

<hr>

[9] Ibid., 355.

"neighbor" or "suppertime" can go dead, or as a word can go dead by being repeated fifteen times. (I have warned against conflating these various deaths and resurrections of our language – and, allegorically, of our relation to our self and to others – elsewhere.)[10]

You will not find Wittgenstein speaking of an allegory of words in these passages. Yet he is speaking of words and of something allegorical or mythological about our use of words. And if we remember the still staggering aphorism that "the human body is the best picture of the human soul," it is certainly fair to suggest that Cavell has prepared us to understand *this* allegory of words. There is a kind of interpretation that elaborates what is given to us as condensed; there is another kind of interpretation (as here) that shows how some very condensed remark arrived at the form of its condensation. Call these different aspects of interpretation, different forms of (interpretive) seeing an aspect of something, here construed as an allegory of understanding the meaningfulness of an expression. Cavell is still interpreting, but he is interpreting (the acts and passions of) interpretation, so he is going to be hard to understand in this region. As is Wittgenstein.

Cavell goes on to remind us of the allegory we were already prepared for by Wittgenstein: "My words are my expressions of my life; I respond to the words of others as their expressions, i.e., respond not merely to what their words mean but equally to their meaning of them."[11] One of these themes haunts *The Claim of Reason* and indeed the bulk of Cavell's work: the idea that the words I have, the words we have at our disposal, will not convey what I mean without my meaning of those words. Whatever "my meaning of my words" turns out to be, we know something of what it means to fail to mean my words or to wish not to have to. Wittgenstein characterizes our efforts to speak apart from language-games; Cavell characterizes the position we then find ourselves in as a place from which the human voice has been evacuated, where the voice that inhabits my words is rendered unnecessary. My meaning of my words does not occur in isolation from what those words mean.[12] Linguistic analysis glimpses this possibility as the difference between the speaker's meaning and the meaning of the

---

[10] Timothy Gould, *Hearing Things: Voice and Method in the Writing of Stanley Cavell* (Chicago: University of Chicago Press, 1998), 45–49.

[11] Cavell, *The Claim of Reason*, 355.

[12] See Cavell, "Must We Mean What We Say?", in *Must We Mean What We Say?*, 1–43.

utterance. Cavell speaks instead of allegory. He knows well enough
the anxiety latent in the idea of "my meaning of my words."

Suppose there is also a question about the other direction – not
from the speaker to the world, but from the conditions within the
world to the speaker. My meaning of my words occurs in a world that
does not merely allow for language but *calls* for speech. It is a world in
which it makes sense to mean our words or fail to, in which the possibility of making sense remains alive. Here, I suggest, we can begin
to discern a further reason for the idea of an allegorical relation as
necessary to express the expressiveness of the human. It is this sense
of the allegorical that might motivate us to look for a unitary theme
in *PI* II.xi – in particular, for thinking of the aspects of things as something that dawns, eventually, over the whole world.

5. LETTING THE ASPECTS OF THE WORLD ALONE

If, from within a Wittgensteinian reading of language-games, one gets
the idea that there is still something in the world beyond or beneath
the world of speech, the world in which language-games are deployed,
then how shall we say what that something is? How but in words can
we point to what lies beyond words? And why, precisely at this point,
do we find ourselves needing recourse to the idea of allegory? What
we seem to require is a kind of general relationship (Cavell sometimes calls it "reading") which might characterize my relation to the
expressions of another human. But this general relationship must fit
on to, or open up, an utterly specific set of expressions – not private
but individual.

It makes no sense for me to think of myself as deciding – in each
case of a possible "other," as the other presents itself to my capacity
for apprehension – whether or not the other's words (and gestures
and actions) are "expressive" of something, call it a mind or soul. Or
rather: There seems to be a kind of gulf that opens up between, for
instance, my general readiness to read the expressiveness of others
as in fact expressive, genuine, metaphysically on the job, and my ability to read your clutching of your hand to your head right now as
"wincing in pain" and not, say, as your being overcome with a sense
of stupidity, having failed to see that the map was upside down. To
characterize the latter ability as I just have seems easier than to say

that for my words to mean something I have to mean something by my words.

Why must we travel through these conceptual thickets (seeing, thinking, interpreting, experience) in order to arrive at so obvious a point about our life with words? Isn't this way of resisting our life with words the main thrust of the so-called private language argument? But then it was always part of the painstaking dismantling of the apparatus by which we took ourselves to be approaching the knowledge of an other that arriving at a formulation was not to be the end of the story. Just as you cannot reduce my doubt of an other to a single form or formula – one that might be corrected by a little more caution, for instance – so you cannot turn the doubt on its head and cure it with a single act of knowledge. The receptiveness or acknowledgment of the other as an Other – as a representative human field of expressiveness – cannot be characterized in the same way as my acknowledgment that your knee is acting up, that your anxiety is real, or that your anticipation of his arrival is making you restless. We sense somehow that our aliveness to an individual moment of expression is connected to our aliveness to human expressiveness as such. But when I come to try to characterize this connection generally I am reduced to gestures or allegory or certain poems.

The difficulty in reading our gestures is visible in some of Mulhall's accounts, where he seems to assimilate the failure to see a particular aspect dawning to aspect-blindness as such. He assimilates precisely what I suggest is best left diverse and unassimilated. To leave ourselves open to the threat of skepticism – a threat intrinsic to what Cavell characterizes as the truth of skepticism – is not to leave ourselves open to one massive failure in our knowledge of the world. And this characterization might bring home to us that our ability to inhabit the world is not founded on our ability to know it. It is to acknowledge our exposure to an unlimited field of failures and inadequacies, to blindness and over-reaching and hopelessness. We are to remain open to the threat of unappeasable knowledge and the paralysis of insight, and this will not be cured in a single bout of philosophical therapy. This openness will be accompanied by a corresponding totalizing wish to slip the bonds of time and correct ourselves in some huge act of continuous seeing (or knowing). We tend to assimilate all our failures to reach the world, sometimes in

our despair of our abilities, sometimes in our despair of the worth of
inhabiting so impoverished a world. This is not a useful preparation
for overcoming our skepticism. It is one of the faces of that skepticism.
This is why I am picking on an apparently small piece of philosophical
misjudgment in Mulhall's work. All this assimilation flows from the
assimilation of aspects to pictures.

Mulhall is led to characterize aspect-blindness as a defect in
one's humanness. The suggestion seems to be this: The aspect-blind
regard a human being's behavior as we would regard the behavior
of a robot, or of something whose behavior is mechanical. Mulhall
suggests that such a thing would be describable in geometrical
concepts:

Geometrically conceptualized behavior would lack imponderable fine
shades, variety, and flexibility of the kind we have been describing; such
concepts would eliminate the loose weave of behavior, utterance, and circumstance that makes up our understanding of genuinely human action
and expression, and that makes it possible for culturally relative paradigms
of expressive behavior to be inflected by the irregularities and variations
of texture that give individual style or character to a particular person's
actions.[13]

This is partly right. If I (as aspect-blind) cannot recognize the expressiveness of the human in general, I will not be able to recognize fine
shades of expression, style, perhaps even character. But I am not sure
that this means I am as one who sees nothing more than robots or
Stepford Wives. Part of the problem with Mulhall's allegory is that he
cannot foreclose the possibility that a world in which we cannot recognize movements as human activity, or acknowledge certain behavior as human expression, might well prove to be a world in which the
noises and movements of robots are also reduced to inexpressiveness.
After all, robots are, at least in the movies, creatures who look and
move and speak in ways very like the ways of the humans we recognize
as human. (In the movies, that is part of the metaphysical pleasure
of robots, as it is part of the pleasure of Vulcans: it gives us a kind of
scale on which to measure what is otherwise quite without measure.)
Mulhall seems not to consider the possibility that while Wittgenstein
would no doubt deplore a merely "geometric" description of a human

---

[13] Mulhall, *Inheritance and Originality*, 173.

being, it doesn't follow that a richer, non-geometric depiction of such a being would yield its humanness, its expressiveness or its consciousness: "Only of a living human being and what *resembles (behaves like)* a living human being can one say: it has sensations; it sees; is blind; hears; is deaf; is conscious or unconscious" (*PI* §281, emphasis added).

The response to skepticism must not foreclose its truth, and its truth does not consist in the proposition that we are in doubt that the other being is a human being. Skepticism's truth is rather that our relation to the other's humanness – its sensations, feelings, perceptions, blindness – is not a matter of knowledge, not even that subtle knowledge that consists of being able to sketch in the "fine shades" of human expressiveness. Any such knowledge and any such ability to appreciate or acknowledge the other being may, in some circumstances, apply to beings that are relevantly like the human in their expressiveness. A world in which we are incapable of appreciating the finer shades of human expression is very likely a world in which we are unable to appreciate the finer shades of robotic expressiveness. Most of us can see that R2D2 evinces more of the expressiveness of a faithful and omni-competent pet, at the same time we see that C-3Po possesses the robotic version of a protective English butler. When human expressiveness becomes entirely unreadable, its animistic and robotic versions are also likely to become unreadable. We need to investigate both what we cannot read and what we are afraid to let ourselves express. Here is the link to the life and death of human expressiveness: We are not normally anxious that we will be reduced to geometric representations of one another but that we will be unable to overcome our desperate fear of expressiveness, and this desperation feeds our self-imposed inexpressiveness. Perhaps Mulhall should think of the destiny of these aspect-blind creatures not as that of "normal" robots but (adapting Thoreau) as those figures fated to lead lives of robotic desperation.

More importantly, the other direction that Mulhall's allegory suggests does not seem valid. My failure to see fine shades of meaning in a face or in some other text – to read *The Ambassadors*, or *Pericles*, or the late poems of Wallace Stevens, or the sorrow in my mother's changing face – does not mean that I have lost all touch with human expressiveness. Of course, Mulhall doesn't quite say this, and there is no reason why his account should insist on symmetry. The fact is, we want that symmetry. His recourse to the idea of aspect-blindness as some kind of global opposite to continuous aspect perception is meant to picture, or allegorize, exactly such a global relation of me to the meaningfulness of the creatures of the world. And why shouldn't he have it?

He *should* have it; but only in allegory. Early in *Being and Time*, Heidegger reminds us sharply not to take the concepts of the everyday (its *existentiale*) as mere aspects, mere transient concepts designed to fit the pragmatism of a day or the *Weltanschauung* of an existentialist or the mood of a literary philosopher.[14] Presumably, Heidegger wants to deny that what he thinks of as an aspect is merely a matter of how something happens to strike you, at a particular time, from a particular angle. (Other philosophers might criticize something as merely an "appearance.") These concepts that Heidegger has excavated from the everyday – Being-in; Being-with-others; understanding; thrownness – are not merely the transient property of a subject, lacking the power to reveal a deeper human essence. But while Wittgenstein may seem to be on an opposite tack, he is no less interested in the relation between the aspects that dawn on us and the world that stays back and remains in the background as precisely what does not strike us or announce itself as underlying our language-games. In insisting on using "aspect," Wittgenstein is insisting that the intimacy of the world, its affinity for us, is not based on its depth. The depth of the everyday is deep enough.

Wittgenstein has almost nothing specific to say about these "fine shades" of meaning and conduct that Mulhall insists on. (Partial exceptions can be found at *PI* 203b and 207a.) Evidently, it is enough for Wittgenstein that they exist, that they are hard to put into words without falsifying them, and that they have important consequences at particular times. By themselves, these shades are not enough to build a human world on: they are not as sturdy as the everyday we live in, however crude. (Mulhall may intend to locate these finer shades within the everyday. But we must remember that the ground of the everyday is "rough" [*PI* §107], even raw – not usually characterized as fine. That does not prevent our sense of the finer shades as emerging from cruder contrasts of dark and light, natural stone and primitive

---

[14] Martin Heidegger, *Being and Time*, trans. John Macquarrie and Edward Robinson (New York: Harper & Row, 1962), 69.

pillar.) If you say that without these shades of refinement the world would be immeasurably impoverished, how can you be sure that Wittgenstein does not mean us to *undergo* this poverty or neediness as the price we must pay to appreciate everyday things, and as part of the path back to accepting the everyday world again, as given? The presentness of the world, in all its roughness and poverty and sublimity, is not a thing to be known or perceived but *accepted*. What is given is a kind of gift, or something bestowed. No doubt the aspect of everydayness, like the aspects of *PI* II.xi, must also strike us (*PI* §129).[15] But the everydayness of things must dawn from within the everyday and the familiar. We have much to learn about the analogy between the ways in which the unfamiliar allows itself to be recognized as familiar (recognizing someone after a long absence) and the ways in which the familiar, what is in front of our eyes, allows itself to be recognized as, after all, familiar. But it remains, so far, an analogy.

Mulhall's fine shades of meaning must surely be related to the stuff of human expressiveness in ways we still need to remember. Perhaps Mulhall wishes to suggest that we have come too late to receive the spark of enlightenment from Wittgenstein's all-too-needy words. It is not the case that only an allegory can awaken this capacity for seeing a world of aspects and affinities. But the allegory we may construct for knowing the fine and the subtle within the all-encompassing, the gross, and the heavy-handed might still provide a kind of philosophical protection or refuge from the sickness of the time. It is, however, part of that protection and that philosophical peace that we be able to discern the true dangers from the false. Those who fear that our only companions are becoming those who cannot detect the shapes of the human spirit from the geometry of robots are trying to characterize a genuine danger: The recognition of the shape of the human depends on nothing more – but nothing less – than the willingness to be recognized as one among the human beings. Perhaps we will be recognized as nothing more than pictures (not aspects) of the human soul. Must this recognition occur solely as an expression of our quiet desperation?

---

[15] The importance for Wittgenstein of being struck by the aspects of the everyday, which are "hidden because of their simplicity and familiarity" (*PI* §129), is discussed by Steven Affeldt in his contribution to this volume.

What aspects occupy you now, I do not know. (You could try to let me know.) Cavell's allegory of words suggests that I cannot know you intimately unless I can know which aspects have dawned on you and are dawning on you now. But the hope remains that the world of human expressiveness, the world of our affinities, will survive some ignorance and a certain gracelessness. That is, perhaps, a beginning, or at least a way to think ourselves back to our beginnings, to the homeland of our words.

4

The Touch of Words

Stanley Cavell

1.

Seeing X as Y, or as like Y, is something not everyone with normal eyesight can be expected to do; yet Wittgenstein says that someone may be blind to that aspect of a "given" X. The thoughts to follow here about the idea of seeing (and failing to see) something as something and its associated concepts – Wittgenstein says the idea brings into play "hugely many interrelated phenomena and possible concepts" (*PI* 199d), which is surely one source of the fascination of this region of the *Investigations* – were forming as I began considering my response to a text of Cora Diamond's that takes up extremities of conflict associated with what she calls "the difficulty of reality," cases in which one's capacity to respond is, for some, put to the test, sufficiently provoked that it threatens to freeze or to overwhelm understanding, while for others it fails to turn a hair. The principal phenomenon she treats is that of understanding our relation to the non-human world of animals, most extendedly the relation or relations in the mass preparation of animals as food for humans, and she approaches it importantly through her responses to a pair of stories by J. M. Coetzee.

These two stories, together with four more and an epilogue, make up a book, variously called a tale and a novel, with the title *Elizabeth Costello*, about a woman, an Australian writer, almost maddened by the relentlessness of her imagination of our food factories, which in

their treatment of animals, to "say it openly … [surround us with] an
enterprise of degradation, cruelty, and killing which rivals anything
that the Third Reich was capable of, indeed dwarfs it, in that ours
is an enterprise without end. …"[1] This quotation is from a speech
Costello is depicted as addressing to an audience at an American college that is doing her the honor of bringing her to the States to give
their (or an) annual lecture. She knows the comparison will be found
offensive by many in her audience, as if what she is experiencing is
correctly expressed by *wanting* to be offensive, to display her condition as horror-stuck. Or should we rather say?: Coetzee knows that
many of his readers will find the comparison offensive, and he puts
the observation, or obsession, into the mouth of a fictional character
to try out how far the vision of ourselves as equal in depravity with the
Third Reich may be preempted and defeated.

Coetzee is careful to have various characters voice their disapproval, to put it mildly, of Costello's comparison of the business of
mass animal butchery with the Nazi organization of the gassing
and burning of Jews. But Diamond, convincingly in my view, takes
Costello's expression of horror with full seriousness. I mean that I do
not read her reading of Coetzee's tale as providing fictional distance
from which to assess the justice, or rationality, of a difficult argument,
but rather as exploring a state of mind whose balance is threatened
by the tortured perception that rationality has come to express irra-
tionality, hence that words are cursed, and asking how one might live
reasonably with such a perception.

The text of Diamond's I am responding to here is her response
to a volume entitled *The Lives of Animals*, in which Coetzee's pair of
stories are reprinted along with responses to them by five writers
from various fields focusing on the title topic. Diamond's attention
to these responses is caught by her sense of their essential neglect
of the moment in which Costello names herself as one among the
wounded animals that she is responding to, a moment Diamond
takes as determinative in what she has to say about Coetzee's words.
Diamond's text is her contribution to a collection of papers about
my work, and I found it so haunting that I used it as the basis of my,
as it were, reciprocal contribution to a collection of papers about her

[1] J. M. Coetzee, *Elizabeth Costello* (New York: Viking, 2003), 65.

work. What follows here is a report and extension of my contribution to that volume.[2]

2.

Elizabeth Costello identifies herself, analogously with Kafka's great ape in "Report to an Academy," as "not a philosopher of mind but an animal exhibiting, yet not exhibiting, to a gathering of scholars, a wound, which I cover up under my clothes but touch on in every word I speak."[3] But Diamond does not use this revelation as a handicap, or a sign of diminished capacity, mitigating the offensiveness of Costello's offense; on the contrary, it is as though Diamond is listening to something the wound is saying, or makes it possible to say, or necessary to say, without mitigation. Then how are we to imagine this wound, exhibited and not exhibited, covered up by her clothes but revealed by every word she speaks, to those who can sense their touch?

We do not imagine, I suppose, that what is covered by Elizabeth Costello's clothes is anything other than an aging, but otherwise undamaged, woman's body; a human body, one among others. The wound is evidently the fact, or fate, of being human, of being woundable as humans are woundable, for example, by knowledge they cannot put away from themselves, of love and of beauty and of pity and of remorse and of horror.

A way of not taking Elizabeth's response seriously is to treat the comparison of food factories with Nazi death camps as a figure of speech, as such merely tasteless in its banality, but invited by such a

---

[2] Coetzee's pair of stories, together with an introduction by Amy Gutmann and reflections on the stories from Marjorie Garber, Peter Singer, Wendy Doniger, and Barbara Smuts, are printed together in J. M. Coetzee, *The Lives of Animals*, ed. Amy Gutmann (Princeton: Princeton University Press, 1999). Diamond's paper appears in *Reading Cavell*, ed. Alice Crary and Sanford Shieh (London and New York: Routledge, 2006). The collection of papers about the work of Cora Diamond, in which my reciprocal response to her paper appears with the title "Companionable Thinking," is *Wittgenstein and the Moral Life: Essays in Honor of Cora Diamond*, ed. Alice Crary (Cambridge: MIT Press, 2007). Diamond's and my papers are now published together, along with essays by John McDowell, Ian Hacking, and Cary Wolfe, in *Philosophy and Animal Life* (New York: Columbia University Press, 2008). The third paper of mine referred to in the closing paragraph of the present text is the revised version of "The Wittgensteinian Event," my contribution to the collection *Reading Cavell*.

[3] Coetzee, *Elizabeth Costello*, 71.

phrase as, say, "The Butcher of Lyon," singling out and allegorizing the work of the Nazi Klaus Barbie. But, then, how are we to take Elizabeth's comparison since she cannot – can she? – mean what she says literally? However literal the "degradation, cruelty, and killing," there are surely those decisive differences everyone must recognize between the cases – not alone the difference between humans and non-humans, but the difference that food factories are not organized with the precise point of degrading and inflicting cruelty. Or is this impertinent? May one not see the show of humanity in food factories as helping humans treat with indifference the matter of turning animals into food on a mass scale? We do not have to, as civilians in Nazi-controlled Central Europe had to – before, during, and after World War II – deny that we know. Our knowledge of the animals simply may in fact not wound us. And this imperviousness seems as terrible, or as maddening, to Elizabeth Costello as the fact itself of inflicting unintentional degradation and cruelty.

It is this double focus of her response, on the appalling and on the indifference to the appalling, that suggests understanding Costello's state as describable by concepts brought into play in Wittgenstein's reflections on seeing aspects. Among these concepts in play, take just the concepts of merely knowing (*PI* 202e), of reading a poem or narrative (I suppose non-fictional as well as fictional) with feeling or merely skimming the lines for information (*PI* 214g), and of a picture as helping me to read with the correct expression (ibid.). Against the background of such ideas I might characterize Diamond as raising the question of what I will call inordinate knowledge, knowledge that can seem excessive in its expression, in contrast to mere or bare or pale or intellectualized or uninsistent or inattentive or distracted or filed, archived knowledge, an opposite direction of questionable, here defective, or insipid, or shallow, or indecisive expression. The appropriateness of response is inherently questionable, one could say perpetually argumentative, in human response and expression, as perpetual as the capacity to talk back. Non-human animals may be temperamental and may balk or shy, but the absence of conversation, within an ambience of communication, lends them their innocence and poignance. With the realm of existence held to be below the human, as with the realm above the human, the judgment, and the judgment of our judgment, of our relation to its inhabitants falls entirely upon us.

The inherent issue of appropriateness in human speech (beginning with the question whether to speak, to destroy silence) – challenging as it were the issue of "adequacy" in making speech realistic, alluding here to Cora Diamond's *The Realistic Spirit* and also to related papers of Sandra Laugier on realism – is bound up with seeing human speech as expressive, expressive of what matters in a human life, what counts for it, which inescapably puts at stake how *much* something matters, how deep or permanent or partial or unreflective our interest is in a given case.

A striking idea among Wittgenstein's remarks about seeing aspects is his saying that the importance of the concept lies in its connection with experiencing the meaning of a word and with our attachment to our words (cf. *PI* 214d, 218g). This is an idea I emphasize in *The Claim of Reason* about Wittgenstein's discussion of seeing-as, in my speaking about our relation to words as an allegory of our relation to others.[4] Some idea of the attachment to our words is indispensable to Wittgenstein's fundamental procedures in the invocation of ordinary language (which, as I often emphasize, highlights the fact of language as *mine*), such as returning words from their metaphysical to their everyday use (*PI* §116), or bringing out the humor in forcing words into inappropriate contexts ("I know how tall I am" – putting my hand on top of my head) (*PI* §279). (How is language mine? Not as a house or a hat is mine. How might I divest myself of it?)

This indispensability of the idea of attachment is alone enough to secure the depth of connection of Part II to Part I of the *Investigations*, to warrant undivided attention to the discussion of seeing aspects. I could imagine that if I had known the *Investigations*, I mean had even read it through once, before writing the material of the essay "Must We Mean What We Say?", I would have concentrated on, or at least wished to include, in justifying Austin's procedures – along with insisting upon, or instancing what it means to speak of, my *knowledge* of my language – an equal insistence upon my attachment to my words, my experience of them in their significance to the world, hence their significance to me. This seems to bring out the stakes in philosophizing out of the ordinary.

---

[4] Stanley Cavell, *The Claim of Reason: Wittgenstein, Skepticism, Morality, and Tragedy* (Oxford: Oxford University Press, 1979), 355.

But consider Wittgenstein's observation (*PI* 218g): "The familiar
physiognomy of a word, the feeling that it has taken up its meaning
into itself, that it is an actual likeness of its meaning – there could be
human beings to whom all this was alien. (They would not have an
attachment to their words.)" I am prepared to take this as a sort of
inside joke of Wittgenstein's, in which the alien human beings are
philosophers, or in which philosophizing itself can tend to alienate
its subject from itself and its world. But this just means that the attachment to our words, for philosophers driven by a certain aspiration to
the purity of philosophy (an aspiration internal to philosophy), is as
apt as not to be precisely what philosophy is to free us from. What we
are attached to, in Russell's memorable phrase, invoked by Quine, is
the metaphysics of the stone age (I assume this captures ideas such
as the sun and moon as rising and falling, objects as "having" properties, ages as having spirits, words as containing meanings, persons as
harboring objects called pains). Could Descartes have written as he
did without an attachment to his words? – and he is one who in effect
chastises our attachment to our words when he finds that words mislead us into saying, for example, that we see objects.

While some philosophers are systematically distrustful of our
attachments to our words (and the foundation of analytical philosophy as symbolic logic's progressive replacement of, or infiltration
into, natural language has for some expressed this settled distrust),
others philosophize out of an ambivalence toward our, that is, toward
any, native tongue. Dewey is for me a memorable case (Heidegger is
another, and I suppose Nietzsche). Dewey will sometimes say, under-
standably perhaps but discouragingly to my way of thinking, that we
have in effect to pry our words away from our experience in order
to see clearly what we mean; then again he will sometimes say such
memorable and helpful things as: "The table is the only *table*," where
he is contrasting scientific objects with everyday objects; or "The
mind *minds*," where he is characterizing human thinking as motivated by specifiable problems. Whether language, and the interests
of humans, reveals or conceals the world, preserves things or plays
with things so that as they are they are changed in it – whether there
is a way things are, and whether that is dependent or independent of
human language and concepts – is a way of forming the (Kantian,
tormenting) questions that *Philosophical Investigations* keeps in motion,

shows a responsibility perhaps to answer locally, daily, accepting that they can never be solved finally, so long as the human being is bound, or rather free, to reflect, to assert its restlessness, to be philosophical, to be human. Human language is such that it is made to claim, and to attack its claim or assertion of, finality – attack both responsible, say realistic, claims of finality or certainty, and hollow, hyperbolic, or say defensive, claims of absoluteness.

The thought I offer for consideration is that, or whether, the concept of our attachment to our words has a further dark side, a contribution to make to what I called inordinate knowledge, a way of understanding what is causing Elizabeth Costello's sense of excruciating isolation, as though she regards madness to be on the other side, her fellow citizens having become disassociated from their words, not knowing what they say and what they hear when they know and do not know that there is a meat packing plant just exactly there, in which animals are killed and cleaned and carved and wrapped and their remainder discarded as waste. It is an inverted hospital run by Satan, in ultimate mockery of the human claim to respect life. (This is in fact not how I felt, however astonished I was, not pleasantly, the one time I saw, hanging in a butcher's window in San Gimignano fifty years ago, a whole pig flayed and gutted. Here was a way of life on display, or something comprehensibly necessary to a way of life that itself is hard but not unacceptable; whereas the factory or meat plant is a way of life hidden, its content placed at Emerson's graceful, that is, invisible, distance.) That each side, eaters and shunners of meat, takes the other to be blind to something they cannot fail just not to know, is what is to be understood.

But isn't the formulation askew from the beginning that undertakes to understand inordinate knowledge as a question of experiencing the meaning of words? Surely it is a question of experiencing, or fixating experience on, a region of reality, on the *fact* of what is happening to animals. The question is whether this is itself denied or revealed by Elizabeth Costello's description of her condition. She says, speaking of her concealed and unconcealed wound, that "it is touched on in every word I speak." Now mightn't a philosopher object that she could possess her wound and say nothing – surely while *I* may need her words (anyway some expression from her) to know of her inordinate knowledge, *she* cannot require it. But then the situation is one in which she must *suppress* her expression, that is to say, suppress *this* expression, and that requires an expression of its own. – But surely, the suppression of the expression can itself be suppressed! – I wonder if this is as easy to do as it is to say. If it is easy, anyway if you can disguise it well enough to keep it hidden from all others indefinitely, then maybe it is *too* easy, that is, maybe the wound doesn't exist. I am impressed by Costello's formulation that "it [the wound] is touched on in *every word* I speak." Every word accordingly touches on, alludes to, activates and expresses, her condition, in its revelations and in its suppressions of revelation, and I do not hesitate to say that it is touched on by her every gesture and posture of her body. Of course you may have to know her well to read her gestures. So may she. And we should consider again, from this corner of things, where the offense lies in the comparison of food factories and concentration camps. We want to preserve the incomparable, the supreme, horror of the camps. But what is the expression of our knowledge, of this supreme horror, let me say, its acknowledgment? What expression is *appropriate* here? How is the wound touched upon differently here, uniquely? (Coetzee will say at the opening of his book: "We push on." We live without answers to the most basic questions of our orientation.) To preserve the inordinateness of this knowledge risks making ourselves unfit for further response, exhausts our capacity for being touched further. It freezes the world; it scalds the capacity to taste.

3.

Here perhaps is a place at least to mention the apparent congruence between Costello's comparison of food factories and concentration camps and a sentence attributed to Heidegger by Philippe Lacoue-Labarthe, quoted by Maurice Blanchot, and discussed by Arnold Davidson in an issue of *Critical Inquiry* devoted to Heidegger and Nazism. Heidegger is reported to say: "Agriculture is now a mechanized food industry. As for its essence, it is the same thing as the manufacture of corpses in the gas chambers and the death camps, the same thing as the blockades and the reduction of countries to famine, the same thing as the manufacture of hydrogen bombs."[5] I

---

[5] Quoted by Maurice Blanchot in "Thinking the Apocalypse: A Letter from Maurice Blanchot to Catherine David," *Critical Inquiry* 15 (Winter 1989): 478.

cannot but imagine that Coetzee knew this citation linking the food industry with, among other things, the death camps and that he meant to be putting Heidegger's words to the test in his novel, in effect to ask whether such a view is credible coming from anywhere but from an old woman, tired almost to death of the responses she receives late in her life of words, crazed by their reality to her and jarred by her imagination into welcoming the offense she may cause. One of Heidegger's best moments in *What Is Called Thinking?* is his description of Nietzsche, in trying to reach his contemporaries with the event of their murder of God: "most quiet and shiest of men, ... [Nietzsche] endured the agony of having to scream."[6] It is illuminating, I find, to think of Elizabeth Costello, in her exhausted way, as screaming. A further detail suggesting the presence of Heidegger's *What Is Called Thinking?* in Coetzee's text is its opening brief paragraph that presents life's journey from a near to a far bank, with which we are able to "push on," as made possible by bridges. Heidegger says early, with respect to the passage from our scientific or intellectualized mentality to philosophical (that is, genuine) thinking, that "There is no bridge here – only the leap."[7] It follows that the opening paragraph of Coetzee's novel describes us, human beings who are pushing on, getting on, going along, as not in a position to think.

Anyone in whose imagination Heidegger survives as a serious person and thinker will have had to find a way beyond the sense that his thought comes to direct itself as an apology for Nazism (despite certain "disagreements" with it), for example in his seeming to equate – in essence; finally; at bottom; after all is said and done; at the end of the day – Hitler's Germany's treatment of the Jews (and others) with Stalin's Russia's treatment of the Ukrainian kulaks in the 1930s, and with America's treatment of the populations of Hiroshima and Nagasaki in dropping atomic bombs, and its declared readiness to drop more and bigger ones. We need to emphasize to ourselves that Heidegger does not equate these events *morally*, attempting to measure their degrees of horror. He equates them in what he calls "essence" with the machine-driven planting and cultivation and harvesting and packing and marketing of fruits

---

[6] Martin Heidegger, *What is Called Thinking?*, trans. J. Glenn Gray (New York: Harper, 1968), 48.

[7] Ibid., 8.

and vegetables. Evidently this is in contrast with, for example, earlier slave-driven sugar plantations, which were visibly harder on workers than mechanized agriculture is. Something has now happened, manifested in these newer holocausts, to the human as such, to its idea of reason or the reasonable.

"In essence" evidently spells out something insisted upon more abstractly in Heidegger's *What Is Called Thinking?*: "Our age is not a technological age because it is the age of the machine; it is an age of the machine because it is the technological age." "The will to make and be effective, has overrun and crushed thought." "The essence of technology is not anything human. The essence of technology is above all not anything technological." "The essence of technology pervades our existence in a way which we have barely noticed so far."[8] (Say that our capacity and desire for thinking has been replaced by material that is planted and cultivated and harvested and packed and marketed by machines, in their "machine essence," apparently for our convenience, but in essence transforming what we find it possible to will and effect.) It is conceivable that someone could equate Heidegger's three cases "in essence" and still maintain that the death camps were the hardest to fathom, reaching, in unexpected flarings of consciousness, the most inordinate horror. But Heidegger himself, I believe, cannot steadily be so conceived. Even after thought has been crushed, we "can learn ... to listen closely," which, being "the common concern of student and teacher," is such that "no one is to be blamed ... if he is not yet capable of listening."[9] Heidegger does not seem interested in guarding against taking a metaphysical vision to license bad behavior or make it blameless – a taking that is Austin's favorite form of intellectual and moral vulgarity and mischief, like producing the fact that life is uncertain as a way of reneging on a promise.

And, since it is Elizabeth Costello's comparison of death camps with food factories that invoked Heidegger's linking of the camps with the agricultural industry, I mark her difference from Heidegger at the point Cora Diamond emphasizes in Coetzee's characterization of Costello, namely in her exhibition of her unexhibited wound. Heidegger has no such wound to confess and by this he is cursed.

---

[8] Ibid., 24, 25, 22.
[9] Ibid., 25.

Where inordinate knowledge is in order he finds that there is something we are still not thinking about. So far so good. But what if this inordinateness is to guide what, and how, we are to think, and perhaps first of all to think why the perception of the inordinate is, or is not, widely shared? Heidegger says we are still not thinking about the essence of the technological, which is not anything technological and not anything human. He would not be the first to perceive the human as subject to takeover, but now neither from above nor from below. In Nietzsche, the human has participated in an event uniquely catastrophic – he calls it the killing of God, but it is to be seen everywhere, in what we accept as ordinary in our lives – in requiring that our response to it will be to re-conceive the human (no longer in contrast with God), by as it were renouncing, reconsidering, renaming, each of our actions and passions, so that suffering is no longer thought of as punishment, and hope and horror are no longer to be looked at as originating from above or from below, but from ourselves, so that every word we speak is a promise and every act a fulfillment, and we will do to others or to ourselves nothing we cannot ourselves redeem. Perhaps then we are in a position of facing for the first time, or in a new way, the task of seeing ourselves, myself and others, as human.

Heidegger may still have taken philosophical thinking about Nazism indispensably far, in case anyone continues to think about its possibility, above all about what made it attractive, about why its promised totality of organization might have seemed the only answer to the chaos, or wasteland, Heidegger perceives coming on, an answer to the impossibility of individual responsibility, to a necessary alteration of human nature and (what Heidegger thinks of as) a people's destiny. Costello's response to the world of dissociated lives is, I think one can say, at the other end of the spiritual universe, to divine the truth of the idea Wittgenstein expresses by saying "No cry of torment can be greater than the cry of one man" (*CV* 45i; a remark from 1944). This seems to accept responsibility for the world, its beginning with me. Which of these responses is likely to be the more effective? Isn't this precisely the question Heidegger claims to deplore?

I am moved to add that ordinary language philosophy is as distrustful of, as stricken by, the actual ordinary as philosophy chronically has been since Plato's representation of it in the Myth of the Cave. This is what I take Wittgenstein to express in saying "What *we* do

is to lead words back from their metaphysical to their everyday use"
(*PI* §116), with the proviso that you might not, without reflection, or
suggestion, tell when the metaphysical has intervened in our lives, as
reported here, for example: "I have seen a person ... strike himself on
the breast and say: 'But surely another person can't have THIS pain!' "
(*PI* §253). But we live in the everyday before words are returned; we
live then in exile from our words, and the return is never at rest. Out
of this perspective one might take Costello's vision of the world as an
allegory of the violence done to the ordinary pervasively, invisibly to
most, by the metaphysical. But in this case the cause is not that we are
shouldered into trying to mean what cannot be meant, but that we are
shouldered out of recognizing our role in meaning what we say.

4.

I began this text by reporting the pressure upon its ideas by another
text I was working on ("Companionable Thinking"), concerned
with how we see ourselves in relation to non-human animals, and
soon I was in effect reporting residues of another related text ("The
Wittgensteinian Event") in invoking Wittgenstein's thought of concepts as guided by interests, something he says evidently in contrast
to the idea of concepts as independent of the makeup of the world
and of ourselves in it. A reason to raise this issue of interests here, if
only sketchily, is that it suggests another way of arriving at the sense
of our attachment to words. The beginning of this train of thought
is taking the metaphysical (as in Wittgenstein's saying "What *we* do is
to lead words back from their metaphysical to their everyday use") as
a state we crave, something Wittgenstein characterizes as "a longing
for the transcendent" (*CV* 15b), an explicit recognition of his affinity with and difference from Kant and from the German Romantics
struggling in the aftermath of Kant.

   It is this longing (itself variously characterized by Wittgenstein,
for example, sometimes as torment, sometimes as restlessness) that
incites the attempt to do what Wittgenstein speaks of as driving us to
speak "*outside* a particular language-game" (*PI* §47), to speak absolutely, or to speak of absolutes. I suppose the most familiar example
of this compulsion is the search for what it is that names name, for the
unchanging essence that makes something knowable, the satisfaction

of the thought that things that have the same name must have something in common – a thought as early as Plato's Forms or Ideas, which later philosophy calls universals. Wittgenstein's well remembered answer is: "Don't say: 'There *must* be something common' … but *look and see*" (*PI* §66). One may well wish to ask: Can this deliberately banal proposal really dispel a philosophical intuition lasting for millennia, that to know what an object is is to know its essence? Shall we look and see?

What does a tall, small round table at which two bar stools are drawn up have in common with a table of numbers displayed on a page, and both with a water table? (I do not suppose that these further tables are metaphorical.) The common thing cannot be simply that they all have an element that is flat, since the sheet of paper on which the table of numbers is printed is flat, and so is the coaster on the bar table, but we don't call each of these a table. Then where does the table idea come in across these three cases? Well, the instances do all have something in common with a common library table – its horizontal stretch of flatness fits the surface of water; that it is mounted on legs or on a stem securely grounded fits the round bar table; its rectangularity fits the table of numbers. But is *this* what we thought we meant in insisting that they *must* have something in common? Didn't we mean something more like: they have it in common *in a common or essential way* – a *same* something that calls out for the concept *in each case*?

It seems that Wittgenstein wants to reveal our intellectual disappointment with our philosophical explanations, such as positing the existence of universals. But his alternative suggestion that what we see among these instances is no more than what he calls a "family resemblance" can seem even more disappointing, although it has evidently satisfied some who are devoted to Wittgenstein's thought. My sense, rather, is that this is only a preparation for his idea that we are right to look for a sense of essence or necessity in our concepts, only we are looking in the wrong place. Essence is, for Wittgenstein, "expressed by grammar" (*PI* §371), what in *The Claim of Reason* I call the schematism of a concept; so to look for a universal for an individual (fixated) term, precisely eclipses the route to its essence, say its unique circulation in its language.[10] And, in the ambience of the concerns of

---

[10] Cavell, *The Claim of Reason*, cf. 77 ff.

the present text, this seems to me a further way of accounting for our attachment to our words.

This is something that may show itself when Wittgenstein considers that "Concepts ... are the expression of our interest, and direct our interest" (*PI* §570). For example: some tables need legs, when our interest is to sit comfortably at them, namely have them come up roughly to our waists (our interest in a coffee table might be served by a closed rectangular box); our interest in the flatness of others is to allow for a significant and accurate measure, as with the water table; and our interest in the rectangularity of a table of numbers is to achieve the linear clarity necessary to check and to interpret them. My declaration "I am wounded" would not refer to a wound, would not, as it were, touch it, unless my use of the word expressed my suffering and alarm and plea for help or for recognition, expressions which we might say call upon the word; my saying "You are wounded" would not refer to or touch your state unless saying it recognized your suffering and expressed my sympathy or my suspicion of your expression. I have in the past spoken of such declarations as acknowledgments. What emerges here is that an acknowledgment is inherently open to the judgment of appropriateness. (I mention in passing another interpretation that I have found possible for Wittgenstein's observation that "Concepts ... are the expression of our interest, and direct our interest." It is to *remind* us of something that we are sometimes led to forget – namely, that we have uses for our words – as when in thinking of the relation of what we say to what there is, we put aside our part in our speech and expect, or demand, that words and world meet, dictate to each other, without my intervention, as if I have no power or responsibility in the matter of the fit between my language and my world. Then the world and its capacities will tell me what, for example, preparing and packing and marketing are, and how to do them more economically, with no moment at which I understand myself to have a say in whether I actually want to be part of these consequences, whether I find my interests to be served by what I serve, what I "do," or the contrary.)

We have turned up what seem opposite criteria for the concept of "attachment to our words." In the aspect case it is the experience of a word, expressed in the idea of its being called forth by an aspect's dawning, that calls forth the concept (the duck aspect in its relation to pictures of ducks); in the case of the draw of essence, it seems to be something like the *absence* of the experience, or distinctiveness, of the word that is required, but also something like its being called forth by (the experience of) the *reality* of what it conceptualizes, that this thing *is* a table (not an *aspect* of a level of water or of a collection of numbers or of a smallish round flat surface made to sit at on a bar stool). Here we come upon the dual service in which grammar and its articulating criteria are pressed in order to reveal to us "what kind of object anything is" (*PI* §373): to show the necessity in grammatical differences (e.g., between "is a duck" and "is now a duck"), and to show the necessity in (or say the internality of) the relation of the realm of language, of concepts, and the realm of the world that incorporate each other (e.g., the necessary coincidence between expecting someone and an environment in which someone is to be expected, or in which hope in her arrival is fading). While there is no closed system of concepts in which the world is revealed to us, our confidence in tracking the shared world is shifted to the improvisation and systematicity of language, where grammar tells us what kind of object anything is because talkers acquire in acquiring grammar the facility to share criteria in which grammar is invited to the individual case ("It is part of the grammar of the word 'chair' that *this* is what we call 'to sit on a chair'" [*BB* 24]).

I have suggested that when Wittgenstein takes up the question, in *Philosophical Investigations*, of knowing how to go on with a series of numbers, he is using this as an allegory of going on with the use of a word in "new" contexts (contexts that seem new before the acceptance of this use). This works both ways. It calls attention to the fact that the series of "next steps" in projecting the word "table" into a series of contexts requires something like a new judgment in each step, a recognition of how the new object counts under the "usual" concept, whereas expanding a series, on the order "Add 2," would not be what it is – would not be arithmetic – if it weren't "automatic," machine-like, which doesn't however mean that it cannot break down in its own way, a way that would seem a lapse in our natural history. It is the peculiar spontaneity in numerical counting, necessary for numerical counting to do what it does (e.g., maintain confidence that you have not left out a step eight steps earlier), that requires that familiar attachment one develops to the words for the sequence of numbers, expressed, for example, by even long-term non-native speakers of English finding themselves reverting to their childhood language when they calculate by hand, or, interestingly, curse, as if to insure that their words maintain their effectiveness, their edge of magic.

That human language wounds as well as names, expresses as well as accuses – put otherwise, that human speech and action is a perpetual resultant of an economy of exchange between the natural and the conventional, that both are necessary to the animal whose conduct (*Handlung*) is shaped by the hand – is a reason I have stressed Wittgenstein's idea of a form of life, or more literally, a life form, as having two directions, or axes, an ethnological and a biological, horizontal and vertical.[11] It is grammar that tells us what kind of object anything is; the associated work of criteria articulates our agreement in language (*PI* §241). I do not guess, for example, what eventual understanding or accommodation will be arrived at between those who think of the relation between the human and the non-human world of animals as one of recognizing that non-human animals have rights, granted in convention and morality, and those who find that the relation is itself fundamentally natural, biological, that animals are our companions; whether accordingly the issue of accommodation will turn more on determining the pertinence and discovery of a just and rational legal order, or, rather, more on finding the trauma and hysteria, or say inordinateness, in acknowledging a reciprocal recognition, seeing them as our others.

That I sense obscurities in what I have written here, which I know I shall want to revisit and to try to clarify, takes me back to the initial improbability I sensed in supposing that two interventions I had committed myself to composing, due roughly at the same date, were interfering with the development of each other precisely because they were linked in ways I could not articulate, except so superficially or arbitrarily as to stultify work on whichever of them I took in hand. When I began from Cora Diamond's sense of the issue of the companionability of

---

[11] See Cavell, *This New Yet Unapproachable America: Lectures after Emerson after Wittgenstein* (Albuquerque: Living Batch Press, 1989), 41 ff.

animals and humans, I was struck by the illumination lent the issue by the feature woven through the concepts Wittgenstein finds in play in investigating the concept, or phenomenon, of seeing something as something – the feature of a specific, extreme alternation of response to one and the same object – an alternation between indifference (or what Wittgenstein reads as "mere" knowledge, say of the common fact that human beings are carnivores, anyway omnivores) and horror (what I call inordinate knowledge, say of the monstrous fact that we accept the manufacture of countless of our companions into food for other of our companions). But when I began on the opposite side of the issue, not from Diamond's examples and descriptions but from Wittgenstein's investigation of the concept of seeing-as, I felt baffled by the distance of the examples of the duck-rabbit and the fallen triangle and what Wittgenstein calls the double cross, etc., from that of food factories and concentration camps. Contrast in size shouldn't affect the precision of concepts. If an atomic explosion can put one in mind of a mushroom, why can a death camp not put one in mind of a mechanized slaughterhouse? But does it? Something is wrong here. A mushroom does not put us in mind of an atomic explosion; a mechanized slaughterhouse may put us in mind of a death camp. Figuration is not reversible. It is clear that man is a wolf to man; it is not clear that a wolf is man to a wolf.

I can accept the suggestion that I may just be "blind" to one aspect of the duck-rabbit figure; but to be blind to the systematic violence of the manufacturing of meat I have to turn a blind eye to the fact, do something to my mind, in order to achieve indifference; indifference has to be maintained, cultivated. But does this give us a measure of the relation between a duck-to-rabbit shift and an indifference-to-horror shift? Are these really illuminatingly comparable "dawnings"? Or is the shock of recognition of the daily work of the mechanized slaughterhouse really like a rabbit darting out and causing the startled production of a name? And aren't matters worse when Heidegger is brought onto the scene? That one *can* be indifferent to certain phenomena is itself already moral blindness, to say the least. But surely in the case of the food factories, this conclusion is argumentative, as it is not in the case of the camps.

But the intrusion of the concept of allegory may contain a hint. I have, I recall, sometimes suggested that Thoreau's description in the

opening paragraphs of *Walden* of his ordinary, unremarkable townsmen as putting him in mind of self-torturing spiritual fanatics is a
piece of allegory, and sometimes spoken of the description as of a
vision visited upon this writer. The immediacy, or intermediary, of
the concept of the visual in this transfiguration does obviously warrant the suggestion that he is *seeing* his townsmen as something, and
here the Wittgensteinian web of associated concepts do seem uncon-
troversially to apply.

In practice I decided to work on my two texts (for the Diamond
volume and for the present volume) simultaneously, or alternately,
and moreover both of them in view of another text I had recently
completed on my reading of Wittgenstein that emphasizes his appeal
to the natural history of the human, including natural, or, say,
appropriate, reactions, letting the texts, as it were, try to find each
other. So yet again I submit myself to the awkwardness of educating
myself in public.

II ASPECTS AND THE SELF

II.1 Self-Knowledge

5

In a New Light

Wittgenstein, Aspect-Perception, and Retrospective Change in Self-Understanding

Garry L. Hagberg

1.

In 1957 Iris Murdoch wrote, with perhaps too much concision, "Man is a creature who makes pictures of himself, and then comes to resemble the picture."[1] And in an earlier diary entry from June 14, 1952, she had written: "There is a lot which I don't put into the diary, because it would be too discreditable – and maybe even more painful." Characteristically, she quickly turns to reflect upon, to refine, and to qualify what she has just written, adding parenthetically, "At least – no major item omitted but certain angles altered – and painful incidents omitted."[2] Still earlier, shortly after having listened to a lecture entitled "The Past" by Elizabeth Anscombe in October 1947, Murdoch, as her biographer Peter Conradi reports, was reflecting on "what she might feel if presented with documentary evidence – for example, journals – about her forgotten past." She then writes a passage that both gives voice to a kind of guarded skepticism concerning self-knowledge and makes a strong claim concerning the *active* nature of our involvement with our past. She writes: "Suppose I were given evidence about what I thought at the

---

[1] Murdoch's diary entries are quoted, contextualized, and insightfully discussed in Peter J. Conradi, *Iris Murdoch: A Life* (New York: W. W. Norton, 2001); this quotation, 272.
[2] Ibid., 274.

time. My diaries, etc. I think I would not accept that evidence. I'd
still feel I didn't know what my past really was." Describing these
diary pages – pages within a diary attempting to advance our
understanding of the degree to which a diary is itself credible,
authoritative, and revelatory – Conradi says, "Over many pages of
reflection, she reaches towards a distinction between a 'frozen' and
an 'unfrozen' past. So long as one lives, one's relationship with the
past *should* keep shifting." Indeed, in those pages Murdoch also put
this point compactly and with emphasis: "*Re-thinking one's past is a
constant responsibility.*"[3]

With these lines Murdoch has brought a number of interlocking
themes into play, and each of these themes articulates a fundamental problem of autobiographical knowledge. How do we go about the
life-defining project of making a "picture" of ourselves, which we
then come to resemble? How does the selectivity displayed in choosing what to include and what to leave out – or semi-wittingly avoid – in
diary-writing determine both the content and the outlines of that picture? How might we characterize, and give more exacting expression
to, the process, a process that is clearly centrally significant for any
project of self-investigation, of altering the "angle" of a life's "major
items"? Skepticism is never just whimsically adopted (not, that is, with
human seriousness anyway); it is *motivated*. So precisely what, we want
to ask, motivates the skeptical stance towards the evidence of which
she writes such that, even with the evidence plainly before us, we find
it plausible to claim that we still would not know "what our past really
was"? And perhaps most importantly, what does it mean to relate to
one's own past as "unfrozen," to have one's relationship with one's
own past keep shifting? How can we more exactingly articulate what
it means, in Murdoch's words, to "re-think" the past?

---

[3] Ibid., 275. A reading of her diary, as we have it in Conradi's biography, shows that
this was for Murdoch anything but a matter for abstract speculation, detached from
life. To take only one example, upon learning of the wholly unexpected separation of
two of her married friends, she writes, "I had thought of them as so indissolubly connected & somehow of that part of my history concerning them as so completely ended.
… An extraordinary sense of time rolling backward. … In some way, the parting of
those two reopens my own past. It is as if they, together closed a door for me, ended
a certain piece of my history, & closed the book. Now that they are parting that force
is no longer exerted." Later, she wrote to one of the separated parties, "I'm very glad
the future contains you," and it is clear that for Murdoch that particular future will be
heavily inflected by a retrospectively revised past. See Conradi, *Iris Murdoch*, 430–31.

In facing such questions we should realize that we do not usually face them alone, but rather with a host of presuppositions, including: (1) philosophical conceptions or pictures, in Wittgenstein's special sense, of selfhood; (2) analogies that both lead and mislead; (3) grammatical similarities between different kinds of cases that lead us to take them as more similar than they are; and (4) epistemological intuitions that import into the proceedings from the outset expectations about what conditions must be satisfied in order to arrive at a true proposition with self-revelatory content. We will see all of these in action as we proceed,[4] but in this paper I will focus primarily upon the last: it is all too easy, when reflecting in a preliminary way about the kind of autobiographical understanding that comes from a grasp of one's past, to conceive of the problem as a polarized epistemological dichotomy. On the first pole (one that has, incidentally, become extremely fashionable throughout the humanities of late), we picture ourselves projecting onto the past the content that we claim to perceive in it, and thus succumb (perhaps unwittingly) to a not-un-familiar variety of self-deception. Here, the narrative self is indeed a narrative construction, and, rather like Hume on causation, what we get ourselves to believe we perceive in our past is of our present retrospective making. Or, on the second pole, we picture ourselves as accurately and non-prismatically perceiving what is in the past in and of itself, where the true self-revelatory proposition is one that is verified through correspondence between present utterance and past fact. Here, the narrative self is one that is constituted not by present

---

[4] I have discussed these first three sources of conceptual difficulty concerning autobiographical writing in a number of recent papers, including: "The Self, Speaking: Wittgenstein, Introspective Utterances, and the Arts of Self-Representation," *Revue Internationale de Philosophie*, ed. J.-P. Cometti, 1:219 (2002): 9–47; "The Self, Reflected: Wittgenstein, Cavell, and the Autobiographical Situation," *Ordinary Language Criticism: Literary Thinking after Cavell after Wittgenstein*, ed. Kenneth Dauber and Walter Jost (Evanston: Northwestern University Press, 2003), 171–98; "The Self, Thinking: Wittgenstein, Augustine, and the Autobiographical Situation," *Wittgenstein, Aesthetics and Philosophy*, ed. Peter B. Lewis (Aldershot: Ashgate, 2004), 215–33; "The Mind Shown: Wittgenstein, Goethe, and the Question of Person Perception," *Goethe and Wittgenstein: Seeing the World's Unity in Its Variety*, ed. Fritz Breithaupt, Richard Raatzsch, and Bettina Kremberg, Wittgenstein Studien, Band 5 (Frankfurt am Main: Peter Lang, 2002), 111–26; and "Autobiographical Consciousness: Wittgenstein, Private Experience, and the 'Inner Picture'," *The Literary Wittgenstein*, ed. John Gibson and Wolfgang Huemer (London: Routledge, 2004), 228–50.

active retrospection but rather by the passive, factually constrained accurate memory of those past episodes of one's life. The very idea of "getting it right," the content of autobiographical verisimilitude, would seem, at first glance, to reduce to precisely this model of objective reportage. Yet Murdoch emphatically asserts that the past, properly understood, should be "unfrozen," and that one has no less than a moral obligation to "re-think."[5] Moreover, she says this without ever so much as giving a hint that one should thus embrace any variety of subjectivist constructionism, that the self-concept that results from an active engagement with one's past is entirely fluid, indeterminate prior to any narrative construction, and contingent upon that construction for its created, and not discovered, sense of stability over time. Perhaps it is the large-scale dichotomy between projectivism on the one pole, and perception on the other, that is false; perhaps the truth of the matter is far too intricate for this intuition-supported dichotomy to begin to accommodate.

2.

We speak, of course, of our understanding of our past, and of the pictures of selfhood drawn and supported by that understanding, in ocular terms. We speak of how we see a situation, of seeing it differently, of tenaciously or intolerantly seeing a circumstance in only one way, and of one's being unable to see it in any other way, and so forth. We similarly have developed a subtle vocabulary concerning how we see ourselves. Although we have been warned of the dangers of unexamined ocular

---

[5] It is clear that Murdoch feels this as a moral imperative throughout her life. At a time of great happiness shortly after her marriage, we find lines stating that life now has "such a quality of simplicity, warmth, and joy," and that it is now strange to read her earlier, much more difficult, and occasionally troubled diary entries. But even here she gently chides herself for not sufficiently engaging in "deep consideration of the consequences of my past actions"; this is evidently a long-ingrained commitment to an active engagement with the past that she clearly feels to be indispensable to a life worth living. And in reference to those earlier difficult entries, she further reinforces this active autobiographical sense in quoting Virgil, to the effect that "the day may dawn when this plight will be sweet to remember." But Conradi shows that the entry is more complex still (and still more illustrative of what she means by an active re-thinking of the past): the lines concerning "simplicity, warmth, and joy" were written "in a later hand and ink" and, as Conradi goes on to say, was thus "a truth grasped retrospectively" (*Iris Murdoch*, 400–1).

metaphors in epistemology and elsewhere,[6] these linguistic practices are enough to suggest that a close scrutiny of the subtleties of visual perception may prove helpful to the questions articulated by Murdoch. Indeed, such scrutiny may show precisely how we can sustain an active or unfrozen engagement with our past and how we see it, while still not forfeiting all hope of satisfying our quite fundamental human desire for self-descriptive accuracy and autobiographical rightness of a kind that avoids an epistemic descent into an "anything goes" narrative constructionism.[7] And it is in Part II, Section 11 of Wittgenstein's *Philosophical Investigations* that we find a most sustained inquiry into visual experience that, as we shall see, proves most relevant to these issues.

Approximately one-third of the way through that section, Wittgenstein arrives at the question, which he puts in the voice of his picture-driven interlocutor, "Is it a *genuine* visual experience?" (*PI* 204g). This follows the discussion of an aspectual shift in seeing that a diagram can be seen as two hexagons, where earlier it was seen as something else. The philosophically recidivistic interlocutor – giving expression to an impulse we can all quite naturally feel at a juncture like this, where an aspect has just shifted – emphasizes "genuine" because he construes the real visual experience as one side of a philosophical dichotomy where accurate perception precludes subjectivized projection. If genuine, so one might think here, the visual experience will be authenticated by what the object seen possesses in and of itself: the criterion for the genuine will here be construed as the replication on an ocular level of the intrinsic properties of the object seen. (The direct analogy to the autobiographical case – to the "second pole" above – is clear enough.) But Wittgenstein does not accept this simple dichotomized picture, of course. He replies, "The question is: in what *sense* is it one [a genuine visual experience]?" (*PI* 204g, emphasis added). He has at this point already discussed the general contrast between two kinds of cases: (1) seeing that an object is an *X*, and (2) seeing that object as an *X* not

[6] See Richard Rorty, *Philosophy and the Mirror of Nature* (Princeton: Princeton University Press, 1979).

[7] I have pursued a fuller elucidation of the concept of "rightness" as it operates in autobiographical contexts in "Rightness Reconsidered: Krausz, Wittgenstein, and the Question of Interpretive Understanding," *Interpretation and Its Objects: Studies in the Philosophy of Michael Krausz*, ed. Andreea Deciu Ritivoi (Amsterdam: Rodopi, 2003), 25–37.

because of what we see, but because of what we know. Here, for the
interlocutor, the former would constitute a case of genuine seeing, the
latter inauthentic because too mind-dependent. Wittgenstein's reply,
in the form of the question "in what *sense* is it one," invites the interlocutor to significantly expand the frame of contemplation, asking him
to consider cases in which we would have occasion to mark a contrast
between the genuine and its opposite. (Incidentally, its opposite might
be called "non-genuine," "inauthentic," "false," "untrue," "inaccurate,"
"prismatic," "distorted," and many other things – no two of which come
to the same thing in context.)

Wittgenstein turns shortly to one case in which we might describe
the act of seeing in question more as one of knowing than of seeing,
where "someone treats the picture as a working drawing, *reads* it like
a blueprint" (*PI* 204i). Here it makes sense to speak of an architect
or engineer seeing much more in a blueprint than one not similarly
trained would see. If one were to insist that the trained eye here sees
much more than is *really* in the line drawing and thus that they "see in"
(as a variant of "seeing-as") more than is there, we could quite readily
understand the contrast in play (or, if not the *contrast* between seeing
and thinking, then certainly the emphasis more on the one than the
other). But this would not constitute, precisely, a contrast (or shift of
emphasis) between *genuine* seeing and one of its opposites: the architect and engineer are able to see what the drawing signifies, what it,
in a manner of speaking, *implies*, without transgressing the bounds
of the genuine. (Indeed, no question of the genuine, precisely speaking, has discernibly arisen.) The dichotomy is, in short, already desta-
bilized: neither intrinsic property–reflecting brute perception, nor
freely imaginative projection, seem to capture what is significant about
this blueprint case. And does the self-interpreting autobiographer,
looking back at the broad outlines – in some ways the "blueprint" – of
his or her life and coming to appreciate the interrelatedness[8] of the
important events in life (of the kind of which Murdoch wrote) by connecting those "dots" with a narrative thread,[9] clearly engage in one or

---

[8] I offer a fuller elucidation of the nature of this interrelatedness in "Davidson, Self-
Knowledge, and Autobiographical Writing," *Philosophy and Literature* 26:2 (October
2002): 354–68.
[9] This metaphor has been developed at length in relation to the problem of explaining how the contours and trajectory of a whole life can make what we can sensibly
refer to as sense; for two particularly insightful studies see Richard Wollheim, *The*

the other? As Wittgenstein's discussion shows even at this early stage, these polarized categories are far too crude: the facts of the case are considerably more intricate. Wittgenstein, a bit earlier in this section, wrote: "The concept of 'seeing' makes a tangled impression." And, resisting the impulse to falsify by over-straightening (and in a manner reminiscent of Aristotle in suggesting that we only look for a degree of categorical neatness consistent with the nature of the field being investigated), Wittgenstein adds, "Well, it is tangled" (*PI* 200a).

Can the criteria for an act of genuine seeing be stated in general terms, and would not any such criterion for genuine seeing generate, *mutatis mutandis*, a criterion for genuine (or true) self-"seeing," that is, autobiographical self-understanding? In seeing "that an animal in a picture is transfixed by an arrow" (*PI* 203b), Wittgenstein asks, imagining the picture to be a silhouette, do we *see* the arrow or do we "merely *know* that these two bits are supposed to represent part of an arrow?" Importantly for the question concerning the possibility of stating general criteria derived from a general model of seeing, Wittgenstein considers both of the following emphatic responses to the silhouette case: " 'But this isn't *seeing*!' – 'But this is seeing!' " (*PI* 203c). These are both, we can see at a glance, rational and defensible responses that we imagine arising in different contexts, that is, where the particular point, or conversational goal, of the response fits into a larger pattern of locutionary interaction: a language-game.[10] And it is within such circumscribed language-games that the particularized and context-sensitive criteria for seeing emerge as salient. "It must," Wittgenstein writes, "be possible to give both remarks a conceptual justification" (*PI* 203). And he asks again, here responding in turn to the second, positive response above, "*In what sense* is it seeing?" (*PI* 203d), the point being that the determinate sense will be given by – and only by – the context of the question and its response. If we can see, on the level of detail in both the blueprint and the silhouette cases, that the responses might intelligibly, rationally, and defensibly go either way, the prospects for a *general* criterion for genuine seeing

Thread of Life (Cambridge: Harvard University Press, 1984), and Richard Freadman, *Threads of Life* (Chicago: University of Chicago Press, 2001).

[10] For a fuller account of this fundamental Wittgensteinian concept and its significance for aesthetic contexts, see my *Meaning and Interpretation: Wittgenstein, Henry James, and Literary Knowledge* (Ithaca, N.Y.: Cornell University Press, 1994), 9–44.

diminish rapidly. What, at this point, shall we say of the analogy to the self-interpretive situation?

Seeing the intrinsic properties or features of an object, and then giving those properties their bluntly factual corresponding descriptions, constitutes the "second pole" model that carries its own (again, far too crude) way of construing autobiographical truth: we look back at the past experience and give it its bluntly factual corresponding description. But if, in both the blueprint and the silhouette cases, we can fully comprehend *both* "But this isn't *seeing*!" and "But this is seeing!," then it is clear that a general, overarching criterion for genuine seeing is perhaps something we could *stipulate*, but not something we could *discover* within the fabric of our experience. The parallel cases – for example, Nabokov as autobiographer in place of the architect or engineer, reflecting on the resonances of his formative early Russian experience as they are sounded throughout his adult life in the United States;[11] or a person engaged in self-investigation who *begins* to see (we might metaphorically say: sees in silhouette) that an early separation trauma fueled his later unacknowledged desire to recapitulate that separation experience but to do so volitionally, that is, to take the role of agent, rather than victim, of separation – would be cases in which the defensibility of the self-interpretation would not derive from a generalized, overarching criterion for the true autobiographical proposition. If a confidante of the person in this last example says (critically) "But that isn't *seeing*!" or (in congratulation for hard-won and successful self-investigation) "But that is seeing!," neither reply is given because the intrinsic properties of an isolated life-event are given accurate description (or not). But it is at this precise juncture vitally important to see that this lack of a generalized, case-transcending criterion does not drive us to the skeptical extremes of post-modern narrative constructionism,[12] that is, back to

---

[11] Vladimir Nabokov, *Speak, Memory: An Autobiography Revisited* (New York: Vintage, 1989; originally published as *Conclusive Evidence* [New York: Harper, 1951]). Here he writes, "the supreme achievement of memory … is the masterly use it makes of innate harmonies when gathering to its fold the suspended and wandering tonalities of the past"; I discuss this in "Davidson, Self-Knowledge, and Autobiographical Writing," 364–65.

[12] See, for example, Richard Rorty, "The Contingency of Selfhood," *Contingency, Irony, and Solidarity* (Cambridge: Cambridge University Press, 1989), 23–43.

the "first pole" picture. Neither reply is given because of an application to the present case of a generic criterion, nor because of a contingent espousing of an arbitrary life-construction. The reply, rather, is given because of a capacious grasp of the life of which the event in question is one significant part, and where the rest of that life is known in sufficient detail to see linkages – linkages[13] reported in that life's narrative – that give that life its teleology, its sense. Such a life would not, indeed could not, be understood in Murdoch's sense as a sequence of "frozen" episodes hermetically sealed unto themselves. And this is true precisely in the way that acts of aspect-perception, and their rightness or wrongness, cannot be described in a brute manner hermetically sealed from the contexts within which they occur.[14] That is a false model of objectivity.

In examining the case of a triangle that can be seen variously (to which we might add: as the Great Pyramid, as the Pope's headgear, as having fallen over on its side, etc.), Wittgenstein writes, "The aspects of the triangle: it is as if an *image* came into contact, and for a time remained in contact, with the visual impression" (*PI* 207b). This reinstates – it gives voice to the impulse to fall back into the long-established grooves of thought – the bifurcation between perception and projection. From within these grooves it naturally seems impossible to get beyond the quandary over how we could conceivably adopt an "unfrozen" view of the past with which we actively engage while maintaining any sense of self-descriptive verisimilitude. Wittgenstein's work

[13] But then the very idea of a linkage, within a life's narrative, is not a simple matter; here too we encounter the perception-versus-projection quandary, and here too that very formulation of the matter requires disentangling. I offer an attempt in "Wittgenstein and the Question of True Self-Interpretation," *Is There a Single Right Interpretation?*, ed. Michael Krausz (University Park, Pa.: Pennsylvania State University Press, 2002), 381–406.

[14] For example, in an entry from 1954 Murdoch writes, "the 'who am I to be jealous?' aspect doesn't stop me being in great pain" (Conradi, *Iris Murdoch*, 379). Whether she is right or wrong, or in different ways both right and wrong, to doubt her right to feel jealousy as an aspect of the experience of emotional pain is a question that could never be answered in a "hermetic" way, i.e., in any way but from a knowledge of the extended and indeterminately bounded context in which the jealousy arises. This also shows, incidentally, that just as in visual experience (where not all perception can intelligibly be described as aspect-perception – we do not see a fork as a fork), not everything in "self-seeing" can be characterized as an aspect: the "who am I to be jealous?" element is (as Murdoch indeed says) an aspect; the pain, by contrast, is not.

in this section is, of course, decidedly not to develop a theory from within these grooves, but rather to become enabled, through detailed examples, to think our way out of them. He writes in a parenthetical remark: "In giving all these examples I am not aiming at some kind of completeness, some classification of psychological concepts. They are only meant to enable the reader to shift for himself when he encounters conceptual difficulties" (*PI* 206a). And so he asks, "Is being struck looking plus thinking?," and he answers, "No. Many of our concepts *cross* here" (*PI* 211e). He gives this stern answer because he has just traversed the following landscape: discussing a person who recounts having looked at a flower without being conscious of its color, and who then says, "Then I suddenly *saw* it, and realized it was the one which ...," Wittgenstein considers the response, "He looked at it without seeing it." And he adds: "There is such a thing. But what is the criterion for it?" Resisting the temptation to posit a single, case-transcending answer, he adds, "Well, there is a variety of cases here" (*PI* 211b). So just as we can speak of looking at the flower without seeing it, we can speak of looking at an episode or event in one's life without at first, or for a long time, seeing it, and then at some point coming to see it. This is precisely analogous to what Murdoch meant by "re-thinking." The past is not changed and yet, only seemingly paradoxically, it is. Is being struck by the newly appreciated significance of an event in our past, like suddenly seeing the color of the flower and recognizing that it is the special one that ..., a phenomenon we can helpfully describe as looking plus thinking? No; many of our concepts cross here. But how *do* we then describe it?

3.

The past is not changed by the active process given a name by Murdoch and given content, by analogy to sight, by Wittgenstein – and yet, in a sense, it is.[15] Wittgenstein writes, "The color of the visual impression

---

[15] This way of putting it has been helpfully described as the "paradox" of aspect-perception that it was Wittgenstein's project in Part II, Section 11 of *Philosophical Investigations* to solve (or rather dissolve); see Stephen Mulhall, *On Being in the World: Wittgenstein and Heidegger on Seeing Aspects* (London: Routledge, 1990), 6–34, and Hans-Johann Glock, *A Wittgenstein Dictionary* (Oxford: Blackwell, 1996), 36–40. Glock succinctly encapsulates the dualism implicit in the Gestalt psychology to which Wittgenstein was in part here responding, a theory that would introduce

corresponds to the color of the object (this blotting paper looks pink to me, and is pink)—the shape of the visual impression to the shape of the object (it looks rectangular to me, and is rectangular)." So far, this in and of itself might lead us to think that the simple perceptual side of the perception/projection dichotomy might suffice after all. But it is what Wittgenstein adds to this remark that complicates the picture, and that gives us an answer to the question which asks in what precise terms we should describe autobiographical re-thinking. He writes next, "but what I perceive in the dawning of an aspect is not a property of the object, but an internal relation between it and other objects" (*PI* 212a). Coming to see an object as an *X* or a *Y* is not reducible to, and not explicable in terms of, the perception of a property intrinsic to that hermetically sealed (i.e., non-relationally embedded) object. But neither is it reducible to, nor explicable in terms of, the projection of a (mind-dependent) property onto the object. Similarly, I would suggest that coming to see, first, that a given past action was an unidentified prototype for subsequent different – yet still in a heretofore undisclosed sense similar – actions, and, second, that that action was self-interestedness masquerading as altruism, is neither just perception nor projection. It is a dawning of an aspect, the seeing of an internal relation, first, between the prototype and its successors and, secondly, between the series of actions and a range of examples involving more self-interest than altruism.

This process is what Murdoch had in mind as re-thinking our way into an unfrozen past, in which the mind's role *is* active – but active in the way one hears that a musical passage is a variation of an earlier theme, not as we, with Leonardo, see landscapes in the myriad cracks of the plaster wall. Imagination is required, but with a distinctive kind of interpretive discipline: "Doesn't it take," Wittgenstein writes, "imagination to hear something as a variation on a particular theme? And yet one is perceiving something in so hearing it" (*PI* 213c). The

two "visual realities," one outward and one inward (where the aspect is reified as a private mental entity). Much of the work undertaken in *PI* II.xi is designed to show that no such private object could serve as the content of an aspect, nor could it serve as a criterion for the correctness of the description of any visual experience. Although it would take a separate paper to show this in detail, I want here to suggest that both the content and the correctness of any autobiographical endeavor will be "public" in the same way that the visual turns out to be in *PI* II.xi.

"something" is not an intrinsic property the description of which is
verified by brute correspondence. It is an internal relation that provides the expanded context within which the particularized criteria
for rightness or wrongness (and the long continuum of possibilities in
between) emerge. If we then ask, "But is it then at bottom really a case
of projection?," or if we ask, "Is it not then at bottom still just perception after all?," this will be only a late-stage manifestation of the polarized dichotomy brought in with our pre-reflective intuitions about the
matter. And as to one or another thing being "at bottom," we should
bear in mind that there is no reason to assume that one language-
game should be prior to, or more fundamental than, another.

It is here that we encounter another, related epistemological intuition that comes into play and that can mislead in its own way. We may
feel an inclination to insist that one language-game *is* prior to, more
fundamental than, another in these cases, and to insist in turn that
this priority is of the first importance in distinguishing the real facts
of the case from the less real interpretation of it. This insistence may
concern either the objects of vision or, here again in direct parallel,
the objects of autobiographical interpretation. Beginning this line
of thought by noting that we do, after all, have to hear the melody
before we recognize it as a variation, and that we have to remember
the large life-incident of Murdoch's kind before we place it into a
pattern of action, thought, and emotion that only emerges on reflection, we may then quickly – too quickly – say that the object of sight
in and of itself, the melody unto itself, and the isolated life event are
fundamental, in a sense more real, and thus objective, whereas the
aspect seen in the object – be it the status as variation in the melody
or the prototypical power of the life event – is not real in the same way
and, thus, is subjective. And that generic distinction, at precisely this
juncture, opens the way for skepticism concerning whether the latter
kinds of things are knowable or not, leading to a general pronouncement against the epistemological legitimacy of seen or heard aspects
or self-interpreted aspects or internal relations. This line of thinking
is mistaken, here again in being far too simple a picture to accommodate the "tangle" here, far too crude to capture the intricacy.

This misguided line of thinking is, I think, not far from
Wittgenstein's thoughts even at the very beginning of *PI* II.xi. His
first words in this section are, "Two uses of the word 'see'." He then

quickly contrasts the case of (1) responding to the question "What do you see there?" (where there are two faces or two drawings of faces) with the answer "I see this" (followed by a description, a drawing, or a copy) with (2) the case of responding with the answer "I see a likeness between these two faces" (*PI* 193a). As Wittgenstein goes on to discuss the difference of category between the two cases, he is careful to never place the one as primary, as real, and the other as secondary, as merely subjective.[16] Of the second category, he writes, "I contemplate a face, and then suddenly notice its likeness to another." And then, like the case we considered above when the seeming paradox emerges where the object seen both does and does not change, he adds, "I *see* that it has not changed; and yet I see it differently. I call this experience 'noticing an aspect'" (*PI* 193c). Here, it is true, the categories are made distinct, but there is, throughout his analysis, never a point where they are described as ordered in a hierarchy of real "knowability."

This, as we can now see, is directly linked to his question concerning the "genuine" visual experience above. His response to that interlocutor's query (voiced in perfect correspondence to the line of thought under consideration here) was not to accept the presumption concerning the fundamental or objective (the genuine) versus the secondary (or the false, the uncertain, etc. – the genuine's opposite), but rather to ask: In what *sense* is it one? This re-shifted our focus back to the relevant particularities of contexts within which the criteria for the genuine and its various contextual opposites emerge *in situ*. And so here, the safeguard against falling back into the grooves will be similar particularities: there may be a difference we want to mark between really having seen an object and not, or really having heard the variation-status of the melody or not, or really having seen that a given life-event laid down a template for a repetition-compulsion or not. But the essential point is that none of these more particularized cases correspond to the generic objective/subjective distinction, nor do they take their expected places on a hierarchy reaching from the unknowable to the knowable. It may emerge in a court of law that I

---

[16] Undermining this view (that the former sort of case is primary) is a fundamental objective in the contributions by Timothy Gould and William Day in the present volume.

did not directly see the bag of money in the hands of the accused
but just saw a fleeting shadow on the subway wall that looked like the
accused with a bag. It may emerge in a musical examination that,
while I can recognize on the score that the melody is a variation on
another, I cannot really hear it as such. And it may emerge that I
am only pretending to accept my confidante's suggestion about the
power of the life-experience, and that I do not really believe it. All of
these cases, again, mark contrasts between the genuine and not, but
none of them, down on the ground of contextual detail that answers
Wittgenstein's question "In what *sense?*," corresponds to the idea that
the one category will be genuine, or objective, or skepticism-proof
perception, while the other only concerns subjective or skepticism-
inviting aspects. The one language-game is *not* primary to the other.

4.

Wittgenstein does not, characteristically, directly repudiate the interlocutor's presumption, but rather, throughout a large number of
examples and detailed considerations – indeed, by disentangling the
tangle – provides the means to "shift" when we need to, that is, to break
the twin molds of the generic objective/subjective and perceived/pro-
jected dichotomies. Contrasted to this underground method, we can
now see that Murdoch's assertion was, for better or worse, more of a
frontal assault on the interlocutor's presumption. By saying, with striking force in her diary entry of October 1947, that even were she presented with "documentary evidence – for example, journals – about
her forgotten past," she would nevertheless "feel I didn't know what my
past really was," Murdoch stands the intuitive presupposition concerning the priority of the one language-game to the other on its head.
Again, Wittgenstein does not do this, for the reason that meeting a
philosophical thesis with its polemical antithesis does not grant the
distinct variety of intellectual freedom, the "shift" to what we might call
our way of seeing, that he is pursuing throughout his writings.[17] But it

[17] For a lucid and thorough study of Wittgenstein's writings emphasizing the cen-
     tral role of visual experience and its nuances (and the significance of these
     for philosophical method and the effecting of a change to our way of seeing a
     problem or whole problem-field), see Judith Genova, *Wittgenstein: A Way of Seeing*
     (London: Routledge, 1995). I further discuss the kind of work that allows the "shift"
     mentioned here in connection with our thinking about first-person description in

is of interest for present purposes just to see that such an inversion *can* plausibly be made. In insisting that she still would not know what her life was like, what her past *really* was, Murdoch is giving priority not to the seeing of the faces before noticing the likeness, not to the hearing of the theme before noticing that it is a variation. She is giving priority, indeed, to just that part of the past that is unfrozen, the part that calls for an active re-thinking. The internal relations that we suddenly, or slowly, come to see, the aspects that dawn on the interrelations connecting life events and that yield coherence, that yield the narrative thread, are for Murdoch the primary parts of understanding a life.

If our first reaction to Murdoch's striking claim is that it is willfully epistemologically perverse, wildly idiosyncratic, or obviously disingenuous and stated for dramatic, polemical flair – if indeed our first reaction is to reply to her claim about the insufficiency of documentary evidence with the question "Well, what more could you want?" – perhaps a new aspect is waiting to dawn on that reaction and its motivations. For it becomes, for a close reader of Wittgenstein's *PI* II.xi, increasingly clear that such a reaction is only the surface manifestation of a buried presupposition concerning the genuine versus its opposite, the real versus the merely fanciful, and, generically, the objective versus the subjective. What more Murdoch wants is, of course, not the written descriptions of the isolated episodes of a life, but rather the content – what we might in this context mark off as the genuine content – of the *sense* of a life. It is widely known that Wittgenstein, throughout his multifarious writings on language and mind, rejected (or, better, undercut) the picture of human experience that both traditional empiricism and behaviorism share, that is, that we subjectively construct the objects of the world out of objectively given raw data. That form of scientistic reductionism seriously miscasts the nature of our perception. And that model, applied to the perception – the understanding – of a life's past would yield only a parallel miscasting of autobiographical reflections, precisely in its suggesting that the raw data of episodic experience is objectively given, and that the subsequent perception of the networks of internal relations connecting them is merely a matter of subjective projection.

"On Philosophy as Therapy: Wittgenstein, Cavell, and Autobiographical Writing," *Philosophy and Literature* 27:1 (April 2003): 196–210.

Yet there remains a further problem. While these reflections may effect, or at least encourage, a "shift" of thought of the much needed liberating kind, still, we want to know: If Murdoch demands a continual re-*thinking*, does this not, in its very terminology, imply that the autobiographical activity she describes, and that is for her nothing less than a moral imperative, is in truth more *thought* than it is "seeing" in a new light a formative past experience? If so, does this not itself diminish the applicability of visual aspect-perception to aspects of selfhood? Wittgenstein voices this problem generically, twelve pages into *PI* II.xi, with the question (asked after a number of examples of aspect-perception): "Was it *seeing*, or was it a thought?" (*PI* 204d). We already know, given the preceding, that this question is too simple in its formulation. Wittgenstein, cueing our alertness to the presence of an underlying simplifying conceptual template or "picture" by voicing a phrase of the interlocutor's that is quickly and explicitly shown to be merely a grammatical manifestation of a picture-driven impulse, writes, " 'The echo of a thought in sight'—one would like to say" (*PI* 212b). The echo of a thought would be, in this sense, a thought that gave the content to what was subsequently seen. But that dualistic way of putting the matter drives a wedge between what we will, in conformity to this bifurcated picture where intellection precedes and shapes sensation, now call (1) the intellectual content of the visual experience, and (2) the purely sensory content of that experience. This is the bifurcation that Wittgenstein's remarks throughout this section intricately dissolve, and it is the bifurcation standing behind the question asking if the work of autobiographical re-thinking is more thought than seeing (and thus if it is, after all and beneath everything else that has been said, still the equivalent in the realm of self-knowledge of Hume's conception of causation).

Wittgenstein shows that there is, apart from the particular cases of the kind considered above, which on inspection do not correspond to the generalized bifurcation and in fact strongly argue against it, no sharp delineation between what we are led to call the intellectual content and the sensory content, between thinking and seeing, between mind and eye. One feels here an impulse to use the word "suffused" as a way of reaching for a general formulation of the relation, that is, the intellectual content suffuses the sensory data in an indissoluble union, but this too should, as Wittgenstein's inquiries here implicitly demonstrate, be resisted: even if better, the concept of suffusion enforces an implicit bifurcation at a prior state now gotten beyond. The word "indissoluble" does the same, and working in concert they would lead us to picture the thought-suffused perception as a result of a prior assemblage of components of sensory and mental ontologies, thus repositioning, near the end of our inquiries, the very picture that empiricism and behaviorism share, as discussed above. The grooves are deep.

If we, with Wittgenstein in *PI* II.xi, shift our way of thinking out of these traditional grooves, we will come to see that the problem that reasserted itself just above, upon realizing that Murdoch is after all calling for re-*thinking*, is not one that should be answered *generally*. It is not genuinely quieted by answering that aspect-perception is primarily cogitation and only subsequently sensory, nor the reverse, nor any other ratio in general. It is true that we can arrange cases on a continuum ranging from, say, Leonardo's cracked-wall "landscapes" on one extreme, to the more disciplined, or restricted, case of the duck-rabbit oscillation (*PI* 194b) in the middle (in that it still requires imagination to see one or the other – whichever one we do not start with), and on the other extreme the "double cross" image (*PI* 207c) (a white cross on a black background or vice-versa) requiring what could be merely an optical switch without a (change of) concept (it is still a cross, black or white). And in that context of ordered cases we might sensibly speak of more thought in the seeing of landscapes than the seeing of the duck, and more thought in the seeing of the duck than in the seeing of the white cross. But here again, it emerges that this is not *at all* to say that this continuum corresponds to a continuum ranging from the objective to the subjective, the perceived to the projected, the fact to the fiction. And autobiographical re-thinking is perfectly analogous to this: we *can* order cases on a continuum, but the criteria for the confirmation, or the hesitant acceptance, or the probability, or the plausibility, or the possibility, or the feared probability, or the minimally plausible, or the highly unlikely, and the wholly disconfirmed sets of connecting internal relations, of recontextualizing juxtapositions, and of re-thought linkages between life-events, will appear *in* context and – exactly as we saw in the visual case – nowhere else. From such a detailed perspective – precisely the perspective Wittgenstein offers with regard to visual experience in

PI II.xi – the attempt to generally state the verification conditions for self-revelatory aspects that dawn in settings of self-investigation will indeed too closely resemble the attempt to repair a torn spider's web with our fingers (*PI* §106). What Wittgenstein called a perspicuous overview of the concept of aspect-perception is gained through a patient, case-by-case consideration of the polymorphous nature of reflective and imaginative seeing, and the more we know of these – as we do at the end of *PI* II.xi – the less likely we are to yield to the impulse to reduce all of these to one paradigm and then to generalize from that.

5.

Murdoch wrote, "*Re-thinking one's past is a constant responsibility*": it should be constant because of new light shed by the ongoing recon-textualization of our past deeds, words, and thoughts, because of the new or deepened ways of seeing ourselves brought in by sets of internal relations awakened by an active retrospection. Wittgenstein's extensive and fundamentally important remarks on aspect-perception show, by analogy, how to answer the questions to which Murdoch's diary entries gave rise at the outset. We make a life-defining picture of ourselves by awakening those sets of relations and connecting the "dots" – the dots being the important life-experiences of which Murdoch wrote – with a narrative thread.[18] And that ongoing work-in-progress then

---

[18] This is not to suggest that the line of demarcation separating important from unimportant life-events is invariably a clear one. What appears to be of great sig-nificance at first glance can recede in retrospect, just as what initially may appear insignificant may emerge, once connected to larger or longer life-themes, or once set in striking contrast to one's situation in the present. To take one example (helpfully suggested to me by William Day), one may find oneself reflecting on *what at the present moment* one takes to be an utterly trivial or unimportant event in one's life, such as remembering that as a child the milk got delivered to your home, to the back door, and that sometimes you would see the milkman and greet him and converse amiably, and sometimes not, and find that it *then becomes* impor-tant in one's self-interpretation – say because you now find it to be a touchstone of sociability and uncomplicated human connectedness that you presently recognize you've lost with your neighbors, store clerks, etc., as if your heart has, gradually over many years, turned cold to the mass of humanity. Thus what may initially appear trivially insignificant as an idle memory may be anything but that (and reverse cases, of retrospective diminutions of the significance of events, could eas-ily be found as well).

becomes a picture we come to resemble, in that it determines which experiences are salient and which are not, thus shaping, at least partially, our subsequent choices in response to the picture, the unfolding narrative. We selectively attend to a life's events accordingly, and we, in Murdoch's sense, can "alter the angle" by controlling the internal relations, the life-structuring juxtapositions, the sets of associations awakened by one aspect or another. A heightened awareness of the deep analogy between visual aspects and the process of seeing ourselves can motivate for us, as I think it did for Murdoch, skepticism concerning the explanatory power of life events *simpliciter*. And this shows us how to understand the past as "unfrozen," and how we might more exactingly articulate the process of Murdochian re-thinking. Wittgenstein in the course of his investigation wrote, "One *kind* of aspect might be called 'aspects of organization'.[19] When the aspect changes parts of the picture go together which before did not"(*PI* 208d). Aspect-perception and autobiographical self-description are, it can gradually dawn on one, two parts of our picture that, indeed, go together.

---

[19] Here again, it helps to keep in mind that Wittgenstein is not working toward a reduction to a single comprehensive account of aspect-perception or seeing-as. On the contrary, he is continually adding layer after layer of complexity, of difference, of case-supported nuance. Brian McGuinness has written, importantly, "The reader feels challenged by all [of] Wittgenstein's writings, but it is an error to hope to reduce their message to a system. Better in the first place to feel their complexity, for in large part this complexity, the amount there is to be thought about in life – not excluding intellectual work – is their message. 'I'll teach you differences', as Wittgenstein used to say (a quotation from *King Lear*)." (Brian McGuinness, "'The Lion Speaks, and We Don't Understand': Wittgenstein after 100 Years," *Approaches to Wittgenstein: Collected Papers* [London: Routledge, 2002], 8.) This fundamental point of interpretation, brought to bear on the present subject, would give us a sense of an ever-expanding overview rather than anything resembling an analysis yielding an account that can then be applied directly from the visual to the autobiographical case. This is a different conception of philosophical progress.

6

The Bodily Root

Seeing Aspects and Inner Experience

Victor J. Krebs

> When you are philosophizing you have to descend into primaeval
> chaos and feel at home there. (*CV* 65b)

From the very beginning of his philosophical work, Wittgenstein was
concerned with "seeing." The *Tractatus'* purpose, for example, was to
change our perspective in order to dissolve philosophical problems
and to bring us, as Wittgenstein himself puts it, "to see the world
aright" (*TLP* 6.54). And in the "Lecture on Ethics," Wittgenstein connects this aim with the ability to see the world as a miracle and not just
as a scientific fact – an ability he suggests we need to cultivate if we are
to make sense of a whole realm of human life that otherwise remains
unintelligible. In the early 1930s in his "Remarks on Frazer's *Golden
Bough*," he sharpens that contrast while trying to show how Frazer's
scientific posture blinds him, blinds us, to the symbolic meaning of
primitive rituals. In all these moments, Wittgenstein is intent on recovering a depth to human experience that he believes is lost to scientific
rationalism. And so he insists on the human significance of "transcendental" (ethical / aesthetic / religious) utterances despite their professed nonsensicality, just as he elaborates on the existential meaning
of primitive rituals even if it is invisible to the scientific eye.

It is symptomatic that, in attempting to treat Frazer's blindness to
this depth, Wittgenstein introduces the very method upon which he
will reconceive his later philosophy. Although the use of "intermediate

cases" (*Zwischengliedern*) and "perspicuous presentations" (*übersichtli-che Darstellungen*),[1] which signals his new method, is originally meant to counteract what Wittgenstein calls Frazer's "spiritual narrowness," the transcription of the almost exact text from the notes on Frazer to the *Investigations* (cf. *PO* 133, *PI* §122) suggests that it is our inability to see beyond the literalist stance typified by Frazer that motivates Wittgenstein's later method, and it reveals that what is at issue here is not just a local or merely anthropological issue, but a general philosophical problem that will become central to the later work. I show in what follows that the generalized blindness involved in Frazer's stance and extended by Wittgenstein to traditional philosophy is a main concern behind the exploration of "seeing aspects." In fact, seeing-as is the name the later work gives to the kind of seeing that recovers the existential depth that Frazer was missing.[2] And the task it demands, of rethinking our conceptions of inner experience and subjectivity, is one that Wittgenstein undertakes in the *Investigations* and radicalizes in his discussions of aspect-seeing.

1. SEEING MIRACLES

A miracle must be, as it were, a *sacred gesture*. (*CV* 50e)

Trapped in the scientific attitude, Frazer assumed that ritual practices result from empirical beliefs or opinions, and so he was unable to see them as any more than superstitions or incipient attempts at science.[3] Wittgenstein argues that Frazer was bound to miss their significance insofar as he attempted to understand and explain them in terms of

---

[1] I follow Stanley Cavell here, who modifies the canonical translation slightly to give "presentations" instead of "representations" for the German *Darstellungen*. Rather than placing the stress on the signifier (as does the German alternative, *Vorstellung*), *Darstellung* places it on the signified.

[2] This recovery gives Wittgenstein's therapeutic purpose an ethical dimension that is lacking in the usual "therapeutic" readings of his philosophy; compare Steven Affeldt's essay in this volume.

[3] I am not too happy with the label "scientific" to characterize Frazer's stance, except for the fact that it clearly identifies it with a well-known mind set; I could equally call it, with Frank Cioffi, an "epistemizing" tendency, or characterize it as the need to reduce everything to information and instrumental use, or to find a foundation for our perception beyond the actual experience – all of which are active in the reductive reading that Frazer makes of human rituals and that Wittgenstein dismantles.

their external relations of rationality or causality. The "Lecture on Ethics" had provided a memorable metaphor of such an attempt, when Wittgenstein asked us to imagine our response to the fantastic event where "one of you suddenly grew a lion's head and began to roar." Suggesting that our immediate reaction "to fetch a doctor and have the case scientifically investigated" would neutralize the real awe and wonder of the event, he concluded that, clearly, "*when we look at it this way* everything miraculous has disappeared," and that, therefore, "the scientific way of looking at a fact is not the way to look at it as a miracle" (*PO* 43, my emphasis). Similarly, the ritual practices studied by Frazer will become significant, Wittgenstein would say, if we only learn to look at them differently. And Wittgenstein's admission, that the nonsensical utterances discussed in his Lecture are "a document of a tendency in the human mind" that he cannot help respecting deeply and would not for his life ridicule (*PO* 44), suggests that he hopes we can learn to see these things differently, to recognize their significance.

Already in the "Lecture on Ethics," he had started to move away from "the scientific way of looking" when he announced his intention to approach his subject not by means of rational explanations but by means of "more or less synonymous expressions each of which could be substituted for the [initial] definition" (*PO* 38). By enumerating them, he explained, "I want to produce the same sort of effect which Galton produced when he took a number of photos of different faces on the same photographic plate in order to get the picture of typical features they all had in common" (*PO* 38). I note that, in wanting "to produce an effect" rather than "logically establish," Wittgenstein is deliberately instating the imagination here as the means by which to see the significance of things beyond their merely logical sense. His various descriptive synonyms[4] are intended to expand and deepen any clear rational definition by working as pictures that, placed beside one another, invite the mind to intuitively establish new relationships and connections – new forms of meaning.

In the same way that I "come to see" that "this man can be terrible" from noticing "his tone of voice and facial expression" (*PO* 147),

---

4 Ethics is the enquiry "into what is good," "into what is valuable," "into what is really important," "into the meaning of life," "into what makes life worth living," "into the right way of living" (*PO* 38).

his general gestures, I come to discern the significance of a ritual practice or of an ethical utterance, not by means of any definition, but in the impression these "pictures" – their tone, their expression, their synonymous affinity, etc. – make on my imagination. The impression (*Eindruck*) that I receive here is so "deep and extraordinarily serious" (*PO* 147) that it transforms the significance of what I see; it feeds my imagination into new connections and relations. Without our scientific spectacles, we begin to see them not just intellectually but also, and primarily, aesthetically. Certain expressive features then produce an impression in us that forces us to ascribe, in an almost reflex response, "the deep and the sinister" to the ritual, for example, or the danger to the man, or the absolute value to the proposition. To grasp their significance is not just to know the history of the ritual or the literal meaning of the propositions, etc., but to vicariously experience them. We begin to see them that way not because we have thought about them (i.e., deduced or inferred something rationally from our experience) – not, in other words, from any form of intellectual deliberation – but, as Wittgenstein puts it, "from an inner experience" (*PO* 147), immediately and imaginatively.

Differently from an explanation that seeks to capture experience in clear-cut intellectual abstractions, these descriptions, pictures, and hypothetical intermediate cases are meant, Wittgenstein points out, to "do nothing but direct the attention to the similarity, the relatedness, of the *facts*" (*PO* 133). They invite the imagination to make and deepen connections[5] so that we begin to attend not to the properties of objects so much as to the "internal relation[s] between [them] and other objects" (*PI* 212a). "Internal" relations such as similarity and affinity, attunement and resonance, physiognomic or mimetic resemblance, etc., suddenly strike us and transform our perception.

Wittgenstein never tires of repeating that he wants to change our way of thinking. And the thinking he is proposing is not about placing what we see within a given intellectual scheme in order to establish its

---

5 That is to say that the "reacquaintance with our meanings" (citing Avner Baz's essay in this volume), the appeal to our ordinary linguistic knowledge ("what we say when" in J. L. Austin), the "elicitation of criteria" (Cavell) intended by Wittgenstein's methods, depends on (and propitiates by imaginative, inner resonance) a mode of awareness that does not issue from the intellect but, as I will want to claim, is rooted in the bodily.

"truth," but rather about becoming aware of the multiplicity and diversity of possible new connections and meanings in our experience. It is the openness to the sensible "impression" that the hypothetical intermediate cases bring about in us that changes our vision and recovers us from scientific numbness. We need "to try to see what happens," Wittgenstein tells us, instead of only "thinking about it" (*PO* 202). We are to connect ourselves in our own imaginative perception, to the vital richness of sensible experience so that we may eventually become capable of seeing, for example, the religious rituals and ethical propositions as manifestations of something other (and deeper) than a faulty or incipient scientific rationality, or the lion's head as "a sacred gesture" rather than just as a scientific puzzle. We could say that Frazer's blindness illustrates a pathology of the human mind, a generalized condition in our time that, because insensitive to an important dimension of human existence, breeds an attitude toward the world that can make everything appear meaningless, "as though it were cheaply wrapped in cellophane and isolated from everything that is great, from God, as it were" (*CV* 50b).

The ethical tone of Wittgenstein's remarks is essential to his thought, a symptom of his need, by his own admission, to see every problem "from a religious point of view."[6] The spiritual intensity of his writings, then, not only testifies to his deep concern about the threatening barrenness of a particular way of doing philosophy, but also constitutes the original *ethos* from which to discern the underlying purpose behind his writings; it allows us to understand the ways in which his perspicuous presentations, his shift from the explanatory to the descriptive mode, are meant to treat Frazer's (and our) spiritual illness.

Seeing in terms of internal relations, then, is not at all about what we might call "literal" reality, neither about the grasp of the actual causal connections that make up what we usually see nor about what we could represent by a diagram. In talking about "internal relations" he is thematizing the ways in which our imagination can reconstitute our experience and transform our actual perception of the facts, even while they show no measurable change. Wittgenstein thus recovers for philosophical reflection that *lived* significance in things that is important

---

[6] M. O'C. Drury, *The Danger of Words and Writings on Wittgenstein* (Bristol: Thoemmes Press, 1996), 79.

beyond the mere increase of knowledge, but is dismissed by philosophy when it identifies itself with science.[7]

2. THINKING WITH THE BODY

Not to know this would be the same as not knowing what the body is. And yet this seems to be knowledge that … philosophy den[ies] (under the guise of affirming it).

Stanley Cavell, *The Claim of Reason*, 340[8]

"One might illustrate an internal relation of a circle to an ellipse," Wittgenstein explains in the 1930s, "by gradually converting an ellipse into a circle; *but not in order to assert that a certain ellipse actually, historically, had originated from a circle … only in order to sharpen our eye for a formal connection*" (*PO* 133). The intention here is the same as that behind his descriptions in the "Lecture on Ethics," and generally behind the later methods as we have elaborated them above. Although Wittgenstein talks about "formal" connections here, he does not mean conceptual (or logical) connections. In fact, he is claiming explicitly that by gradually converting an ellipse into a circle he does not want to make us intellectually understand anything (their causal history, for instance). He wants us to *see*, "to sharpen our eye" to what he calls here "formal connections." Furthermore, when in his drafts for the second part of the *Investigations*, written about twenty years later, Wittgenstein uses the same, only slightly modified example to illustrate seeing what he there starts calling "internal relations," the slight change indicates more clearly that he is not talking about the grasp of conceptual connections. There he introduces a child as his interlocutor and emphasizes in this way that the learning (and seeing) of internal relations (or formal connections) is not a propositional matter: "One might say to a child, for example, 'Look, when you put these two stones together

7 See above, note 3, and also my "'Descending into Primaeval Chaos': Philosophy, the Body, and the Pygmalionic Impulse," *Mythos and Logos: How to Regain the Love of Wisdom* (Amsterdam and New York: Rodopi, 2004), 141–60, for a diagnosis of this identification.
8 Stanley Cavell, *The Claim of Reason: Wittgenstein, Skepticism, Morality, and Tragedy* (Oxford: Oxford University Press, 1979).

you get a circle'. ⌒⌣ Is he learning an empirical proposition? (Here I am purposely talking about a child, not an adult)" (*LW* I §760). The rhetorical question "Is he learning an empirical proposition?", talking about a child and not an adult, indicates that it is not a propositional lesson but rather a visual, imaginative, intuitive exercise that is intended. The child's incipient language skills make his grasp of the internal relations more naturally an experiential rather than a propositional matter; we could say that he is being more trained than instructed at this stage.

That the understanding of internal relations is an experiential, rather than a linguistic, matter may wrongly suggest that it involves an ineffable private grasp in the depths of the soul, as it were; but it is one of the lessons of the *Investigations* that the presumed separability or independence of articulated experience from language is bogus – it leads us directly, for example, into the "hellish idea" of private experience, which Wittgenstein considers one of the main roots of philosophical confusion (*PO* 204). No, in learning to see internal relations we are exactly neither outside nor inside language. We are not yet learning a concept, nor are we having yet an articulated experience. We are on the verge of both. As Cavell points out, when we signal toward an object while saying a word to children who are still coming to a mastery of their language, "it may be (fully) true *neither* that what we teach them is (the meaning of) a word *nor* that we tell them what a thing is. ... To say we are teaching them language obscures both how different what they learn may be from anything we think we are teaching, or mean to be teaching; and how vastly more they learn than the thing we should say we had 'taught'. ... 'Learning' is not as academic a matter as academics are apt to suppose."[9]

Even though we may eventually be able to conceive and talk of the perception of internal relations in terms of logical connections or empirical propositions (the internal relation, we are told, may be seen as "the clothing of a formal connection" [*PO* 133]), Wittgenstein is distinguishing at this stage the act of understanding involved in seeing connections from any intellectual operation. He is pointing toward the intuitive leap that makes articulated experience possible, making us

---

[9] Ibid., 170–71.

realize that this transition of silence into speech, of sensible experience into linguistic consciousness, which, as we will see, is integral to the experience of seeing an aspect, depends on a contingent fact that, far from being rationally explicable, is nothing short of miraculous.[10]

When Wittgenstein speaks of "internal relations," he connects them frequently to the gestural or the expressive. At one point, for instance, he proposes to vary the geometrical example of the sphere and ellipse, claiming that its purpose would be served just as well by the gestural relations that give meaning to the lines composing a face. "That proposition would not have to be a geometrical one," he writes. "Its purpose could be to confirm that the face composed of *these* lines *now* gives *me* the impression of sadness" (*LW* I §762). The point of the geometrical proposition is here taken up by that of a subtle gesture. *Esprit geometrique* gives way to *esprit de finesse*.[11] And, speaking of how we can register the difference in our perception before and after we recognize an old friend in the approaching man – that is, when we suddenly see new aspects in our perception – he says that it would be registered in the different way we would draw a picture of him (PI 197g). Our drawing would tell of our new perception in its deliberate details and nuances (and other generally imponderable but decisive evidence for the eye that sees), just as the way a person is able to mimic a smile registers the fact that she recognizes it for a smile (*PI* 198e). These are just a couple of the multiple instances where Wittgenstein suggests that the kind of understanding involved in seeing internal relations is not only conceptual but also sensible and mimetic – or perhaps better said: that the conceptual is at the same time, and sometimes primarily, sensible and mimetic.

[10] (Compare: "Not that one could now say: Yes, now it is all simple – or understandable. It is absolutely not *understandable*, it is just not *not-understandable*" [*DB* 239].) Miraculous in the sense of spontaneous and unexplainable. The fact that seeing aspects is subject to the will, as William Day stresses (see his essay in this volume), underscores the ethical nature of Wittgenstein's explorations and shifts their philosophical aim from the resolution of problems to the achievement of awareness and the broadening of its range, from the search for accuracy of representation to the intensification of "interest and relevance" (citing Juliet Floyd's piece in this volume) – in other words, from scientific control to grammatical insight.

[11] Blaise Pascal, *Pensées*, fragment 21 (*Oeuvres complètes*, ed. Jacques Chevalier [Paris: Gallimard, 1954]).

3. ASPECTS AND GESTURES

Yes, there really have been people like that, who could see directly into the souls of other people.

Ludwig Wittgenstein in conversation with M. O'C. Drury[12]

"I contemplate a face," Wittgenstein writes, "and then suddenly notice its likeness to another. I see it has not changed; and yet I see it differently. I call this experience 'noticing an aspect'" (*PI* 193c). Noticing aspects is precisely that understanding that consists in "seeing connections" – the very understanding (of internal relations) that Wittgenstein has made the object of his method at least since Frazer, whose antecedents we have traced back to the use of descriptions and images in the "Lecture on Ethics," and whose connection to the gestural we have just elaborated. It should not be surprising, therefore, that when he explicitly addresses the case of seeing aspects he starts talking again about the imagination. Wittgenstein tells us, for instance, that noticing an aspect is "related to *forming an image* [*Vorstellen*]" (*LW* I §733). We see aspects, he says, according to "*the fiction* we surround something with" (*PI* 210d); "It is as if an *image* [*eine Vorstellung*] came into contact, and for a time remained in contact, with the visual impression" (*PI* 207b). And we are told further that "there is a close kinship" between forming an image and "'experiencing the meaning of a word'" (*PI* 210c), as if to make clear that the imagination concerned brings in a certain sensible or bodily density. Let me elaborate.

Early on in the discussion of seeing aspects, Wittgenstein draws a grammatical parallel between the experience we have at the dawning of aspects and the jolt of surprise at a sudden perception. If I look at an animal and I am asked about what I see, he begins, I simply utter a report – "A rabbit," for example. But if, for instance, while looking out the window a rabbit suddenly appears before me running across the landscape, I *exclaim* "A rabbit!" In other words, when I look at a rabbit ordinarily my mind takes in the habitual image without any emotion, abstract(ed)ly, and I utter my words almost mechanically. But when I

---

[12] Drury, "Conversations with Wittgenstein," in Rush Rhees, ed., *Recollections of Wittgenstein* (Oxford: Oxford University Press, 1984), 108.

notice that a rabbit that had not been there before is suddenly there now, I am awakened and moved to the point of almost spitting out words that are forced from me (*Er entringt sich uns*) as a cry is by pain. The connection between my experience of aspects and my utterance is compared here to the intense and immediate connection between pain and its expression. Now, the experience Wittgenstein imagines with the rabbit is also compared to that we have typically with pictures, when (as we say) they suddenly "become alive" to us, an experience he characterizes as "seeing aspects."[13] But what is at stake in these examples – the surprise, the emotion, the seeing of aspects – is a difference in what we may call the degrees of bodily engagement behind our utterances of perception, engagement that reaches its highest intensity in the original immediacy of the exclamation and its lowest in the silence of habit or indifference. Wittgenstein refers to the heightened experience involved as "a seeing-as which only takes place while I am actually concerning myself with the picture as the object depicted" (*PI* 205g), and he suggests it is an experience that needs a new concept. We need a concept, in other words, that registers the aspectual perception that results from the immediate connection between sensible awareness and thought.

Wittgenstein explicitly distinguishes "image" [*Vorstellung*] from "picture" [*Bild*] earlier in the *Investigations*, and he claims that, for example, in the language-game with pain (i.e., when someone tells me he is in pain), *of course* pain plays a part, "only not as a picture" but as an image (*PI* §300). He is distinguishing the kind of awareness that results from a merely mental grasp (where I have disconnected my understanding from my experience) from that which is also anchored in the body. And it is the latter that better serves him in talking about the meaning of psychological words like "pain." The image of pain, like the image of the rabbit suddenly triggering my exclamation, immediately informs my use of "pain" in the language-game, not like a picture that produces an abstract experience susceptible to doubt, but as an impression anchored in my memory. I agree with Cavell, therefore, when he suggests that Wittgenstein's appeal to the *image* of pain is

---

[13] The experience mentioned here of surprise and heightened awareness is stressed especially when Wittgenstein articulates this kind of seeing with diverse modifications of the German verb *Bemerken: auf etwas aufmerksam werden, die Aufmerksamkeit auf etwas richten.* Compare *LWI* §§719, 682, 692; *PI* 205i, 210d.

meant to emphasize the immediacy between the impression (the experience, the affect) and the expression.[14] The appeal to an image, in other words, is meant to do away with the mental gap, generated by a representation (a "picture"), between the verbal expression and the experience that it expresses. Whereas the *picture* of pain refers us to the mediation of reflective thought in the act of perception, the *image* of pain refers us instead to the immediacy of "internal," bodily perception. Of course Wittgenstein is not speaking here of seeing aspects, but his emphasis on the role of imagination in aspect-perception – particularly when he speaks of it as the result of "the contact" between our visual impression and an image, as if our seeing were informed by the impression we have retained in our sensible memory – allows us to say that he is locating the experience of aspect-seeing at the same point of contact between thought and sensation, in a sort of Kantian "play" between reason and bodily memory,[15] highlighting what we might characterize as an aesthetic awareness of experience. So when Wittgenstein claims that where we notice an aspect "an image makes contact with our visual impression," he is using a metaphor to refer to the way in which our sensibility and memory inform our perception; he is moreover giving us an image of how what we see in the empirical plane can be transfigured and relocated to the realm of aspects.

The impression that the relevant experience (of pain, of hesitancy, of childishness, etc.) produces in me is (re)constituted in the spontaneous articulation of my bodily awareness made possible by the concepts I have acquired in my life in language. A single face can therefore not only *mean* (intellectually) different things to different people, but actually be *perceived* differently by each. For each literally fashions a different world that is defined by the experiences they have had and by the way these have been stored in memory as concepts. A child, for example, may see a smile but not yet perceive the irony of the smile, if he has not yet achieved the sophistication of experience or acquired the conceptual resources to enter into that world. He is too innocent still, he has neither the experience nor the words. But he may keep the impression in store as an image that may eventually spring forth when

[14] I am referring to Cavell's famous discussion of Wittgenstein's parable of the boiling pot in *The Claim of Reason*, 332–43.
[15] See Immanuel Kant, *Critique of Judgment*, Trans. J. H. Bernard (New York: Hafner Press, 1951), §9, Ak. 217.

the place has been made possible in his tongue by new experiences and new words. These will shine a light and grant awareness to the re-membered image. I can see someone else's behavior *as* pain-behavior, therefore, and any event as invested with a significance, *if* I have made the relevant past experiences conscious, that is, if I have woven them into the web of concepts, images, memories, and words with which I receive all new impressions, and in terms of which my body learns to respond both physically and verbally to its perceptions.[16]

Learning and using language is for Wittgenstein at some level as spontaneous and corporeal as learning and making new gestures. And the connection between sensibility, words, and actual perception is decisive in seeing aspects: "Anyone who did not have our concepts of 'hesitant', 'childish', 'vulgar', could not *sense* the handwriting or the facial expression the way we do" (*LW*I §741). Once we have them, once we have assimilated these experiences – of hesitancy, childishness, vulgarity – as complex *linguistic* gestures, something in the object we perceive connects to our sensibility, resonates within, and triggers a response, an "inner experience" that wrenches from us a verbal expres-sion, just as pain elicits a cry from a baby in pain or a sudden joy calls forth a glittering bodily gesture. A *behavior* of sensation, Wittgenstein will say, is substituted by an *expression* of sensation (*RPP*I §313).

Seeing aspects is not the same as normal seeing. I do not perceive the meaning of a gesture, the grace of an arabesque, the virility of a voice, etc., as I do the shape of the table or the color of the carpet. They belong to different categories of objects of sight (cf. *PI* 193a). And what I see when I see an aspect is not explained by reproducing what I have seen, for it remains beyond any literal representation I can make of the perceived object. My concept in such cases, Wittgenstein says, is not a "purely" perceptual (aural, visual, etc.) concept, where we would reproduce exactly what we see, ignoring all "other" relations (cf. *LW*I §749). It includes a residue of meaning that is actualized by the bodily engagement of our words. As Merleau-Ponty says of a gesture, what I see when I see an aspect is "not *given*, but *recaptured* by an act on the specta-tor's part." The communication and comprehension of aspects, too,

---

[16] There is a shift, therefore, in our conception of perception where, in place of our usual tendency to think of perception as a judgment, we begin to see judg-ment, as Sandra Laugier puts it, "as itself a kind of seeing" (see her essay in this volume).

"comes about through the reciprocity of my intentions and the gestures of others, of my gestures and intentions discernible in the conduct of other people."[17] In other words, I communicate or apprehend an aspect as I do a gesture, not by grasping intellectually, but through empathic projection, which belongs rather to the bodily.

"The whole difficulty," writes Merleau-Ponty, "is to conceive this act clearly without confusing it with a cognitive operation";[18] and Wittgenstein adds that "what tells us that someone is seeing [aspects] is ... certain gestures ... : fine shades of behavior" – not any kind of intellectual knowing, in other words, but "knowing one's way about" (*PI* 203b). In this imponderable, physiognomic expressiveness or gesturality, we see something that the physical object by itself cannot show us, but which *we* can complete from our own experience and thus perceive "internally," aspectually. As Wittgenstein says about the significance of rituals (which we can extend to seeing-as), the principle by which aspects can dawn is "found in our own soul" in "an instinct we have," or belongs to "our thoughts and our feelings" (*PO* 58, 73, 78; cf. *LC* 84–85).

4. RE-MINDING THE BODY

The purely corporeal can be uncanny. ... So-called "miracles" must be connected with this. (*CV* 50e)

In making the distinction between image and picture, Wittgenstein is therefore also identifying two different sources for my utterances. I can speak "from the head," mediated by representations, and I can speak immediately, from my own bodily consciousness. Wittgenstein insists again and again on the animal or instinctive root of language, on conceiving primitive language-games as instances of "primitive thinking,"

---

[17] Maurice Merleau-Ponty, *Phenomenology of Perception* (New York: Routledge, 1999), 185. We could extend what we are saying here about the perception of human expressiveness to the seeing of aspects in general by adding that seeing aspects in things involves adopting an animistic attitude toward the world, seeking a rapprochement to what Cavell calls "an intimacy with existence" (see his *In Quest of the Ordinary: Lines of Skepticism and Romanticism* (Chicago: University of Chicago Press, 1988), 4): assuming the world, in other words, as inhabited – in the material presence of its objects – by an intention. Compare my "Against Idolatry and Toward Psychology: A Review of Ray Monk's *Ludwig Wittgenstein: The Duty of Genius*," *The San Francisco Jung Institute Library Journal* 12, no. 3 (1993): 36ff.

[18] Merleau-Ponty, *Phenomenology of Perception*, 185.

where the primitive reaction "may have been a glance or a gesture, but it may also have been a word" (*PI* 218b). Even choosing our words is imaged by Wittgenstein as a bodily matter:

How do I find the "right" word? How do I choose among words? Without doubt it is sometimes as if I were comparing them by fine differences of smell. ... I ought to have to wait until a word occurs to me anew. This, however, is the queer thing: it seems as though I did not have to wait on the occasion, but could give myself an exhibition of it, even when it is not actually taking place. How?—I *act* it.—But *what* can I learn in this way? What do I reproduce?—Characteristic accompaniments. Primarily: gestures, faces, tones of voice (*PI* 218h–219a).

Wittgenstein is echoing here Merleau-Ponty's observation that knowing and uttering words is not the expression of a mental process but simply their incorporation as "modulations and possible uses of my body," so that when I choose a word to express myself, I simply "reach back for [it] as my hand reaches towards the part of my body which is being pricked."[19]

The idea of an original word that substitutes for instinctive behavior, and then extends that instinct into the subtle body of language, informs Wittgenstein's vision and describes the process by which new experiences are made possible from such linguistic "extensions."[20] Indeed, Wittgenstein's discussion suggests that it is our connection to the sensible root of the language we use, our *aesthetic* sensitivity in calling things by words, that makes us capable of seeing aspects. It is, in particular, our "attachment to [our] words," as he refers to our affective or bodily connection, that is responsible for our being able to see language internally, thus revealing a word's "familiar physiognomy" and giving us "the feeling that it has taken up its meaning into itself, that it is an actual likeness of its meaning" (*PI* 218g). When we see only externally, in terms of causes and reasons, we don't *experience* the meaning of our words. They can then become disconnected from their bodily or gestural root, "cold, lacking in associations," no longer "an acorn from which an *oak tree* can grow," as Wittgenstein so vitally imagines it (*CV* 52d, c).[21] The importance of "seeing aspects," as he

---

[19] Ibid., 180.
[20] See Victor J. Krebs, "The Subtle Body of Language and the Lost Sense of Philosophy," *Philosophical Investigations* 23, no. 2 (April 2000): 147–55.
[21] Ultimately, "aspect-blindness" results from this disconnection. I agree with Edward Minar and William Day (see their essays in the present volume) that aspect-blindness,

remarks, is found "in the connection between the concepts of 'seeing an aspect' and 'experiencing the meaning of a word'" (*PI* 214d). The concept of seeing aspects thus highlights the importance of bodily awareness in language and perception.

It is precisely the disconnection from our sensible experience that is responsible, in Wittgenstein's mind, for the pseudo-problems that plague philosophy. Wittgenstein's methods – not only his constant appeal to instances of primitive language-games, but also his perspicuous presentations of grammar, his exercises of imagination, his appeal to intermediate cases, his admonishments against explanation and theory, and his insistence on description and "looking to see" instead of merely thinking – can be seen as a response to this, as an attempt precisely to reconnect our words to their sensible root, to make us capable of perceiving the world in its sensuous richness again. They are meant not to explain anything, or to answer questions about the meaning of our words or the essence of language, but to quicken the memory that is blocked, to help us to resist the literalizing impulse that possesses us "when we philosophize." They are intended to resist the inclination we have to transform our difficulty (in seeing what we have before us) into a problem that must be explained away or "resolved," which thus leads us to disconnect our mental understanding from our experience.

5. EM-BODYING THE INNER

Not ... for opposed positions to be reconciled, but for the halves of the mind to go back together.

Stanley Cavell, "Knowing and Acknowledging," 241

"Noticing an aspect" involves "a particular visual experience [*Seherlebnis*]" that Wittgenstein connects explicitly to that other experience [*erleben*] we can have of the meaning of a word: for example, when the word "bank" feels differently when it refers to the bank where I

---

understood as a *total* condition, is obviously an imaginative construct. It is a figure meant to highlight an intermittent possibility, a condition *within* our life with language. Insofar as it names the condition of detachment whereby we disconnect our words and grow deaf to their tone and rhythm, blind to their physiognomy and gestural dimension, aspect-blindness already presupposes that which it is meant to deny. It is something which, as Cavell points out, we must learn – the same way we must learn not to love – or it is something we come down with, like a disease.

keep my money and to the river bank; or when we feel the absurdity or incongruence (the example is Wittgenstein's) that Goethe's signature could have belonged to Kant (we might think, perhaps, of Pavarotti's voice belonging to Al Gore); or even when our familiarity with a word shrinks away after we repeat it many times. The visual experience we have when we see aspects is the same type of experience as these, and it has important consequences – and not just for understanding the phenomenon of "seeing aspects" and its connection to the body. It involves a systematic effort to rethink "the inner" in Wittgenstein's later work, which means battling against the almost absolute possession of our modern minds by the Cartesian concept of the subjective that seems to reduce every reference to the inner into something mental or private. As Richard Moran has noted, "Recent philosophy typically rejects the picture of the mind as immediately transparent to itself, and then tacitly takes this rejection to be equivalent to rejecting the very idea of introspective access, thereby ceding the very concept of first-person awareness to its Cartesian interpretation."[22] The mentalism or psychological internalism which we unconsciously adopt – perhaps from a deeper propensity than that resulting from mere historical conditioning – keeps experience and the inner virtually sequestered, making it difficult if not impossible to understand them philosophically in any other way. It is, of course, precisely in his desire to dissociate himself from that tradition that Wittgenstein insists that when talking about this queer "experience" of seeing aspects or of linguistic meaning, we are not talking about an *inner experience,* in the same way that he insists that when we talk of thinking we are not talking about psychological processes that accompany our words. But at least as (if not more) important as his systematic and sustained rejection of the mentalist reduction of subjectivity is Wittgenstein's constant appeal to our own "inner" experience and to the imagination.

There is something new, then, in this discussion of "experience" that moves beyond and completes the well-known Wittgensteinian rejection of internalism. Although he rejects the Cartesian interpretation of subjectivity, Wittgenstein does not on that account discard the subjective, but rather returns once and again to the "experience of the meaning of a word," and he insists on "the visual experience"

[22] Richard Moran, *Authority and Estrangement: An Essay on Self-Knowledge* (Princeton: Princeton University Press, 2001), 4.

that accompanies the seeing of aspects. He asks us, moreover, that we pay attention to what we want to say when we speak about "experience," suggesting that there is something important that we need to recover from our expression. And he is continuously making us imagine ourselves in the actual situations by means of his elaborate descriptions to evince the appropriate words from us, always countering our inclination to resort to a private experience.

Wittgenstein has us consider, for example, what it means for two people to have the same experience of thinking about someone upon hearing a word, and he proposes it could mean that upon hearing the words each person has the same inner conversation with himself (*PI* 217e). Although this explanation has the virtue of giving voice to our natural inclination to imagine the inner on analogy with the outer, Wittgenstein wants to distance himself from the allure of internalism. So he proposes that we think instead that the experience consists in an inclination to make a gesture so that, upon hearing some word, it is not inner words that I produce. I simply look at you with a spontaneous gesture. But when you ask me *later*, "Why did you look at me at that word, were you thinking of ... ?" (*PI* 217g), I explain myself, utter new words that flow directly from that same experience, saying that, "I thought of so-and-so," or that I suddenly remembered "that night at the Caffè Florian." Both descriptions that Wittgenstein tries out to characterize the inner – the one about my internal dialogue as much as the one that appeals to my gesture – give voice to the same "experience." But the gesture eliminates the mental representation suggested by the mention of "inner words" and brings to light the important fact – which we verify imaginatively – that until the moment I articulate myself in a verbal explanation, the "experience" is *expressively full* even if *representationally* it is as empty as a gesture.[23]

Nothing is happening "inside me" when I have these experiences, and my words are as little the expression of an inner experience as is the expression "I have it on the tip of my tongue" (*PI* 219e). But,

---

[23] It also shows that the explanation I am inclined to give ("I thought of" or "I suddenly remembered") arises as spontaneously and groundlessly as the gesture did. We could also say: What contains those words is the same as what contains the gesture. They both arise from a silence that precedes language, and it is to this prelinguistic silence, this potential directionality or objectless intention, that the experience refers.

it is necessary to insist, this does not mean for Wittgenstein there is no "inner activity" to which our mention of "experience" gives voice. It is just that this inner activity (I want now to say: this image)²⁴ has no content, even if it is indeed an experience. It is not a something, but not a nothing either (*PI* §304). It acquires a content only in the way in which (and when) our words and our actions – that is, our verbal and non-verbal behavior – begin to articulate it (*PI* 220c). When pronouncing the words that express this type of "experience," we are not then really describing anything, but making sophisticated gestures (*PI* 218b–c). The words with which we express ourselves in these cases, we could say, are signaling a corporeal directionality already present in our original gesture, and about which we become gradually more aware as it acquires concreteness in those words and in our actions, in the diverse and diffuse consequences, and in the ponderable and imponderable evidence that is wholly open to the other (cf. *PI* 218h).²⁵

Wittgenstein's constant appeal to the imagination, and to the gestural and mimetic, calls our attention to this existential fullness, thus recovering for philosophical thought and reflection the metaphorical fertility of our sensuous experience which goes undetected by the objectifying eye that seeks to understand only in terms of inner states and mental representations. What we need – Wittgenstein told us as early as the time of the *Tractatus* – is to learn to look at things "as a miracle." Only through a radical change in attitude – one that takes into account our sensible/affective relation to experience – would we come to understand those peculiar and at the same time so deeply rooted phenomena of human experience, such as ethical and aesthetic propositions and religious rituals, whose meaning became indiscernible to the quintessentially modern attitude staged in the *Tractatus*.²⁶

---

²⁴ I have developed the notion of image involved here in *Del alma y el arte: Reflexiones en torno a la cultura, la imagen y la memoria* (Caracas: Editorial Arte, 1997).

²⁵ The experience is not directly related to what I say; it is not the same as the meaning of the words, but it is related *indirectly* to those meanings through what those words *evoke* in me, by what Wittgenstein calls their "field [*Feld*]" (cf. *PI* 219b). Therefore, it is in virtue of, but also beyond, their literal or conventional meaning that these extensions are possible. This sense of "experience" seems to be intimately related, then, to the constitution of what Wittgenstein calls the "'secondary' sense of a word" (*PI* 216e).

²⁶ I say "staged" because I agree with the proponents of the New Reading of the *Tractatus* (Conant, Diamond, Floyd, et al.) that Wittgenstein is attempting to introduce, here

Our inability to understand our utterances on such occasions lies in our (acquired) incapacity and (natural) resistance to connect ourselves more deeply than through the intellect, to enter into the realm of self-revelation and vulnerability that such expressions demand. The notion of aspect-seeing, then, at the same time as it reminds us of an extended form of perception, can present us with a task we seem to systematically avoid because of an almost constitutional tendency of our own nature; a tendency institutionalized in certain habits of thought that were strengthened in modernity, and that Wittgenstein identifies in philosophy as difficulties not of the intellect, but of feeling and volition (*PO* 161). If, as I am inclined to think, the investigation into seeing aspects is the culmination of an effort on the part of Wittgenstein to forge in his philosophy a new way of seeing, then his underlying concern is the recognition of the constitutive role of the bodily or affective in the meaning of our words, and in our perception of the world and others in it. Without an affective investment, without interest and commitment, our words become unintelligible and empty; *with* that commitment words begin to show other manners of signification beyond the realm of literal meaning and correspondence. Thinking becomes for Wittgenstein a matter of continuous conversion, of overcoming our resistance to the sensible – resistance that may be explained, as Cavell has suggested, by the anxiety caused by the possibility of failure in expressing what we uniquely experience beyond what our sedimented concepts articulate – and reconnecting our words with their bodily root.

To express ourselves in this context is not the same as making a demonstration or providing a rational justification. It is more akin to making a confession, to expressing something by which I reveal myself spontaneously (both to myself and) to the other. And, as Wittgenstein points out,

> the criteria for the truth of the *confession* that I thought such-and-such are not the criteria for a true *description* of a process. And the importance of the true confession does not reside in its being a correct and certain report of a process. It resides rather in the special consequences which can be drawn from

too, the imagination as a method of philosophical reflection in order precisely to overcome this intellectual rigidity, even if he fails to achieve his aim there. See my "'Around the Axis of our Real Need': On the Ethical Point of Wittgenstein's Philosophy," *European Journal of Philosophy* 9, no. 3 (December 2001): 344–74.

a confession whose truth is guaranteed by the special criteria of *truthfulness* (*PI* 222f).

Confessions, just like the utterances with which we express our experience of aspects, are not meant to establish any factual truth. Wittgenstein says they are reactions "where people can *come in touch with* one another [*in der sich die Leute* finden]" (*RPP* I §874).

Philosophical discourse is thus relocated, displaced from the realm of the true and the false, the correct and the incorrect – the assertion of literal truths – to the realm of aspects, of "connections" or internal relations we perceive between things, where they begin to acquire a new significance. Wittgenstein's proposal involves a change in attitude, a deliberate grammatical openness and receptivity to the natural gesturality of language and the underlying, pulsating activity of the body.[27]

[27] I would like to thank Avner Baz, Gordon Bearn, and Bill Day for their valuable comments and suggestions to previous versions of this chapter.

II.2 Problems of Mind

7

(Ef)facing the Soul

Wittgenstein and Materialism

David R. Cerbone

1.

Consider the following remark, from one of Wittgenstein's late (1950) manuscripts. The one-sentence remark reads: "It is as if he became *transparent* to us through a human facial expression" (*LW* II 67b). This sentence appears within a short series of remarks wherein Wittgenstein is ruminating on the idea of a human being "who had no soul." As is the case elsewhere in his later writings, part of the upshot of this series of remarks is the difficulty of connecting anything definite or determinate with such an idea, thus calling into question the very idea of an idea here. The immediate context of this sentence is an attempt to describe such a "soulless" human being, and Wittgenstein finds himself resorting to rather familiar imagery of mechanical, uniform movements characteristic of an automaton. Even the thrashing and writhing of such a being, Wittgenstein declares, if carried out in a sufficiently mechanical fashion, might still not bespeak the presence of a soul; the being we are imagining would, in this way, fail to be "transparent," not so much by remaining opaque, but by having nothing further to discern beneath the surface (except maybe more machinery). If, however, the play of the face were sufficiently nuanced, the idea of a soul would begin to find a place in our imagining of this being, and likewise the "possibility" of such a being nonetheless lacking a soul would begin to evanesce.

My particular interest in this remark lies not so much in its place in these immediate surroundings, but in some of the more general implications of the connection it forges between the concept of transparency it invokes and the expressive character of the human face. In particular, I would like to try to measure those implications against some of the general tendencies I discern in contemporary philosophy of mind. In particular, I have in mind here those positions in the philosophy of mind that see themselves to be committed to materialism or physicalism, and who see this commitment as dictating a more or less radical revision of our conception of ourselves (with eliminative materialism being perhaps the most radical). The importance of Wittgenstein's remark extends beyond these positions to encompass as well views in the philosophy of mind that run directly counter to them. I have in mind here the kind of view that promulgates a conception of mind, especially of consciousness, as an elusive, mysterious wholly "inner" phenomenon, possibly untouchable by the natural sciences. (Holders of this sort of view, e.g., Thomas Nagel[1] and Colin McGinn,[2] have been rather impishly labeled "the new mysterians"[3] by their detractors.) Such opposing views in the philosophy of mind are, I would suggest, made for each other, since they share as common ground a conception of what it takes for mental concepts to be fully and without qualification legitimate: If mental concepts were in order as they stood, it would be in virtue of there being such mysterious, irreducibly subjective states available only to the subject whose states they are, i.e., there would be such things as "qualia," "raw feels," and so on. Though I will concentrate in what follows on materialist theses in the philosophy of mind, the distance between Wittgenstein's views and those theses should in no way be taken to indicate his proximity to the mysterian views that are typically opposed to materialism in contemporary philosophy of mind.

---

[1] See, for example, Thomas Nagel, "What Is It Like to Be a Bat?" *Philosophical Review* 83 (October 1974): 435–50.
[2] See, for example, Colin McGinn, "Can We Solve the Mind-Body Problem?" *Mind* 98 (July 1989): 349–66.
[3] The phrase was originally coined by Owen Flanagan, though Daniel Dennett has since deployed it approvingly as well. See, for example, the latter's *Consciousness Explained* (Boston: Little, Brown, and Company, 1991), 273.

2.

Here is what one might consider a tension in Wittgenstein's later philosophy, but which is, I want to suggest, a source of its strength: on the one hand, Wittgenstein is unrelenting in his attempts to turn us away from an "occult" or "magical" conception of the mind, as a place or realm where meaning happens, where reference is effected, where explanations come to an end not with satisfaction, but out of desperation. This aspect of Wittgenstein's philosophy is, of course, what brings upon it the charge of behaviorism, and one reason why Cavell, for example, declares that Wittgenstein's philosophy "takes the risk of apsychism."[4] On the other hand, Wittgenstein's later philosophy, especially his later later philosophy (Part II of the *Investigations*, the later manuscripts on the philosophy of psychology), insists on the legitimacy of the concept or category of the *soul*, of talking about and treating others as ensouled without any desire to demonstrate that, say, all talk about the soul is really just talk about the body: "Am I saying something like, 'and the soul is merely something about the body'? No. (I am not that hard up for categories)" (*RPP* II §690). Taken together, difficult as that may be to do, these two tendencies provide a way of thinking through or past the current deadlock in the philosophy of mind, since they suggest a kind of blindness on the part of both sides to the debate in the philosophy of mind to the "transparency" afforded by "a human facial expression." That is, for materialist and mysterian alike, the play of the face, the ebb and flow of gesture and expression, none of that is central or even relevant to settling questions concerning the "status" of the mind, to the question of whether or not a being "has" a soul.

Consider as an example the following remark made by Daniel Dennett, in response to what he perceives as the stubborn unwillingness by many to envision or allow the possibility of consciousness in a machine, *viz.*, a computer:

If you look at a computer – I don't care whether it's a giant Cray or a personal computer – if you open up the box and look inside and see those chips, you

---

[4] Stanley Cavell, *The Claim of Reason: Wittgenstein, Skepticism, Morality, and Tragedy* (Oxford: Oxford University Press, 1979), 400. The passage from which this phrase is taken reads: "Wittgenstein takes the risk of apsychism, the risk that his understanding of the human body (as, for example, a picture) is unnecessary, or insincere, or dead. If this is behaviorism in disguise then a statue is a stone in disguise."

say, "No way could that be conscious. No way could that be self-conscious". But the same thing is true if you take the top off somebody's skull and look at the gray matter pulsing away in there. You think, "That is conscious? No way could that lump of stuff be conscious".[5]

Whatever difficulties arise for our powers of imagination when confronting the inner workings of a machine are, for Dennett, precisely the same as those which arise when confronted with the inner workings of someone's skull, that "lump of stuff" one sees "pulsing away." And since we "know" that the brain is conscious despite the feelings of incredulity that may occasionally beset us, so too might it be the case that a computer is conscious. What Dennett fails even to mention here is that these kinds of difficulties generally do *not* arise on those occasions when we refrain from removing the tops of one another's skulls. That is, we don't find ourselves beset with the same feeling of incredulity when we look at one another intact, as it were. Try pointing to a friend, or to a child or spouse, and saying "No way could that be conscious." The exercise would be akin to the one Wittgenstein suggests in the *Investigations* at §420: "Say to yourself, for example: 'The children over there are mere automata; all their liveliness is mere automatism'. And you will either find these words becoming quite meaningless; or you will produce in yourself some kind of uncanny feeling, or something of the sort."

J. J. C. Smart's philosophy of mind provides an earlier and more resolute example of the kind of blindness to the outer that Dennett's remark displays, and it is instructive, I think, to consider it in some detail. Informed by a more thoroughgoing materialism, according to which "there is nothing in the world over and above those entities which are postulated by physics," Smart construes all mental states and events as identical to states of the brain and nervous system.[6] In so identifying mental states and events, Smart allows nothing in the way of irreducibly mental categories or laws. There are, he thinks, no special principles that apply exclusively to psychology as such: what laws there are are laws of physics.

---

[5] Daniel C. Dennett, "Can Machines Think?" *Brainchildren: Essays on Designing Minds* (Cambridge: MIT Press, 1998), 24.
[6] J. J. C. Smart, "Materialism," *Essays Metaphysical and Moral: Selected Philosophical Papers* (Oxford: Blackwell, 1987), 203–14.

Cartesian dualism, with its fondness for irreducibly mental substances and properties, is one of Smart's principal targets, but he is opposed as well to various fellow travelers in the materialist tradition. In particular, Smart sets his sights on behaviorism, the idea that mental states and events are "outer" states of the body. The argument Smart gives against behaviorism turns on an appeal to a piece of science fiction, though Smart regards the fictional aspect as only temporary: As science progresses, the fictional scenario will, he thinks, be fully realizable. The scenario is none other than one familiar from discussions of skepticism, that of the otherwise disembodied brain kept alive and stimulated in its own special vat. Such an envatted brain tells against a behaviorist interpretation of mental states, Smart thinks, because we can very well imagine, and so understand, this brain as having a full repertoire of psychological states and events – particular episodes of thought, say, or various kinds of sensation – all the while lacking in any outward manifestation in behavior. Since there can be psychological states and events without any manifest or expressive behavior, then psychological states are not behavioral states and events. They are instead, in keeping with Smart's overall position, states and events of and in the brain.

The success of Smart's argument turns on the ease with which we can imagine the scenario he describes, but what exactly are we to imagine here? And how far does our success in imagining anything go toward establishing the "nature" of psychological states or the true meaning of psychological concepts? Suppose we find ourselves in Smart's imagined laboratory, confronted with this brain. How are we to tell the story? Minimally, one imagines standing there, in the company of one or more of the attending scientists and technicians, who eagerly point out how things are with the brain. In imagining this, one is led to wonder as to the scientists' basis for their confident proclamations. After all, to the untrained eye, i.e., to the one being led around, the brain is simply there, afloat in its pool, no more active than a dead fish floating at the top of an aquarium. The scientists, we are to imagine, have a trained eye, one more discerning with respect to unencumbered brains, but even the scientists avail themselves of something *beyond* the brain itself. No doubt there will be instruments, devices, apparatus, replete with displays that the specialist, but perhaps not the layman, may *read*, and these serve to inform the scientists of the brain's condition. Imagine, for example, there being a display which glows one color or another depending on the "mood" of the brain – red, say, when angry, blue when sad, green when indifferent, and so on. The colors, the scientists assure us, play the same role for the envatted brain as smiles, frowns, and the like do for us. We can further imagine there being other, more complicated displays, ones which "translate" patterns of activity deep within the brain into more recognizable patterns: one might just as well imagine sentences of English as oscillating blips or other more abstract read-outs.

If we push the attempt to imagine the scenario in this way, the behaviorist at whom Smart's argument was directed may feel himself to have been cheated. After all, with all of these elaborate means of display, it is difficult to see how this is an example of psychological states *without* any overt manifestation. To be sure, the usual manifestations – the smiles, frowns, tears, and so on – are missing, but various surrogates have been found, and it is these which give us a purchase on the idea that something is going on with and for this brain that we are willing (still) to call psychology at all. Kick away the crutch of these displays, and one is back to the imagery of the floating fish. Moreover, the behaviorist will want to be told just how these displays work in terms of how they are connected with what is happening within this brain. In particular, what ensures that the scientists have made the proper connection between what appears on the screens and what's going on "in there"? One answer might be that the scientists have studied how the brain works when it is "hooked up" in the usual ways with (the rest of) standard human bodies: having isolated patterns which are productive with respect to various overt displays and reports on the part of ordinary human subjects, the scientists have designed their displays to respond analogously in this case. Thus, whatever it is that produces a frown in an ordinary human subject is just the same pattern of neurological activity that produces a red light in their envatted subject. Such a response, however, might be taken as only further grist for the behaviorist's mill, since he will point to the pivotal role played by all of those "overt manifestations" in the scientists' isolation of the relevant neural patterns which are "productive" of them. Again, the behaviorist will insist, it is the outward activity that is informing the inner activity, and so Smart has not offered any kind of argument to the effect that behavior is the dispensable element in psychology.

But here Smart (or our imagined scientists) might reply in turn that the displays are, after all, just a crutch, something which *we* need (both in thinking about, as well as imagining ourselves in, this novel situation) in order to *tell* how things are for this brain, but they certainly aren't something the *brain* needs for things to be a certain way with and for it, and certainly not in order for it to know what way things are. All such things are "observational data whereby the psychologist can postulate what goes on in the central nervous system."[7] It would thus be ludicrous to think that by turning off the screen the brain is thereby deprived of thoughts or sensations, its "mental experiences," any more than we should think that all thinking ceases whenever someone loses the ability to speak (or is merely left alone in a darkened room). Though the displays do help us to get a handle on the idea that psychological states are brain states, they are indeed only a crutch to facilitate proper understanding: Once that understanding is achieved, we can see them as indeed peripheral. As Smart puts it, we can see "that what is important in psychology is what goes on in the central nervous system, not what goes on in the face, larynx and limbs."[8] His scenario of the brain *in vitro* brings this out "vividly."

Despite this insistence on the importance of "what goes on in the central nervous system," Smart is perhaps not quite so resolute. In describing the scenario, Smart himself talks of "suitable electrodes inserted into appropriate parts of the brain," which work so as to give the brain "the *illusion* of perceiving things" and also of having "pains, and feelings of moving its nonexistent limbs, and so on."[9] The brain thus has *appendages*, both actual (the electrodes and all that go with them) and virtual (the "nonexistent limbs"); though they need not be the usual ones, they still provide ways in which it remains "in touch" with what surrounds it, and enable it to express and so inform those around it of what goes on for it. But notice that again we are beginning to cheat in the way the behaviorist complained about before: we are once again smuggling in something beyond the brain in and of itself in order to make out the idea of its having a psychological life, of there being some way things are *for* it. Despite Smart's self-avowed

[7] Ibid., 210.
[8] Ibid.
[9] Ibid.

blindness to the outer, his own attempts to motivate his scenario still manifest some reliance on it.

Consider some of Wittgenstein's remarks from early on in Part II of the *Investigations*. In Section i, Wittgenstein notes in the first remark that "the phenomena of hope are modes of this complicated form of life," and in the subsequent remark, that " 'grief' describes a *pattern* which recurs, with different variations, in the weave of our life" (my emphasis) (*PI* 174a,b). Though someone's grief may be a fact about that person, it is not a fact solely in virtue of the events in that person's brain, or even in virtue of his or her outward behavior. Whatever brain events and behavior as may be salient here are so only insofar as they are located within the broader "weave of our life." These remarks may be usefully applied to Smart's appeal to a brain in a vat as a way of explaining our puzzlement in the face of such a scenario. That is, when presented with this envatted brain, the puzzle we confront is one of just whether and how this brain and whatever is happening with it constitute continuations of the patterns of our everyday lives. While it appears dogmatic, armchair science run amok, to declare the brain in a vat to be in principle bereft of a psychological life, any step away from that dogmatism must do something by way of attempting to "weave" the "life" of this brain into the patterns already constituted by our ongoing lives. Whether this can be intelligibly done or not cannot be settled in advance of actual attempts (and it seems clear at least that Smart has done little in that direction).

In a pair of passages from his manuscripts, Wittgenstein again describes the concept of hope as something embedded in human life:

Someone says: "Man hopes." How should this phenomenon of natural history be described?— One might observe a child and wait until one day he manifests hope; and then one could say "Today he hoped for the first time." But surely that sounds queer! Although it would be quite natural to say "Today he said 'I hope' for the first time." And why queer? One does not say that a suckling hopes that ..., but one does say it of a grown-up.—Well, bit by bit daily life becomes such that there is a place for hope in it.

In this case I have used the term "embedded," have said that hope, belief, etc., were embedded in human life, in all of the situations and reactions which constitute human life. The crocodile doesn't hope, man does. Or: one can't say of a crocodile that it hopes, but of man one can.

But how would a human being have to act for us to say of him: he never hopes? The first answer is: I don't know. It would be easier for me to say how a human being would have to act who never yearns for anything, who is never happy about anything, or who is never startled or afraid of anything. (*RPP* II §§15–16)

The questions and difficulties that arise in trying to work up Smart's sketch of a scenario may be taken as illustrative of these remarks, and in the following way: Though it has not been my intention to defend the behaviorist, the extent to which the behaviorist might feel "cheated" at least shows that in trying to imagine the brain in a vat as having a psychological life, we end up looking beyond the confines of the brain and its neural activity alone. By appealing to displays, outputs, inputs, scientists who "read" the brain and "engage" with it, we end up *embedding* the brain in a larger context, and in doing so, we strive as much as possible to approximate "the situations and reactions which constitute human life." Does this brain in a vat hope? Can it? Wittgenstein's remarks do not so much provide an answer to these questions one way or the other, but show instead what is involved in even thinking about an answer. Telling a story in which the answers to these questions are in the affirmative requires more than isolating a pattern of neural activity in this isolated brain corresponding to patterns of neural activity associated with hope in normal human beings (if such patterns there are). Rather, one ends up telling a story such that hope has a place in the life of a brain in a vat, so that we can understand what it might hope for, how it might express or otherwise manifest its hopes, how those hopes might be realized or disappointed, and so on, and all of that involves more than reciting facts about the brain's continued neurological functioning. The idea that hope and psychological states more generally are "embedded" in human life does not preclude the possibility of Smart's brain in a vat. Rather, it tells against the particular interpretation of that possibility which Smart's position demands: namely, that the brain's psychological life is *just* a matter of its neural states and nothing else. This is not behaviorism exactly, but a conception of the psychological that refuses the narrow categorizations Smart's materialism allows.

3.

Smart's exceedingly thin descriptions of the brain in a vat leave the brain we are imagining in a state of opacity. That is, nothing in the scenario as Smart describes it serves to render the brain "transparent" in the manner that a human facial expression does. Our (or at least my) imaginings retain an aura of incredulity of the kind described by Dennett as long as we fix our attention solely on this brain. It is only when Smart begins to "cheat" in the direction of the outer that the "inner life" of this brain begins to take shape, since it is those outer phenomena that allow us to begin, at least, to "weave" together the life of this envatted brain with our own lives.

In the *Investigations*, Wittgenstein writes: "What am I believing in when I believe that men have souls? What am I believing in, when I believe that this substance contains two carbon rings? In both cases there is a picture in the foreground, but the sense lies far in the background; that is, the application of the picture is not easy to survey" (*PI* §422). The likening of the idea of human beings having souls to ways of representing chemical structure can be found at various points in Wittgenstein's later philosophy. In another of the 1950 manuscripts, he writes: "We would like to project everything into his inner. We would like to say that *that's* what it's all about. For in this way we evade the difficulty of describing the *field* of the sentence. It's exactly as if one said that 'Benzene has the structure ⬡' means: the atoms are arranged *in this way*" (*LW*II 82e–f). In the case of the chemical diagram, the picture lies in the foreground and serves as a structural representation of the chemical's internal composition. The application, however, is "not easy to survey," at least not without sufficient knowledge of chemistry and chemical notation. In particular, one cannot simply project the structure of the picture into the molecule, as though one would really find rings in there, only very small ones, so that if, say, one's fingers were correspondingly small, they could be worn as jewelry. Considerable care is thus needed in explicating the content of the belief that a substance contains two carbon rings: Moving from the pictorial or diagrammatic representation to the internal structure of the substance is sufficiently complicated as to prevent a straight or literal construal of the belief. I think it would also be incorrect to say that the belief should be construed metaphorically: The belief that there are two carbon rings *is* a belief about the substance's internal structure, but the connection between the imagery of rings and the real structure of the substance is indirect, mediated by the details of the chemical theory which gives the notation its sense and to which the notation is subservient.

In the case of belief in souls, a picture likewise lies in the foreground: the human being as having an *interior*, an *inner* life of thoughts and feelings, things which may be kept hidden or revealed, expressed or denied. Wittgenstein does not want to disabuse us of these notions, of such a picture, any more than he would question the legitimacy of talking of carbon rings and the like. Remark 423 in the *Investigations* provides reassurance: "*Certainly* all these things happen in you." But at the same time, he does not wish the *pictorial* character of these notions to be overlooked. The remark continues: "And now all I ask is to understand the expression we use.—The picture is there. And I am not disputing its validity in any particular case.—Only I also want to understand the application of the picture." Just as we should not read the diagrams of chemistry as straight depictions of molecular structure – artists' renderings, as it were, of what we should find in there – so too should we not expect to find all the thoughts and feelings that are part and parcel of being ensouled populating the (literal) insides of a human being. To look inside for the soul is as misguided as looking for the rings of carbon in a molecule: In both cases, the picture is being misapplied.

In the *Investigations*, shortly after the remarks just cited, Wittgenstein writes:

"While I was speaking to him I did not know what was going on in his head". In saying this, one is not thinking of brain-processes, but of thought-processes. The picture should be taken seriously. We should really like to see into his head. And yet we only mean what elsewhere we should mean by saying: we should like to know what he is thinking. I want to say: we have this vivid picture – and that use, apparently contradicting the picture, which expresses the psychical. (*PI* §427)

Smart's scenario of a brain in a vat gives us the insides of a human being, at least the insides of the skull, with all of the outsides stripped away (all the periphery of "face, larynx, and limbs"), but getting inside the head in *this* manner takes us, if anything, further away from what we want to apprehend when we want to know what someone is thinking, what is going on in his or her head. Finding only that "gray matter pulsing away," we are left wondering whether the category of thought even applies any longer, let alone what particular thoughts there might be. The disappointment is perhaps akin to what one might feel upon not finding rings, literal rings, within some molecules with which one was familiar through diagrams alone. Though Wittgenstein counsels us to take the picture of thought in the head seriously, Smart's scenario provides a cautionary tale of how *not* to do so.

In Part II of the *Investigations*, Wittgenstein writes: "The human body is the best picture of the human soul" (*PI* 178g). With this statement we might compare: The hexagonal ring is the best picture of a benzene molecule. In both cases, the statements are open to dispute, and along various lines. One could, in each case, claim to have a *better* picture of the soul or the molecule. Chemists may very well dispute how best to represent or diagram molecular structure; another picture may perhaps prove more accurate, useful, illuminating, or even just elegant. More drastically, we might imagine that chemists give up on molecular theory more generally, so that there is nothing left to have a picture *of*. In this more extreme case, the hexagonal structure may still be the best picture, but the picture would lose much of its importance. One might likewise find something other than the body to be the best picture of the soul. Black and white horses struggling against one another might strike one as more fitting, or perhaps "a rarified I-know-not-what, like a wind, or a fire, or ether, which had been infused into my coarser parts," as Descartes imagined his opponents holding (though such a picture is much harder to render with any precision).[10] One might understand Smart to be disputing Wittgenstein's claim by proposing a picture of his own: The human brain is the best picture of the human soul. But Smart does not tell us how to *apply* this picture, how to read it without looking beyond the limits of the picture. We don't (yet?) see the brain *as* the soul, even if we believe, as I take it most of us do, that having a soul, i.e., being a being who thinks, feels, imagines, dreams, suffers, and exalts, is intimately bound up with having a properly functioning brain. Even if the human brain turns out to be the best picture of the human soul, it still would be wrong to say that the brain just *is* the soul, as though the picture and what it depicts coincided, as though the brain were, and could only be, a picture of itself.

Perhaps this last conclusion is unwarranted. Like the imagined chemists who, in the extreme, forego chemical diagrams altogether,

[10] René Descartes, *Meditations on First Philosophy: In Which the Existence of God and the Distinction of the Soul from the Body Are Demonstrated*, trans. Donald A. Cress, 3d ed. (Indianapolis: Hackett, 1993), 18.

who abandon their theories of molecules and molecular structure altogether, the picture of human beings as having interiors in a sense other than the insides of the body may lose its grip. In such a case, the human brain would perhaps be the best picture of the soul, but only by indeed being a picture of itself. The eliminative materialist is someone who urges us in this direction, who sees all of our folk-ish mind- and soul-talk to be empty, irrational superstition, something we would be well advised to discard.[11] Thus when Wittgenstein asks, "What am I believing in when I believe that men have souls?" the eliminative materialist finds the question doubly problematic, defective not just for the belief professed, but for the very profession of *belief* as well, as this is one of the concepts or categories to be "eliminated." Not only are we no longer to believe in the soul; we are to stop believing in belief altogether.

Despite the self-contradictory ring of this last formulation, the eliminativist is well aware of, and unimpressed by, such clever remonstrations, seeing them as no better than similarly clever defenses of the "medieval theory" of "vital spirit." The adherent of the medieval theory argues that the claim that there is no vital spirit is "incoherent" since, if it were true, the claimant would then lack vital spirit, and so would be dead.[12] The analogy is, however, forced, a conflation of *explanans* and *explanandum*, since those who reject the notion of vital spirit do not reject the very idea of *being alive*, but only a particular explanation of what being alive consists in. A true analogue to the eliminativist in the medieval case would be one who proposed abandoning the distinction between life and death, between the living and the non-living altogether. He would thereby be rejecting not just one picture of what being alive comes to, the picture of the body as infused with an immaterial spirit, but questioning whether there is anything in reality to be pictured.

In the same section where Wittgenstein writes of the body as the best picture of the soul, he also says: "My attitude towards him is an attitude towards a soul. I am not of the *opinion* that he has a soul" (*PI* 178d). Read one way, this remark suggests less distance between Wittgenstein and

---

[11] The version of eliminative materialism most central to my discussion is that found in Paul M. Churchland, *Matter and Consciousness*, rev. ed. (Cambridge: MIT Press, 1988).

[12] See ibid., 48.

the eliminativist than one might have thought, since, as far as opinions go anyway, there is nothing that Wittgenstein has that the eliminativist is out to eliminate. At the same time, Wittgenstein is here noting how all of the ideas bound up with the idea of a soul (for example, belief, desire, fear, sensation, joy, and pain, to name just those on Paul Churchland's hit list)[13] inform his orientation toward "him," toward those whom he encounters and with whom he engages. Wittgenstein's engagement with the eliminativist is thus less than straightforward, precisely because of the eliminativist's overly narrow understanding of the human body as a picture of the soul. For the eliminativist, the outward, visible body is the effect, the externalized result, of a series of internal states and processes. The outward body is something of a guide or map, an imprecise one to be sure, for finding or figuring out what these states really are. All of the "folk psychology" bound up with the idea of the soul (such as, again, belief, desire, fear, sensation, joy, and pain) is one way of following the map, and according to the eliminativist, this way does not get us very far. Science, the eliminativist contends, is slowly revealing this depiction of the human interior to be hopelessly defective, as nothing corresponding to all of these folk ideas are being found inside the body (*viz.*, inside the brain).

By contrast, notice how Wittgenstein treats the question of how to locate joy, one of those concepts slated for elimination by the eliminative materialist:

"I feel great joy".—Where?—that sounds like nonsense. And yet one does say "I feel a joyful agitation in my breast".—But why is joy not localized? Is it because it is distributed over the whole body? Even where the feeling that arouses joy is localized, joy is not: if for example we rejoice in the smell of a flower.—Joy is manifested in facial expression, in behavior. (But we do not say that we are joyful in our faces). (Z §486)

That joy is not "localized" renders dubious the idea that what joy picks out is an "internal state." Indeed, as Wittgenstein sees it, we need to be wary of thinking of these concepts as designating *anything*. As he notes in the passage following the one just cited:

"But I do have a real *feeling* of joy!" Yes, when you are glad you really are glad. And of course joy is not joyful behavior, nor yet a feeling round the corners

---

[13] See ibid., 44.

of the mouth and the eyes. "But 'joy' surely designates an inward thing". No. "Joy" designates nothing at all. Neither any inward nor any outward thing. (Z §487)

4.

According to the eliminativist, the conceptual repertoire of folk psychology is a kind of hypothesis concerning the internal workings of human beings. In our dealings with one another, we infer the states picked out by such concepts, and the basis of our inference is the "behavior" we observe. Such "states" are thus not anything we perceive: We do not really see one another's joy or anger, sorrow or elation, any more than we usually see one another's brains. The eliminativist, by casting our ordinary psychological concepts in the role of a theory about the inner workings of the human body (treating joy, for example, as an "inward thing"), denies precisely the kind of transparency Wittgenstein attributes to the face.

Wittgenstein's appeal to transparency is bound up with his more general interest in the concept of seeing as it appears in his many discussions of aspect-perception. One principal motive of Wittgenstein's preoccupation with seeing aspects is to root out the prejudice that there is one fundamental kind or way of seeing, that there is something that we "really" or "directly" or "immediately" see, with all the rest being somehow superadded by the mind, by some kind of thought processes. Wittgenstein, in other words, wants to remind us of the multiplicity inherent in the concept of seeing:

The concept of "seeing" makes a tangled impression. Well, it is tangled.—I look at the landscape, my gaze ranges over it, I see all sorts of distinct and indistinct movement; *this* impresses itself sharply on me, *that* is quite hazy. After all, how completely ragged what we see can appear! And now look at all that can be meant by "description of what is seen".—But this just is what is called description of what is seen. There is not *one genuine* proper case of such description—the rest being just vague, something which awaits clarification, or which must just be swept aside as rubbish. (*PI* 200a)

In the paragraph immediately following the one just cited, Wittgenstein connects the conceit that there is "one genuine proper case" of description to materialism, at least insofar as materialism takes material objects and properties to be, unlike emotions and attitudes, what we really or directly perceive:

Here we are in enormous danger of wanting to make fine distinctions.—It is the same when one tries to define the concept of a material object in terms of "what is really seen".—What we have rather to do is to *accept* the everyday language-game, and to note *false* accounts of the matter *as* false. The primitive language-game which children are taught needs no justification; attempts at justification need to be rejected. (*PI* 200b)

In keeping with this general perspective, Wittgenstein frequently rejects the idea that emotions and attitudes, all the inflections of consciousness bespeaking the presence of a soul, are things that we *infer* from more "neutral" data;[14] we see them as directly as bare "facial contortions" and the like, indeed perhaps more so. As Wittgenstein writes:

Consciousness in the face of another. Look into someone else's face and see the consciousness in it, and also a particular *shade* of consciousness. You see on it, in it, joy, indifference, interest, excitement, dullness etc. The light in the face of another. Do you look within *yourself*, in order to recognize the fury in *his* face? It is there as clearly as in your own breast. (*RPP* I §927)

To insist that we do not really see such things, that such things are not given in our perceptual experience, is to invoke a distorted, highly problematic model of perception indicative of the kind of blindness to the outer characteristic of materialist philosophies of mind. At the same time, however, Wittgenstein's insistence on the legitimacy of talking of "seeing" in these contexts should not be read as a *vindication* of such talk. The tension in Wittgenstein's stance is signaled

---

[14] Dennett's heterophenomenology is an example of the kind of approach to consciousness Wittgenstein wants to reject. On Dennett's conception, heterophenomenology is designed to meet the "challenge" of constructing "a theory of mental events, using the data that scientific method permits" (*Consciousness Explained*, 71). Given the austerity of what is permitted, heterophenomenology does not, strictly speaking, study conscious phenomena, since it is neutral with respect to the question of whether there are any: its subject matter is instead reports of conscious phenomena, the actual transcripts produced in a laboratory setting recording what the "apparent subjects" say about their "experience." Indeed, even taking the noises emitted by these apparent subjects to amount to things they say is already a bold leap beyond the given: "The transcript or text is not, strictly speaking, given as data, for … it is created by putting the raw data through a process of interpretation" (ibid., 75).

in the following, difficult passage: "Naturally the question isn't: 'Is it right to say "I *see* his sly wink."' What should be right or wrong about that, beyond the use of the English language? Nor are we going to say 'The naive person is quite right to say he *saw* the facial expression'!" (*RPP* I §1069).

I mentioned before Cavell's remark that Wittgenstein's later philosophy "takes the risk of apsychism." Wittgenstein's rejection of the final formulation in the above remark is risky insofar as it deprives the soul of any kind of factual guarantee, immune from doubt and safe from extinction. On the latter danger, consider one of Dennett's stated ambitions in *Consciousness Explained* of "threaten[ing] with extinction" certain "phenomena of consciousness" that depend on concepts Dennett thinks are outdated, confused, and/or unscientific.[15] The phrasing here is intriguing, since to talk of "extinction" implies that prior to the threats of Dennett and others, these "phenomena of consciousness" *were* real. (Only species of animals that really roam the earth can be threatened with extinction; purely mythological ones cannot, though people may, for various reasons, stop believing in them, or even talking about them. The best picture of a unicorn or dragon may eventually hold little interest for anyone.) What kind of threat, then, is Dennett leveling and how are we to understand the target of his threats? Dennett's own likening of conscious phenomena to economic phenomena (monetary value, inflation, and so on)[16] suggests that their reality is sustained by our collective interactions, our attitudes toward one another (compare: My attitude toward this piece of paper is an attitude toward something valuable), and these interactions are not sacrosanct, but instead are liable to change both through deliberate efforts and through less mindful forms of cultural drift. The soul is no more secure than the five dollar bill: that can be either dark or heartening, depending on one's confidence in the almighty buck.

Wittgenstein himself explores this kind of dependence, and with it, the possibility of changes in our conceptions of the mental, even wholesale ones. Writing on the particular example of our concept of lying and the myriad connections between this concept and

---

[15] Dennett, *Consciousness Explained*, 24.
[16] See, for example, Appendix A (for Philosophers) to *Consciousness Explained*, 457–63, especially 460.

our practices of distinguishing truth-telling from lying, detecting dishonesty in one another's gesture and expression, and debating, sometimes without resolve, whether someone has been truthful or not, Wittgenstein invites us to consider the possible consequences of introducing more exact, mechanical procedures, which bypass altogether these many nuanced dimensions of our concepts of honesty and dishonesty. As the passage makes clear, such a replacement is far from inconceivable. What is less clear is how we would go about deciding whether this is a change we would want to make:

And now the question remains whether we would give up our language-game which rests on "imponderable evidence" and frequently leads to uncertainty, if it were possible to exchange it for a more exact one which by and large would have similar consequences. For instance, we could work with a mechanical "lie detector" and redefine a lie as that which causes a deflection on the lie detector. So the question is: Would we change our way of living if this or that were provided for us?—And how could I answer that? (*LW* II 95a)

"My attitude toward him is an attitude toward a nervous system/a brain/a neurophysiological system." What attitude *is* that? What way of being oriented toward one another is entailed by such an attitude? Again, how is such a picture to be applied? Perhaps we should ask instead, how are we to live without having any picture at all, without any sense of the human body, the human face, as transparent? Nothing in Wittgenstein guarantees that we will not someday find ourselves living this way, though the net effect of his remarks is to make such a wholesale change in attitude appear far less inevitable, as somehow necessitated by the steady progress of the natural sciences.

By way of a conclusion, I want to cite two final remarks. In each case, I must confess that I am omitting a great deal of the surrounding remark, though I am reasonably confident that I am not thereby distorting the words: "Grief, one would like to say, is personified in the face. This is essential to what we call 'emotion'" (*RPP* II §570); "it is as if the human face were in a way translucent and that I were seeing it not in reflected light but rather in its own" (*RPP* II §170). These remarks are but two examples of Wittgenstein's appeal to the face, to its translucency and transparency. The face, for Wittgenstein, is the exterior by and through which our "interior" comes to light; the face depicts or pictures our interior in a way that is, Wittgenstein notes, "essential." The interior personified by the face, rendered transparent by it, is not the blood-and-guts of our corporeal insides, but another, categorically distinct dimension of our existence, one perhaps better understood as *ethical* rather than theoretical. Contemporary materialism, by contrast, is, or strives to be, blind to the multi-dimensional character of our existence. Hard up for categories, the materialist can see in the face only the outward effects of the workings of the brain, a set of "data" pointing inward toward the "lump of stuff" "pulsing away" within the skull, rather than a translucent, transparent medium through which the soul is made manifest.[17]

[17] Versions of this chapter were presented at a conference on Wittgenstein and Levinas at Indiana University and to the Auburn Philosophical Society at Auburn University. I am grateful to the members of both audiences for their comments and criticisms. I would also like to thank William Day and Victor Krebs for their comments and suggestions, and, above all, their patience.

8

Wittgenstein on Aspect-Seeing, the Nature of Discursive Consciousness, and the Experience of Agency

Richard Eldridge

> We find certain things about seeing puzzling, because we do not find the whole business of seeing puzzling enough. (*PI* 212f)

1.

Consciousness or awareness is possessed by at least a wide range of higher chordates. But genuine discursive consciousness is possessed – at least in its complex forms – only by human beings. Only human beings can, so it seems, be aware of seeing a given object *as* this or that, under one or another concept. The ability to be thus aware informs our perception, giving it both a judgmental character and a relation to self-consciousness. We typically see or hear *that x* is *F*, over and above simply taking in sensations. There is for any one of us always the potential to step back from our conceptually structured, judgmental perceiving so as to become explicitly aware that it is I who have judged that *x* is *F* (rather than, say, *G*). This openness to awareness of one's own role in judgmental perceiving further opens for us the possibility of a normative question arising. Am I correct so to have judged? This question does not arise for other higher mammals. They do not thus call their own being into question.

Historically, the apparently special character of human judgmental consciousness has motivated a variety of attempts to explain it, including at least Plato's theory of the immortal soul's ability to recollect eternal Forms, Aristotle's theory of *nous* as actively instancing essences both in us and in things, and Augustine's theory of the *scintilla animae*. Kant proposes, somewhat obscurely, that a spontaneity of reason stimulates the understanding to produce from its own resources the pure or nonempirical concepts of substance and causality that then figure as part of the implicit substructure of the more ordinary empirical concepts we form. ("Cup," for example, is a substance-concept; "break" is a causal verb.)

More recently the leading contenders for an explanation of the fact – if it is a fact – of the special character of human discursive consciousness have been various forms of materialist naturalism: symbolic representations theory and connectionism. Sometimes a generally Kantian stance is naturalized, so that the structure of our sorting practices is "wired in" (no longer the product of a spontaneity, and no longer bound up with the standing possibility of self-awareness), as in Chomsky and other forms of post-Piagetian, naturalistic symbolic representations theory. Sometimes an empiricist-associationist stance is naturalized, and judgmental responsiveness to things is taken to arise only out of networks of neural connections, again without reference to either spontaneity or self-awareness.

When the relations between discursive consciousness, on the one hand, and spontaneity and self-awareness, on the other, are thus broken, then the very idea that we are capable of *judging* that thus-and-so is threatened. We seem then not to be responsible for what we do, but to be mere sensing and responding animals (like the dogs and frogs with whom we share the earth), incapable of even so much as raising the question whether we are correct to judge as we do. Judgments, structured by concepts, about how things are, are reduced to complexities of purely caused response. This idea – that human judgment does not properly exist as judgment – seems fantastically implausible. But then just what *are* judgment and discursive consciousness? And how can they possibly arise in us?

Wittgenstein's work – early and late – clearly fits into the tradition of philosophical investigations of the nature and basis of discursive consciousness. The picture theory of meaning in the *Tractatus* and the analysis of the proposition into simple names corresponding to simple objects are put forward to elucidate how truth-value-bearing propositions and thoughts are possible. "There *must* be something identical in a picture [whether proposition or thought] and what it depicts, to enable the one to be a picture of the other *at all.*" [*In Bild und Abgebildetem muss etwas identisch sein, damit das eine überhaupt ein Bild des anderen sein kann.*] (*TLP* 2.161, emphases added.) Here the "must" and "at all" (*überhaupt*) indicate that the necessity involved is transcendental or conceptual. It is, so the argument runs, not thinkable that genuine representationality and truth value–bearing judgmental structure could be set up otherwise, in thought or in language. Wittgenstein's resolute determination to keep transcendental or purely conceptual investigations – philosophy or philosophical logic – separate from empirical science as the investigation of contingent states of affairs means, however, that no causal-material explanation of what the elements of pictures (in either thought or language) are, and how they interact with simple objects, is on offer. It is a transcendental or logico-philosophical necessity that there are simple names (in thought and in language) that can be arranged in a way that corresponds to (shares a pictorial form with) an arrangement of simple objects. *What* these simple names (and simple objects) specifically are, and *how* the relevant correspondences are set up, must take care of itself. *That* they must exist and must be able to stand in relations of correspondence is, in contrast, something that is necessary in order for there to be truth value–bearing thoughts and propositions at all.

In *Philosophical Investigations* these *specific* claims about what is transcendentally or logico-philosophically necessary are subjected to criticism. The full-blooded representationality or judgmental-discursive character of both thought and language are – it is now proposed – matters not of any "substructure" of simple names and simple objects lying underneath the surface, but matters rather of words having a role within a public language as a matter of common practice. "This role is what we need to understand in order to resolve philosophical paradoxes" (*PI* §182). "A person goes by a sign-post [i.e., is able to use a word, understands] only insofar as there exists a regular use of sign-posts, a custom" (*PI* §198). "To understand a sentence means to understand a language. To understand a language means to be master of a technique" (*PI* §199). "'How do sentences manage to represent?' ... Nothing is hidden" (*PI* §435).

Once we see this – that nothing but the mastery of a technique laid down in common, public practice could enable one to assert, judge, or state, or to wish, command, hope, fear, or envy, as opposed to having a life only of mere sensory awareness – then we are, so it seems, to cure ourselves of our temptation to look for a "deeper" quasi-scientific or metaphysical explanation of discursive consciousness, full-blooded representationality, judgmental awareness, or our life with language. We are, it seems, to *stop* hunting for the "superlative fact" that under-lies and explains these phenomena, to stop groping after "a super-expression" or "a philosophical superlative" that might describe this putatively explanatory superlative fact (*PI* §192).[1] Here the role of com-mon practices and techniques in making language meaningful and making propositional attitudes possible remains, for Wittgenstein, a philosophical, logical, or grammatical fact, not simply one empiri-cal fact among others to be investigated and explained causally. The emphasis remains on what *must* be in place – a technique, a common practice, a custom in using words – in order for there to be discursive consciousness, understanding, judgmental awareness, propositional attitudes, and words with meanings at all.

Notoriously, this stance (especially insofar as it is urged as a thesis or conclusion) has occasioned considerable disappointment and hos-tility in contemporary philosophy, and for good reason, at least *prima facie*. Language and discursive consciousness are, at least in their full-blooded forms, specific to biologically evolved human beings; linguis-tic and cognitive performances are generated *by* human individuals. Surely there must, it seems, be some further explanation available of the nature and basis of these feats, in the individual and in the spe-cies. Indeed, numbers of readers of Wittgenstein have themselves, in the grip of a wish for something deeper, undertaken to go beneath noting our grammar and linguistic practice, in the hope of explain-ing what makes that practice what it is. As a result we are sometimes told that Wittgenstein himself held that what *counts as* understanding

---

[1] That Wittgenstein is urging this stance of attention to the ordinary on himself, in the face of his own temptations otherwise, as much as on us as a kind of statable thesis or dogma, but that it is – for him and for us – all but impossible consistently to remain in this stance, and finally that peace in relation to the ordinary comes, when it comes, fitfully and through the dawning of a sense of gratitude for one's human life (rather than via a discovery of its essence) is the argument of my *Leading a Human Life: Wittgenstein, Intentionality, and Romanticism* (Chicago: University of Chicago Press, 1997), drawing extensively on Stanley Cavell's reading of *Philosophical Investigations* in *The Claim of Reason: Wittgenstein, Skepticism, Morality, and Tragedy* (Oxford: Oxford University Press, 1979).

(discursive consciousness) consists in reacting in a way that is simply natural (Stroud), in deciding to do this or that (Dummett, Rorty), in doing what the community has laid down as correct (Kripke), or in fluent conformity to fixed "internal relations" (Baker and Hacker).[2]

Cognitive science of all kinds has not been slow to sketch possible explanations and to undertake to fill in their details through empirical research. As Jerry Fodor cogently remarks, why can't we ask questions such as "What (causally) makes the linguistic form 'red' apply to red objects?"[3] It does not so apply in all cultures; it does for us, we who are able to speak English. When we apply the word "red" correctly (or incorrectly), *we* are doing something. Just what are we doing, and how do we do it? "How does one become 'master of a game' (*PI* §31)?"[4]

When these questions do not receive any clear address or answer from within Wittgensteinian thinking, then cognitive science and neuroscience, with their material causal explanations, will rush in to fill the gap. Happily, there is a kind of address or answer to these questions – and one quite different from what is envisioned in naturalist, conventionalist, and communitarian misreadings of *Philosophical Investigations* – in the text of *Philosophical Investigations* itself, in the discussion of seeing-as in Part II, Section 11 and in related remarks about coming to experience the meaning of a word. These remarks (if we can follow and make sense of them) have considerable promise for filling in a picture of what we are *doing* when we are judging, understanding, entering into a propositional attitude, ordering, wishing, hoping, or fearing: participating in all the phenomena of discursive consciousness – and a picture that is *not* "metaphysical" (in referring what *we do* to something else), material-scientific, naturalist-causalist, or conventionalist.

In order to see just how these remarks offer such a picture and to begin to assess its plausibility, it will be helpful first to turn to the recent work of a cultural-developmental-cognitive scientist (if that is not too much of an oxymoron) who has drawn extensively on

---

2 See Eldridge, *Leading a Human Life*, 91–112 for description of these readings, criticism of them, and an alternative.

3 See Jerry A. Fodor, *The Language of Thought* (New York: Thomas Y. Crowell, 1975), 2–9 for this argument in favor of the sense of this causalist question.

4 Compare the discussion of Fodor's causalism in Eldridge, *Leading a Human Life*, 150.

Wittgenstein's work on seeing-as. In *The Cultural Origins of Human Cognition*, Michael Tomasello has surveyed the existing studies of primate "cognition" and of human cognitive development.[5] Drawing on these studies as well as on Wittgenstein, Tomasello has developed a persuasive account of just what we do in learning language and in learning to understand under concepts. This account is not simply causalist, not simply conventionalist, and not in any sense homuncularist-intellectualist. After tracing Tomasello's account of the details of this learning process, we will then be in a position to turn to the details of Wittgenstein's discussion of seeing-as, ready to be alert both to how seeing-as plays a fundamental role in learning to understand and to how seeing-as and learning to understand are *things that we do*, as opposed to things that merely happen in us. We will be able then to follow Wittgenstein's thoughts about the (co-)dawning of discursive consciousness and agency and about the human circumstances, plights, and possibilities that come with these dawnings.

2.

Tomasello's story runs as follows. "Individual human beings possess a biologically inherited *capacity* for living culturally."[6] To say that they have a (second-order) capacity, rather than an explicit first-order ability,[7] for living culturally is to say that they are the kinds of beings who *can learn* to produce fluent, conceptually structured, cultural performances, not that they come into the world already explicitly able to produce them. There *is* a biological contribution to becoming a concept-mongering, acculturated being, but that contribution does not take the form of already possessing concepts in any way.

The development of explicit linguistic, conceptual, and cultural abilities then depends crucially on ontogenetic-developmental

---

[5] Michael Tomasello, *The Cultural Origins of Human Cognition* (Cambridge: Harvard University Press, 1999). Many of the studies cited by Tomasello are his own; others are by eminent researchers including Savage-Rumbaugh, Rumbaugh, Nelson, Premack, Woodruff, Meltzoff, and Gopnik.

[6] Ibid., 53 (emphasis added).

[7] Aristotle distinguishes capacities or second-order abilities to acquire abilities from explicit, first-order abilities in *Physics* 8.4.255a30 ff.

processes "by which human children *actively* exploit and make use of both their biological and cultural inheritances."[8] These

historical and ontogenetic processes ... are enabled but not in any way deter-mined by human beings' biological adaptations for a special form of social cognition. ... It is these processes, not any specialized biological adapta-tions directly, that have done the actual work in creating many, if not all, of the most distinctive and important cognitive products and processes of the species *Homo sapiens*.[9]

Two crucial dimensions of these processes are that they involve chil-dren actively doing something, and that they require and involve *iden-tification* with other *human beings as havers of a point of view*. Members of other species likewise identify with conspecifics, and they may "pick up" behaviors via patterning, in the way that songbirds, for example, will pick up a species-typical song. But the identification of human children with other human beings is, in contrast, both deeper and point-of-view–related. "Human beings 'identify' with conspecifics more deeply than do other primates. This identification is not something mysterious, but simply the process by which the human child understands that other persons are beings like herself – in a way that inanimate objects are not, for example – and so she sometimes tries to understand things from their point of view."[10] Hence the process of the development of linguis-tic and cognitive skills on the part of the child is a process of *sociogenesis*; it requires other havers of points of view. So-called "wild children," or children otherwise biologically growing up under conditions of severe deprivation of human interaction, do not develop sophisticated lin-guistic and cognitive skills; many autistic children master them only in part; and other species do not master them at all.[11]

Other primates do respond to their environments in sophisticated ways that involve both rich sensory awareness and differential response or classificatory abilities. They remember the locations of things in their environment, assume object persistence, match small numerosi-ties, recognize and represent relations of kinship and rank, cooperate in problem-solving tasks, and more.[12] What they do *not* do, however,

---

[8] Tomasello, *Human Cognition*, 11, emphasis added.
[9] Ibid.
[10] Ibid., 14.
[11] Ibid., 14, 8.
[12] Ibid., 16–17, 19.

is "view the world in terms of ... underlying causes and intentional/ mental states. ... Nonhuman primates are themselves intentional and causal beings, they just do not understand the world in intentional and causal terms."[13] Underlying their failure so to understand the world is the fact that nonhuman primates "do not participate in extended joint attentional interactions in the same way as human children."[14]

In contrast, children engage soon after birth in "protoconversations" with adults, that is, "social interactions in which the parent and infant focus their attention on one another – often in a face-to-face manner involving looking, touching and vocalizing – in ways that serve to express and share basic emotions."[15] By the age of nine to twelve months, children engage in "joint attentional behaviors that seem to indicate an emerging understanding of other persons as intentional agents like the self."[16] Within these joint attentional behaviors, a "referential triangle of child, adult, and the object or event to which they share attention" is set up.[17] Crucially this referential triangle involves the joint focusing of attention on a thing or event *construed* in a certain way within the game. *That* (the soft plush item on the floor) is a rabbit, or Pooh's friend, or the one who is resting from hopping, or the toy Aunt Sadie gave you, as the context may be.

One comes – all at once – to be able to use words to refer to things, and distinctly and self-consciously to *conceive* of things in particular ways, in and through participation in joint attentional behaviors and referential triangles. Hence "linguistic reference is a *social* act in which one person attempts to get another person to focus her attention on something in the world" that has been construed in a certain way within the context of the scene.[18] As the child moves

---

[13] Ibid., 19.

[14] Ibid., 36.

[15] Ibid., 59. Compare R. G. Collingwood on the development of personhood, point of view having, and cognitive and linguistic skills in the child through a complex play of contestation and expression with an adult, in *The Principles of Art* (Oxford: Clarendon Press, 1938), 239–41.

[16] Tomasello, *Human Cognition*, 61.

[17] Ibid., 62. Compare Donald Davidson on referential triangles in "The Second Person" and "The Emergence of Thought," *Subjective, Intersubjective, Objective* (Oxford: Clarendon Press, 2001), 107–21 (see especially 117–21) and 123–34 (see especially 128–29).

[18] Tomasello, *Human Cognition*, 97.

within these scenes from an initial biologically supported mimicry and into more flexible and evolving play, in which objects are construed and reconstrued as this or that, genuine, self-conscious point-of-view–having develops. The child becomes aware that this object can be construed- or conceived-as this or that, in this or that changing context of goals, aims, and emotions, and so she comes to be aware both of the multiple kinds of things objects are, and of herself as a construer and conceiver.[19]

What Tomasello calls the *internalization* of a linguistic symbol, which is initially used by the adult within a joint attentional interaction, as a symbol involves the learning all at once of words, concepts (construals of the ways things are), point of view, and of self and other as havers of points of view. This internalization takes the child well beyond the kinds of merely perceptual representations that she otherwise shares with other higher chordates:

As the child internalizes a linguistic symbol – as she learns the human perspectives embodied in a linguistic symbol – she cognitively represents not just the perceptual or motoric aspects of a situation but also one way, among other ways of which she is aware, that the current situation may be attentionally construed by "us", the users of that symbol. The way that human beings use linguistic symbols thus creates a clear break with straightforward perceptual or sensory-motor representations, and it is due entirely to the social nature of linguistic symbols.[20]

Genuine linguistic symbols are hence something more than apt response–based sensory-perceptual representations. Instead they have, in Tomasello's phrasing, "human perspectives embodied" in them:

In different communicative situations one and the same object may be construed as a dog, an animal, a pet, or a pest; one and the same event may be construed as running, moving, fleeing, or surviving; one and the same place may be construed as the coast, the shore, the beach, or the sand – all depending on the communicative goals of the speaker. ... As perspectively based cognitive representations, then, linguistic symbols are based not on the recording of direct sensory or motor experiences, as are the cognitive

---

[19] Compare Cavell on language-learning in "Learning a Word," *The Claim of Reason*, 169–80.
[20] Tomasello, *Human Cognition*, 126.

representations of other animal species and human infants, but rather on the ways in which individuals choose to construe things out of a number of other ways they might have construed them, as embodied in the other available linguistic symbols that they might have chosen, but did not.[21]

Genuine symbolic representations or linguistic symbols (as opposed to perceptual representations only) are, then, all at once public, intersubjectively shared, and perspectival, i.e., saturated with "embodied construals" of how things are, which are salient in relation to certain goals, purposes, and contexts of joint attention. Unlike either mere perceptual representations or animal signals, they embody an available construal of things, and they enable genuine communicative action through their use. The availability of these symbolic representations to a now developed genuine subject, in possession of explicit cognitive and linguistic skills, marks the difference, in Aristotelian terminology, between a being with *phantasia* or sensory awareness alone, and a being for whom *phantasia* is informed and structured by *nous*, whose awareness is then fully discursive. But this difference in the structure of awareness – the emergence of the very life of a person – is brought about neither by the agency of *nous*, nor by biology plus causal conditioning alone, but instead by a sociogenetic process involving the development from mimicry to participation in joint attentional interactions. Full-blooded, discursively structured consciousness comes by way of developing through attentional interactions the skill of using genuine symbolic representations that embody construals.

3.

At first blush, there are significant differences between Tomasello's story of the development of discursive consciousness, self-consciously influenced by *Philosophical Investigations* though it is, and Wittgenstein's investigations into aspect-seeing. Tomasello's account is built up out of observations available in the primate observation and child development literatures. That account is part of an empirical inquiry into what is going on as a matter of fact. Wittgenstein, in contrast, reminds

[21] Ibid., 8–9.

himself (and us) that "Our problem is not a causal but a conceptual one. ... What is at issue is the fixing of concepts [*Begriffsbestimmungen*]" (*PI* 203e, 204g).

Looked at more closely, however, these differences are less striking. To begin with, Tomasello's story is *not* itself derived from *experimental* results, but is instead developed out of conceptually self-conscious *observation* of what children (and primates) do (and don't do). What we *do* in learning language is neither reduced to, nor explained by, purely material processes, according to Tomasello. What we do involves the development and exercise of an ability (based on a prior innate capacity) in actual practice. Nothing is hidden, one might say.

Conversely, Wittgenstein connects his investigation of aspect-seeing more closely with the learning of language than might initially meet the eye. He remarks at one point on "a game played by children: they say that a chest, for example, is a house; and thereupon it is interpreted as a house in every detail. A piece of fancy is worked into it" (*PI* 206e). This remark suggests that the appearance of fancy (invention; *Erfindung*) within game-playing in the life of a child is akin to seeing an aspect. When we then further notice the remark that seeing an aspect bears "a close kinship with 'experiencing the meaning of a word'" (*PI* 210c; see also 214d), then the suggestion is not far off that it is *by* exercising fancy (inventiveness, imagination) within the context of game-playing that children come to learn language at all (by catching on to the aspects of things that are "embodied" in words).

Even the remark about the fixing of concepts (*PI* 204h) itself admits, in context, of two different, compatible readings. What is at issue is, first, what the concept (or various concepts) of *seeing* and *visual experience* are – that is, what it makes sense, conceptually, to compare these phenomena to, and how to understand them – but also, second, how concepts get fixed at all within our seeing: how does our seeing itself come to be discursively structured, how do concepts get fixed (determined; *bestimmt*) *in it*.

This latter reading is decisively reinforced, repeatedly, throughout the discussion of seeing an aspect. That discussion begins by noting a difference between "two uses of the word 'see'": one in which one might report having had a piece of sensory awareness by saying, "I see this," accompanied by a description or drawing or copy; and one in which one sees "a likeness between these two faces" – i.e., two things (faces) are compared with one another (*PI* 193a). This difference between two kinds of seeing resembles the difference in English (and German) between "see" (*sehen*) as it takes an object accusative ("I see *x*"), and "see" as it takes a propositional accusative ("I see that *x* is *F*"). The achievement described in the latter, propositional accusative form is necessarily conceptually structured in a way that the former having of a visual impression need not be.[22] (A frog can see the fly, but not see that that is a fly – does it see that it is a bluebottle or a May fly? – and cannot be implicitly aware of itself as so seeing. It cannot report the content of its awareness in the form of a proposition, even to itself.) Wittgenstein notes that there are two kinds of seeing in question here: what one might call seeing as mere visual awareness, and "discursive" seeing or seeing informed by conceptualization, wherein a noticed aspect can be reported. About noticing an aspect, he observes that "It must be possible to give both remarks [both 'But this isn't *seeing*!' *and* 'But this is seeing!'] a conceptual justification" [*Beide müssen sich begrifflich rechtfertigen lassen*]: both ways of speaking must admit of being conceptually justified; both must be regarded as conceptually legitimate (*PI* 203c). And this is as much as to say that there are two concepts of seeing that must be distinguished. One is the having of visual awareness, without any conceptualization; the other involves "a modified concept of *sensation*" (*einen modifizierten* Empfindugsbegriff) (*PI* 209h), where sensing (seeing and hearing) *include* that one notices or recognizes something (for example, recognizes a face as timid: "*ihn [ein Gesichtseindruck] als furchtsam ... erkennt*" [*PI* 209h]). This latter kind of sensation involves having concepts as part of its very structure, in a way that having visual awareness alone does not. We are, Wittgenstein writes, "interested in the concept [of noticing an aspect; that is, of discursively informed experience]

---

[22] The remark at *PI* 193a both notes and muddies a contrast between a more simple, accusative, "mere" visual awareness, on the one hand, and visual recognition under a concept, on the other, since it contrasts two uses of "see" on the part of an already competent language-user. Nor is it any part of Wittgenstein's project to trace a material-causal history of concept acquisition. Normal visual perception on the part of competent language-users just is conceptually structured. But as Wittgenstein later notes, recognitive visual awareness involves "a modified concept of sensation" (*PI* 209h) from that which we might reasonably take other chordate mammals to possess.

and its place among the concepts of experience" [*seine Stellung in den Erfahrungsbegriffen*] (*PI* 193e).

That is to say, seeing-as involves a different *kind* of experience, or experience in a different sense than having sensory awareness alone. Thus it is, Wittgenstein writes, "not part of perception" or "does not belong to perception" [*Das "Sehen als …" gehört nicht zur Wahrnehmung*] (*PI* 197a) – there is more to it than takes place in sensory awareness alone. "And for that reason it is like seeing and again not like"; it "seems half visual experience, half thought"; "if you are having the visual experience expressed by the exclamation ['Now I see it as a …'], you are also *thinking* of what you see" (*PI* 197a,d,c). When I suddenly recognize [*erkenne*] an acquaintance in a crowd, "is this a special sort of seeing? Is it a case of both seeing and thinking? or an amalgam [*eine Verschmelzung*] of the two, as I should almost like to say?" (*PI* 197h). Unlike mere sensing, seeing-as "demands *imagination*" or "requires *power of imagination*" [*braucht es* Vorstellungskraft] (*PI* 207h).

Within the fusion of seeing and thinking that is noticing an aspect, there are *not* two separable stages: first the perception, then the concept application. It is all immediate within the act of seeing-as. "No squeezing, no forcing [of a perceived object into an interpretation held apart and ready for it] took place here" (*PI* 200e). "So we interpret [what we notice an aspect of], and *see* it as we *interpret* it" (*PI* 193f).

What Wittgenstein calls "the 'continuous seeing' [*stetigen Sehen*] of an aspect" (*PI* 194b) is, for us who have come to be able to use language, the normal form of seeing. It is distinguished from explicitly noticing an aspect shift, or what Wittgenstein calls "the 'dawning' of an aspect" [*das Aufleuchten eines Aspekts*; its flashing or lighting up] (*PI* 194). The philosophical interest of this latter experience of the dawning of an aspect is that it makes evident, to and for us, who are now already conceptually conscious, something of what the experience of *coming to be discursively aware of things* is like.

The dawning of an aspect is not just a matter of "perceptual" or "mental" or "neural" events occurring in me. Crucially, it involves my actively placing the object seen in a context of comparisons: seeing "a likeness" [*eine Ähnlichkeit*; a similarity] (*PI* 193a), not just seeing an object. For example, when I see the duck-rabbit as a rabbit, then I would, if I were asked to explain my perception, set about "pointing to all sorts of pictures of rabbits, [and I] should perhaps have pointed to real rabbits, talked about their habits, or given an imitation of them" (*PI* 194d; see also 196a ff.). I set the object seen in a certain field of comparisons, within my very act of seeing.

This setting of the object seen within a field of comparisons is something I do in relation to other objects and pictures of objects in the world. What Wittgenstein calls the "organization" [*die Organisation*] (*PI* 196b ff.) that I bring to the seeing of an object *as* such-and-such is *not* any framework or pattern "inside" my mind or brain. It is, rather, an organization or arrangement that I see *in* or *among* the things that I discursively see. When I am able to achieve such an organization or arrangement of the objects of my experience, then I have a power to respond to things that I had previously lacked. When I say, "Now I see it as a ..." then "the very expression which is also a report of what is seen, is here a cry of recognition" [*ein Ausruf des Erkennens*] (*PI* 198a). There is a kind of triumph in accession to felt power in the entry into concept-suffused perception.[23] Now I can and do "*describe* what I am seeing differently" (*PI* 202b). I can actively connect this with that, within an organized field, rather than having sensory experience simply "come to me." I can and do now turn my attention on this or that, attend to this or that, notice or see *that* this is (like) that.

How do I do this? Again, not through the occurrence of "inner processes" alone of any kind, but through picking up on resemblances and on patterns of attention to them that are associated with words. "The substratum of this experience [of noticing an aspect, and so also of coming to 'see discursively' at all] is the mastery of a technique" (*PI* 208e). It is the mastery of the technique of attention to comparisons, of seeing likenesses, that makes discursive experience possible:

"Now he's seeing it like *this*", "now like *that*" would only be said of someone *capable* [*imstande*] of making certain applications of the figure quite freely [with fluency; *mit Geläufigkeit*]. ... It is only if someone *can do* [*kann*], has learnt, is master of, such-and-such, that it makes sense to say he has had *this* experience. (*PI* 208e, 209a)

Hearing a word with understanding is like this as well. ("The importance of this concept [of aspect-blindness] lies in the

---

[23] Compare, again, Collingwood on the emergence of a sense of self-as-agent out of mere sensory awareness, through the organization effected by picking up on patterns of attending, in *The Principles of Art*, 203–6, 234–41.

connection between the concepts of 'seeing an aspect' and 'experiencing the meaning of a word'" [*PI* 214d].) Experiencing the meaning of a word – hearing it with discursive understanding – likewise involves (internalized) mastery of a technique of making connections between this word and various possible contexts of use, associated with various construals embodied in the word as a tool in use. "*Hearing* a word in a particular sense. How queer that there should be such a thing! Phrased *like this*, emphasized like this, heard in this way, this sentence is the first of a series in which a transition is made to *these* sentences, pictures, actions. ((A multitude of familiar paths lead off from these words in every direction))" (*PI* §534). Language itself, Wittgenstein observes, is "a labyrinth of paths. You approach from *one* side and know your way about; you approach the same place from another side and no longer know your way about" (*PI* §203). The skill of knowing one's way about is a matter of knowing what one can do next – mastering the technique for it – in such a way that one immediately sees or hears these words as leading to these next possible responses. This kind of discursive understanding of words – knowing (in seeing and hearing) what *can* come next – is like understanding a theme in music: knowing what can (or even must) come next *in it*:

> Understanding a sentence is much more akin to understanding a theme in music than one may think. ... Why is just *this* the pattern of variation in loudness and tempo? One would like to say "Because I know what it's all about". But what is it all about? I should not be able to say. In order to "explain" I could only *compare* it with something else which has the same rhythm (I mean the same pattern). (One says, "Don't you *see*, this is as if a conclusion were being drawn" or "This is as it were a parenthesis", etc.). (*PI* §527, second and third emphases added)

One must learn actually to hear or see *in* the words or notes that are present in experience the *possibilities* (sometimes even the necessities) of further transitions to just this or that. "What happens when we learn to *feel* [*empfinden*] the ending of a church mode as an ending?" (*PI* §535). – We are then part of a form of life and able to move fluently within it, masters of a particular technique for making connections, itself internalized within the very act of attentive, discursively informed perception.

4.

The development of this explicit ability to hear or see in words or notes possibilities of connection to further words or notes is a matter of learning actively to *do* something, of developing an explicit ability out of an innate capacity on the basis of training in response to samples, within scenes of joint attentional interaction. The abilities that are thus developed are holistic, not modular. It is true that deaf children can learn language (both to "speak" ASL or another sign language, and to read and write English), and people who are unable to carry or recognize a tune can be fluent native speakers. As a result of brain injury, subjects can develop an inability to recognize faces, while retaining their linguistic abilities. To this extent, these abilities can be modularized. Nonetheless the development of any one of these abilities is not a strictly self-contained modular phenomenon. The abilities to hear words with discursive understanding, to recognize pictures as pictures of such-and-such (to see aspects), to hear a melody with understanding, to count, to recognize and respond to facial expressions, to repeat nursery rhymes, and more, all inform and feed off one another. Massive deficits in some areas tend to generate massive deficits in other areas, as in many cases of autism, in which the inability to respond to facial expressions of emotion undermines the development of language.

In moving from innate capacity to explicit ability to make connections (within the very act of discursive perception), seeing others as persons with points of view is crucial. *PI* §§536–39 compare experiencing the meaning of a word and hearing the development of a melody with seeing timidity, say, *in* a face, and this comparison recurs throughout Part II, Section 11: for example, in discussions of reacting to the expression of a human face (*PI* 194c), of recognizing a face as timid or as sad (*PI* 209h, d), and of recognizing "a genuine loving look" on the basis of "imponderable evidence" (*PI* 228b–d). One must catch on to what is done by other people as they respond discursively to things, to their ways of noticing and responding to aspects. In order to move into explicitly discursive consciousness, "What has to be accepted, the given, is—so one could say— *forms of life*" (*PI* 226d).

The fluent abilities that one acquires through such acceptance, achieved *via* participation in joint attentional interactions, confer on the thus emergent subject of experience (in a new sense of "experience") a kind of power. Wittgenstein's image is that of being able to move along a path ("A multitude of familiar paths leads off from these words in every direction"), or of knowing how to go on. One becomes a subject *of* experience rather than only passively subject *to* experience.[24] One is *able* to *notice*, actively, the aspects of things.

  Coming to have this ability brings with it certain risks and also certain possibilities of satisfaction in the rightness of fitting words or things into contexts. The risk is that things themselves do not guarantee the aptness of connecting them one with another in a certain way. It is possible that certain (though not all) of the connections one makes will be repudiated or found opaque by others, especially when the concepts under which connections are made are abstract and "philosophical." (How can you call that love or respect or fairness or meaningful or syntactically organized or convincing?) But then it is also possible to feel satisfaction in the aspects of things that one notices and in the genuineness of the connections that are thus seen or heard. It is possible for a noticing of an aspect to take the form of an *exclamation* (*PI* 197b), involving a kind of immediate "Aha!" experience in seeing something as something.

  In the exercise of this ability, there will always be *some* possibilities both of novel noticings (jokes? metaphors? invitations of intimacies?), and of noticings that are felt to be wayward or incoherent, by others or by oneself upon reflection (failed jokes? failed metaphors? failed invitations?). Distinct success is possible. One can see conceptually what is there to be seen. But the exercise of the abilities to see conceptually and to make connections between experiences (words, notes, faces, objects) always remains at the edges loosely bounded, at the edges quite unlike the ability to grasp "internal relations" between words and concepts that are "fixed." And the possibility of (further, other) action at the edges always surrounds action in noticing as such. ("A *multitude* of familiar paths lead off from these words in *every* direction.") Some may be blind to the aspects of things that others see, may be blind to the aspects of things that I see.

---

[24] See Robert B. Pippin's development of this distinction in his "Hegel's Ethical Rationalism" in Pippin, *Idealism as Modernism* (Cambridge: Cambridge University Press, 1997), 425.

Aspect-seeing centrally involves doing something: mastering a technique and acting according to it (or extending it), as a result of "taking to" joint attentional interactions. In so describing aspect-seeing, and in casting it as lying at the heart of discursive consciousness, Wittgenstein is defending both the priority of practice over theoretical representation and the irreducibility of agency to material processes. The ability actively and agentively to see one thing as another develops as one "takes to" a going practice. It is not and cannot be the result of material processes alone, though it is "built on top of" sensory-motor awareness that includes genuine "world-intake." Neither conceptual practice nor anyone's actively "taking to it" can be reduced to independent and self-subsistent material or mental processes.

Hence Wittgenstein's treatment of aspect-seeing offers us a way of thinking about human discursive consciousness that is neither mentalist, nor materialist, nor social constructivist, nor any kind of explanation. It is rather an elucidatory redescription of what we do when we employ concepts within acts of seeing. In developing this redescription, which includes attention to the roles of agency and interaction with other persons, Wittgenstein places the idea of a person as an agent among agents – with all the anxieties, wishes, fears, desires, moods, and possibilities of felt satisfaction that come with coming to be an explicit participant in conceptual practice – at the center of thinking about discursive consciousness. Wittgenstein's elucidatory redescription will not be to everyone's liking. It is, again, *not* a material explanation of how discursive consciousness arises in and through natural processes alone. It is rather, one might say, an invitation to see human mindedness, discursive consciousness, as *like this*: to notice *its* aspects. This invitation is "grounded" in a survey of the phenomena of discursiveness. It does not have the status of a command, grounded in pure rational-intellectual access to things in themselves, to see a discovered material or mental "essence." This invitational, elucidatory redescription of discursive consciousness is apt to regard itself as "one of the heirs of the subject that used to be called 'philosophy'" (*BB* 28) – an intimate offering to us of a way of looking at ourselves.

III ASPECTS AND LANGUAGE

9

The Philosophical Significance
of Meaning-Blindness

Edward Minar

1. PLACING *PHILOSOPHICAL INVESTIGATIONS* PART II, SECTION 11 IN CONTEXT

We need to realize that what presents itself to us as the first expression of a difficulty, or of its solution, may as yet not be correctly expressed at all. Just as one who has a just censure of a picture to make will often at first offer the censure where it does not belong, and an *investigation* is needed in order to find the right point of attack for the critic. (*OC* §37)

Wittgenstein's philosophical criticism, he suggests here, calls out a sensitivity to language comparable to the aesthetic sensibilities of the art critic. "It is so difficult to find the *beginning*" (*OC* §471). The sources of this difficulty, Wittgenstein holds, lie in philosophical blindness to the very sensitivity that his way of philosophizing elicits. Directing us in how to follow the path of his writing, he advises that "we do not *command a clear view* of the use of our words"; to do so, we need a "perspicuous representation" which "produces just that understanding which consists in 'seeing connections'." "The concept of a perspicuous representation," he adds, indicates "the way we look at things" (*PI* §122). In beginning at the beginning, we must be prepared to acknowledge that the words with which we are inclined to enter philosophy may obscure the nature of our "real need" (*PI* §108), and to alter our ways of thinking about and of expressing our philosophical confusions. "A philosophical problem has the form: 'I don't know my way about'" (*PI* §123). Understanding Wittgenstein's instruction, and engaging in the task of reorienting ourselves, will involve openness to aspects of language bracketed when we treat it as akin to a calculus of rules (or ask what must be added to such a calculus to conjure life into it). Much of the work of Wittgenstein's writing involves searching for words in which we can render our confusions intelligible. Our words thus freed, we overcome the prospect that, absent a certain philosophical grounding for our uses of words, we will be left voiceless. We might say that reading Wittgenstein is meant to lead us toward an acknowledgment of our "attachment to ... words" (*PI* 218g).

In this chapter, I explore how Wittgenstein's investigations of aspect-seeing and related topics in Part II, Section 11 of *Philosophical Investigations* contribute to our understanding of his views on the nature of philosophical conflicts and confusions, of his diagnosis of our "tendency to sublime the logic of our language" (*PI* §38), and of his own critical methods. In this long discussion, Wittgenstein moves from the apparent paradoxicality of aspect-shifting to the "raggedness" of the concept of seeing, to our relation to pictures, to experiencing the meanings of words (and the failure to do so, "meaning-blindness"), to the role of agreement in various language-games, to our capacity to read others and to let ourselves be read by them. Neither the dialectical structure (if any) of this sequence of topics nor the remarkable extent of his attention to the concept of aspect-seeing, receives much explanation. Aspect-seeing, Wittgenstein implies, is internal to our relation to pictures (*PI* 214a). Attention to the dawning of aspects brings out differences in the "objects" of sight (*PI* 193a) and shows that the concept of seeing is variegated and "tangled" (*PI* 200a). Under the spell of a too-simple conception of perception as objects impressing themselves on a passive medium, "we find certain things about seeing puzzling, because we do not find the whole business of seeing puzzling enough" (*PI* 212f). How the confusions about perception under scrutiny here relate to Wittgenstein's overarching purposes remains, however, largely unsaid.

Part of what is at stake is how philosophy occludes our vision of our uses of words. In the dawning of an aspect, after all, one perceives "likenesses" (*PI* 193a) and "internal relations" (*PI* 212a), which have in a sense been hidden not by obstacles in the scene itself, but by barriers in us, by our failure to "see connections" (*PI* §122). Aspect-dawning is (at least) a metaphor for the kind of understanding a perspicuous

representation of our uses of words is to produce. In my view, *PI* II.xi
prepares and refines an approach to the question, "Why does philosophy resist recognizing the ground that lies before us as the ground?"[1]
It deepens Wittgenstein's efforts to expose the reasons philosophy is
anxious about our ability to make sense of ourselves and the world.
This anxiety stems from the fact that intelligibility appears to rest
on nothing deeper than our agreements in judgment (*PI* §242) – a
"basis" which appears, at least from within the pictures of mind and
meaning that Wittgenstein is trying to uproot, to rely on our all-too-
human capacities for imagining and seeing connections.

Most critical discussion of *PI* II.xi has focused on the early
parts of the section, where seeing-as is the central concern.[2] Here
Wittgenstein is mostly occupied with undoing the apparent paradoxicality involved in the phenomenon of aspect-shifting, where I
see that the "object" of sight has remained the same, and yet want to
say that it is seen differently (*PI* 193c). His treatments undoubtedly
add a nail to the coffin of a picture of experience which supports
the idea of private impressions or sense-data serving as the foundations of knowledge and meaning. They thus comprise an important
addition to the Part I criticism of the intelligibility of the notion of
a private language: We come to realize that the fantasy of the mind
as populated with private objects goes with a distorted philosophical
view of the role of visual experience.[3] This leaves unclear, however,
to what particular and hitherto unexplored aspects of the picture of
mind under scrutiny in Part I of the *Investigations* this line of thought
responds. Further, focusing on the differences between objects
of sight does not provide a specific understanding of the relation
between the early pages of *PI* II.xi and Wittgenstein's emerging concern with aspect-blindness, experiencing the meaning of a word, and
the role of agreement in our language-games. What (if anything)
unifies this section as a whole?

---

[1] On not seeing the ground before us as the ground, see *RFM* VI, §31.
[2] A notable exception is the writing of Stephen Mulhall. See *On Being in the
World: Wittgenstein and Heidegger on Seeing Aspects* (London: Routledge, 1990),
Chapters 1–3, and *Inheritance and Originality: Wittgenstein, Heidegger, Kierkegaard*
(Oxford: Oxford University Press, 2001), 153–82.
[3] A good account of this aspect of the dialectic of *PI* II.xi can be found in Marie
McGinn, *Wittgenstein and the Philosophical Investigations* (London: Routledge, 1997),
Chapter 6 (see, e.g., 202).

An important clue occurs near the middle of the section. In the course of examining the role of images in the perception of aspects, Wittgenstein points out that seeing aspects requires a capacity for imagination – for example, for relating the object seen to other objects not currently in view. He then turns to the question of whether there could be aspect-blind human beings, people "lacking in the capacity to see something *as something*" (*PI* 213f), "blind," for example, "to the *expression* of a face" (*PI* 210a). Remarking that "aspect-blindness will be *akin* to the lack of a 'musical ear'" (*PI* 214c), sensing some important parallels with respect to the involvement of imagination, he continues: "The importance of this concept lies in the connection between the concepts of 'seeing an aspect' and 'experiencing the meaning of a word'. For we want to ask 'What would you be missing if you did not *experience* the meaning of a word?'" (*PI* 214d). One way, then, of advancing with the question of Wittgenstein's preoccupation with seeing-as is to look at the philosophical significance of the possibility of *meaning*-blindness. The meaning-blind person might not have the experience of an ambiguous word like "bank," "March," or "till" taking on one meaning rather than another. He or she would not "feel that a word lost its meaning and became a mere sound if it was repeated ten times over" (*PI* 214d). Similarly, the meaning-blind would not make sense of the idea of a name fitting a character or a face (Cf. *PI* 215f). What is the importance of these possibilities? One might think that the phenomena absent in the imagined cases, familiar though they may be in the normal course of things, are incidental to our ways of dealing with words.

Wittgenstein seems to agree, but does not think this is the end of the matter. He writes:

When I supposed the case of a "meaning-blind" man, this was because the experience of meaning seems to have no importance in the *use* of language. And so because it looks as if the meaning-blind could not lose much. But it conflicts with this, that we sometimes say that some word in a communication meant one thing to us until we saw that it meant something else. First, however, we don't feel in this case that the experience of the meaning took place while we *were hearing the word*. Secondly, here one might speak of an experience rather of the sense of the sentence, than of the meaning of a word. (*RPP* I §202)

Of course we should not be led by experiences of meaning into thinking that some inner item accompanying the use of a word is needed to lend it meaning. Nevertheless, our inclination to speak of our knowledge of meaning in perceptual terms is not accidental; and it becomes a live question whether our capacities for experiencing the meanings of words indicate something deep in our relation to language. The stakes begin to seem high:

> The familiar physiognomy of a word, the feeling that it has taken up its meaning into itself, that it is an actual likeness of its meaning—there could be human beings to whom all this was alien. (They would not have an attachment to their words.)—And how are these feelings manifested among us?—By the way we choose and value words. (*PI* 218g)

Would the meaning-blind person be capable of carrying on a life in language?[4] To what extent would that life be consonant with, even indistinguishable from, our own? And how do the answers contribute systematically to Wittgenstein's engagement in philosophy as "a battle against the bewitchment of our intelligence by means of language" (*PI* §109)?

2. RHEES ON THE SIGNIFICANCE OF ASPECT-SEEING

Some useful starting points are to be found in the writings of Wittgenstein's student Rush Rhees, in particular his preface to the *Blue and Brown Books* and the chapter entitled " 'Seeing' and 'Thinking' " in his notes on *On Certainty*. In the 1958 preface, Rhees is specifically concerned with how *Philosophical Investigations* represents an advance in Wittgenstein's understanding of the nature of philosophical problems over the "middle period" *Blue and Brown Books*. He holds that "the discussions of 'seeing something as something'" are concerned with "the principal theme of the *Investigations*," which is "the relation between language and logic" (and in particular the tendency – wellspring of philosophical confusion – to think that uncovering the underlying logic of language shows what makes language possible). Also, "Wittgenstein in the *Investigations* is making these discussions into an exposition of the philosophical difficulties, in a way that he has not done in the Brown

---

4 The importance of locating linguistic activities in the textures of our lives is a central theme in the writings of Rush Rhees; see Rhees, *Wittgenstein and the Possibility of Discourse* (Cambridge: Cambridge University Press, 1998). See also Cora Diamond, "Rules: Looking in the Right Place," in *Wittgenstein: Attention to Particulars*, ed. D. Z. Phillips and Peter Winch (London: Macmillan, 1989).

Book" (*BB* xiv). Rhees's notes on "'Seeing' and 'Thinking'," dating from 1970, are meant to "show that Wittgenstein's discussion of 'seeing different aspects' is part of his discussion of language and understanding," in particular that *PI* II.xi contributes to Wittgenstein's campaign against the idea of propositions as fixed entities made up of "ultimate meanings or constituents," there to be unearthed by analysis.[5]

According to Rhees's "'Seeing' and 'Thinking'," by calling attention to aspect-seeing, itself a variegated notion, *PI* II.xi brings out the "raggedness" (*PI* 200a) of the concept of seeing and the limitations of the empiricist tendency to explain "objects of sight" in terms of sense-data, private objects, or other ostensibly raw "thises." "If the idea of 'seeing' is not as unitary or simple as analysis in terms or sense-data suggests – if the concept of seeing itself stands in need of conceptual analysis – it does not have the unquestioned character that seems to qualify it as the basis for all meaning."[6] If meaning lay in verifiability by the "given," say, then analysis would show precisely what the meaning of a proposition is and guarantee its availability. By bringing out that the concept of seeing is indeed "tangled" and "in need of conceptual analysis," Wittgenstein's investigation dislodges the specific ideas that only inner objects of acquaintance can really be referred to and that analysis will show what we "really mean" on that level. Moreover, it throws into high relief questions about the motivations behind a picture of meaning that would demand the kind of sharpness of meaning that a sense-data–based analysis was supposed to reveal. By calling attention to aspect-seeing and thus debunking a quite natural conception of the fundamental level of analysis, *PI* II.xi contributes to Wittgenstein's project of exposing our tendency to "sublime the logic of our language" (*PI* §38).

In the preface to the *Blue and Brown Books*, Rhees tries to show how the investigation contributes to the diagnosis of this tendency. The reading of Wittgenstein's progress that unfolds in Rhees's preface to the *Blue and Brown Books* has two main strands. First, while middle Wittgenstein realizes that the picture of an underlying logical unity to language, into which we tap as a source of intelligibility, is a fantasy, he lacks a sufficiently deep and convincing explanation of how we are led to think of

---

[5] Rush Rhees, "'Seeing' and 'Thinking'," *Wittgenstein's On Certainty: There – Like Our Life*, ed. D. Z. Phillips (Oxford: Blackwell, 2003), 19.

[6] Ibid., 17.

language in this way (*BB* xiii, referring to *PI* §38). In the Blue Book in particular, he attributes our confusion to a scientistic "craving for generality" (*BB* 17) and not, as later, to the notion that what we mean must "satisfy requirements" of sharpness and determinacy by relating properly to a pre-existing logical structure (see *BB* xiii–xiv). Not only does the earlier critique leave unexplained the sources of our craving for generality, it does nothing to connect philosophical puzzlement specifically to language – clearly a desideratum even for middle Wittgenstein.

Rhees's second point directs us where to look for a more particular and satisfying diagnosis and for the reasons behind our dissatisfaction with the earlier diagnosis. Middle and late, Wittgenstein holds that meaning lies in use.[7] His comparisons between using words and making moves in a game are supposed to pull us away from looking inward, to mental accompaniments of our uses of words, for the source of words' meanings.[8] Rhees is alive to the possibility that this emphasis on investigating use will be subject to what amounts to a behaviorist misinterpretation, on which use by itself would amount to nothing more than mere patterns of acting and reacting. This misunderstanding is particularly prone to arise when, as in the Blue Book, language-games have been compared with different "notations," and when understanding and speaking have apparently been conflated with "operating with signs": " 'You make it look just like operating a mechanism'," someone might object. " 'And if that is all there is to it—just the mechanism—then it is not a language' " (*BB* xv). We now want to ask what we need to add to make the mechanism a language, or perhaps we acquiesce in the behaviorist reduction of our activities to patterned noise-makings and the like. Neither alternative is promising.

Perhaps it should be enough to turn us away from this impasse to say with Wittgenstein that "to imagine a language is to imagine a form of life" (*PI* §19). As Rhees is quick to remind us, signs get their meaning in "intercourse with other people" (*BB* xv) and, therefore, neither from mere regularities in behavioral response, nor from some inner ingredient added to such patterns. One still might worry, however,

---

[7] See, for example, *BB* 5: "The mistake we are liable to make could be expressed thus: We are looking for the use of a sign, but we look for it as though it were an object *co-existing* with the sign"; see also *PI* §43, §189, 176f.

[8] See, for example, *PI* 175–76 and 181b–c.

about whether our interpersonal dealings have been conceived in a way that leaves them "too mechanical." And this leads us to our problem: "The objection is that someone might ... make the signs correctly in the 'game' with other people and get along all right, even if he were 'meaning-blind'." The meaning-blind person, we are to imagine, "could 'react with words' to the sentences and other utterances he encountered, and to situations too, and react correctly." So appeal to shared forms of life and so on doesn't alleviate matters. Rhees asks: "Can we *not* imagine that," i.e., the meaning-blind person getting along all right? He thinks that "Wittgenstein was not sure" (*BB* xv). Yet the question *seems* to demand an answer, and there are considerations that speak to both sides. Certainly Wittgenstein himself has qualms about the capacities of the meaning-blind. We feel a strong pull toward the intuition that the meaning-blind person is missing something, that he or she makes "a less lively impression than we do, behaving more 'like an automaton'" (*RPP* I §198), that he or she is "as it were sleep-walking" (*RPP* I §178). On the other hand, we decide against the meaning-blind with some hesitation, lest we fall prey to the dangers of identifying some particular "inner" experience as essential to the meaning of a word in the face of Wittgenstein's well-advised warnings against doing so.

Here, then, is where we are: If, on Wittgenstein's view, the meaning-blind person's understanding of the language just *is* ours, then that view seems to deaden our lives in language. Wittgenstein is well aware of this risk. If, on the other hand, the understanding of the meaning-blind person does differ from ours, we may be inclined to withhold the honorific "meaningful" or even "genuinely linguistic" from his actions with words. As Rhees puts it, it will be "as though understanding were something outside the signs; and as though to be a language it needs something that does not appear in the system of signs themselves" (*BB* xv). It may well seem that we are going to have to conjure up some special experiences or thoughts or inner somethings of some kind to say how and why the meaning-blind would be different. And *that* will seem to conflict with the idea that meaning is use. No wonder, then, that we are not sure about how even to look for an unequivocal answer to the questions, "If a man were 'meaning-blind', would that make any difference to his use of language? Or does the perception of meaning fall outside the use of language?" (*BB* xvi). Note that on Rhees's way of phrasing the latter question, the "perception," the "experience," the element that the meaning-blind person would be missing, would be separable from the rest, an ingredient which seems alternately like the vital one and like mere flavoring. This vacillation does indeed lead us to wonder whether, as Rhees says, "there is something wrong with that last question [does the perception of meaning fall outside the use of language]; something wrong about *asking* it" (*BB* xvi). If correct, Rhees's remark challenges the *point* of pressing on the question of whether we can really conceive of meaning-blindness – of the significance of such image-mongery (cf. *PI* §390).

Wittgenstein, then, delivers no direct answers to the questions we want to pose about meaning-blindness. This should not be surprising, because such questions seem to presuppose an essentialist conception of language. On such a conception, there must be an account, available independently of detailing particular lives with or without some component feature that typically accompanies our linguistic activities, as to whether this "ingredient" is genuinely necessary for full-blown language-use. In emphasizing the raggedness of the concept of seeing, *PI* II.xi challenges the applicability of the essentialist picture by uprooting an important source of its appeal – the idea that language hooks on to the world through the uniform mediation of what is given in experience. In addition, the treatment of meaning-blindness shifts the focus of criticism to something deeper, to the whole idea of definite requirements that a "system of signs" would have to satisfy to count as language. With respect to our questions about the significance of meaning-blindness, Wittgenstein would surely remind us to "*look and see*. ... Say what you choose, so long as it does not prevent you from seeing the facts. (And when you see them there is a good deal that you will not say)" (*PI* §66, §79). This advice is not mere methodological good sense. When we look and see, rather than approach the phenomena through the lenses of abstract requirements on what language must be, the need to account for our abilities to make sense in the monolithic and uniform way sought on the essentialist picture is supposed to dissolve.

This is only to sketch one broad aspect of Wittgenstein's anti-essentialism; the label is potentially misleading. For our purposes, the important thing is that Rhees's reading of the significance of *PI* II.xi brings out that Wittgenstein's systematic concern with aspect-seeing, "experiencing the meaning," and meaning-blindness does not betoken an attempt to isolate a basic or essential aspect of language; rather, it forestalls a global misunderstanding of his seminal idea that meaning lies in use. This misunderstanding is symptomatic of a deep-seated philosophical tendency to abstract from our actual linguistic dealings in the hope of discovering the grounds and limits of intelligibility. A philosophy that tries to ferret out the underlying ground of our capacity to mean *begins*, Wittgenstein suspects, with a posture of meaning-blindness. Philosophy starts with a picture of our capacity for responding to the world by putting it to words as somehow lifeless and mechanical, and then adds whatever elements (if any) are necessary to breathe life, or to secrete meaning, into the proceedings (cf. *PI* §432).

In particular, by stipulating a match in "mere response" between the meaning-blind person and us, this picture sharply delimits our alternatives: *Either* our relation to language is just like that of the constitutionally meaning-blind, *or* there is something in us that adds "real" sense, genuine intelligibility, into the mixture – an experience, an interpretation, a "private rule," in any case something that "must mean something to *me*," as Rhees puts it (*BB* xvi). On the first horn, we may still enjoy what Rhees calls "perceptions of meaning," but they would be "external to language"; the "attachment to words" manifested in "the way we choose and value words" (*PI* 218g) would be merely an incidental, parochial feature of *our* lives in language.

The picture in question would restrict the terms available for describing our uses of language from the outset, hindering our view of the phenomena of use and rendering Wittgenstein's admonition to "*look and see*" futile. Given these self-imposed restrictions, we will find nothing, no meaning, there in the use to see. (Insofar as the picture prejudges the possible approaches to the problem by taking for granted a divide between the merely external and the privately internal, it parallels a temptation in the case of seeing-as: We think that *something* internal, an "'inner picture'" [*PI* 196d], "a quite particular 'organization'" [*PI* 196b], or an interpretation, must be added to what we "really see" as the result of "the influence of the object" [*PI* 199g] to yield aspect-seeing.) Whereas if we consider how the lives that we imagine for those who suffer from various states we might call "meaning-blindness" would differ from ours, we come to realize the futility of looking *behind* the use for the "ingredient" that constitutes our linguistic dealings as meaningful. We come to this without *denying* that something crucial to these dealings is registered in the inclination to say that "meaning is a physiognomy" (*PI* §568), something we see in the use. What in our lives is blocked from view by the posture of meaning-blindness, and why are we nonetheless tempted to adopt this life-denying stance?

3. MEANING-BLINDNESS AND THE PHILOSOPHICAL AVOIDANCE OF MEANING

To give a general characterization of meaning-blindness and the com-plementary notion of "experiencing the meaning of a word" would be, at best, systematically difficult. As we have seen, aspect-seeing is related to the ability to notice similarities, as when I am struck by a likeness between two faces. Wittgenstein speaks in this connection of a "difference of category between the two 'objects' of sight" (*PI* 193a), a "this" or its properties on the one hand, and an "internal relation between … objects" (*PI* 212a) on the other. Now we *talk* of aspect-see-ing, of seeing something as something, when the possibility of aspect-shifting has been called into play. The occasions on which we *express* an experiencing of the meaning of a word (or the failure so to experi-ence) are parallel to those on which aspect-shifts are noticed or where there is an awareness of alternative ways of seeing. Both kinds of occa-sion are exceptional; those in which we express the experiencing of the meaning of a word arise for the most part when, for some reason, the word is being considered outside the ordinary contexts of its use. Although experiencing the meaning of a word thus *looks* like a rather particular and isolated phenomenon, apparently one having little directly to do, if not conflicting, with meaning considered as use (see *RPP* I §358), having such experiences is predicated on the place of the word in our language-games: they arise because the word has taken on relations to a whole field of linguistic possibilities. Again: "The familiar physiognomy of a word" – what it manifests, what we experi-ence in its use – lies in "the feeling that it has taken up its meaning into itself, that it is an actual likeness of its meaning" (*PI* 218g). *This* much experiencing of the meaning has *not* been divorced from use, in that we would not have this particular experience, characterizable in this way, unless we had a grasp on the use of the word.

What, then, is it to be meaning-blind? Particular examples of meaning-blindness appear to be, *contra* what Rhees seems to say ("Wittgenstein was not sure" [*BB* xv]), readily conceivable, if relatively limited in extent and importance. The meaning-blind person will be baffled by the request to say "till" and mean it as a verb (*PI* 214d); will not have the feeling that a word "lost its meaning and became a mere sound" on repeated utterance (*PI* 214d); will not be tempted to think that differences in spelling make small differences in pro-nunciation, thus betraying a lack of "sensitiveness" to "changes in the orthography" (*RPP* II §§571–72); will not cotton on to the idea that the name "Schubert" fits the particular composer (*PI* 215f; see *RPP* I §243, *RPP* II §246) or share in the feeling that Wittgenstein expresses in writing, "Goethe's signature intimates something Goethian to me. To that extent it is like a face" (*RPP* I §336); will not make anything of the question whether Tuesday or Wednesday is fat or lean (*PI* 216c–d). Generally speaking, these local phenomena of meaning-blindness occur when, as happens, someone fails to make sense of the question, "In which (if any) of its meanings has a word been experienced?" Familiar though experiencing the meaning may be, when someone does not "get it," we are not normally inclined to say that he or she is lacking something critical to linguistic understanding *per se*. Or so it appears if we take it to be antecedently clear what the question of whether he or she understands language has in view. If, for example, we have focused our attention on whether the person would apply words to the same items as we do, we may very well not find anything lacking in his or her performance.

In asking whether meaning-blindness is really imaginable, Rhees must be aware of all this. What he is worrying about in doubting the conceivability of meaning-blindness must, then, go beyond the local examples. After all, they betoken a mere occasional failure to "see," and neither the lack of a sense nor a mental defect. In the case of the repeated word losing its meaning, we might say that the person has been blinded to something in the word, but then the example seems to presuppose that the word begins as something already imbued with meaning and that blindness cannot be the person's normal state. What happens when we try to conceive of people who have a genu-ine incapacity, who *never* undergo the relevant experiences and never could? Wittgenstein wonders at the fact that "in all the great variety of mankind we do not meet such people as this" (*RPP* I §179). What might a more global "meaning-blindness" be thought to involve?

We need to ask what the lives of the individuals with the imagined disability would be like, how their ways would differ from ours. Here are some possible cases: (1) Wittgenstein calls attention to various processes involved in reading a poem or narrative with feeling: "The sentences have a different *ring*. I pay careful attention to my intonation. ... I can ... give a word a tone of voice which brings out the meaning of the rest, almost as if this word were a picture of the whole thing" (*PI* 214g). No doubt not everyone appreciates the nuances of expressive readings. If someone were, however, utterly unable to comprehend tones of voice – to discern a *mis*emphasis in tone, for instance – in what kinds of conversations could he or she engage? (The hearer is not necessarily missing something about the "mental state" of the speaker; see *RPP* II §247.)

(2) Wittgenstein writes of seeing an arbitrary mark as a letter of an unknown alphabet, and imagines a variety of ways in which the mark could deviate from the letter written correctly. "I can see it in various aspects according to the fiction I surround it with," he says. "And here there is a close kinship with 'experiencing the meaning of a word'" (*PI* 210c). I take it that it would not generally be said that when I read, I am seeing letters under an aspect, just as it would not generally be said that when I hear a word, I experience its meaning. Nevertheless, in reading, I go on the internal relation between the radically different marks that could count as "h"s, just as in listening I hear noticeably different sounds as utterances of "knife" or of my last name. Can we imagine reading and listening without such recognitions? In trying to do so, we envision different relations to letters and words from those we enjoy in our normal linguistic trafficking.

(3) Wittgenstein writes: "Anyone who cannot understand and learn to use the words 'to *see* the sign as an arrow'—that's whom I call 'meaning-blind'. It will make no sense to tell him 'You must try to *see* it as an arrow' and one won't be able to help him in *that* way" (*RPP* I §344). This is not to say that there will *be* no help for him; perhaps someone will be able to instruct him in how to react to the sign. But we need to fill in a story about how he would learn, and on at least some developments, it will be at best unanticipatable how far the training will take him into the general practice of going in the direction of

an arrow. It remains undetermined in what circumstances we should ascribe to him an *understanding* of the sign.

(4) Wittgenstein asks how one teaches a child, "Now take *these* things together!" and "Now *these* go together" (*PI* 208c), for example in the process of showing the child how to add and subtract. The child is taught to *see* "aspects of organization" as he becomes fluent in various ways of grouping objects. Here "it is only if someone *can do*, has learnt, is master of, such-and-such, that it makes sense to say that he has had *this* experience" (*PI* 209a), that is, has seen the relevant aspects. Wittgenstein worries that it may "sound crazy" for a particular experience (like seeing a configuration of ten objects as twice five, or one side of a triangle as the base) to depend on the "mastery of a technique." He wants to say that here "the *concept* of seeing is modified" (*PI* 208e, 209a), extended beyond its application to a *this* that happens to register in the visual field. The particular technique in question would not be learned in the way we learn it were the learner not also capable of being brought to *see*, for example, that *this* grouping of objects and *that* grouping have the same number. Being led to certain experiences and coming into the technique as we have it go hand in hand.

(5) Would a meaning-blind person have the thoughts and experiences characteristic of taking a speaker to mean something or someone in particular from the beginning of his or her speech? Typically, we can make sense of the question, "Did you know right at the beginning whom I was talking about?" even though there is nothing in our accompanying thoughts or experiences that determines whom we take the speaker's referent to be. Could the meaning-blind? Wittgenstein is inclined to say, "No": "And now if he does not understand such a question—shall we not simply judge him to be mentally defective? I mean: shall we not simply assume that his thinking is not really *clear*, or that he no longer remembers what he was thinking then?" (*RPP*I §197). Consider the case: "He heard ... that N was dead and believed that this meant his friend N; then he realizes that it is not so. At first he looks upset; then relieved" (*RPP*I §204). Wittgenstein asks of this: "What am I to say now—that the meaning-blind man is not in a position to react like that?" (*RPP*I §205). Not quite – it depends on how we develop the case. The meaning-blind person could with the requisite background and information come to disambiguate names and determine what

the speaker is saying. But he or she would have to *come to* this; he or she lacks the thought, experience, and imagination to anticipate the meaning in the way envisioned – in the lightning speed of thought Wittgenstein suggests. His or her reactions would be less fluid than ours and, as responses to the speaker, would take on a different cast or meaning. In the form of life of the meaning-blind, the relations of hearer and speaker would be radically different.

These examples call for further exploration. The questions they raise are not meant to be rhetorical. Their moral is that as we work through the phenomena of meaning-blindness, exploring the various things that a meaning-blind person would not get – that is, experience – and extending these deficits by imagining a *complete* lack of the experiences and capacities involved, what we envision becomes increasingly less familiar and less easy to absorb seamlessly into our "forms of life." Insofar as such people would not respond as we do to matters of tone and expression, Wittgenstein is inclined to emphasize their strangeness, even their "mental defectiveness":

And now the question arises whether for the same reasons it wouldn't be totally misleading to speak of "form-blindness" or "meaning-blindness" (as though one were to talk of "will-blindness", when someone behaves passively). For a blind man just is someone who does not have a *sense*. (The mental defective—e.g.—can't be compared to the blind man). (*RPP* I §189)

Certain forms of passivity show a failure to avail oneself of the possibilities in a given situation, to "own" one's will, but they do not require that the will-blind person be insensitive to some particular ingredient calling for action in that situation. Similarly, meaning-blindness is more akin to an attitude, to a lack of receptivity or responsiveness, than to the absence of a sensory modality. When we move toward the extremes of meaning-blindness, the behavior we imagine begins to seem increasingly alien and mechanical:

But it is true: with mental defectives we often feel as if they talked more automatically than we do, and if someone were what we called "meaning-blind", we should picture him as making a less lively impression than we do, behaving more "like an automaton". (One also says: "God knows what goes on in his mind", and one thinks of something ill-defined, disorderly). (*RPP* I §198)

The meaning-blind may prove incapable of modifying familiar concepts, or of improvising on novel occasions, or even of making judgments that involve projecting a word with its customary meaning into new, non-stereotypical situations, of seeing new uses as extensions of old ones. The more we read their familiarity and liveliness out of the picture, the less apparent it is what the possibilities we are trying to imagine really amount to, and the less clear it is whether we should say that they really speak language. We do not know how to arbitrate these matters. While we are tempted, Wittgenstein thinks, to account for whatever is lacking in these people by positing *something* in us which they must be missing – the senses or ideas or experiences, the whatevers, that inform our livelier and more thoughtful relation to the words we use – our questions have taken on a certain unreality.

We should be wary, that is, of drawing conclusions about the nature of language that go beyond describing how what the meaning-blind do with words differs from our sayings and doings. "For is it even certain that anyone who understands our language would be inclined to say that each word has a *face*?" (*RPP* I §323). The meaning-blind person, presumably, would not, or at least would not take this in the way we do. Wittgenstein thinks that forcing a verdict on whether he or she really understands diverts attention from "the most important thing—what general tendency in us is this inclination part of?" (*RPP* I §323). Although this "tendency to regard the word as something intimate, full of soul, is not always there," we should not therefore look at the use of the word as something "mechanical" (*RPP* I §324). The place to look for the soulfulness of the word is in its use, not in an occult something somehow superadded to it.

4. MEANING-BLINDNESS AND THE RECALCITRANT PUPIL

I turn to a further example which is not presented as directly related to experiencing the meaning of a word but in which the significance of our "agreement ... in judgments" (*PI* §242) is at stake. In *PI* §185, Wittgenstein asks us to consider a child who cannot get the hang of the rule "add two" past 1000, regardless of the examples, explanations, and cajolings we supply.

He writes 1000, 1004, 1008, 1012. We say to him: "Look what you've done!"—He doesn't understand. We say: "You were meant to add *two*: look how you began the series!"—He answers: "Yes, isn't it right? I thought that was how I was *meant* to do it."—Or suppose he pointed to the series and said: "But I went on in the same way". (*PI* §185)

What are we to say of this apparently incorrigible "+2" kid? There is something he seems unable to get. He does not pick up on the pattern, grasp the point of calling *this* step the same, appreciate the internal relations between the steps. To say that the kid is meaning-blind would be about as useful as saying that he must be wired wrong. And it would be misleading in an important respect: He need lack no particular experience, the having of which does not presuppose the mastery of the technique we are trying to teach him. Still, doesn't he fail to *see* something, the whole range of connections that give these words (not only the series of numerals, but our explanations and so on) their place in a particular practice? It is in the spirit of the practice of following rules like "+2" that we want to say he is missing something already *there*; we may be inclined to express this as "the steps are really already taken" (*PI* §219). If, as is liable to be the case, there might seem to be a certain dogmatism in this, a refusal to so much as *try* to explain in independently intelligible terms what the kid is missing, this is because the patterns and connections already there in the practice cannot be apprehended prior to one's beginning to gain a mastery of it.[9]

In the dialectic of Wittgenstein's treatment of rule-following, we are drawn to look behind the practice of following a rule for an *interpretation* that would determine how it is to be followed. Because any rule that was expressed in public terms could itself be misinterpreted, we seek that interpretation *inside*, in a "private rule" constituting what the original rule-expression *really* means. (On the picture Wittgenstein opposes, this private rule might supply the mysterious missing "ingredient" that the otherwise meaning-blind initiate into a practice would require for understanding.) This stratagem not availing, a private rule proving incapable of determining *anything* (any determinate course of action), we are in danger of oscillating between the fantastical idea that there is really nothing to meaning

---

[9] And yet this does not give a reason to think that the patterns and connections are not really there. An illuminating comparison could be made with judgments of beauty, on which see Stanley Cavell, "Aesthetic Problems in Modern Philosophy," in *Must We Mean What We Say: A Book of Essays* (Cambridge: Cambridge University Press, 1969), 88–89, especially footnote 8.

above mere verbal behavior (as on Kripke's "skeptical" interpretation of Wittgenstein on following rules),[10] and insistence on an ineffable private basis for meaning. Wittgenstein's response to this impasse is that "there is a way of grasping a rule" – and more generally, of understanding an expression – "which is *not* an *interpretation*, but which is exhibited in what we call 'obeying the rule' and 'going against it' in actual cases" (*PI* §201). This understanding, not itself contained in a further rule or interpretation, is manifested in individual *judgments*. For Wittgenstein, agreement in these judgments could be said, if anything could be said, to ground the meaningfulness of our proceedings (cf. *PI* §242). Agreement in judgment cannot be a matter of matching bare behavioral responses, because what makes judgments the same from case to case presupposes the sharing of the forms of life into which the practice of making the judgments is woven. "Not agreement in opinions but in form of life" (*PI* §241) is what agreement in judgments amounts to. Who partakes of this agreement? Those who "agree in the language they use." To agree in language *is* to share in form of life. If the circle here seems too small, it may be because we are still seeking the wrong kind of explanation. We had wanted an answer to the question of what grounds meanings that would guarantee that someone outside the relevant practices, blind to their significance, would understand. Rather than seeking such an explanation, Wittgenstein teaches us to see how the meaning, far from having to be breathed into a rule, lies in its use.

5. PHILOSOPHICAL CRITICISM AND OUR LIVES IN LANGUAGE

In "Aesthetic Problems in Modern Philosophy," Stanley Cavell compares the Wittgensteinian aspiration to "bring words back from their metaphysical to their everyday use" (*PI* §116) to aesthetic judgment, observing that "Kant's 'universal voice' is, with perhaps a slight shift of accent, what we hear recorded in the philosopher's claims about 'what we say'."[11] I end by juxtaposing a particular moment from our

---

[10] Saul Kripke, *Wittgenstein on Rules and Private Language* (Cambridge: Harvard University Press, 1982).
[11] Cavell, "Aesthetic Problems," 94.

exchange with the child who fails to get it about following the rule "+2," with some things Cavell says about what he calls the "logic" of aesthetic judgment. After the failure of our explanations and pleas to get him to go on in the right way, we shall be inclined to say to the child, "But can't you *see* ... ?" (*PI* §185, my italics) and to traverse essentially the same ground again. In the case at hand, these efforts are of "no use." Nothing we do convinces or forces the child to go on in our way. As a result we attempt to locate the problem (now, *between* us and him) in his lack of "insight" (*PI* §186). Subliming this notion, we are drawn into the emptiness of private rules, "insight" into which, it turns out, would yield no more guidance in how to go on than an arbitrary "new decision ... at every stage" (*PI* §186). The alternative is to bear in mind that failure to reach agreement with the child is a particularity of our relation to him, to recognize that the problem may lie as much in our inability to show him as in his incapacity to see. There will be other occasions on which appealing to what is there to be seen *will* result in the desired uptake. Here Wittgenstein reminds us of the extent to which agreement can be taken as a foregone conclusion – the limits of the "we" with whom we can add or otherwise converse.

Here, by way of a parallel, is Cavell on a feature he finds to be internal to the practice of making critical claims: "It is essential to making an aesthetic judgment that at some point we be prepared to say in its support: don't you *see*, don't you hear, don't you dig?"[12] What is immediately striking is that, while this support often calls on an intimacy with the audience, there is, as with the child, no guarantee that the intended audience *will* see – or even appreciate that there is something to be seen. "The best critic will know," Cavell continues, "the best points. Because if you do not see *something*, without explanation, then there is nothing further to discuss. Which does not mean that the critic has no recourse: he can start training and instructing you and preaching at you. ..."[13] Again, all of which mirrors the exchange with the child, from the temptation to think that if only one could provide more and deeper explanation or interpretation, then mutual understanding and agreement

[12] Ibid., 93, my italics.
[13] Ibid.

would be secured, to the anxiety that attends facing up to the facts
that the other may not yet reside in the same universe of discourse
and that our means (if any) for "converting" him to our way of looking at things will run the dangers of coerciveness and moralism. "At
some point, the critic will have to say: This is what I see. Reasons –
at definite points, for definite reasons, in different circumstances –
come to an end."[14]

I have claimed that the temptation to try to ground our linguistic practices in a deeper something that predetermines the limits
of the meaningful starts with what I called the posture of meaning-
blindness – with a picture of those practices that takes their surfaces
to be available to the meaning-blind – and then pursues what must
be added – something like "interpretation," hidden beneath the
surfaces – in order to constitute genuine meaning. In starting with
this picture, we blind ourselves to the lives in which different activities count as learning languages, speaking them, communicating in
them, modifying them, inventing them, etc. The need to recover language from beneath the surfaces of what we do is our projection.
We still need a diagnosis of why we are confused in this way. It represents a beginning to say, following Wittgenstein and Cavell, that
we find in our reliance on our agreements a source of anxiety about
our relations to others, and that we do what we can to avoid taking
responsibility for these agreements and relations. We might add that,
in abstracting from the weave of our lives, philosophy resists acknowledging an aesthetic dimension in language – not just that meaning
and understanding involve a particular intuitive or sensory or experiential aspect, but that the patterns, connections, and saliencies
that make up the agreement in judgment in which our understanding resides are no more (and no less) "out there" than the subjects
of aesthetic claims. Philosophy as Wittgenstein practices it proceeds
by engaging our understanding of language, our appreciation, so to
speak, of our form of life.[15] It thus opens us to the facts of our lives in

---

[14] Ibid.

[15] On how Wittgenstein's writing engages and draws on, and thus lays open, our
linguistic capacities, see Edward Minar, "Feeling at Home in Language (What
Makes Reading *Philosophical Investigations* Possible?)," *Synthese* 102 (March
1995): 413–52.

language by testing our agreements, agreements that we are power-less to identify, let alone to compel, from a perspective outside the practices of putting the phenomena themselves into words. In trying to do so, we have deprived ourselves of the sensibility that makes us capable of understanding each other in the first place.[16]

[16] Thanks to William Day and Victor Krebs for suggestions and improvements.

10

Wanting to Say Something

Aspect-Blindness and Language

William Day

Man hält mich auf der Straße oft für blind. (*RC* III §280)

INTRODUCTION

The mystery of why Wittgenstein takes an interest in the concept of aspect-seeing may be trumped only by the enigma of why he introduces the concept of aspect-blindness. After twenty pages of examining the place of aspect-seeing among our concepts of seeing and thinking, he announces that

the question now arises: Could there be human beings lacking in the capacity to see something *as something*— and what would that be like? What sort of consequences would it have?—Would this defect be comparable to color-blindness or to not having absolute pitch? – We will call it "aspect-blindness"— and will next consider what might be meant by this. (*PI* 213f)

Wittgenstein adds parenthetically that what he has in mind is specifically a "conceptual investigation." This is his preferred name in Part II for the general method of the *Investigations* that has come to be called, and that he tends to describe in Part I as, grammatical investigations (cf. *PI* §90). But the ensuing discussion of aspect-blindness, which covers no more than a page, does not follow the pattern of other grammatical investigations. Wittgenstein's interest here seems to outstrip what such an investigation can accomplish. When in other contexts he imagines human beings in some way different from us, such as the builders in *PI* §2, he does not ask, as he does of the aspect-blind, whether there could *be* such people. More than once he raises questions (will the aspect-blind be able to do such-and-such) that he says he will not try to answer. And his conclusion to the discussion – "Aspect-blindness will be *akin* to the lack of a 'musical ear'" (*PI* 214c) – is itself a simile, and so (grammatically) implies that he is able to say what it means, to find other words; but explanations are not forthcoming. There is, in short, no final word on which one can rest, at least none that offers the sort of revelatory turn of thought one finds elsewhere in the *Investigations*. Compare, for example, the epigrammatic remark near the end of Part II: "I can know what someone else is thinking, not what I am thinking. It is correct to say 'I know what you are thinking', and wrong to say 'I know what I am thinking'. (A whole cloud of philosophy condensed into a drop of grammar)" (*PI* 222b). With the concept of aspect-blindness it seems Wittgenstein wants to create rather than dissipate a cloud of philosophy.

This has often struck me as the obvious and natural way to begin thinking about Wittgenstein's discussion of aspect-blindness in the *Investigations*. Yet most commentators on these pages not only begin without such doubts but read the discussion of aspect-blindness as *conclusive* of something. It is no surprise that they do not agree on what the discussion proves, nor agree on so much as what the discussion is about.[1] Is it about the strangeness, the less-than-humanness, of the aspect-blind, or about how the aspect-blind resemble human types we know well? Is Wittgenstein's intent to explain the experience of aspect-seeing, or is he more interested in the way we normally, unremarkably see things? Is his concern at bottom what, if anything, we are doing in seeing what a picture is a picture of, or what, if anything, we are doing in meaning the words we say?

---

[1] Compare the discussions of aspect-blindness and meaning-blindness in Rush Rhees, Preface to *BB*; Joachim Schulte, *Experience and Expression: Wittgenstein's Philosophy of Psychology*, trans. Joachim Schulte (Oxford: Oxford University Press, 1993); Stephen Mulhall, *On Being in the World: Wittgenstein and Heidegger on Seeing Aspects* (London: Routledge, 1990); Paul Johnston, *Wittgenstein: Rethinking the Inner* (London: Routledge, 1993). Rhees is the only one among these for whom Wittgenstein's settled attitude towards the possibility of aspect-blindness remains in doubt.

My guiding thought in what follows is that the capacity to be struck by a change of aspect underlies the possibility of (acquiring) human language – and *so too* does aspect-blindness, not as it is suffered continually by the aspect-blind, but as it is experienced endemically by us. We would not speak as we do, nor have the interests and desires that we do, if we did not see or hear aspects of the world that others fail to see or hear, and if we did not fail to see or hear aspects of the world that others see or hear. For that reason we can neither fully imagine aspect-blindness, nor fail to find ourselves imagined, pictured, by it. And this ambivalent reaction to the possibility of aspect-blindness is, I take it, what Wittgenstein asks us to notice, as if it shed light on our condition as creatures who converse. The same conclusion is suggested from the other direction, as it were, by noticing that what we could not but assent to – what we could not see or hear differently – would not be so much as worth saying; and what is not worth saying cannot be meaningfully said. "*Theses* in philosophy," i.e., claims made in the name of philosophy to which everyone would agree (*PI* §128), are possible only in a world in which everyone is, or has become, aspect-blind. And yet philosophy's attraction to such a world – a world of perfect, mutual intelligibility – in the face of the seemingly intractable problem of meaning, is merely one manifestation of the no less endemic human failure to take an interest in one's own way of seeing or hearing things. What Wittgenstein asks of us in this instance, I take it, is not that we notice our ambivalent reaction to some particular possibility, but that we notice *simpliciter*, allow what we see or hear to strike us.

The present essay continues in three sections. In the first I make good my claim that being struck by aspects of the world underlies our ability to acquire language, implying that continual aspect-blindness is unimaginable as a human possibility. Nonetheless, as I argue in the second section, we grow to become inured to aspects of the world, and so likewise grow to overlook the extent to which our "being in the world" is internally related to our seeing, and desiring, aspects. It is in *this* way that aspect-blindness can be seen as natural to us. In the final section I consider how Wittgenstein's writing, loosely describable as a series of "reminders" (*PI* §§89, 90, 127), in fact models for the reader her forgotten desire to be struck by aspects of the world.

1. COMING TO SPEAK

We can find our way with aspect-blindness most easily if we begin by noting what aspect-blindness is not. The distinguishing characteristic of the aspect-blind is not that there are some aspects the aspect-blind will not see (e.g., the rabbit aspect of the duck-rabbit) or at least recognize (e.g., that the schematic cube represents a cube). The aspect-blind are not even said to be incapable of seeing different aspects of an object at different times: the duck-rabbit can appear to them as a duck at one time and as a rabbit at another. But they will not describe these different aspects as aspects of the same object, for they will not see them (experience them) as *of* the same object. What characterizes aspect-blindness is the failure to say or show that one has been struck by a change of aspect; it is the failure to experience an aspect *dawn*.

This suggests various consequences if we imagine the aspect-blind as a tribe, a people. (Wittgenstein's question is always about *Menschen*, human beings, more than one. His interest in the aspect-blind, as with the builders in *PI* §2, has to do in part with how they would talk to *each other*.) For a community of aspect-blind people, "seeing the same object" would always entail seeing what we would call the same aspect of the object.[2] Thus the aspect-blind would always understand themselves to agree, where we only usually agree, on the look a (given) thing presents, and a (given) thing would maintain its look. Further, for such a community, seeing what we would call a different aspect of an object would always entail seeing a different object. Thus they would always fail to see, where we only sometimes fail to see, a different aspect appearing to someone else; they could not obey the command, "Now see the figure like *this*" (cf. *PI* 213e). Since the aspect-blind would understand any disagreements over the look that an object presents as evidence that they were seeing different objects, their language-game here would be similar to ours when we speak of seeing hallucinations, dream-images, phantasms, etc. Such objects, in other words, would not exist for them.

---

[2] To be more precise: seeing the same object would entail seeing the same aspect of the object for those objects that we would say "have" more than one aspect. Otherwise the aspect-blind, like us, would just see the object. (One doesn't take the cutlery at a meal for cutlery; a fork doesn't have a fork aspect. Cf. *PI* 195b–c.)

In trying to imagine a people who never see objects differently from one another, or such that no object ever struck them differently unless the object itself changed, we should ask not only whether we can imagine a community with the concepts of "seeing" and "object" altered in this way, but whether we can imagine them as having concepts, as speaking to one another, as having things to say. Our interest in these questions lies in their relation or connection to how *we* come to speak to one another, why we should have things to say. In approaching these questions I hope to bring out the naturalness or humanness of aspect-dawning experiences by considering what in my reading is an unremarked implication of such experiences. It is in particular not to be found, to my knowledge, in Wittgenstein's later writings. But it is prepared by his interest throughout the *Investigations* in the learning of language, particularly when we pair that interest with his observation that aspect-seeing is, like imagining, subject to the will (*PI* 213e). Specifically, I want to suggest that the capacity to "see" "aspects" is a condition of our growing into language, of our coming to speak the same language as our elders, to agree "in language" and "in judgments" and "in form of life" (cf. *PI* §§241–42). Thus while I don't claim to be explicating here what Wittgenstein thought, I imagine myself to be following along one of his criss-crossing paths of thought.

It is often taken as an implication of the concept of aspect-seeing that the ability to be struck by an aspect presupposes (in some sense I am not confident in characterizing) the ability to see continuously. Thus Stephen Mulhall writes, for example: "The possibility of experiencing aspect-dawning is a function of our general attitude to pictorial symbols when an aspect-change is not in question";[3] "Any particular experience of aspect-dawning, in making us aware that we can see a given entity as a *new* kind of object, thereby highlights the fact that we are *already* regarding it as a particular kind of object."[4] The idea seems all but demanded by the "seeing *x* as *y*" schema: One cannot see a *y* (an aspect of something) without an *x* (something continuously or unambiguously *there*, something seen-as). This would mean that one can't experience the dawning of an aspect before one

---

3 Mulhall, *On Being in the World*, 31.
4 Ibid., 136.

has (continuous-seeing) concepts, before one can speak. And yet Wittgenstein is happy to present an example that suggests that we can imagine otherwise (namely, the "double-cross") (*PI* 207c).[5]

To say that aspect-dawning presupposes continuous seeing goes hand in hand with the thought, which Mulhall is not alone in giving voice to, that the experience of an aspect dawning "is a very specific and relatively rare one."[6] Insofar as Mulhall's pointing this out serves his overriding interest in minimizing the philosophical significance of aspect-dawning experiences,[7] its motivation is understandable. But it is otherwise not clear why he and others should want to *assert* it, or what their doing so should be taken to mean. "Aspect-dawning is rare" is part of the grammar of "aspect-dawning." To assert that aspect-dawning is rare seems to me redeemable, at best, by seeing it as an invitation to imagine otherwise, to carry out the conceptual investigation that complements Wittgenstein's discussion of aspect-blindness. Let us, then, imagine a people for whom aspect-dawning comes as standard equipment, a people who never simply "regard" something as something (cf. *PI* 205e–g) but for whom aspects of a thing are *continually* dawning, aware that no one else, for the most part, is seeing what they see in the way they see it. (*We* might think of this as a state of perpetual hallucination.) Various consequences for the lives of these people suggest themselves, few of which will tempt us to view their heightened sensitivity as a gift. Could they, in particular, be described as agreeing in judgments among themselves (cf. *PI* §242)? It is not clear that they could even so much as have a language, since they could not *name* things: How would someone for whom the aspects of the world are continually in flux attach a label to a thing (cf. *PI* §§15, 26)? To imagine such people simply underscores the grammar of our concept of aspect-dawning: Being struck by an aspect requires that one not be struck continually (in that respect it is like falling in love), and so it implies or anticipates an unequal balance of the familiar and the unfamiliar (in that respect it suggests a kinship to Freud's concept of the uncanny).

---

[5] "One could quite well imagine," he says, someone reporting the change of aspect of the double-cross by pointing to, say, an isolated black cross, and that this could be imagined "as a primitive reaction in a child even before it could talk" (*PI* 207f).

[6] Mulhall, *On Being in the World*, 136.

[7] Cf. ibid., 123.

But is that enough to make the grammar of aspect-dawning perspicuous? If we are willing to maintain that creatures who see *only* aspects could not manage to attach a label to a thing, and so could not form a community of speakers, we ought to consider whether the aspect-blind, given the parity in their (dis)ability, could do these things. To arrive at a place from which to consider this question, we can ask how *we* ever come to attach a label to a thing, to speak a first word. The answer will reveal that, notwithstanding the "seeing *x* as *y*" formulation, continuous seeing is not conceptually prior to aspect-seeing.

Imagine a toddler who has just learned his first few (maybe four) words, the words his parents subsequently write down in his baby book, one of which is "ball." The child reverses phonemes and it comes out "bloh" (at first his parents think he is saying "block"): not an auspicious-sounding step into language, and it may not be right to imagine it as the first step, but it is a step. Now consider the change that has taken place for this child, not only by weighing the changes you can see but by considering the change in the child *through* the concept of seeing – that is, by sketching what you imagine the child now sees. – But isn't that mistaking an empirical question for a conceptual one? Isn't it, in fact, like trying to get the result of an experiment by imagining the experiment, and then imagining the result (cf. *PI* §265)? – But as I mean the question "What does the child now see?", there is no empirical experiment to carry out, at least none that I can imagine. Nor am I forgetting Wittgenstein's warnings against the conjuring trick of imagining an inner process or state (*PI* §308). What I would *like*, admittedly, is for the child to tell me what has changed for him, beyond what I already know (namely, that he now "says" "ball") – and of course he can't tell me. But, in fact, my interest in the child's "bloh" extends no further than Wittgenstein's interest in "noticing an aspect" – that is, no further than finding "its place among the concepts of experience" (*PI* 193e). And I take it that the child's "bloh" *is* the expression of an experience, an exclamation of sorts. (I will simply assert that it is not an assertion, nor an avowal, description, or "perceptual report." Could it be a command, as the builder's "block" at *PI* §2 looks to be? I might say this later, perhaps, when the child – whom I now adopt as mine, since he is – utters it loudly and somewhat crossly, and cries if I do not "obey" him. But

at present I'm imagining a time in the child's life when he utters his
"bloh" excitedly, sometimes repeatedly, and when my repeating it or
something like it back to him – doubtless excitedly, and probably with
the ball already at hand – seems response enough.) I understand my
interest, in short, to be conceptual.

The toddler, for the first time in his brief life, says "bloh": What
else, if anything, has changed? Before he "started to talk," my saying "ball" did not elicit much of a response from him, at least none
that I could see. Now not only does he frequently say "bloh" when I
say "ball," but he uses "bloh" in ways I can make sense of, not least
when he repeats "bloh" over and over, which I understand as a kind
of delight, call it the delight of first words. His world, the world he sees
and otherwise experiences, now has a ball or balls "in" "it." But didn't
it before? Surely the first time he said "bloh" was not the first time he
saw a ball, as if as soon as he saw one he could see immediately that it
was one. Like other toddlers, he has been playing with a ball or balls
for months before he said "bloh" – reaching for them, grabbing them,
putting them in his mouth, tossing them, shrieking when I roll them
back to him, etc. On the other hand, to imagine that he was seeing
a ball all along would seem to imply that he already had the concept
"ball" and lacked only a (our) label for it. And is that any more coherent? It *is* a conception of language – one that Wittgenstein attributes
to Augustine (though he has others in mind too, including the early
Wittgenstein) and that he comes to criticize in these terms: "Augustine
describes the learning of human language as if the child came into a
strange country and did not understand the language of the country;
that is, as if it already had a language, only not this one. Or again: as
if the child could already *think*, only not yet speak. And 'think' would
here mean something like 'talk to itself'" (*PI* §32). But "talking to
oneself" has its own range of looks, assumptions, and implications,
and this child shows none of these. He does not mutter, for instance,
but babbles – and not particularly, or ever, *to* himself.

If the child's first "bloh" betokens neither the first time he sees
a ball nor the first time he gives a name to an object he has seen all
along, then what does it betoken? As I imagine it, it must betoken that
the ball or balls he has been playing with (reaching for, putting in his
mouth, etc.) and our repeated utterance of the word "ball" – which
the child now hears as *one* (sort of) utterance, and as (close to) the

same utterance *he* now makes – together have undergone a change of aspect for him. The ball he sees is not yet the ball that I and his 4-year-old sister see, which we may tell one another is round, red, shiny, the size of a grapefruit, etc. Likewise, or consequently, his "bloh" is not yet our "ball," nor would it be if the two utterances sounded identical. We become aware of this when we notice how little he can *do* with his word (for now). But I think one can describe the child, in his first tentative or delighted or contented utterances of "bloh," as "experiencing the meaning" of "ball" (cf. *PI* 214d ff.), by which I mean to say that a word's meaning begins for him necessarily as the experience of its meaning, as finding a new home in its utterance. So there is something the child can do with his word more readily than we can after all.

The experience of having an aspect dawn, or of being struck by something, or of seeing the familiar in a new light, is thus as intimately and pervasively joined to the human form of life as talking. Rather than assert, with Mulhall and others, that continuous seeing is conceptually prior to aspect-seeing, I find it more felicitous to say that continuous seeing – a taking for granted the furniture of the world – presupposes an ability (interest, desire) to be struck by aspects of the world, to find the face of the world change in answer to one's gaze.[8] – Would this mean that aspect-seeing is *conceptually* prior to continuous seeing, or simply that it is developmentally prior, an incidental fact about us, like the tails we grew in the womb? If, impressed by the "seeing *x* as *y*" schema, one insists that aspect-seeing is no more than developmentally prior, then one is probably willing to separate the fact that humans speak from the fact that humans must come to speak.[9] A willingness to separate here is not unlike the skeptic's willingness to separate the words we speak from the occasions of their use. But it is part of Wittgenstein's method of "bring[ing] words back

---

[8] No less a thinker than Rousseau in his "On the origin of languages" argued for not unrelated reasons that figurative meaning precedes the literal, that our first utterances are signs of a sudden aspectual vision. ("That is how the figurative word is born before the literal word, when our gaze is held in passionate fascination.") See *Jean-Jacques Rousseau and Johann Gottfried Herder: On the Origin of Language*, trans. John H. Moran and Alexander Gode (Chicago: University of Chicago Press, 1966), 12–13.

[9] Stanley Cavell's reading of the opening sections of the *Investigations* is to some extent an unfolding of the thought that "what language is is bound up with our ideas of what acquiring language is." See Cavell, "Notes and Afterthoughts on the Opening

from their metaphysical to their everyday use" (*PI* §116) that we ask ourselves how we come to learn, or in what contexts we are first at home with, the meaning of a given word. In extending the application of this methodological question to consider in general the contexts in which a repeated sound becomes a first word, I am proposing that the remarks on aspect-seeing continue the preoccupation with the conceptual or grammatical conditions of learning to speak evident in the opening sections of the *Investigations* (cf. *PI* §§5–7, 9–10, 26ff.). It is worth noting in this regard that Wittgenstein's initial example of "noticing an aspect" is the experience of seeing a likeness in a face – an experience whose home for us is, I think we can say, the face of the mother.[10]

To return to the condition of the aspect-blind, we should now recognize that among the consequences of aspect-blindness would be (if not the absence of language, then) the inability to grow into language, to learn to speak. Early in his remarks on aspect-blindness Wittgenstein says that he "do[es] not want to settle" the question whether the aspect-blind will be able to notice the similarity between, or the identity of, faces (*PI* 213f) – so that even the question of recognition, as of a mother's face, is left up in the air. This is understandable, since to settle such a question seems more like deciding the aspect-blind's fate than investigating the concept of their possibility. Wittgenstein's ambivalence reminds us that when we examine a concept by inventing forms of life we may not be able to say which (other) facts of nature will be altered or implicated. Yet he adds reassuringly that the aspect-blind "ought to be able to execute such orders as 'Bring me something that looks like *this*'." This too is understandable, since the aspect-blind have not been conceived as blind to what a thing unambiguously is. But another reason Wittgenstein may want to say this is because executing the order, "Bring me something like this," is enough like what the builder's assistant in *PI* §2 is said to be able to do (e.g., when the builder calls out "Block" or "Slab"). And the

---

of Wittgenstein's *Investigations,*" *Philosophical Passages: Wittgenstein, Emerson, Austin, Derrida,* The Bucknell Lectures in Literary Theory, vol. 12 (Oxford: Blackwell, 1995), 144 ff.

[10] Wittgenstein speaks initially of the likeness between two *different* faces, but he soon mentions, in addition, the experience of seeing a familiar face in the one before me (*PI* 193c) – that is, of seeing someone's face as hers, recognizing her. (Cf. *PI* 197g.)

aspect-blind have not been conceived at the outset as *more* primitive and dull than the builder and his assistant.

But mightn't the aspect-blind be *as* primitive? A curious feature of the language-game of *PI* §2, and a feature typically unremarked, is that the builder's assistant does not speak.[11] He could, conceivably, be simply a trained animal, his execution of the builder's orders a kind of circus act. It needn't be an unattractive life: While we may still picture his master, the builder with his four words, as moving about sluggishly or half-wittedly,[12] the builder's assistant may look to us as suddenly carefree in his dumb, dog-like obedience. Could he be, in fact, better off than his master? Lacking language, the builder's assistant simply lacks all human possibilities; the builder, on the other hand, looks to have had human possibilities somehow foreclosed, stopped short. Which of these we find to better approximate the condition of the aspect-blind will depend on whether we picture the aspect-blind as already having a language they could not have learned or acquired (Augustine's picture, the philosopher's ideal) or as simply lacking the prospect of language altogether. Either way, I am suggesting, aspect-blindness appears unimaginable (for now) as a (full, real) possibility for us, creatures who *come to* language.

2. DESIRING ASPECTS

In countering Augustine's description of language acquisition as "grasping" the connection between word and thing, or as "gradually learning to understand" that connection (cf. *PI* §1), the picture according to which acquiring a first word is undergoing a change of aspect describable as experiencing its meaning suggests that learning to talk is

---

[11] When in *The Brown Book* Wittgenstein extends the builder's language along the same lines as he will at *PI* §8 – most notably, by introducing numerals that the assistant must "know by heart" – he says explicitly, "Here *both* the parties use the language by speaking the words" (*BB* 79; my emphasis).

[12] As suggested by Rhees, "Wittgenstein's Builders," in *Discussions of Wittgenstein* (Bristol: Thoemmes Press, 1970), 83; Warren Goldfarb, "I Want You to Bring Me a Slab: Remarks on the Opening Sections of the *Philosophical Investigations*," *Synthese* 56 (1983): 269–70; Cavell, "Declining Decline: Wittgenstein as a Philosopher of Culture," *This New Yet Unapproachable America: Lectures after Emerson after Wittgenstein* (Albuquerque, N.M.: Living Batch Press, 1989), 62–64; and Cavell, "Notes and Afterthoughts," 145–47.

conceptually connected to one's (the child's) taking an interest in one's experience, particularly in one's experience of words themselves.[13] I don't mean here an interest in the utility of words, their being more serviceable for expressing a desire or a state of mind than crying or cooing or thrashing about, as Augustine notes. Rather, I have in mind an interest in whatever changes the dawning of words brings about in the child's desires – changes that themselves must be desired by the child if he is to continue to grow into language. If a child can speak, not only is it safe to say with Rush Rhees that "he has got something to tell you,"[14] but we can assume that he desires what the dawning of words do: He desires the world that his embryonic utterances inevitably constitute. Absent that desire, there is literally nothing he can say.

If "to desire the world that one's utterances inevitably constitute" is understood seriously, with one's full imagination, the question has to arise: Where does this desire in us go? It is a question that leads to unsettled regions of philosophy, where desire tends to arrive with excessive baggage. The question is not about the loss of the child's babbling instinct or about some adult's recovered delight in words, but about the loss of the babbling's immediate offspring, the delight's primogenitor, next to which the adult's delight bears the tint of nostalgia. It is a question about the naturalness for humans, or for a certain stage of the human, to become inured to the aspects of the world, as well as about our constitutional forgetfulness of this. Said otherwise, my question is about our constitutional failure to register that our relation to the world (every feature of that relation, I might say) rests on our desiring aspects (of it). (How this claim sits alongside Stanley Cavell's signature claim that our relation to the world is not one of knowing but of something like accepting or acknowledging[15] will have to await another occasion.) If the experience of having an

[13] "Taking an interest in one's experience" is Cavell's locution; see Cavell, *Pursuits of Happiness: The Hollywood Comedy of Remarriage* (Cambridge: Harvard University Press, 1981), 12. The importance of this notion for an understanding of Emerson and Thoreau is a central element of Cavell's reading of them and of the tradition of moral perfectionism that he finds exemplified by their writing. See in this regard my "Knowing as Instancing: Jazz Improvisation and Moral Perfectionism," *The Journal of Aesthetics and Art Criticism* 58 (Spring 2000): 99–111.

[14] Rhees, "Wittgenstein's Builders," 80.

[15] Cf. Cavell, "The Avoidance of Love: A Reading of *King Lear*," in *Must We Mean What We Say? A Book of Essays* (Cambridge: Cambridge University Press, 1969), 324;

aspect dawn is as pervasively joined to the human form of life as
talking, then why does the child, in growing into language and so
coming to continuously-see the furniture of the world – not only its
objects but its human attitudes, expressions, exchanges, occupations,
preoccupations, ... – why does the child grow out of the interest or
desire to be struck by aspects of the world?

Nietzsche, the fearless philosopher *par excellence* at dissecting
human desire, seems to dispose of this question early in his career
when he says, in effect, that losing interest in our experience is the
price we pay for language:

Every concept comes into being by making equivalent that which is non-
equivalent. Just as it is certain that no leaf is ever exactly the same as any
other leaf, it is equally certain that the concept "leaf" is formed by dropping
those individual differences arbitrarily, by forgetting those features which
differentiate one thing from another. ... Now, it is true that human beings
forget that this is how things are; thus they lie unconsciously in the way we
have described, and in accordance with centuries-old habits – and precisely
because of this unconsciousness, precisely because of this forgetting, they arrive
at the feeling of truth. ... As creatures of *reason*, human beings now make
their actions subject to the rule of abstractions; they no longer tolerate being
swept away by sudden impressions and sensuous perceptions; they now generalize all these impressions first, turning them into cooler, less colorful
concepts in order to harness the vehicle of their lives and actions to them.
Everything which distinguishes human beings from animals depends on this
ability to sublimate sensuous metaphors into a schema, in other words, to
dissolve an image into a concept.[16]

Nietzsche cannot quite mean what this says, or have in mind some
alternative deal that could be struck, since it is literally inconceivable
what would be gained by experience, or left of it, if we lost the concept of it. But his suggestion that acquiring concepts (and what he
calls the drive to truth) is the beginning of the end of our desire for
what strikes us, calls to mind a feature of *PI* II.xi that I take to be no
accident, *viz.*, that the bulk of Wittgenstein's examples of noticing an

The Claim of Reason: Wittgenstein, Skepticism, Morality, and Tragedy (Oxford: Oxford
University Press, 1979), 241.

[16] Friedrich Nietzsche, "On Truth and Lying in a Non-Moral Sense," *The Birth of Tragedy
and Other Writings*, ed. Raymond Geuss and Ronald Speirs (Cambridge: Cambridge
University Press, 1999), 145–46.

aspect – aside from those few drawn from experiences of art, which I address briefly at the end of this essay – are objects and activities of childhood. There are puzzle-pictures, flipped figures, games of "What do you see?", games of make-believe in which, for example, a chest is a house, and lessons in rudimentary arithmetic ("Now take *these* things together!" *PI* 208c). There are also, to be sure, games that children of a certain age will not be able to play – for example, obeying the command to see *this* angle of a triangle as its apex or *this* segment as its base – games for which "the substratum ... is the mastery of a technique" (*PI* 208e). Indeed, with some responses to art – Wittgenstein mentions finding certain themes of Brahms to be extremely Kellerian while being unable to say why they should strike him this way (cf. *LC* 32) – the substratum might rather be called a culture (cf. *LC* 8–11), or "the whole field of our language-games" (*Z* §175; cf. *CV* 51e–52a and *RPP* I §433). I might characterize the lesson of these cases of aspect-seeing by saying: our very conception of our experience, and so the sort of striking something that this or that moment can trigger, is itself transformed by our growing into language, transformed every bit as much as our concept of "ball" or "block" (or "bank" or "Boston" or "baby") is transformed.

But despite the ways in which our grown-up responses to art, for example, answer to or echo our interest or desire to be struck by aspects of the world, the fact I mean to observe is that we inevitably harden to, or become inured to, that interest. The child who, in growing into language, is learning what to do with such experiences as lay behind his first words, learns equally well to forget such experiences. Perhaps it should be said (taking our cue from Nietzsche's use of "unconsciously") that he learns to repress them. After he takes his first steps into language and can say his first several dozen words, there may be no encouragement from those around him for what merely strikes *him*, what then and there may be striking to him alone. When he pronounces one of his words in a non-ordinary context (says "bloh" when I put an ice cube in his hands), I may "correct" him – encourage him to say "ice cube" or "cube" or "cold" – even as I find his "error" understandable, even metaphorically suggestive. One might imagine the child finding this new response to his utterance (my "correcting" him) itself striking. But one cannot say beforehand or in general whether the child will experience these encounters over time as what we would call encouragement (to our ways of seeing the world) or as admonishment (for not yet having mastered our ways).

I don't mean to stress in these considerations the element of maliciousness (of society, the legislators of language, toward the fledgling or unconventional language-speaker) that seems to reverberate in the young Nietzsche.[17] Perhaps the elders in Augustine's picture can be seen as malicious, indoctrinating him into "the stormy fellowship of human life."[18] Perhaps Nietzsche has them in mind, or someone like them. And certainly, if the child's loss of interest or desire in seeing aspects *is* an instance of repression, it will be tied to something like an experience of malice. (And perhaps ignorance and cluelessness about a child's desires are expressions of malice.) In any event – and I take this to be Nietzsche's point as well – the loss of interest in the world's aspects is no less a part of our natural history than having that interest. What is not a (necessary) part of that natural history – and what makes Nietzsche's observation Nietzschean – is the appreciation that something has been lost.

If the cost of our growing into language is the dissipation of our originary desire for aspects, of our interest in what may here and now strike us alone, then of course this describes our relation to our words no less than to the world. Something like evidence for this can be gleaned from our initial disorientation on reading Wittgenstein's brief discussion (*PI* 216c–g) of the secondary sense of a word: "Given the two ideas 'fat' and 'lean', would you be rather inclined to say that Wednesday was fat and Tuesday lean, or *vice versa*? (I incline decisively towards the former)" (*PI* 216c). Here is a glimpse of our pre- or extra-grammatical life with words.[19] It is almost as if the maturing human, in departing that life, comes to adopt the philosopher's static view of the connection between words and their systematic implications, and begins to imagine that the field of our words has in every instance and in each utterance long since been surveyed. But then, from the standpoint of our loss of interest in our experience, aspect-blindness will seem to us not unimaginable as a human possibility at all, but quite familiar, a kind of fixed literal-mindedness in taking in

[17] Cf. ibid., 143.
[18] Augustine, *Confessions* (trans. Albert C. Outler) 1.8.
[19] Cf. Cavell, *The Claim of Reason*, 355.

the world. We will not picture the aspect-blind as hesitant, stumbling, stiff automata,[20] but as visibly indistinguishable from us: people we think we have met, or been.[21] "Anomalies of *this* kind are easy for us to imagine" (*PI* 214b) because people who have "an altogether different relationship to pictures from ours" (*PI* 214a) could be, in effect, any one of us at any given time.

As a consequence, and in contradistinction to my conclusion from the last section, I want to suggest that our response to the possibility of aspect-blindness is in fact ambivalent: Aspect-blindness is neither (fully, really) imaginable to us nor (fully, really) foreign to us. This may reflect our ambivalent conception of ourselves as both imaginative and unimaginative, both spirit and flesh. Insofar as we see aspect-blindness as familiar, we thus imagine ourselves, or recognize ourselves, as unimaginative, the all-too-human creatures we see in Nietzsche's mirror. The suggestion here is not that aspect-seeing is *commensurate* with imagining: unlike imagining, aspect-seeing works with a perception. Still, the lesson that emerges from Wittgenstein's discussion of the differences among kinds of aspects (*PI* 207–8) is that seeing a change in aspect requires, at a minimum, that one can imagine something (see especially *PI* 207b, 207h, and *RPP* II §508).

But an equally telling connection between aspect-seeing and imagining for our present purpose is that, as noted earlier, both are subject to the will (*PI* 213e). It follows that our intermittent occasions of finding the world striking are the natural expression of our imagination in the world, or the projection of our imagination on the world: a kind of epitome of our freedom. Should we then notice that Wittgenstein places this observation (the feature shared by imagining and aspect-seeing of being subject to the will) in the *Investigations* immediately before introducing the concept of aspect-blindness (with the words "The question *now* arises: Could there be human beings lacking the capacity to see something *as something* ...", first emphasis mine), as if his interest in the concept of aspect-blindness were prompted by an interest in willing, or rather in our propensity to relinquish our wills, to make ourselves blind to the aspects of

---

[20] Cf. Mulhall, *On Being in the World*, 89.
[21] This is the view Joachim Schulte adopts in explicating Wittgenstein's related notion of meaning-blindness. See Schulte, *Experience and Expression*, 68–70.

things? If we are meant to notice this, then Wittgenstein's apparent reticence to say something conclusive over the following two pages about the possibility of the aspect-blind opens the possibility that this conceptual investigation is meant to lead (gently, not against our will) to considerations of matters of the will. In what remains I will sketch a way of reading the later Wittgenstein that attends to his interest in the connection between his philosophical project and matters of the will.

3. WRITING AND WILLING

I have suggested that Wittgenstein's interest in the concept of aspect-blindness develops out of a preoccupation (found in Part I of the *Investigations*) with our attraction to the familiar philosophical ideal of perfect, mutual intelligibility that is the prize we would gain with the "solution" to the problem of meaning. The image of a community of aspect-blind people answers perfectly to that impulse in philosophy which stipulates the elimination of my part in what I see, my responsiveness to it and my responsibility for it (call this philosophy's antipathy toward aesthetics) – an impulse that asks us finally to relinquish our will. In wanting now to claim that, for the later Wittgenstein, a task of philosophy is to model in one's writing an interest in one's experience, I am guided by three or four comments he makes on the role of the will in that peculiar use of language called philosophical writing. I will set these comments down here, beginning with a summary statement by one of Wittgenstein's biographers:

He often remarked that the problem of writing good philosophy and of thinking well about philosophical problems was one of the will more than of the intellect – the will to resist the temptation to misunderstand, the will to resist superficiality.[22]

Lying to oneself about oneself, deceiving yourself about the pretense in your own state of will, must have a harmful influence on [one's] style; for the result will be that you cannot tell what is genuine in the style and what is false. This may explain the falsity of Mahler's style; and it is the same danger that I run myself.

[22] Ray Monk, *Ludwig Wittgenstein: The Duty of Genius* (New York: Free Press, 1990), 366.

If I perform to myself [think that I'm writing as such a man would], then it's this that the style expresses. And then the style cannot be my own. If you are *unwilling* to know what you are, your writing is a form of deceit.

If anyone is unwilling to descend into himself, because this is too painful, he will remain superficial in his writing.[23]

These thoughts, if not their tone or favorite musical whipping-boy, are Nietzschean, and few can answer their bidding. But at present I want to highlight only the following aspect of Wittgenstein's thought: What stands in the way of "knowing what you are" is not only the refusal to look at what you are, but not knowing how or where to look: and arriving at these locales ("descending into yourself") depends on an interest in one's experience. "Lying to oneself about oneself" would not be a threat to philosophical or musical style if it were as easy to spot in oneself as lying about one's age. Spotting it requires a will to self-knowledge, which is not a matter of exerting willpower toward a given goal but of being willing to look for what one is without knowing the cost of finding out. (That was Meno's paradox, and his sticking-point – though of course he didn't know it; and Socrates couldn't tell him.) The peculiar look of Wittgenstein's later style has often been mentioned. Less often do his readers observe the peculiar demands on will and judgment evident in his style, particularly in its unrelenting venting of doubting voices – not only voices of skeptical doubt but other, accusatory voices raising the suspicion that the direction taken by the protagonist at this juncture is no longer one that he continues to will, but is instead a direction he may be finding simply less resistant or more familiar.[24] To disregard these demands in reading the *Investigations*, or to regard them as of merely biographical interest, would be like reading Augustine's *Confessions* for merely biographical interest.

If a genuine style rests on a kind of watchfulness for self-deception – not a paranoid suspicion of it, which may itself be a kind of self-deception – then it rests on one's interest or desire to notice, to watch

---

[23] Quoted in Rhees, "Postscript," *Recollections of Wittgenstein*, ed. Rush Rhees (Oxford and New York: Oxford University Press, 1984), 174.

[24] "Is it a case of both seeing and thinking? Or an amalgam of the two, as I should almost like to say? The question is: *why* does one want to say this?" (*PI* 197h); "I should like to say that what dawns here lasts only as long as I am occupied with the object in a particular way. ('See, it's looking!') – 'I should like to say' – and *is* it

for, one's watchfulness: a kind of double- or aspect-seeing. As with writing, so with reading: one does not know, in taking up a text like the *Investigations*, what the temptation to misunderstand will prove to be, or where the temptation to superficiality will lie, so that one can make preparations to overcome it. (Before the duck-rabbit flips for you the first time, it looks just like a line drawing of a duck, or of a rabbit.) Then how does one come to know how to proceed in reading it? Since Wittgenstein characterizes good philosophical writing as writing that shows "a genuine style," he may think that one comes to recognize this, to know it, in much the same way that one comes to know "the genuineness of expressions" in others:

Can one learn this knowledge? Yes; some can. Not, however, by taking a course in it, but through *"experience."*—Can someone else be a man's teacher in this? Certainly. From time to time he gives him the right *tip.*—This is what "learning" and "teaching" are like here. ... What is most difficult here is to put this indefiniteness, correctly and unfalsified [i.e., genuinely], into words. (*PI* 227h–i)

Can we conceive the *Investigations* as a series of tips on reading the *Investigations*? We can characterize its writing, in any event, by noting that it does not draw conclusions about matters unseen (the glue that binds world to language, or language to meaning, or speaker to speaker) so much as prepare connections to be seen (a "series of examples" that "can be broken off" [*PI* §133]) while recognizing that seeing the connections asks for a reconstituting way of looking.

As an instance of this, consider what I am asked to see in the following remark from Part II of the *Investigations*: "What is fear? What does 'being afraid' mean? If I wanted to define it at a *single* showing—I should *play-act* fear. Could I also represent hope in this way? Hardly. And what about belief?" (*PI* 188d–e). I am asked to try these questions and answers out on myself, but not only in the way that any philosophical claim asks this of me, to examine and assess its truth – in this instance, by seeing whether I agree that the most salient features of

so?" (*PI* 210d); "But wait! Do I ever really say of an ordinary picture (of a lion) that I see it as a lion? I've certainly never heard that yet. And yet here I've been talking about this kind of seeing!" (*LW* I §§675–76); "But I have kept on saying [e.g., at *PI* 230b] that it's conceivable for our concepts to be different than they are. Was that all nonsense?" (*RC* III §124).

hope cannot be shown by play-acting, as those of fear can. I am certainly also asked to consider whether Wittgenstein's answer to his first question helps to dispel the thought that "I am afraid" principally refers to a state of mind, and whether his second set of questions diminishes the appeal of the thought that "I fear that *x*," "I hope that *x*," and "I believe that *x*" function similarly as propositional attitudes, or that their dissimilarity is that the first two refer to emotive states while the last does not. Beyond weighing Wittgenstein's words against my experience, however, I am invited to weigh my experience in light of his words, to try on a method – Wittgenstein likens it to a therapy (*PI* §133) – for returning to an interest in my experience, in the words I speak and in my part in voicing their justification, when that is required of me. But this method requires that I dissolve or destroy the barriers to my interest in my experience, the (philosophical) problems I have constructed to keep my real interest, and what satisfies my real need, out of my everyday thoughts and speech, out of my sight (cf. *PI* 206a). On the other hand, if I am looking for grounds for our understanding, or rules to which I can appeal, or a theory, whether out of hope or out of fear, then even the remarks from the *Investigations* just quoted will answer to my imagined interest when read a certain way, *viz.*, out of that hope or fear.

But then where does Wittgenstein place his hope that he will be understood? The potential for despair is illustrated in a remark of his that links his deep involvement with music to his well-documented fear or conviction that his teaching would fall on deaf ears and before blind eyes. At the time he was at work on the remarks on aspect-seeing, Wittgenstein told his friend Maurice Drury, "It is impossible for me to say in my book one word about all that music has meant in my life. How then can I hope to be understood?"[25] Of course it is possible to make too much of this remark, but one shouldn't be so impressed by that fact that one overlooks the danger of making too little of it. For its tone of despair, to mention its most obvious feature, asks us to take it seriously, however in the end that is to be done.[26] Elsewhere I have noted various paths to follow from Wittgenstein's remark

[25] M. O'C. Drury, "Conversations with Wittgenstein," in Rhees, ed., *Recollections of Wittgenstein*, 160.

[26] It is true that Wittgenstein's remark, as remembered by Drury, could be read as saying that his life with music is important (only) to understanding *him*. But if that is

about the role of the meaning of music to an understanding of the *Investigations*.[27] Here I conclude with just *one* important trail: Toward the end of Part I of the *Investigations* Wittgenstein has this: "We speak of understanding a sentence in the sense in which it can be replaced by another which says the same; but also in the sense in which it cannot be replaced by any other. (Any more than one musical theme can be replaced by another)" (*PI* §531).

Can we ask how we are asked to understand this, or any other, sentence in the *Investigations* – whether in the sense in which it can be replaced by another which says the same, or whether in the sense in which it cannot be replaced by any other? And what does it mean, after all, to read a sentence in the sense in which it cannot be replaced by any other? It means, I take it, to read it with an interest in one's experience (of it). Can one conceive this as one's commission in taking up a philosophical text? How can a text ask for that, give the reader the right tip, if finding oneself encouraged to an interest in one's experience presupposes an interest in one's experience, a readiness to be struck by what passes before one's eyes, meaning, here, the words on the page? "It is not impossible that it should fall to the lot of this work, in its poverty and in the darkness of this time, to bring light into one brain or another—but, of course, it is not likely" (*PI* Preface). What is the darkness of this time, if we are not instructed by this remark to reflect on the time of our reading it?[28]

what one takes it to say, then one must account for the fact (an implication of this particular voicing of despair) that Wittgenstein would care to place the singular hope of his being understood on what is, by most accounts, a work of philosophy.

[27] Day, "The Aesthetic Dimension of Wittgenstein's Later Writings," unpublished manuscript.

[28] I thank Steven Affeldt, Avner Baz, and Victor Krebs for conversations and comments touching on aspects of the present chapter.

IV ASPECTS AND METHOD

IV.1 Therapy

11

On Learning from Wittgenstein, or What Does It Take to *See* the Grammar of Seeing Aspects?

Avner Baz

> Like Freud's therapy, [Wittgenstein's writing] wishes to prevent understanding which is unaccompanied by inner change.
>
> Stanley Cavell, "The Availability of Wittgenstein's Later Philosophy"

INTRODUCTION

Many who write about Wittgenstein these days speak of his philosophy as a form of therapy that does not present us with some heretofore unknown truths, but rather aims at dispelling confusions and at returning us to a knowledge that we couldn't have failed already to possess. I suppose that at this level of generality there is nothing incorrect in this characterization. The real difficulty in coming to terms with Wittgenstein's teaching, I find, emerges when philosophers turn from talking *about* that teaching to actually *doing* philosophy that's supposed to proceed in its light. And that difficulty seems to me to tell, perhaps more than anything else, of the kind of teaching that Wittgenstein's teaching is.

My procedure in this paper will be to attempt to illuminate the nature of the difficulty by attending carefully to the way it manifests itself in a recent article by Stephen Mulhall on Wittgenstein's remarks on seeing aspects.[1] I find Mulhall's interpretation of Wittgenstein's remarks on aspects to be a good example for a reading of Wittgenstein that takes itself to be alive to the question of the nature of Wittgenstein's teaching, but that in effect represses the kind of work undertaken by Wittgenstein's remarks. The purpose of the first part of this paper will be to characterize that work more precisely, by looking closely at Wittgenstein's remarks on aspects. I will argue that Wittgenstein's remarks are meant to bring us back to, or project us into, situations of speech, or anyway situations in which words are called for – *particular* words – whereby we are meant to discover things about the meanings of the words we utter, things that we cannot have failed to know, and yet things that are, for some reason, hard to *see*. I will further argue that this is *essential* to the teaching of these remarks – that, apart from effecting, or enabling, a re-acquaintance with the meaning of our words, their teaching does not happen. There is no *result* that these remarks aim at that can be had apart from the work they call upon us to do on ourselves. And that means, I will argue, that Mulhall's account, however interesting and even at times insightful it may be in its own right, is essentially unfaithful to Wittgenstein's teaching. Purporting to deliver us once and for all from puzzlement to clarity concerning the experience of aspect-dawning, Mulhall's interpretation looks to find in Wittgenstein's remarks a very different kind of satisfaction, or say peace, from that which they are designed to enable. And the satisfaction it arrives at, I will argue in the second part of this paper, is the kind of satisfaction that Wittgenstein's procedures actually aim to help us overcome.

LEARNING FROM WITTGENSTEIN: I

Let me begin with what Mulhall claims to have found in Wittgenstein's remarks on aspects. The central claim is that Wittgenstein's true

---

[1] Stephen Mulhall, "Seeing Aspects," *Wittgenstein: A Critical Reader*, ed. Hans-Johann Glock (Oxford: Blackwell, 2001), 246–67. Mulhall's account in this article is a somewhat abridged version of the account that he gives in *Inheritance and Originality* (Oxford: Oxford University Press, 2001). Without denying the interest of some of the ideas that appear in the book but not in the article, I have not found substantive differences between the two texts on the issues that concern me in this chapter – namely, how Wittgenstein's remarks on aspect-perception are supposed to work and what kind of understanding they are designed to provide.

interest in his remarks on seeing aspects lies not in what Wittgenstein calls "the dawning of an aspect," but rather, and contrary to appearance, in a particular attitude that, according to Mulhall's Wittgenstein, is our typical relation to things in our world – at the very least to pictures, to words, and to people. This attitude, according to Mulhall, is what Wittgenstein calls "the continuous seeing of aspects." It then turns out that this attitude is *also* what Wittgenstein means by "regarding (something as something)" and, most strikingly, what he also means by "seeing." This attitude is characterized, according to Mulhall, by the "immediacy" and "lack of hesitance" with which we perceive the meaning of things, by our taking their significance or exact nature "for granted"; it contrasts with what Wittgenstein, according to Mulhall, calls "knowing," which in turn is characterized by hesitancy, and by the perceiver's taking his description of what he sees to be just one interpretation among many possible ones. The capacity to experience the dawning of an aspect turns out, in Mulhall's reading of Wittgenstein, to be "simply one (admittedly striking) manifestation of – one criterion for – a person's general relation to pictures [and analogously to words and to people] being one of continuous aspect perception."[2] Mulhall argues that it is only against the background of "continuous aspect perception" that what he calls "the inherent paradoxicality" of the experience of the dawning of an aspect can be "accounted for."

So far as I can see, Mulhall's recent account is essentially a reassertion of his earlier, extended account in *On Being in the World*.[3] In a previous article of mine, I criticized Mulhall's original account – criticized it, for the most part, *as an interpretation of Wittgenstein* – and I tried to present what I wouldn't exactly want to call a "reading" of the remarks on aspects, but an alternative understanding of what Wittgenstein means by "aspect" and by "seeing an aspect."[4] In this paper, my aim, as I said, is to situate that initial disagreement that I discovered I had with Mulhall's reading of Wittgenstein within a wider context – the context of the question of how Wittgenstein's remarks

---

[2] Mulhall, "Seeing Aspects," 254.

[3] Mulhall, *On Being in the World: Wittgenstein and Heidegger on Seeing Aspects* (London and New York: Routledge, 1990).

[4] Avner Baz, "What's the Point of Seeing Aspects?", *Philosophical Investigations* 23 (April 2000): 97–121.

are to be read, or the question of what learning from Wittgenstein requires. For while my disagreements with Mulhall, as I presented them in that earlier paper – concerning, among other things, what Wittgenstein means by "aspect," by "seeing an aspect," by "seeing and not merely knowing," and by "continuously seeing an aspect" – still seem to me substantial and worth stressing, it has become increasingly clear to me that my disagreement with Mulhall goes deeper than how we each understand this or that term of Wittgenstein's, and even deeper than where we each locate the significance of the seeing of aspects.

I have presented what I take to be the gist of Mulhall's interpretation of Wittgenstein in one paragraph. I may have misrepresented or left out this or that aspect of that interpretation. (In particular, I need to say more, and will do so in the second part of this paper, about how exactly Mulhall's account is supposed to "dissolve" the "paradox of aspect-dawning"). But I don't think that I was wrong in taking Mulhall's interpretation to *be* paraphrasable in something like a paragraph. After all, he himself says that Wittgenstein has "his views" (or "his position") on the subject of aspect-seeing, and further suggests that these views are capable of being "formulated" and "justified."[5] But now, let us ask, if Wittgenstein does have views on the subject of aspect-seeing, and if Mulhall's presentation of Wittgenstein's views is faithful, why doesn't Wittgenstein ever just *say* what Mulhall claims he says? And why did he feel the need to write *hundreds* of remarks on the seeing of aspects, if what he really was trying to say can be put in twenty pages or so (which in turn are paraphrasable in a paragraph)?[6] If the purpose of the remarks, or of some of the remarks, were simply to remind us of the smooth and unhesitating way with which we "generally respond to pictures in terms of what they depict" or "treat pictures in terms of what they depict," and to suggest to us that, given this basic attitude that we have to pictures, "our paradoxical sense of the dual-aspect figure changing even though we know that it remains

---

[5] Mulhall, "Seeing Aspects," 246–47.
[6] I should actually have said "ten pages," because for the sake of clarity and simplicity I am going to focus almost exclusively on the first part of Mulhall's article. The other two parts, addressing the connection between "seeing aspects" and "experiencing the meaning of a word," and the "seeing of aspects" in human beings, would have to be similarly treated. But not this time.

unaltered becomes entirely unsurprising,"[7] then Wittgenstein certainly chose an odd way for making his point. Is there no connection between the peculiar form of Wittgenstein's remarks and their teaching? What is happening in these remarks? How do they work?

Part II, Section 11 of the *Investigations* opens with a distinction between two uses of the word "see," to which there correspond two "objects" of sight. According to my understanding of the remarks on aspects, the first object of sight is what we ordinarily describe, report, inform another person of, alert someone to, raise a question about, etc. In short, it is what we ordinarily can be said to see. The second object of sight is what Wittgenstein will call "an aspect"; it is characterized, in part, precisely by the fact that it makes sense for us to *call upon* someone to see it who is standing there and is seeing the object as clearly as we do: " 'I see a likeness between these two faces'—let the man I tell this to be seeing the faces as clearly as I do myself" (*PI* 193a).

Mulhall, so far as I can see, has no real use for Wittgenstein's initial distinction between the two uses of the word "see" and the two "objects of sight" corresponding to them. For he ultimately is going to want to call, in Wittgenstein's name, most of what we typically see[8] – what we describe, inform others of, attract someone's attention to, … – "aspects." And the inter-subjective dimension – To whom are we addressing ourselves in giving expression to an aspect, and why? What puts us in a position to address him or her in this way? What would count as an appropriate response on his or her part to our exclamation? What can he or she do with what we say? – also plays no part in Mulhall's understanding of what seeing an aspect is (means).[9] This, I suppose, is why he chose to open his article by quoting the *third*

---

[7] Mulhall, "Seeing Aspects," 254.

[8] At least when it comes to pictures and drawings, to human expression, and to words – though, following what he takes to be a lead from Heidegger, Mulhall has wanted to extend the term "aspects" to refer to basically everything we see.

[9] Part of my contention, in that earlier paper of mine, against some prominent readers of the remarks on aspects, including Mulhall, is that while they heed Wittgenstein's continual urging and take the peculiar forms of expression, with which we give voice to the experience of noticing an aspect, as the outward criteria of the "inner" experience, they then neglect almost entirely the situation(s) of speech, the context(s), the language-game(s), within which those expressions find their life, hence meaning. To attain clarity with respect to one of our concepts of experience requires more than merely reminding ourselves of a particular isolated form of words that we use to give voice to our experience. We need also to remind ourselves of "the occasion and

remark of *PI* II.xi, and to say about it that *it* "introduces" the topic of aspect-seeing.[10] This shift of focus – from the inter-subjective *context*, the language-game, within which the expression of the seeing of an aspect assumes its sense, to the *experience* – is fatal, or can be.

But I'm already going too deeply into my original disagreements with Mulhall. I want to remain on the more general level of how Wittgenstein's remarks are to be read, learned from. So let me note that immediately following those introductory remarks Wittgenstein says that the *causes* of the experience of noticing an aspect are of interest to psychologists – that is, not to him – and that we (that is, he and anyone who cares to try to join him) are interested in "the concept and its place among the concepts of experience" (*PI* 193e). Here are some of the concepts whose interrelations, mutual affinities and distances, Wittgenstein's remarks in *PI* II.xi invite us to assess: "seeing" (and, or versus, "*seeing*"), "seeing a property of the object" (as opposed to "seeing an aspect"), "being struck," "noticing," "interpreting," "knowing" ("merely knowing"), "seeing something as something," "treating something as something" (*alsbehandeln*), "regarding something as something" (*alsbetrachten*), "taking something as (or for) something" (*fürhalten*), "conceiving [*auffassen*] something in one way or another" (as opposed to "*seeing* it as this or that"), "seeing something three-dimensionally," "looking without being aware," "being conscious of," "thinking," "recognizing," "seeing something without recognizing it," "imagining," "feeling" (as in "one *feels* the softness of the depicted material"), "concerning one's self with what one sees," "paying attention." If I were now to urge that the purpose of the remarks on aspects just is to attain a perspicuous representation of the concept of "the dawning of an aspect" and its place among our concepts of experience, I suppose this would be welcomed with a shrug: *Of course* this is what Wittgenstein is interested in![11] But I find that it is not yet clear *how* Wittgenstein conducts his conceptual inquiry, and hence that we are not yet clear on *what* he is after.

purpose" of these phrases (*PI* 221e). "It is necessary to get down to the application" (*PI* 201a), to ask oneself "What does anyone tell me by saying 'Now I see it as ...'? What consequences has this information? What can I do with it?" (*PI* 202f).

[10] Mulhall, "Seeing Aspects," 246.
[11] And yet I should say that the commentaries I'm familiar with, including Mulhall's, feature very few of the above "concepts of experience."

What we need now, I feel, is some further evidence for the how and what of Wittgenstein's conceptual inquiry into noticing an aspect. Consider the following sample – by no means exhaustive, but I think representative – gathered in the order of appearance from the remarks of *PI* II.xi (I try to present the quotations in a way that increasingly abstracts from what might be called the *content* of Wittgenstein's remarks, in order to bring out what might be called their *form*):

1. If you say "Now it's a face for me," we can ask: "What change are you alluding to?"
2. I see two pictures, with the duck-rabbit surrounded by rabbits in one, by ducks in the other. I do not notice that they are the same. Does it *follow* from this that I *see* something different in the two cases?
3. I am shown a picture-rabbit and asked what it is; I say "It's a rabbit." Not "now it's a rabbit." I am reporting my perception.
4. The change of aspect. "But surely you would say that the picture is altogether different now!" But what is different: my impression? My point of view?—Can I say? I *describe* the alteration like a perception; quite as if the object has altered before my eyes.
5. Someone suddenly sees an appearance which he does not recognize. ... Is it correct to say ... ?
6. Now, when I know my acquaintance in the crowd, perhaps after looking in his direction for quite a while,—is this a special sort of seeing? Is it a case of both seeing and thinking? Or an amalgam of the two, as I should almost like to say? The question is: *why* does one want to say this?
7. How does one tell that human beings *see* three dimensionally?
8. If later I see ... can I say ... ?
9. If you ask me what I saw, perhaps I shall ... ; but I shall mostly. ...
10. Look at all that can be meant by "description of what is seen."
11. What does it mean to say ... ? Is it enough that ... ? What is the expression of ... ?
12. What does anyone tell me by saying ... ?
13. What does it mean for me to look at ... and say ... ? Does it simply mean ... ?

14. But this is seeing! *In what sense* is it seeing?

15. Of course I might also have seen the picture first as something different, and then have said to myself "Oh, it's two hexagons!" So the aspect would have altered. And does this prove that I in fact *saw* it as something definite?

16. "Is it a *genuine* visual experience?" The question is: in what sense is it one?

17. This is one meaning in calling it. ... But can I say in the same sense ... ?

18. And does the child now *see* the chest as a house? "He quite forgets that it is a chest; for him it actually is a house. ..." Then would it not also be correct to say that he *sees* it as a house?

19. If someone said ... he might still be meaning very different things.

20. Someone tells me: "I looked at the flower, but was thinking of something else and was not conscious of its color." Do I understand this?—I can imagine a significant context.

What do we call ... ? How do we tell ... ? What makes you want to say ... ? Would it be correct to say ... ? How might we understand someone who said ... ? Inviting the reader to say, and thereby find out, what he or she would want to *call* something, what word or words he or she would choose to employ in a particular case, and then asking the reader to reflect upon his or her choice and try to account for it – this is the Wittgensteinian elicitation of criteria. In the remarks on aspects we are repeatedly invited to test out our words, see whether and how we want to employ them in the face of the different cases, all more or less familiar, that Wittgenstein presents us with. And then we are asked to account for our choice – which doesn't necessarily, or exactly, mean to justify our choice, for it really is more a matter of getting clear on what our choice *is*, what it amounts to. And the implied claim is that we don't know in advance – part of our problem is precisely that we *think* we know in advance – what we will find; and hence, that the structure of the region of human experience which these words are used to articulate, though in a sense familiar, is something that we don't yet clearly see.

"Let the use *teach* you the meaning," Wittgenstein urges (*PI* 212e), as he similarly urges us in many other places. "Don't think that you knew in advance what [a particular word or expression] means!" (cf. *PI* 212e). What could be more familiar and better understood in Wittgenstein than this call? Mulhall himself has insisted on something like this on behalf of Wittgenstein at various places in his writings. But now I want to suggest that Mulhall and others have insisted on this as what might be called "Wittgenstein's contribution to our understanding of the concept of meaning," not as something that is internal to the philosophical work that happens in Wittgenstein's remarks. Whatever understanding or revelation we are offered in Mulhall's account of the seeing of aspects, that understanding or revelation is not arrived at by reminding ourselves of the uses of our words – by our struggling in this way with the temptation to think that we know *in advance* what our words mean. It would be impossible to guess, going solely by Mulhall's reading of Wittgenstein's remarks, that so many of them end with a question mark.

"What we have ... to do is to *accept* the everyday language-game, and to note *false* accounts of the matter *as* false" (*PI* 200b; see also *PI* §§654–56). How hard can accepting the everyday language-game be? It turns out to be extremely hard. We are tempted, for example, to suppose that we already know what seeing is, and hence what we *must* mean by "seeing." As against this temptation, Wittgenstein urges us to remind ourselves of how we use the word "seeing," hence of what we, on different occasions, mean by "seeing," and hence of what seeing, for us anyway, *is*. A great many of the remarks on aspects exhibit this struggle to attain clarity, "*in despite of* an urge to misunderstand [the workings of our language]" (*PI* §109). And why should such a work of reminding ourselves of something we already know require hundreds of remarks? Well, it turns out that what we already know is immensely subtle and complex, no less complicated than the human organism (cf. *TLP* 4.002).[12]

It is also the case that the lures of misleading pictures and false explanations are powerful and hard to resist. For example, it is very tempting to suppose, when an aspect strikes us and we see something

---

[12] Compare *PI* §156: "The use of this word in the ordinary circumstances of our life is of course extremely familiar to us. But the part the word plays in our life, and therewith the language-game in which we employ it, would be difficult to describe even in rough outline."

in a way we've never seen it before, that before the new aspect dawned we had been seeing the thing all along under some *different* aspect. It is tempting, in other words, to suppose that there is, that there must be, some continuous version to the seeing of aspects.[13] And the problem is not that this supposition is just flatly wrong, but that it is not yet clear what we mean, what it is we are supposing. Our problem, as I might put it, is that we only *think* we know what we mean – what we must mean – and this blinds us to what we *do*, or might, mean.

And since *this* is our problem, it may help us to ask ourselves, with Wittgenstein, whether the fact that I have just been struck by an aspect, and now see the object in a way I have not seen it before, "prove[s] that I in fact *saw* it as something definite" (*PI* 204f). Or it may help us to consider Wittgenstein's suggestion that while there is no doubt about the possible aptness of the "never" in "I've never seen this in that way before," the "always" in "I have *always* seen this like that" is not equally certain (see *RPP* I §512); or that when we say "I've always seen it in this way" what we really mean to say is "I have always *conceived* (*auffassen*) it *this* way, and *this* change of aspect has never taken place" (*RPP* I §524); or that when you say "I have always seen it with *this* face" you still have to say *what* face, and that as soon as you add *that*, it's no longer as if you had *always* done it (*RPP* I §526); or that to say of a real face, or of a face in a picture, "I've *always* seen it as a face" would be queer, whereas "It has always been a face to me, and I have never seen it *as something else*" would not be (see *RPP* I §532); or that "If someone were to tell me that he had seen the figure for half an hour without a break as a reversed F, I'd have to suppose that he had kept on *thinking* of this interpretation, that he had *occupied* himself with it" (*RPP* I §1020); or that "If there were no change of aspect then there would

---

[13] This insistence will be further encouraged by the choice of the duck-rabbit, and other similarly ambiguous figures, as one's paradigmatic examples of aspect-seeing. For in the case of those figures there seems to be an obvious candidate for what the other, preceding, aspect was. Not that it is at all clear in *what* sense we were "seeing" the duck aspect, say, before the rabbit aspect dawned! But think of being struck by the similarity between two faces, for example, and you will find less appealing the idea that the aspect that dawns always replaces some other aspect that was seen continuously. (Here is a place where Mulhall wants to be able to offer a *general* answer to a question that, as can be seen in the text, Wittgenstein would always seek to answer by reminding us or himself of the different contexts in which it would make sense for us to say that we or others saw the picture continuously as one thing or another, before we were struck by the new aspect.)

only be a *way of taking* (*Auffassung*), and no such thing as *seeing* this or that" (*RPP* II §436).

Disentangling a philosophical puzzlement can require the kind of patience and concentration and persistence that disentangling a Gordian knot made of delicate threads would require. It also requires resistance to false senses of satisfaction. But in Wittgenstein, the threads are nothing more, nor less, than grammatical threads – our everyday ways of making sense, of putting our world into words, or trying to; and disentangling them is always done, as it is done in the examples given in the previous paragraph, by reminding ourselves of what we couldn't have failed to know.

LEARNING FROM WITTGENSTEIN: II

But if it meant this I ought to know it. (*PI* 194a)

But now, what about Mulhall's dissolution of the "paradox" of aspect-dawning? For after all, if there is indeed a genuine paradox which Mulhall manages genuinely to dissolve, then perhaps one does not need to take Wittgenstein's torturous way in order to arrive at a clear view of the phenomena of aspect-dawning; perhaps there is no need for the kind of potentially endless work that I've suggested is undertaken by Wittgenstein's remarks; perhaps we need no more than to be reminded of "the very general fact that human beings relate to, treat, regard pictures as pictures (as representational objects)."[14] (Why is this very general fact about us, whatever exactly it amounts to, something that we need to be *reminded* of? Is it supposed to be a fact that we know, but for some reason have been failing to acknowledge, or see? Is it a fact of which it is, for some reason, *hard* to remind ourselves? After all, it seems that all that being reminded of it, and having it become a forgone conclusion, requires is simply for Mulhall to propose it to us, or for him to have Wittgenstein propose it to us.)

So let us consider Mulhall's "therapeutic dissolution"[15] of the paradox of aspect-dawning:

---

[14] Mulhall, "Seeing Aspects," 253.
[15] Ibid., 255.

If, in general, we do not simply recognize that pictures depict and what they depict but rather take their pictorial identity (as a picture of *x* rather than *y*) for granted in our dealings with them, if we generally respond to pictures in terms of what they depict, then we will of course tend to regard a picture-duck as being as different from a picture-rabbit as a duck is from a rabbit; and we will accordingly be tempted to give expression to the sudden realization that the picture-object before us is both a picture-duck and a picture-rabbit in terms which suggest that the picture-object itself has altered – that a pictured duck has been transformed into a pictured rabbit, one sort of picture-object into another, very different sort. In short, against the background Wittgenstein encapsulates in his notion of continuous aspect perception, our paradoxical sense of the dual-aspect figure changing even though we know that it remains unaltered becomes entirely unsurprising; what else would one expect from people who relate to pictures and picture-objects in terms of what they depict? … Understood as simply one manifestation of a general tendency to treat pictures in terms of what they depict, the apparent paradoxicality inherent in the ways in which we give expression to experiences of the dawning of an aspect dissolves.[16]

The first question I wish to raise is what sort of an account this account is meant to be. Is it supposed to be a *conceptual* account, having to do with things we sometimes find ourselves "tempted" (or inclined, or compelled, or called upon …) to say, and with what we (could possibly) mean in saying them? Or is it, rather, an empirical or causal account, having to do with *why* we "tend" to have certain peculiar experiences, why it sometimes seems to us (why we sometimes "have the sense")[17] that what we see has changed, even though we know it hasn't changed? Put otherwise, my question is how the "puzzlement" induced by the experience of "everything has changed and yet nothing has changed" is supposed to disappear in the light of Mulhall's account. Is it supposed to disappear through our finding, as it were, "another dimension," (*PI* 200f) in which the concept of "seeing" – as it is employed and manifested in, for example, "I *see* his likeness to his father" or "I *see* the sphere floating" – has "room" (*PI* 200f)? Is it supposed to disappear at least partly through our coming to see how puzzling some things about what we call "seeing" are, which until now we have failed to find puzzling enough (cf. *PI* 212f)?

[16] Ibid., 253–54.
[17] Ibid.

Or is it, rather, supposed to disappear in the way that, say, our puzzle-ment over certain forms of hallucination is supposed to disappear in the light of psychological theories of psychic mechanisms? It seems that Mulhall's account wants to be, or thinks of itself as being, the former sort of account. And yet it seems to me to follow, in many of its moments, the grammar of the latter sort of account. And the result is that it ends up being neither, or a confusing combination of both.

As we just saw, Mulhall wants, as part of his dissolution of the para-dox of aspect-dawning, to be able to talk about a particular typical attitude that we have toward drawings and pictures. But what exactly is this attitude? What does it mean to say about someone that "he takes the specific pictorial identity of a picture (as a picture of x rather than y) for granted," or that "he has the general tendency to treat pictures in terms of what they depict"? Does it simply mean that if we showed him a schematic drawing of a face and asked him, "What's that?", he would in all likelihood say something like "a face," "a picture-face," or "a drawing of a face"? But that would only show that he knows what a drawing of a face *is*, what "a drawing of a face" means. Is this what the dissolution of the paradox comes to, that given that we know what a drawing or a picture of x is – can tell one when we see one – our sense (or our saying) that everything has changed even when we know that nothing has changed becomes entirely unsurprising?

Mulhall knows, of course, that this could not be what the dissolu-tion of the paradox comes to. First of all, he himself acknowledges that "a picture-object (like a picture) just is the sort of thing that is cor-rectly described by describing what it represents,"[18] which means that describing pictures and drawings in terms of what they depict could not, in itself, account for a certain "capacity" that most, but possibly not all, people have, for being struck by aspects. Mulhall also knows that the sense of paradox arises precisely because the person does not merely say, "Oh, this could also be a picture of a rabbit," but rather says something like, "*Now* it's a rabbit," "Everything has changed," or "I *see* it differently." So what Mulhall feels he needs is a *specific*, yet typical, relation that we have to pictures or drawings – one in which we, as it were, *see through* them to what they depict; and he wishes to conceive

---

[18] Ibid., 251.

of it as a *general* category of relation to pictures and drawings, such that the dawning of an aspect would amount to something like a *switch* from one relation to another *within* this general category. Mulhall claims that this general category of relation is what Wittgenstein calls "seeing," and he further claims that this category is contrasted, in Wittgenstein's remarks, with another category, that of "knowing":

> We distinguish seeing from knowing what a picture represents in terms of the immediacy with which a description of what it represents is forthcoming even after only a glimpse of the picture, of whether that description is proffered as one amongst a number of possible interpretations, and of whether any faults in that description make sense in terms of what it depicts.[19]

In my earlier paper I argued that Mulhall's distinction between "seeing" and "knowing" corresponds to no distinction that might exist in our language between "seeing" (in whichever of its ordinary senses) and "knowing" (in whichever of its ordinary senses), and that Wittgenstein says nothing that would justify attributing such a distinction to him. But one may presumably postulate whatever meaning one wishes for his words; and there may be no harm in doing so, provided one manages to avoid confusing oneself and others. Of course, one would not thereby become free of one's dependency on our shared criteria; for, having postulated what one is going to mean by "seeing," one would now have to be prepared to say what he or she means by – what he or she is going to count as – "immediacy" ("smoothness," "unhesitance"), "proffering one's description as one amongst a number of possible interpretations," and "a fault in the description that makes sense in terms of what the picture depicts."

Let us suppose that this can coherently be done. We now have a concept of a certain specific relation to pictures and drawings, and we can go on to apply that concept. We show someone a schematic drawing of a face and we ask him "What's that?" If he answers "A face," "A smiling face," "A picture-face," or "A drawing of a (smiling) face," and if we find that we wish to count his response as "(more or less) immediate" (he does not "hesitate" before answering), and if it seems to us that he doesn't take "face" or "smiling face" to be "one amongst a number of possible interpretations of the drawing," then we will call his relation to the drawing "continuous aspect perception." And then,

---

[19] Ibid., 253.

sure enough, we will discover that most people's relation to pictures is the relation that we have decided (following Mulhall) to call "continuous aspect perception."[20]

But now suppose that the person looks once again at our drawing and exclaims: "Ha! Had you asked me, when you first showed me this drawing, what type of a person it represented, I suppose I would have said that it represented a meek person who is humbly, if also somewhat self-deceptively, accepting the blows of fate; but now, all of a sudden, he strikes me as having the expression of a complacent businessman, stupidly supercilious, who though fat, imagines he's a lady killer.[21] I see, of course, that the drawing hasn't changed, and yet I see it differently." And suppose further that even though the experience he expresses is altogether familiar to me – I know exactly what he is talking about, I myself have occasionally been struck by aspects in the past and can also bring myself to see the two aspects he speaks of – I find myself puzzled and intrigued by the possibility of such a shift in one's seeing of the same thing. I want to understand the experience of aspect-dawning, and I turn to Mulhall's account for enlightenment. Recall that we have already established that my friend's relation to drawings is one of "continuous aspect-seeing" – he "responds to drawings in terms of what they depict."

According to Mulhall, the next thing I'm supposed to realize is that, given his general relation to drawings, it is no wonder that he should be "tempted to give expression to his sudden realization that

[20] In "What's the Point of Seeing Aspects?" I say what I understand Wittgenstein to be talking about in the one place in the *Investigations* in which he talks of "continuous seeing of an aspect." I understand Wittgenstein to use "continuous seeing of an aspect" to refer to something far more specific, and far less central for him, than what Mulhall has made it out to be. I understand it to refer to the state of someone who is unaware of the ambiguity of an ambiguous figure, say the duck-rabbit. If we then asked him, about the duck-rabbit, "What's that?", he would say simply "a duck" (say); and then it would make sense *for us*, who know that the picture can be seen in more than one way, to say about him that he is continuously seeing the duck aspect of the duck-rabbit. Such a person, Wittgenstein says, would simply be describing his perception (*PI* 195a, 195h), whereas about what he calls "seeing-as" he says that it is "not part of perception" (*PI* 197a). I make this point in "What's the Point of Seeing Aspects?" by saying that even the "aspect-blind" – defined by Wittgenstein as those who lack the capacity to see something *as* something – should be perfectly capable of "continuously seeing an aspect," thus understood.

[21] This second description of an aspect is taken from *BB* 162. The first description is mine. I invite the reader to look at that drawing and see the two aspects.

the picture-object I showed him is both a picture-meek-man and a picture-complacent-businessman in terms which suggest that the picture-object itself has changed – that … one sort of a picture-object [has been transformed] into another, very different sort." Do I understand that? First of all, it is not at all clear that I am well described as "tempted" to express myself as I do when an aspect dawns on me, any more than I am tempted to express bewilderment when I'm bewildered, or surprise when I'm surprised. Is there some better judgment, or wisdom, against which I express myself in the way I do? Is there any reason for me to refrain from thus expressing my experience, other than a certain (mis)conception of what "seeing" *must* mean? Nor do I find that the terms of my expression *suggest* that the object itself has changed, any more than my saying, "Now it's clear," about a theorem you've just explained to me suggests that the theorem itself had changed (though if I said the same words in response to your question about the weather, I would very likely be suggesting, or rather saying, that the weather had changed).

Next I think we need to figure out what exactly is meant by "his sudden realization that the picture-object *is both* a picture-meek-man and a picture-complacent-businessman." Does it mean that he suddenly realizes – it all of a sudden occurs to him – that it *could serve* as either of them, *be taken or interpreted* to be either of them? Or does it mean that he found he could *see* it as one or the other? If it means the latter, then Mulhall's resolution of the paradox presupposes the very concept it purports to be explicating, and we are exactly where we started: He says he sees it differently, even though he also sees that it hasn't changed, *because he really does see it differently, even though he realizes that it hasn't changed.* This, as Wittgenstein says, "really means: This expression is justified!—(For taken literally it is no more than a repetition)" (*PI* 201g).

So I suppose Mulhall must mean something like the former understanding: The man suddenly realizes that the drawing can be, can represent, two sorts of character, or two different facial expressions. But since each of the two competing interpretations induces a particular kind of attitude – a way of standing toward and responding to the drawing – what he discovers is that he can relate to the drawing in two different ways. Let us further grant that the two moments – the one of interpreting the drawing in a particular way, and the one of regarding or treating it as we interpret it – need not always come separated and in this order. Let us grant that a particular interpretation may reveal itself to us *in* (our discovery of the possibility of) a (new) way of regarding or treating the object. This would mean that Mulhall's dissolution of the paradox proceeds as follows: We tend to express the dawning of an aspect by saying that everything has changed, even though we know that the drawing or picture has not changed, *because* we really do have a "sense of the dual-aspect figure changing even though we know that it remains unaltered";[22] and we have the sense that the figure itself has changed, *because* our relation to it – the way we treat or regard it – has changed.

But if Mulhall's dissolution of the paradox is meant to work along the above lines, then I think at least the following four worries arise: (1) Mulhall's proposed criteria of "continuous aspect perception" – one's immediate and unhesitating response, etc. – have been of no use to us or to him.[23] If Mulhall indeed meant to capture with his criteria a way of treating or regarding something, then his criteria failed to come in contact with what he was trying to capture. For responding immediately and unhesitatingly to the question, "What's that?", taking the identity of the objects we encounter for granted, offering correct descriptions, or descriptions that if wrong are wrong only in certain ways but not in others – none of this *means* that we are regarding, or treating, the drawing in any particular way. It only means that we know what drawings are, and what drawing this particular one is.

(2) Even if we disregard Mulhall's proposed criteria for his notion of "continuous aspect perception" and take it, as he clearly wishes us to, to mean something like "treating" or "regarding" the drawing in a particular way, we will not thereby come any closer to a satisfying understanding, let alone dissolution, of what may be called "the paradox of aspect-dawning." For the "seeing" of aspects is *not* "the way we treat or regard things." What constitutes the peculiarity of the seeing of aspects, what perhaps lies at the root of the difficulty of attaining a clear view of what Wittgenstein calls "aspects," is precisely

---

[22] Mulhall, "Seeing Aspects," 254.
[23] They are also nothing like the criteria that the Wittgensteinian investigation is designed to elicit. But that's a point for another occasion.

the fact that the seeing of an aspect, conceptually, goes *beyond* treating, or regarding, something in a particular way.[24] This is why we should have no problem understanding someone who said: "You can think now of *this* now of *this* as you look at it, can *regard* it [my emphasis] now as *this* now as *this*, and *then* [my emphasis] you will see it now *this* way, now *this*" (*PI* 200d).

Elsewhere Wittgenstein reminds us of one of the typical criteria of seeing something as something: exclaiming, in a particular situation, "Now it's a house!" (*PI* 206g). This exclamation of "Now ... !" signals that the person is not, or not only, treating or regarding the thing in a particular way, but is seeing it in a particular way. "Seeing," unlike "regarding" or "treating," is, grammatically, "a state" (*RPP* II §43; cf. *PI* 212d); like paying attention to something, it has a determinate and, normally, limited duration, and it can be interrupted. So in the expression of the dawning of an aspect, the same form of words that in other contexts would have been used to say how the person is treating or regarding the thing is being used to say something different, to give voice to an experience: "The expression of the aspect is the expression of a way of taking [*Auffassung*] (hence, of a way-of-dealing-with [*Behandlungsweise*], of a technique); but *used* [my emphasis] as description of a state" (*RPP* I §1025). "Seeing something as something" does not mean "treating, or regarding it as, something."

(3) If it did – if Mulhall were correct in equating, as he does, "seeing something as something" with "responding to or regarding it as something"[25] – then the dawning of an aspect would not be the philosophically puzzling phenomenon that it is. If, by giving voice

---

[24] Having said that, I should add that the phenomena of seeing aspects do reveal a most intimate connection between how we see things and how we, as it were, bodily take them up into our field of potential engagement. These sorts of connection have most deeply and persuasively been explored and argued for by Maurice Merleau-Ponty. The relation of his work to Wittgenstein's seems to me to be a very promising direction of philosophical investigation, provided that we don't lose sight of the huge difference between Merleau-Ponty's method of inquiry and Wittgenstein's. My point here is that the connections between our attitude to things and the aspects under which we can *see* them are *not conceptual*, and that confusing the conceptual distinctions is bound to make us misplace the significance of the phenomenological investigation.

[25] See Mulhall, "Seeing Aspects," 262.

to the seeing of an aspect, we meant to say no more than that we are treating or regarding the object in a particular way – if in saying, "Everything has changed and yet nothing has changed," we meant to say no more than, "the thing has not changed, but my attitude toward it, the way I treat or regard it, has changed" – then there would have been no puzzlement to begin with. That we can regard the same thing in different ways, relate or respond to the same person or house or piece of furniture in different ways, is not puzzling in the same way that our sometimes seeing the same thing in different ways is. Faced with children who as part of their play "interpret a chest as a house in every detail" (*PI* 206e), seeing that for them, as we might wish to put it, "the chest actually is a house," we may very well admire and even wonder at their powers of imagination and at their freedom in using them; but we are not going to be puzzled in the way that it is quite natural to become puzzled in the face of the (conceptual) possibility of *seeing* the chest as a house. It is precisely the way in which the concept of "seeing" forces itself upon us in the case of the dawning of an aspect that makes the seeing of aspects so philosophically puzzling.

(4) So Mulhall's "dissolution of the paradox" has left "the paradox" untouched. Given what he may have entitled himself to claim, in his remarks concerning the way we treat or regard drawings and pictures, his "dissolution of the paradox" really comes to something like the following:

If we generally respond to pictures in terms of what they depict, then of course how we tend to regard a picture-duck should be expected to be as different from how we tend to regard a picture-rabbit, as how we tend to regard a duck is different from how we tend to regard a rabbit; and we will accordingly (be tempted to?) give expression to the sudden realization that the picture-object before us is both a picture-duck and a picture-rabbit in terms suggesting(?) that (we found) we are capable of two different responses, or relations, to the picture-object – that the very same drawing that we earlier regarded as a pictured duck we now (realize we can) regard as a pictured rabbit.

Aspect-dawning, thus understood to consist in a shift in how we treat or regard the drawing, indeed ceases to be puzzling and intriguing; it indeed becomes "entirely unsurprising"; what else would we expect from people who tend to regard drawings and pictures in terms of what they depict? But understood in this way, it also ceases to be what Wittgenstein is investigating in his remarks on aspect-seeing.

If my analysis of Mulhall's account is correct as far as it goes, his predicament is the following: He wants to be able to speak of a continuous relation that we have to pictures and drawings, against the background of which aspect-dawning would be discovered to be "unsurprising" – just what one would expect. But it turns out that any relation to the picture or drawing short of seeing it under some aspect is bound to leave the *dawning* of an aspect floating outside its reach, as mysterious as it ever was. So it appears that an account of the kind Mulhall has been looking for must either fail to come in contact with what it presumes to explain, or else presuppose it. And by that I mean: Either we take our general relation to pictures and drawings (however exactly we wish to conceive of it) to be different from our relation to them when an aspect dawns on us, in which case that general relation can perhaps be *causally* related to the dawning of the aspect but cannot help us to become clearer on *what* "the dawning of an aspect" means; or else that general relation to pictures and drawings is taken to be basically an extended version of our relation to them when an aspect strikes us, in which case we'd better first get clearer on what the latter relation is. Because one thing we are going to discover is that the seeing of an aspect, in the sense Wittgenstein most cares about in his remarks, cannot, grammatically, be *continuous*: "It is as if the aspect were something that only dawns, but does not remain; and yet this must be a *conceptual* remark, not a psychological one" (*RPP* I §1021; see also §1028).

Finally, I want to return to the question of what sort of an account Mulhall's account is, or might be. Faced with the (various) phenomena of aspect-dawning, Mulhall has, in effect, been asking not, "How can sense be made of our saying that we see something differently even though we know it hasn't changed?", but rather "How come we have this seemingly queer experience in which the very same thing all of a sudden seems to us to have completely changed, even though we know it hasn't?" To this question Mulhall in effect answers: "What has in fact changed is our relation to, our attitude toward, the thing." I've been trying to show that it is not clear how we are supposed to understand this answer. As a *causal* explanation of the experience of aspect-dawning, there may be nothing wrong with such an answer to such a question – just as there may be nothing wrong with our saying to our friend who tells us that, even though nothing in her world has changed, *everything* has changed, "Of course it seems to you that everything has changed, for your attitude has changed!" It should be noted, however, that an account of this type presupposes our understanding of the concepts involved and of the utterances in which they are employed; it does not in any way explicate them.

It would be different if we said, "To speak of everything changing is an inaccurate and misleading way of expressing oneself. What the person really means is that *her attitude* has changed. This is all she could possibly mean when she says that everything has changed, for the thing itself clearly has not changed, as she herself acknowledges." *This* would be an attempt to *conceptually* dissolve the puzzlement generated by the other's form of expression. I have tried to show that in the case of aspect-seeing (just as possibly also in the case of the person to whom the world seems different), this way of trying to dissolve the paradox would end up distorting that which it attempted to clarify. For it misses altogether the point of our giving voice to the dawning of an aspect. (When I call upon you to see the likeness of one face to another, I am not inviting you to share with me a new way of relating to that face (though possibly this is part of what I expect from you), but rather I am inviting you to *discover* something – to *see* something – in this face.) Instead of painstakingly recovering the domain to which the expression of the seeing of aspects belongs, such a conceptual account squeezes it into some other domain, which, though connected to the domain we are looking for in various intricate ways, is also importantly not identical with it.

I said that perhaps Mulhall's account might work as a causal explanation of the dawning of aspects in *some* cases.[26] But the important

---

[26] I say "some cases" because his account appears to be particularly tailored to pictures and drawings, and possibly to representational objects more generally, whereas it should be quite clear (even if we went just by Wittgenstein's own examples) that aspect-dawning – roughly characterized as the experience expressible by, "I see that the thing has not changed and yet I see it differently" (cf. *PI* 193c) – can happen virtually anywhere and with anything, and specifically also in contexts where no relation of depiction or representation exists. Consider seeing (being suddenly struck by) the likeness of one face (or place or situation) to another; seeing a (real) face as timid (as in *PI* §537); hearing a bar as an introduction; seeing a chest as a

thing, for Wittgenstein, is not to explain these and other similar experiences, but to explore their grammar; in part so that certain forms of explanation will lose their charm. Seeing aspects in representational objects, which is a sort of experience that assumes a variety of forms, itself belongs to a much wider type of experience – one characterized by things suddenly appearing to us in a new light, striking us as different from what we took them to be. Wittgenstein, as I understand him, tries, in his remarks on aspects, to arrive at an unobstructed overview of the conceptual domain within which those varied experiences assume their sense.

And in the light of what Wittgenstein's remarks on aspects enable us to see, I find that my sense of where the significance of aspect-dawning lies runs counter to (though is perhaps not incompatible with) Mulhall's. Whereas for Mulhall, aspect-dawning acquires its significance by revealing our basic relation to the world to be unproblematic – something that we all have already earned for ourselves as a matter of course – I find that aspect-dawning reveals our basic relation to the world to be one in which we are continually in danger of losing our world, *by*, as it were, taking it as a matter of course. My sense of the matter is that our relation to the world, as revealed by the dawning of aspects, is one in which we continually have to restore an intimacy with the world – an intimacy that is forever at stake, and that if taken for granted is bound to be lost. The continual danger, in other words, is that, succumbing to habitual and convenient ways of treating, or regarding, things, we will lose our ability to *see* them.[27]

---

house; seeing an M as an upside down W, or an F as facing right, or left; having everything suddenly strike us as unreal; seeing the double-cross as a black cross against a white background, or *vice versa*; seeing a (real, say wooden) triangle as pointing to the right; seeing a house as squatting in the moonlight (this example is from Faulkner's *Light in August*); seeing an old and familiar armchair as faithfully and submissively awaiting to serve one. How are we to fit Mulhall's "dissolution of the paradox of aspect-dawning" to cases of noticing an aspect in a non-pictorial object?

[27] I would like to thank Bill Day and Victor Krebs for some very inspiring and encouraging conversations. I would like to thank the members of the University of Chicago Wittgenstein Workshop for a stimulating and enlightening discussion of the essay. Special thanks are owed James Conant, who went over a draft of this essay and made many helpful suggestions.

12

The Work of Wittgenstein's Words

A Reply to Baz

Stephen Mulhall

I'm grateful for the chance to respond in public to Avner Baz's most recent essay on my work – primarily because it gives me an opportunity to express my gratitude for his willingness to engage with that work in detail, and to re-engage with it over the years; it's heartening to know that a gifted and dedicated philosopher considers such an investment of time and effort to be worth his while. I'm also glad to see that, particularly in the present essay, he finds himself focusing on issues surrounding Wittgenstein's work on seeing aspects that are also central to my own most recent attempts to go over this ground, more than a decade since I first staked out a set of claims about it. Since, however, he seems to judge that these re-presentations of my original thoughts about Wittgenstein's work bring those issues into focus precisely by failing properly to observe the methodological precepts that (we both assert, and accept) are integral to its teaching, I hope I will be forgiven for finding this portrayal of my failings rather more than disheartening. Such a rebuke is, after all, particularly pointed when addressed to someone who has made it his business (in the larger book in which my recent words on seeing aspects find their place, and elsewhere) to address exactly such rebukes to other writers on Wittgenstein. For some reason, recalling that those who live by the sword, die by the sword, doesn't serve to blunt its edge.

Baz develops so many questions of content and method in his essay (and in the essay which preceded it) that it is impossible for me to respond to every matter of moment that they bring out. So I propose, in my reply, to follow the rough division of his own essay into two parts: I will first address his concern that my account of Wittgenstein systematically represses the distinctive kind of work that his remarks undertake to effect, and only later turn to his more specific disagreements with the interpretative claims I make about how best to understand what is philosophically bewildering about the experience of aspect-dawning and about how best to respond to it.

Before I begin on this task, however, I want to make one general point about the status of my own interpretation of Wittgenstein, as I understand it. Although I consider my reading of his remarks on seeing aspects to form a coherent whole, and hence to give a total reading of the material, I do not take it to be exhaustive or exclusive. In claiming that I have identified one way of making sense of Wittgenstein's interest in this material, one way in which his varied body of remarks on the topic might be seen to hang together, I do not take myself to be committed to denying that there might be other such ways, other equally coherent and total readings of his remarks. Hence, I do not regard the validity of my own reading as dependent upon my ability to demonstrate the invalidity of other readings which may align and juxtapose Wittgenstein's remarks in very different ways to my own; on the contrary, I would expect there to be more than one such alternative reading, and I would welcome their elaboration by others (perhaps even by myself, on another occasion). One implication of this point is that I see no need, and in fact I have no desire, to contest Avner Baz's own, alternative way of understanding what Wittgenstein might be driving at in his persistent, exhausting preoccupation with this material. On the contrary: I would encourage him to work it out in rather more detail than his essays have hitherto been able to accommodate, so that it might thereby become assessable as another, noncompeting way of seeing Wittgenstein's work here as an articulated whole. The remainder of this essay will accordingly restrict itself to defending the coherence of my own reading against Baz's critique.

1. FORM AND CONTENT

Baz claims that my reading of Wittgenstein on seeing aspects represses something to which my writings elsewhere on Wittgenstein and Cavell at least appear to be attentive: the fact that "apart from effecting, or enabling, a re-acquaintance with the meaning of our words, [Wittgenstein's] teaching does not happen." Since Wittgenstein's concern is to bring us back, or project us into, situations in which particular words are called for, and thereby to allow us to discover things about the meanings of the words we utter – things that we cannot have failed to know, but which are hard to see – "there is no *result* that [his] remarks aim at that can be had apart from the work they call upon us to do on ourselves."

I have no wish to quarrel with this (necessarily) very general account of the internal relation between Wittgenstein's teaching, his writing, and its reading. But why does Baz think that my writings on seeing aspects are "essentially unfaithful" to it?

In the first main section of his paper, he offers the following considerations in support of his judgement. First, he claims that my interpretation of Wittgenstein's remarks is essentially paraphrasable in something like a paragraph; and hence, that it attributes views or positions to him that he could have simply, directly said. (In something like a paragraph? Or in something more like a twenty-page essay?) Second, he claims that my interpretation has essentially no use for Wittgenstein's initial distinction (in *PI* II.xi) between two uses of the word "see" and the two objects of sight corresponding to them, and instead treats the discussion as beginning with the third remark of *PI* II.xi (concerning the experience of noticing an aspect). Third, he claims that my reading represses the fact that Wittgenstein's remarks invite us to test out our words, to see whether and how we might want to employ them in a variety of familiar contexts, and to account for our choices. My interpretation, as it were, eliminates all of Wittgenstein's question marks; whatever understanding of Wittgenstein it gains "is not arrived at by our reminding ourselves of the uses of our words – by our struggling in this way with the temptation to think that we know *in advance* what our words mean."

Before I address the details of these criticisms, two preliminary reminders might prove helpful. The first is that there is a structural obstacle in the way of determining exactly what weight to attach to the precise forms and general organization of Wittgenstein's remarks in Part II, Section 11 of *Philosophical Investigations*, and indeed of the writing that constitutes the whole of that part of the book. The problem is that these remarks went through far fewer stages of revision

and re-arrangement than did the remarks that make up Part I.[1]
Hence, although we simply do not know with what degree of satisfaction Wittgenstein regarded the state in which those remarks have
been presented to us by his editors and literary executors, his treatment of what is now Part I suggests that the text of Part II, as we have
it, would have been subject to further revision if its author had lived
long enough to do so. We certainly cannot take it for granted that
the text of *PI* II.xi, as we have it, in either its fine details or its overall articulation, is in a state that Wittgenstein would have considered
either satisfactory or final.

I should perhaps emphasize that this conclusion is not the result
of applying a general interpretative principle to the effect that any
adequate account of Wittgenstein's writing must anchor and orient
itself in the history of its construction, refashioning, and publication. My point is rather that the author of *Philosophical Investigations*
did not live to see his book into print; and whilst we have good reason to think that Part I as eventually published had reached a state
that Wittgenstein considered to be satisfactory, we are on far shakier
ground in making the same claim about Part II. Hence, even a reader
of *PI* II.xi who shares Baz's view that the form of Wittgenstein's writing is internal to its teaching, and who is open to the possibility that
the smallest detail of its formulations might be made to bear significant philosophical fruit, could be forgiven for hesitating to place the
same degree of hermeneutic pressure on the prose of any sections
in Part II as she might on the remarks of Part I. Can one, for example, confidently exclude the possibility that (at least some range of
instances of) Wittgenstein's liberal use of question marks in *PI* II.xi
reflects the provisional and tentative state of his reflections on his
material, his persisting uncertainty about what exactly to say and how
to say it, rather than a considered and weighty methodological commitment? Once again, I am not claiming that the first answer to this
question should be preferred to the second; I am rather struck by the
fact that Baz does not even consider that there might be a question
here worth asking.

---

[1] A more detailed account of these matters is to be found in G. H. Von Wright, "The
Troubled History of Part II of the *Investigations*," *Grazer Philosophische Studien* 42
(1992): 181–92.

My second preliminary reminder concerns the history of my own texts rather than those of Wittgenstein; and I am led to this immodesty by Baz's passing remark at the outset of his paper that, "So far as I can see, Mulhall's recent account is essentially a reassertion of his earlier, extended account in *On Being in the World*." Is it overly sensitive of me to detect in this remark the implication that any self-respecting author might reasonably have been expected to have deepened or modified, or at least in some way to have allowed a decade's worth of teaching, reading, and thinking to effect some change in, his initial understanding of his material? And of course, I am unwilling to think of myself as so utterly lost to my own experience. That is why it matters to me that what appears as one chapter in *Wittgenstein: A Critical Reader*[2] also appeared (virtually simultaneously) as the concluding sections of Part One of my *Inheritance and Originality*[3] (where it is prefaced by a claim that it constitutes an extension, revision, and reinflection of my conclusions in *On Being in the World*).[4]

Baz, in an attached note, mentions this fact about the material he discusses but regards it as essentially insignificant. In my view, however, a number of vitally important issues and themes that, whilst there to be seen in the *Critical Reader* version, had necessarily to remain either implicit or undeveloped in that relatively cramped context, become rather more explicit, indeed the subject of deliberate and fairly elaborate thematization, in the more ample surroundings of *Inheritance and Originality*, which (amongst other things) provides a detailed reading of the first 243 sections of Part I of the *Investigations* as a kind of determining background for the reading of *PI* II.xi with which that part of my book culminates. In my view, it is the thematizations and elaborations that this context makes possible that are most pertinent to understanding the ways in which my conception of seeing aspects has been refined and modified over the last decade, ways which I would view as directly relevant to exactly the issues upon which Baz focuses his critique. I don't mean to deny that the *Critical Reader* article should

---

[2] Stephen Mulhall, "Seeing Aspects," *Wittgenstein: A Critical Reader*, ed. Hans-Johann Glock (Oxford: Blackwell, 2001), 246–67.

[3] Mulhall, *Inheritance and Originality: Wittgenstein, Heidegger, Kierkegaard* (Oxford: Oxford University Press, 2001), 153–82.

[4] Mulhall, *On Being in the World: Wittgenstein and Heidegger on Seeing Aspects* (London and New York: Routledge, 1990).

be able to stand on its own two feet (although I would say that not every significant issue can be raised, let alone dealt with, in every context); nor do I mean to demand that anyone who wishes to engage with my views on seeing aspects has to have read everything I have ever written on the topic. But it is clear from Baz's paper (e.g., in note 1) that he has in fact read (at least some of) *Inheritance and Originality*; and I would have expected him, as much as anyone, to acknowledge that a reader is likely to see more of (to see more in, to see further aspects of) what an author is attempting to achieve in a given text when its immediate context is one that the author himself was also in a position to fashion. Hence, I will tend to base my defense of my "recent account" of Wittgenstein on seeing aspects on the version that concludes Part One of *Inheritance and Originality*. I can thereby bring out more clearly the features of that account that might have been harder to discern (although I believe that they are nevertheless discernible) in the *Critical Reader* version to which Baz refers.

What, then, of his charge that my account represses the philosophical work that Wittgenstein aims to effect with his words? It will surprise no one to learn that I am unimpressed by his claim that my reading is essentially paraphrasable in something like a paragraph. Since I found it painfully hard to compress even its central contentions into the context of the *Critical Reader* without significant loss, I am rather inclined to take the fact of Baz's one-paragraph paraphrase to indicate that he has missed the full complexity even of what survived this compression. So the heart of our disagreement must rather lie in his more specific claims about the precise turns my reading takes.

Let's begin with Baz's contention that I repress the true beginning of Wittgenstein's discussion (a particularly serious charge in the context that *Inheritance and Originality* constructs, with its obsessive interest in properly locating the points at which philosophical texts begin their work). First, it is worth noting that, in my original discussion of this material,[5] I gave the matter of what Wittgenstein calls "the categorical difference between the two 'objects' of sight" (*PI* 193a) sustained attention, in my discussion of two later but related remarks from *PI* II.xi: "If I saw the duck-rabbit as a rabbit, then I saw: these

---

5 Ibid., 28–30.

shapes and colors (I give them in detail)—and I saw besides some-thing like this: and here I point to a number of different pictures of rabbits.—This shows the difference between the concepts" (*PI* 196h); "The color of the visual impression corresponds to the color of the object (this blotting paper looks pink to me, and is pink)—the shape of the visual impression to the shape of the object (it looks rectangu-lar to me, and is rectangular)—but what I perceive in the dawning of an aspect is not a property of the object, but an internal relation between it and other objects" (*PI* 212a). Perhaps Baz thinks that these passages do not distinguish the same two objects of sight as are men-tioned at the outset of *PI* II.xi, or do so in a way that Wittgenstein wishes to question; or perhaps he wishes to avoid any passage in which Wittgenstein himself appears happy to use a phrase ("internal relations") that he holds in some suspicion (for reasons that remain somewhat opaque to me). Since, however, I don't hold that taking the beginning of a text seriously requires that one's treatment of it should occur, in full, at the beginning of one's commentary, and since my original discussion of this passage argues that the categorical distinc-tion at stake in it can directly be connected to the issues I see raised in the idea of "continuous aspect dawning" (for that attitude is, on my account of the matter, in part made manifest in one's tendency to sort an object with others as one of their kind – picture-rabbits with rab-bits, Louis XV chairs with Louis XV paintings rather than Bauhaus chairs, and so on), I feel that Baz has simply overlooked my attempt to treat the issue he accuses me of overlooking.

Why, then, did I choose to omit this original discussion from my recent, condensed recounting of my reading as a whole?[6] In part, because I take the initial importance of the categorical distinction to be brought out in the third remark of *PI* II.xi, where Wittgenstein says: "I contemplate a face, and then suddenly notice its likeness to another. I *see* that it has not changed; and yet I see it differently. I call this experience 'noticing an aspect'" (*PI* 193c). This passage surely encodes the categorical distinction Baz emphasizes, together with the two uses of the word "see" (distinguished by italicization in the second sentence) that are noted before anything else in *PI* II.xi. But it draws

---

[6] That I did so is noticed and discussed by Timothy Gould as well, in his contribution to the present volume.

immediately from those paired distinctions the sense of paradox in the experience of aspect-dawning that I claim to be what engenders our philosophical bewilderment, and to which I take Wittgenstein's ensuing discussion to be (before all, if not exclusively) responsive. Hence, by talking of this remark as the beginning of the discussion, I don't see that I have occluded anything coming before it, or any of the philosophical work of Wittgenstein's words; and since Baz himself repeatedly declares in his paper that the business of clarifying the concept introduced in this remark (by clarifying its place amongst the concepts of experience) is Wittgenstein's central concern in *PI* II.xi, I see no good reason why he should disagree with my way of framing that concern.

A more important difference between Baz and myself can also be seen to come out even at this initial stage, however. This has to do with his sense that Wittgenstein's dominating mode of discourse throughout *PI* II.xi is one of setting questions for his readers: The point is to invite his reader to say what she could want to call something, what words she would employ in a particular situation, and then to ask her to reflect upon her choice and try to account for it. I don't wish to deny that such invitations and questions accumulate along the way in *PI* II.xi, and that they have important work to do; but it is worth remembering that there are many remarks in *PI* II.xi that don't match Baz's template. The remark I quoted above from *PI* 212a is one excellent example. How much room for individual judgement is left for us there? But the opening remark of *PI* II.xi is equally to the point: it does not, after all, ask us whether we would be inclined to acknowledge two different uses of the word "see" here, or to distinguish *categorically* between two "objects of sight" (itself hardly an everyday expression, of whose grammar Wittgenstein might be thought merely to be reminding us). And in the third remark of the section, Wittgenstein explicitly says that "I call this experience 'noticing an aspect'"; suddenly apprehending the likeness between two faces is not what *we* call "noticing an aspect," and certainly not what *is* called "noticing an aspect." The phrase is, rather, Wittgenstein's – a coinage of his own for experiences of a kind that do not seem to have their own, handy, generic labels of which we might be reminded.

And in this respect, the opening of *PI* II.xi sets (at least one of) the dominant tones of the section as a whole. As I note at the outset of all three of my discussions of this material, this section of the *Investigations* introduces an unprecedented number of newly minted terms – "picture-objects," "continuous seeing-as," "regarding-as," "aspect-blindness," and so seemingly endlessly on. My way of working into Wittgenstein's treatment of this topic is to invite my reader to be struck by this highly unusual fact about Wittgenstein's philosophical prose, and to lay out as clearly as I can what I take the point of each specific coinage to be. In short, I take this dimension of Wittgenstein's prose to be asking questions of its reader in the absence of any question marks – questions to which my prose declares itself to be offering answers; and I take many of Wittgenstein's ways of deploying even such familiar terms as "seeing" and "knowing" here in the same spirit – as projections of those terms in decisively unfamiliar ways that are designed to bring out and put together phenomena that typically go unnoticed, and certainly are not seen as hanging together.

Hence, when Baz claims that "Mulhall's distinction between 'seeing' and 'knowing' corresponds to no distinction that might exist in our language between 'seeing' (in whichever of its ordinary senses) and 'knowing' (in whichever of its ordinary senses)," I take it that he is here overlooking the highly distinctive kind of work that Wittgenstein intends his words to perform. In fact, Baz might be said to provide one way of characterizing that work earlier in his paper, when he talks of Wittgenstein as not only bringing us back to situations of speech but also projecting us into them, so as to discover something about the meanings of the words we utter – *if* that formulation is meant to include such cases as being asked to find a way of making sense of a familiar word in an unfamiliar context, to understand what a speaker might mean to be bringing to our attention thereby, by understanding how the ordinary sense or senses of that word might lead us to find its employment in this new context apt or compelling.

This sense of ordinary words as projectable in ways that go beyond, that put pressure on, their commonly established routes of significance is hardly evident in Baz's just-cited comment about my use of "seeing" and "knowing," however; it rather implies that projecting a word beyond its already-established uses takes it outside our language (or is it outside language as such?). But even if we set that aside, a fundamental point remains. My commentary on Wittgenstein's words explicitly identifies, and attempts to respond to, an unusual mode of philosophical work that they labor to carry out. I am prepared for a reader to find my claim that this is the case, and certainly my claims as to the specific kind of work they are intended to do, unconvincing; but I was unprepared for any of them entirely to miss the fact that this is what I am claiming.

So much I took to be an obvious dimension of my work from its outset. But when constructing my condensed recounting of that work for the *Critical Reader*, and particularly for *Inheritance and Originality*, I found myself able to provide a further, explicit, and more specific characterization of the work I was attributing to Wittgenstein's prose. The argument goes in two stages, the first of which emerges when I give more forceful emphasis to a point that was central even to my account in *On Being in the World*, when my discussion moves from pictorial aspects to the significance of meaning-blindness. As is familiar, Wittgenstein here introduces the phenomenon of "secondary sense" (once again, hardly a familiar use of our ordinary words). He declares that secondary uses of a word do not illustrate but rather presuppose (even while transforming) its primary use, that no other word would do to express my inclinations in this context, and that candidate causal explanations of that inclination are irrelevant (at least for Wittgenstein's purposes). In discussing these claims, I point out that "any experience of aspect-dawning – whether linguistic or pictorial – is doubly dependent on the inclination to take over an expression from its standard technique of use and employ it as the immediate expression of an experience."[7] This is what happens when we express our realization that there is a face in a puzzle-picture by saying that we see a change in a picture's organization even though we know that no actual rearrangement of its parts has occurred; and more generally, whenever we talk of "Now I'm seeing it as …", when we know that the relevant picture-object has not changed, the concept of seeing is modified in a way whose point depends upon a sense that its original meaning necessarily comes along with the word itself. Similarly, when we talk of saying the word "bank" outside any discursive context and meaning a riverbank, we employ the term "meaning" in a way which unmoors it from its standard links to distinguishable techniques and

---

[7] Mulhall, *Inheritance and Originality*, 167.

contexts of use; and to talk of such things as "experiences of meaning" is itself to employ the word "meaning" outside its usual contexts of use. Hence, I claim, the language of aspect-dawning experiences in general "is an instance of what Wittgenstein means by primary and secondary senses" of words.[8]

The second step of my argument follows fairly directly if one accepts, as I do, that so much of the language Wittgenstein finds that he needs in order to articulate and prosecute his interest in aspect-seeing was not ready-to-hand, but rather had to be coined by him. My most explicit elaboration of this step is taken in a long paragraph that is also the culmination of the whole of my reading of the *Investigations* in *Inheritance and Originality*.

In Part I of the *Investigations*, Wittgenstein's denial of the idea that rules of grammar approximate to calculi with fixed rules – his sense of the play of language – finds its methodological expression in imagining language-games (conjuring up fictional contexts which invite the projection of our concepts in unpredictably controlled ways), in coining metaphors and similes, and in the liberating resonances of aphorism. This reflexivity culminates, at the culmination of his discussion of rule-following, in his uncovering of symbolic or mythological modes of meaning words – modes which Part II of the *Investigations* shows to be re-describable as secondary senses of terms (which must be distinguished from metaphorical uses of them). But of course, this re-description emerges from a grammatical investigation of aspect-perception and its ramifications which is permeated and governed by a phalanx of new coinages – a body of terms whose sense trades upon and yet goes beyond their ordinary grammar – that itself exemplifies the phenomenon of secondary sense. In short, in a more systematic way than ever before, Wittgenstein explores the capacity of language to generate secondary meanings, its openness to gestural or mythological senses, precisely by deploying it. And he shows thereby that, just as the grammar of our words can make possible modes of projecting meaning that go beyond the projection of rules, so a grammatical investigation can discover new ways of establishing philosophical self-possession, by allowing itself

[8] Ibid.

to be informed by a certain transfigured sense of the necessities and limits of grammar – one in which the word "grammar" (and so the idea of grammatical structure) is discovered to tolerate projection into a context which is intolerant of rules. This suggests that grasping our second inheritance of language at once requires and makes possible our second inheritance of Wittgenstein's method; and it further implies that the way in which we take up that re-inheritance is itself a touchstone of intimacy – with Wittgenstein, and with one another.[9]

Some of the outcroppings of ideas in this passage (which refer back not only to the immediately preceding discussion but to all that precedes that discussion in this book) need more of a gloss than I can give here; but that merely reinforces my earlier reasons for resisting Baz's claim that the essence of my reading of seeing aspects can be summarized in a paragraph. More pressingly, however, I want to ask: How can a reading of this material that culminates in a characterization of its prose as exploiting, and hence relying upon, the very dimensions of language use that it takes as its subject matter be taken to effect a repression of the specific work of that prose – the ways in which its deployments of words relate not only to their topic but to their readers, and thereby force us to reconceive our relation to those words, and thereby to the philosophical method they at once exemplify and put under examination? If Baz feels that even this kind of saying on my part needs to be backed up by some kind of showing – that these claims about the internal relation between Wittgenstein's words about aspects and the work they do on their readers remain essentially unacknowledged in the words by which they are advanced – then he might look more closely at my ways of using such terms as "gesture," "physiognomy," and "grammar," and in particular at my little mythology of our first and second inheritances of language.[10] I can well imagine that my particular claims here about the work of Wittgenstein's words, as well as my ways of making those claims, might elicit controversy and disagreement. I find it harder to imagine how one might read my most recent writings on this topic without seeing that I make them.

[9] Ibid., 181.
[10] Ibid., 178.

2. RESOLVING THE PARADOX

In the second main part of his paper, Baz aims to cast doubt on the success of my attempt to resolve or dissolve the sense of paradox attendant upon the experience of aspect-dawning. Primarily through a detailed discussion of a specific example of aspect-dawning, he aims to establish four claims: (1) that my proposed criteria of "continuous aspect perception" are of no use to me in that task; (2) that what I clearly wish to mean by "continuous aspect perception" – which is not what my proposed criteria capture – is of no more use to me in that task; (3) that my ways of using Wittgenstein's terminology in this area in fact elide what is genuinely philosophically puzzling about aspect-dawning; (4) hence my discussion fails to make contact with what it presumes to explain. More precisely, he judges that it can at best be understood as a species of causal explanation of aspect-dawning – precisely the genus that Wittgenstein begins his remarks by identifying as the kind of approach to this material that holds no interest for him.

In my view, this whole structure of nested claims falls to the ground because Baz fails properly to characterize my notion of "continuous aspect perception." In fact, his whole discussion of my dissolution of the paradox goes off the rails virtually at the outset, where, in the course of attempting to clarify my proposed criteria for that notion, he treats two related though distinct claims of mine as virtually synonymous: "What does it mean to say about someone that 'he takes the specific pictorial identity of a picture (as a picture of x rather than y) for granted', or that 'he has the general tendency to treat pictures in terms of what they depict'?" All that Baz is able to extract from my formulations is the claim that continuous seeing of an aspect is evinced not just by the ability to describe a picture in terms of what it depicts (which simply amounts to the ability to recognize pictures as pictures), but the ability to do so immediately and unhesitatingly. He then proceeds to construct his putative counter-example on this understanding of my position. But it is in fact a misunderstanding of my position; and it was my knowledge that my position as advanced in *On Being in the World* had been so misunderstood (by Baz himself in his earlier article, amongst others, which suggests to me that his own position has not essentially altered in the intervening years) that led me to stress the inadequacy of such a reading (with respect to my own claims, and to those of Wittgenstein) in both of the more recent versions of my work on this topic.

This is why I spend so much time at the beginning of my recent remarks on the fact that, and the way in which, Wittgenstein introduces the concept of "continuous seeing" of an aspect at the beginning of his discussion, quite as if it is a contrast term without which his investigation of aspect-dawning will not properly be oriented. He cites the example of a picture-face, and then offers the following commentary:

> In some respects I stand towards it as I do towards a human face. I can study its expression, can react to it as to the expression of the human face. A child can talk to picture-men or picture-animals, can treat them as it treats dolls.
>
> I may, then, have seen the duck-rabbit simply as a picture-rabbit from the first. That is to say, if asked "What's that?" or "What do you see here?" I should have replied: "A picture-rabbit." If I had further been asked what that was, I should have explained by pointing to all sorts of pictures of rabbits, should perhaps have pointed to real rabbits, talked about their habits, or given an imitation of them.
>
> I should not have answered the question "What do you see here?" by saying: "Now I am seeing it as a picture-rabbit." I should simply have described my perception: just as if I had said "I see a red circle over there." (*PI* 194c–e)

I take Wittgenstein to be stressing three interrelated points in this passage. First, when we see a picture-object, we see what it depicts – describe it in terms of what it depicts, not as an arrangement of marks inviting interpretation. Second, our grasp of what a picture-object is typically comes out in the ways in which we unquestioningly relate it to that which it depicts – for example, by acting as if pointing to, or even imitating, real rabbits is as good a way of explaining what I see as is pointing to other pictures of rabbits (i.e., grouping a picture-rabbit with rabbits rather than with pictures). Third, we also relate to such picture-objects in the kinds of ways in which we relate to the objects they depict – recoiling from the malevolence of a picture-face, or feeling cheered by its glowing happiness.

Despite the fact that my discussion begins by explicitly distinguishing these three implications of Wittgenstein's remarks, Baz's summary of it simply runs them together. When he glosses my phrase about "taking the specific pictorial identity of a picture for granted," he takes it to refer to the first of these three points, when in fact it refers to the second; and his gloss on my talk of "treating pictures in terms of what they depict" makes it hover between the first and second points, when in fact it refers to the third. The consequence of this misapprehension is that my third point goes missing altogether, and with it a central component of my notion of "continuous aspect perception."

I argue that it is this third point that Wittgenstein is returning to when he offers us one of his most striking coinages: "Perhaps the following expression would have been better: we *regard* the photograph, the picture on our wall, as the object itself (the man, landscape, and so on) depicted there" (*PI* 205e). Kissing the photograph of a loved one; feeling ashamed before the icon of a saint; being struck with awe at the immensity of the night sky in Van Gogh's "Starry Night" – people who respond in such ways to pictures are not mistaking the pictures for what they depict; they rather exhibit the adult version of the child's natural tendency to talk not only to dolls, but to picture-faces. Wittgenstein's point in invoking them is two-fold. First, while such reactions are perfectly familiar parts of human experience, they might have been otherwise: "We could easily imagine people who did not have this relation to such pictures. Who, for example, would be repelled by photographs, because a face without color and even perhaps a face in reduced proportions struck them as inhuman" (*PI* 205f). And second, such reactions constitute an extreme manifestation of the general human tendency to take it entirely for granted that pictures depict something or someone; the very idea of such responses would never occur to us unless the general shape of our lives with pictures were not deeply informed by an unhesitating responsiveness to what they depict.

We might combine these points in the following way. Such "regarding-as" reactions would have no place in the lives of those who merely know that pictures are meant to be representative, who tend to describe them in terms of lines and color patches and then draw inferences therefrom. Indeed, even those who not only perceive and describe pictures in terms of what they depict, but also relate to them immediately and unhesitatingly as pictures (for example, when asked to describe a glimpsed drawing of a transfixed animal, they might make mistakes, but mistakes about the kind of animal or kind of weapon depicted, not about the organization of pencil-lines on paper [cf. *PI* 203f]), might not be inclined to feel ashamed under the gaze of an icon. The fact is, however, that human beings do have such inclinations; as it happens, our form of life is pervaded with practices and modes of response that manifest the kind of relation to pictures that includes all three aspects or dimensions implicit in Wittgenstein's initial introduction of the concept of "continuous seeing-as," and that he explores elsewhere in much more detail. My notion of "continuous seeing-as," following Wittgenstein's, is meant to incorporate all three of those aspects.

Why, then, remind us of these very general facts about the place of pictures in our lives? What is the philosophical significance of such armchair anthropology, such remarks on the natural history of mankind? My intuition is that Wittgenstein is here putting into practice the methodological implications of a remark that (as Baz reminds us) he makes fairly late in *PI* II.xi: "We find certain things about seeing puzzling, because we do not find the whole business of seeing puzzling enough" (*PI* 212f). In other words, Wittgenstein aims to dissipate our sense of bewilderment about the apparently paradoxical turns of phrase through which we give expression to aspect-dawning experiences, by inviting us to relocate that specific kind of experience against the broader background that is constituted by the general role of pictures in our lives – a role that can itself be seen as deeply puzzling from a certain perspective, and would be so regarded by creatures who, for example, were repelled by pictures, although we are not normally struck by this fact about ourselves and our form of life.

Our openness to aspect-dawning experiences – our willingness to give expression to the dawning of a new pictorial aspect of a picture-object in terms which have their original home in contexts where they would register an actual change in the perceived object – bewilders us because we maintain our desire so to express ourselves in the face of our knowledge that nothing about the picture-object has changed, and because it seems that all that strikes us in such experiences is the fact that one pictorial figure has two pictorial uses. Suppose, however, we locate this disorienting phenomenon within the broader range of our relations to pictures elsewhere in our lives. A picture-rabbit is something we see as hanging together with real rabbits; we might explain what it depicts by imitating a real rabbit or pointing to real rabbits; a child might treat it in the ways it treats its stuffed rabbit or its pet rabbit in the yard, and so on. A picture-duck hangs together in analogous ways to ducks. The common pictoriality of these pictures in fact links them with rather different regions of our experience of, and responsiveness to, the world we inhabit; for it is in terms of *what they depict* that we respond to them, to the point at which we naturally transfer responses appropriate to what is depicted to their depictions – so our modes of response to each picture-object will be as different as are the things they depict, and so will our sense of their specific place in our world. Hence, when it suddenly dawns on us that this particular picture-rabbit is also a picture-duck, when we express our experience quite as if it registers the picture-rabbit's actually becoming a picture-duck, our sense that everything about it has changed (despite our knowledge that nothing has changed) can be seen as an unusually extreme expression of our general tendency to regard a picture of a rabbit as being as different from a picture of a duck as a rabbit is from a duck. It is, in effect, a further species of our "regarding-as" response to pictures; and hence is to be understood as part of the general relation to pictures that I (and, I hold, Wittgenstein) call "continuous seeing-as."

I can, therefore, understand why Baz thinks he sees a circularity in my attempted resolution of the paradox of aspect-dawning, and also why he is anxious about its possible dissolution into a merely causal account of the phenomenon; for it is central to my strategy for dissolving the paradox that I present our openness to such experiences as one (although not the only) striking manifestation of the ways in which we regard pictures as the objects they depict, and thereby as showing that our general relation to pictures is one of continuous aspect perception. But there is in fact nothing viciously circular about this strategy, because there is nothing viciously circular about an attempt to resolve our sense of bewilderment about a specific phenomenon taken in isolation by perspicuously representing it as forming part of a larger whole – as one manifestation of the distinctive role of pictures in our lives. And by the same token, relating aspect-dawning to continuous aspect perception as part to whole does not involve claiming that our general attitude of continuous aspect perception is the immediate or proximate cause of aspect-dawning experiences. My idea is not that we are open to such experiences because we have a certain psychological predisposition to them; it is rather that our openness to such experiences is part of what is involved in having the attitude of continuous aspect perception – that it constitutes a particularly striking manifestation of one aspect of the role pictures play in our lives.

I suppose it is just possible that part of Baz's reason for thinking that my strategy threatens to resolve into a species of causal explanation can be traced to the fact that it rests on reminding us of some very general facts about our form of life – features of it that might have been otherwise. But I hope it is plain that my account nowhere concerns itself with the causes of aspect-dawning experiences in the sense in which experimental psychology or neuroscience might approach the matter; after all, if it did, then one would have to level the same charge at Wittgenstein every time he recalls us to certain simple, familiar facts about our life with language in the service of dissolving philosophical confusions:

The aspects of things that are most important for us are hidden because of their simplicity and familiarity. (One is unable to notice something— because it is always before one's eyes.) The real foundations of his enquiry do not strike a man at all. Unless *that* fact has at some time struck him.— And this means: we fail to be struck by what, once seen, is most striking and powerful. (*PI* §129)

The strategy of my writings on seeing aspects, both early and recent, is to reduce our sense of puzzlement about aspect-dawning by relocating it in the broader context of our lives with pictures; that context is hidden from us (and by us) because of its simplicity and familiarity – it evades our notice precisely because it pervades our form of life. If, however, in overcoming our bewilderment about aspect-dawning, we must allow ourselves to be struck by what I call continuous aspect perception, I do not wish to deny that in so doing we will come to see something striking and powerful about ourselves and our lives – something that might itself create not only a sense of wonder but one of bewilderment. The remainder of my account of seeing aspects is designed to respond to that possible bewilderment by further contextualizations of the phenomena that might provoke it. Hence, I relate continuous aspect perception to its analogue in the realm of linguistic meaning; and continuous meaning perception to the seam in human experience at which individuality and sociality meet, the realm of the otherness of the other, the ways in which our connectedness with others can seem at once unpredictably deep and irremediably fragile; and I relate these issues in turn to what I want to call our inhabitation of the world (its promise of nextness to us, and its threatened distance from us).

Since each such contextualization in effect recontextualizes its predecessor, there is a sense in which much of the significance I perceive even in the ground we have so far explicitly covered is left unrecovered in the absence of the full account I try to provide elsewhere. There is no possibility of undertaking such a full accounting in this context; but my gesturing toward it is meant at once to underline my sense that my reading of this material resists paraphrase, and to warn against the tempting thought that even my attempt to resolve the paradox of aspect-dawning can be reduced to a single paragraph. And I hope that the present set of remarks might succeed, where my earlier writings appear to have failed, in making some real progress toward bringing the work of my own words on seeing aspects into view.[11]

[11] I wrote this chapter during my time as John Findlay Visiting Professor at the Philosophy Department at Boston University. I would like to thank the members of that department for inviting me to take up that position, and the Warden and Fellows of New College, Oxford, for making it possible for me to accept that invitation.

13

On the Difficulty of Seeing Aspects and the "Therapeutic" Reading of Wittgenstein

Steven G. Affeldt

1.

The distinctive character of Wittgenstein's manner of writing, early and late, must play an important role in accounting for the diverse ways in which it has been approached and engaged. Indeed, there is arguably no other philosopher about whom the question of how to approach his texts – how to understand their aims, methods, modes of criticism, compositional structure, and the like – is as widely regarded as decisively important to a correct appreciation of what they say, and as perennially a matter of dispute. In recent years, however, something approaching an orthodoxy concerning this matter has begun to emerge among interpreters of Wittgenstein. Informed by his remark that "there is not *a* philosophical method, though there are indeed methods, like different therapies" (*PI* §133), this approach to his work has been designated "therapeutic."

A useful account of this "therapeutic" reading is offered by Alice Crary in her Introduction to *The New Wittgenstein* – a volume of essays the editors regard as exemplifying this approach.[1] For my purposes at this point, the following three contrasts with what Crary calls "standard" approaches to reading Wittgenstein provide a sufficiently

---

[1] *The New Wittgenstein*, ed. Alice Crary and Rupert Read (London: Routledge, 2000). While my comments on this "therapeutic reading" are keyed to Crary's discussion, I do not intend them to be limited to it. Her discussion is helpful in offering a clear explication of an approach to reading Wittgenstein that is exemplified by, but not generally as explicitly theorized in, a great deal of writing on his work.

accurate, if general, sense of its nature. First, "standard" readings of Wittgenstein understand him to be addressing meaningful philosophical claims and to be showing them to be false, misleading, incomplete, or in some other way unsatisfactory. The "therapeutic" reading, in contrast, takes Wittgenstein to be addressing merely apparent claims that are actually strictly meaningless, and it understands one of his central ambitions to consist in showing that these apparent claims have as yet been given no sense whatsoever. Second, the "standard" reading takes his work to have important philosophical consequences in that it contests mistaken views and replaces them with more adequate views: replacing, for example, an account of the objectivity of agreement in language in terms of universals with an account in terms of agreement in judgments. On the "therapeutic" reading, however, since Wittgenstein is simply showing apparent claims to be strictly nonsense, abandoning them is "*without consequences*," and to think otherwise is "a sign that we are still participating in the confusion Wittgenstein seeks to address."[2] Finally, as is already suggested by these first two contrasts, on the "standard" reading, Wittgenstein's aim in philosophy is quite traditional: replacing mistaken responses to meaningful philosophical questions with correct responses. However, on the "therapeutic" reading, the aim of his philosophical work is far more radical: it consists entirely in freeing us from the idea that there are any meaningful philosophical questions of the sort we had imagined that stand in need of the kinds of responses we had sought to provide. As Crary puts it, his aim is to bring "us to the recognition that certain words we are tempted to utter in philosophy are nonsense, that they fail to say anything that we want to say."[3]

These distinguishing features of the "therapeutic" reading are clearly interwoven, and each is integral to its "therapeutic" character. The last, however, seems most central. Wittgenstein's work, on this reading, is therapeutic in that, by showing us that claims we are tempted to make in philosophy are empty and do not satisfy us, it frees us from the grip of those claims and the intellectual entanglement they bring.[4]

---

[2] Ibid., 4.

[3] Ibid., 7.

[4] Crary also emphasizes that Wittgenstein's work is therapeutic in *how* the recognition of emptiness is achieved (ibid., 7). At this point nothing I will say depends upon this, but I return to the matter more fully in section 4.

This approach to reading Wittgenstein is powerful, compelling, and certainly more accurately captures his methods and aims in both major periods of his work than the "standard" reading. However, at least with respect to Wittgenstein's later period, I find it importantly limited. In saying this I don't, in the first instance, mean to quarrel with what it *does* say – although I will raise some concerns on this score. Rather, I have in mind the following two limitations. First, there are important dimensions of Wittgenstein's later philosophy about which the "therapeutic" reading is silent; it does not seem to recognize (the importance of) these dimensions, and it does not provide the resources needed for exploring them and learning from them. Second, in failing to consider these dimensions, the "therapeutic" reading is both unable to show how Wittgenstein's work possesses any genuinely therapeutic power and unable to capture the depth and force of its broadly moral urgency.

To develop these claims, I turn in Sections 2 and 3 to a consideration of some specific passages from *Philosophical Investigations* centered on the difficulty of seeing certain kinds of aspects. This will allow me to sketch, in at least some detail, one central dimension of Wittgenstein's later work that I do not find recognized or taken into account by the "therapeutic" reading, and which, it seems to me, must be. I will then return, in section 4, to the "therapeutic" reading and articulate my sense of its limitations somewhat more fully.

2.

When thinking of Wittgenstein on seeing aspects it is natural to think first and primarily of the remarks in Part II, Section 11 of *Philosophical Investigations*. And, indeed, they contain much that is importantly distinctive about his engagement with this matter. However, there are a number of other remarks in *Philosophical Investigations* concerned with aspect-seeing, and exclusive attention to the remarks in *PI* II.xi may blind us to important aspects of Wittgenstein's interest in these issues in those remarks themselves as well as elsewhere.

Accordingly, while I will briefly consider some central examples of aspect-seeing in *PI* II.xi, I want initially to focus upon *PI* §129. There Wittgenstein writes:

The aspects [*Aspekte*] of things that are most important for us are hidden because of their simplicity and familiarity. (One is unable to notice something—because it is always before one's eyes.) The real foundations of his enquiry do not strike a man at all. Unless *that* fact has at some time struck him.—And this means: we fail to be struck by what, once seen, is most striking and powerful.

The location of this charged passage, near the close of an extended set of remarks concerning the methods required by Wittgenstein's new conception of philosophy and articulating his new understanding of the difficulty of its fruitful practice, heightens its power and its claim on our attention. However, the mere appearance of the word "aspects" is not sufficient to justify aligning the concerns of *PI* §129 and the concerns of the remarks in *PI* II.xi. Such a justification depends upon the use of the word "aspect" in *PI* §129 giving it a sense sufficiently close to the sense of the word as used in the more canonical remarks of *PI* II.xi. To see that it does, or at least how it might, we must recognize that in speaking of the aspects of things that are most important for us, Wittgenstein is invoking not something different from the things we notice, but some aspect of what we do notice. It has to be recognized, that is, that he is not directing us to look elsewhere but to look differently, that he is seeking to transform not the direction but the manner of our vision. For if this is recognized, then the use of "aspect" in *PI* §129 will closely follow many of its uses in *PI* II.xi and will invite such exhortations as "You have to see it like *this*," or "Try seeing this as related to that."

I cannot argue for this reading of *PI* §129 here. I will simply note that it coheres with one of the central methodological moves of *Philosophical Investigations* as a whole. Wittgenstein (often) writes in response to a sense that the possibility of various phenomena – for example, meaning, understanding, naming, following a rule, knowing another – has become mysterious to us, and that our efforts to account for their possibility – for example, by supposing underlying mental acts, universals, a pure logical order – only make matters more mysterious. A central part of his method, then, consists in seeking to dispel this mysteriousness of phenomena by recalling our attention to the ordinary circumstances in which they are said to occur and the criteria for them. He directs our attention differently to what is evident: the ordinary circumstances of phenomena of which we are aware but which we, for various reasons, dismiss as merely incidental or irrelevant.

If this reading of *PI* §129 is accepted, then it will invite an expanded understanding of the significance of the remarks in *PI* II.xi. In particular, it will invite understanding those remarks as more than simply an investigation into a circumscribed set of issues in the philosophy of perception. But further, and for my purposes more importantly, it will also enable us to recognize that Wittgenstein must be concerned with issues of aspect-seeing throughout *Philosophical Investigations*. For while admittedly highly general, it is nevertheless accurate to say that Wittgenstein is throughout concerned with how and why the aspects of things that are most important for us are hidden, and with how those aspects may be made available and their significance appreciated.

Of course, even if we grant that Wittgenstein must be concerned with aspect-seeing throughout *Philosophical Investigations*, how we understand the nature of that concern remains open. How we settle this matter will depend upon whether we construe central questions raised by *PI* §129 narrowly or broadly. I mean, for example, questions surrounding the scope of "us" and "we" in the phrases, "the aspect of things that are most important for us," and "we fail to be struck by," as well as how we should respond to the questions, "Important for what?" and "What is the nature of the enquiry Wittgenstein has in view in speaking of 'the real foundations of [a person's] enquiry'?"

If these questions are construed narrowly, Wittgenstein's pervasive concern with aspect-seeing will be correspondingly narrow. It will be directed exclusively toward philosophers engaged in investigating, for example, "the concepts of meaning, of understanding, of a proposition, of logic, of the foundations of mathematics, states of consciousness, and other things" (*PI* ix). Its aim will be to encourage attention to the specific uses of words, to the concrete circumstances of their use, to the role of natural reactions and forms of life, and the like. And its importance will be simply that, apart from attention to such matters, philosophers will fall victim to confusion, error, or emptiness.

Such a narrow construal of these questions is perfectly legitimate. Wittgenstein is, after all, clearly concerned with philosophers examining perennial philosophical questions and, in particular, with why these questions *are* perennial – with why philosophy has produced so much confusion and nonsense and so little illumination. However, it is equally legitimate to construe the questions raised by *PI* §129 broadly. For recalling Wittgenstein's continuous aim of revealing the philosopher as an exemplar of pervasive human drives, temptations, fantasies, desires, and disappointments, we may read *PI* §129 as addressing a general and recurrent human blindness to what is most important: to the bases of the significance and intelligibility of our experience, activity, speech, and our lives quite generally. So understood, Wittgenstein's perception in *PI* §129 will be closely allied with Romantic investigations of our recurrent human failure genuinely to experience our world and to appreciate the significance of (events in) our lives. Further, his project in *Philosophical Investigations* will be closely allied with Romantic projects of enabling such experience and in that way enabling a recovery, or discovery, of the significance of (events in) our lives.[5]

This broader construal of *PI* §129 intensifies the question of what impedes the availability and appreciation of the aspects of things that are most important for us. And it is this question that I want to explore, even if, of necessity, only partially.[6]

Of course, *PI* §129 itself may seem to provide the beginnings of a couple of gratifyingly clear responses to this question. On the one hand, the idea that the most important aspects are hidden "because of their simplicity and familiarity" may seem to suggest that the difficulty lies simply in a type of blindness to what is habitually present. And, indeed, such blindness may occur. We fail to notice, after a while, a stack of newspapers in a corner of the kitchen, or muddy shoes beside the back door. Or, as Heidegger emphasizes more than Wittgenstein, skill in carrying out some action can render its individual steps transparent and,

---

[5] Stanley Cavell was the first to articulate this connection, in Part Four of *The Claim of Reason: Wittgenstein, Skepticism, Morality, and Tragedy* (Oxford: Oxford University Press, 1979), and he has returned to it most recently in "The *Investigations*' Everyday Aesthetics of Itself," in *The Cavell Reader*, ed. Stephen Mulhall (Oxford: Blackwell, 1996). Beyond Cavell's, explorations of these relations that I have found helpful include Timothy Gould's "Finding the Everyday Again" (unpublished) and Richard Eldridge's *Leading a Human Life: Wittgenstein, Intentionality, and Romanticism* (Chicago: University of Chicago Press, 1997).

[6] It also intensifies the question of how Wittgenstein's writing may effect a recovery of experience and significance. While what I will develop bears on this question, I cannot explore it directly or systematically here.

in a sense, invisible. And, on the other hand, this passage may seem to suggest that our difficulty lodges in the fact that we do not understand what will meet the needs of our enquiry and so simply fail to consider the possibility that the simple and familiar aspects of things may do so.

Each of these suggestions construes our difficulty passively and as due to a more or less simple oversight or confusion. So construed, in order to make the most important aspects available, Wittgenstein's writing must simply draw our habitually blinded gaze toward them and show us that and how they are important for us.

But these suggestions cannot, I think, be accepted. I will simply mention two reasons why. First, to suggest that our difficulties may be so swiftly and directly dispatched renders the quite distinctive character of Wittgenstein's writing mysterious if not adventitious. He does call philosophy "description" (*PI*§124) and remarks that it "simply puts everything before us" (*PI* §126). However, if we grant that the nature of Wittgenstein's writing is determined by the difficulties it engages, then the character of the text itself shows that the work of description and simply putting everything before us cannot themselves be simple matters. Second, these suggestions miss Wittgenstein's continuous preoccupation with the human drive to repudiate the ordinary or the everyday.[7] He discloses this drive in, for example, our being "dazzled by the ideal" (*PI* §100), desiring something "pure and clear cut" (*PI* §105), so that we are, therefore, "dissatisfied" with the ordinary (*PI* §105) since it mars our wish for sublimity (*PI* §94). For Wittgenstein, then, the simple and familiar, understood as the ordinary or the everyday, are precisely not passively overlooked but are actively repudiated. Accordingly, our difficulty in seeing the most important aspects cannot be passively construed or, again, swiftly and easily dispatched.

I will develop more fully below one line of thought, related to, but distinct from, the ideas just broached, regarding our active role in the difficulty of appreciating the aspects of things that are most important for us. However, I want to approach it by turning to some remarks in *PI* II.xi and considering what light, if any, they shed on the nature of our difficulty.

---

[7] Revealing and investigating this continuous preoccupation of Wittgenstein's later work is central to all of Cavell's writing on him, marking what he argues is Wittgenstein's struggle with skepticism.

Leaving aside Wittgenstein's investigation of the possibility of complete aspect-blindness, there are a number of examples in *PI* II.xi in which we may encounter difficulty in seeing some aspect. I want to specify a couple of features of some of these examples. Consider first the most familiar example from *PI* II.xi, the duck-rabbit. I begin with this example both because it is the most familiar of Wittgenstein's examples of seeing aspects and because its central features are shared with his further examples of the schematic-cube, the triangle, and the double-cross. What I say about it, then, will also apply to these further examples.

Restricting ourselves to the case in which the duck-rabbit is presented in isolation rather than amid a number of line drawings of unambiguous duck-profiles or rabbit-profiles, and also disregarding as irrelevant for our purposes various individual biographical or psychological factors that might incline one to see simply the duck or the rabbit aspect, one may yet encounter difficulty in seeing one or the other aspect and, hence, in seeing the figure as embodying both – as *having* different aspects. Further, this difficulty may be temporary, recurrent, or, in principle, permanent. In any of these cases, however, we are readily able to explain the difficulty: There is a clear aspect that one *is* seeing, and since it is not possible to see both aspects at once, the fact that one is seeing the aspect of the duck, say, prevents one's seeing the aspect of the rabbit. As Cavell puts it, one aspect eclipses the other.[8] In such cases, then, in order to see one of the figure's aspects one has to blind oneself to the other. As I've said, this same type of explanation applies to possible difficulties in seeing aspects of the schematic-cube, the triangle, and the double-cross. In each case what impedes seeing a given aspect is that there is another clear aspect to be seen and one is seeing it.

A second, more diffuse, set of examples in which there may be a difficulty in seeing something *as* something includes seeing the specific character of a pictured smile if the picture is upside down (*PI* 198f), seeing the mirror image of the word "Pleasure," written in cursive script, as the word "Pleasure" (*PI* 198g), and, an example not derived from *PI* II.xi, seeing a picture of a man walking up a steep

---

[8] Cavell develops this thought in Part Four of *The Claim of Reason* (see especially 368–69).

path leaning on a stick as him sliding down the path in that position (*PI* 54).

With such examples Wittgenstein means to call to mind, by disrupting, the intimacy with which seeing is bound up with our embodiment, expectations, natural reactions, forms of life, and facts about our natural and social worlds. But then in these cases as well, whatever difficulty we may encounter is readily explained. Since what we (naturally) see is importantly structured by features of our embodiment, expectations, natural reactions, and the like, and since these cases run counter to or disrupt them, the very features that ordinarily enable seeing block it in these cases. In order, for example, to see a picture of a man walking up a steep path leaning on a stick as him sliding down the path, we must break free of our natural expectation that such a posture bespeaks exertion to move against the force of gravity and friction, we must (try to) imagine people for whom it comes natural to slide down a path in this posture, and this will, in turn, involve imagining a world in which human bodies (their shape, flexibility, capacities for balance, etc.) and physical forces are such as to *allow* naturally sliding down a path in this posture.

Consider, finally, a third set of examples from *PI* II.xi. These concern seeing the expression of a face (as sad, timid, quizzical, exasperated), hearing the mood of a melody (as plaintive or serious), or recognizing the likeness between the faces of a father and son (*PI* 209–210). In such cases, one sees the faces or hears the melody – indeed, one may be able to draw perfect likenesses of the faces or write the notes of the melody – and yet fails to see or hear the aspects in question. We might say that the individual sees or hears what is before her, yet, failing to recognize it *as* what it is, misses the aspect that is most important.[9]

In such examples, failure to recognize the relevant aspects seems to be explained in one of two ways. On the one hand, failure to recognize, at a certain age, a face (or melody) as happy or sad, or a tone of voice as approving or disapproving, seems to be explained (only) by a quite significant divergence in natural reactions or fairly basic human capacities. On the other hand, the ability to recognize a melody as plaintive may depend upon experience or training in music, and the

[9] I am grateful to Avner Baz for pressing me to consider this last set of examples.

ability to recognize a face as quizzical or like another may depend upon special familiarity with the person(s) involved. The failure to recognize these aspects, then, simply bespeaks a lack of such special experience, training, or familiarity.

Do the kinds of explanations brought to light by these sets of examples help in understanding the difficulty raised in *PI* §129 of seeing the aspects of things that are most important for us?

The last examples discussed may initially seem especially helpful, for they focus upon what we might call, not altogether happily, recognizing the significance of what is before us. However, I think that they are not helpful. The reason, briefly, is this. In *PI* §129 Wittgenstein is concerned with the failure to notice and appreciate what can be, and should be, noticed and appreciated by any (normal) human (of a certain age); by any of "us." However, this is not the case with these examples. For, as I have noted, they direct attention either to individuals with special training or familiarity, or to individuals whose natural reactions or basic human capacities are sufficiently divergent to raise questions about the extent to which they can be regarded as (normal) members of the "we" for whom Wittgenstein claims to speak.

Do the other two types of explanations help? Perhaps. But if they do, they do so in a surprising manner.

Consider, first, explanations centered on relations between seeing and embodiment, natural reactions, and so on. If explanations of this sort are to account for our difficulty, then Wittgenstein must be suggesting that our expectations, natural reactions, forms of life, and the like, as they stand, are radically disordered or perverted in such a fashion that, rather than enabling appreciation of the most important aspects, they impede it.

The thought of the human as continuously, if not irredeemably, subject to perversity is by no means foreign to *Philosophical Investigations*. It is expressed, for example, in the thought that we are possessed of a "drive to misunderstand" (*PI* §109) and so turn away from our "real need" (*PI* §108). However, the judgment of recurrent human perversity depends upon the thought that it is *possible* to recognize and follow our real need – even if we recurrently refuse to do so. While perverse, we are not permanently and necessarily out of harmony with ourselves and our world. Accordingly, this kind of explanation is not much help in understanding the difficulty of seeing the aspects that are most important for us.

What then of the idea that one aspect eclipses another? Is this type of explanation helpful? Is there some other clear aspect of things that we are seeing in the scenario of *PI* §129?

The answer to this question is not obvious, and I think we should say "not quite yes and not quite no." This much seems clear, however. If what impedes our appreciating the aspects that are most important is our seeing some other aspect, the situation is nevertheless importantly unlike the cases of duck-rabbit, the schematic-cube, the triangle, or the double-cross. In these cases it is clear *what* the eclipsing aspect is and *how* seeing it eclipses the other aspect(s). But neither of these matters is clear in the case of *PI* §129. Concerning the aspects of things that are most important for us, it is unclear that there is another readily specifiable aspect of the things to which we attend, and it is, therefore, unclear how seeing it might eclipse the most important aspects. Would the suggestion be that it is the things themselves to which we attend that block our recognizing the aspects that are most important? But it is clear neither how the things to which we attend could do this, nor, if they do, that another *aspect* of them impedes us. Wittgenstein finds the phenomenon of understanding, for example, to be an occasion for recurrent self-mystification, in large part because we recurrently fail to appreciate its most important aspects. But it is not *clear* that anything about the phenomenon as such eclipses them. As noted above, in *PI* §129 it seems that we are attending in the wrong manner to what lies fully open to view. But we do so without what is open to view readily suggesting another way of seeing it that could eclipse the most important aspects.

I do want to suggest, however, that these aspects are eclipsed – that their being hidden is not due to passive oversight or simple confusion. And, in particular, I want to suggest that what eclipses them is not a nothing, but not a something either.[10]

---

[10] Clearly, I am adapting and reversing the famously obscure remark from *PI* §304. To an interlocutor's protest that "you again and again reach the conclusion that the sensation is a *nothing*," Wittgenstein responds: "Not at all. It is not a *something*, but not a *nothing* either!"

3.

To begin to explain what I mean, I want to turn to Wittgenstein's first example in *Philosophical Investigations* – the shopkeeper in *PI* §1. It is presented as follows:

Now think of the following use of language: I send someone shopping. I give him a slip marked "five red apples". He takes the slip to the shopkeeper, who opens the drawer marked "apples"; then he looks up the word "red" in a table and finds the color sample opposite it; then he says the series of cardinal numbers – I assume that he knows them by heart – up to the word "five" and for each number he takes an apple of the same color as the sample out of the drawer. – It is in this and similar ways that one operates with words.

This is a quite peculiar and jarring example of the "use of language" or "operating with words."[11] It is as peculiar and jarring as is, on a certain reading, the opening passage from Augustine in which he describes his learning language as if he were an isolated, unnoticed, and unaddressed observer of his elders' speech and movements, more of a specter haunting the house than a babbling, laughing, crying, young child. There is an air of the surreal in Wittgenstein's example, perhaps most sharply crystallized in the shopkeeper looking up the word "red" in a table and finding the color sample opposite it. But notice two further features of the example. First, there is no mention of the shopper and shopkeeper speaking to one another during this transaction and, in my experience, if asked, readers usually say that they do not. Second, the shopkeeper is explicitly described as *saying* the series of cardinal numbers, a detail that, in the context of imagined silence between the shopper and shopkeeper, invites the impression that, like children of a certain age, the shopkeeper *must* say the numbers aloud to keep them straight. These features of the example work to present our use of language as mechanical, as consisting in deriving from "dead signs" (*PI* §432) operations to be performed – as,

---

[11] It is, of course, possible to read it otherwise. In his essay "Logic in 3D" (unpublished), Kelly Jolley argues, roughly, that the truncated quality of the example is meant to "disperse[] the fog" (*PI* §5) and allow us to recognize that the logical role of different words is a function of their uses. I find his reading compelling. My claim is that mine is as well – and, perhaps, more helpfully motivates the interlocutor's ensuing questions.

in short, *operating* with words.[12] There is no sense that we have a life with words, or that they have a life for us. Our relation to words is indistinguishable from our relation to signs of an unfamiliar code.[13]

I suggest that Wittgenstein has deliberately crafted a jarring example in which language use appears lifeless and mechanical, and has done so, at the opening of his investigations, precisely to call to mind (by contrast) the vitality of our life with words – our familiarity with them, our attachment to their look and sound, their prolific and fluid associations, the ease with which we employ them, their coming to meet us in speaking, and more. He aims to call all of this to mind for at least two reasons. First, it must form a touchstone for any adequate philosophical reflection on language. But second, and for present purposes more importantly, he wants to allow us to recognize the reality of our life with words as remarkable.[14]

In the light cast by this example, we are impressed not only by the remarkable character of our life with language, but by the fact that words, marks, sounds, gestures, are taken as significant at all, as communicating, and as directed toward things or others. In terms of Augustine's passage, we might say that we are impressed by the remarkable fact that they are taken as expressing desire. For as the shopkeeper example is presented, one wonders why he takes it that he is to do anything when presented with the slip of paper, or, indeed, why he takes it that an extended arm holding a slip of paper counts as *offering* it to him. (Does he have another chart depicting actions to take in response to various positions of others' arms? Or does he, perhaps, also know *this* by heart?)

---

[12] A further source of this impression is blunted by Anscombe's translation. Wittgenstein's German says that signs "stand on the slip" (*auf diesem stehen die Zeichen*), and this odd locution adds to the sense that they are dead or mute – merely standing there.

[13] This relation to words is akin to that of those who do not "experience the meaning of a word" (*PI* 214d) or do not feel that a word "has taken up its meaning into itself" (*PI* 218g). About the latter Wittgenstein says that "they would not have an attachment to their words."

[14] This is distinct from, for example, the idea that a proposition is "something very queer!" (*PI* §93), which expresses the sense that the possibility of a proposition is mysterious. Wittgenstein aims to dispel the sense of the mysterious, but not that of the remarkable. Indeed, as I am beginning (obliquely) to suggest, he regards the sense of the mysterious as, in part, produced by a flight from the remarkable.

The interlocutor's questions – "But how does he know where and how he is to look up the word 'red' and what he is to do with the word 'five'?" – express something of this puzzlement and so, indirectly, a recognition of the remarkable character of our ordinary life with language. However, they are somewhat misdirected. For as I've suggested, the question provoked by this example is rather: "How does it happen that the shopkeeper takes anything to be significant at all, to express desire?"

I am working to suggest that this example's deliberately mechanical and lifeless presentation of our use of language evokes a sense of an abyss of contingency, or the merely natural, in the fact of human language as we know it; a sense that Wittgenstein registers more explicitly in claiming that "Commanding, questioning, recounting, chatting, are as much a part of our natural history as walking, eating, drinking, playing." As in this remark from *PI* §25, I want to claim that the example in *PI* §1 is, ultimately, meant to direct our attention toward the myriad natural conditions on and for our life with language – conditions as manifold and specific as those on and for our human forms of walking, eating, drinking, and playing.[15] I want further to claim that these conditions represent one instance of the aspects of things that are most important for us. They are important for us not only for narrowly philosophical purposes, helping us to avoid confusion and emptiness about the working of language, but also important more broadly. For as Wittgenstein's work shows – and as is illustrated in Augustine's oddly spectral depiction of himself – a failure to appreciate these conditions produces endless self-mystification. We become not simply confused, but lost (*PI* §123).

However, the direction of our attention toward these conditions is blocked. The aspects of things that Wittgenstein constructs his example to bring before us are eclipsed. What eclipses them?

The *sign* of what eclipses them is the interlocutor's question: "What is the meaning of the word 'five'?" I take this question to mark the first appearance of a specifically metaphysical voice in *Philosophical*

---

[15] Stanley Cavell has developed this theme most fully in "The Availability of Wittgenstein's Later Philosophy," in *Must We Mean What We Say? A Book of Essays* (Cambridge: Cambridge University Press, 1969), 44–72, and in *The Claim of Reason*, Chapter VII, "Excursus on Wittgenstein's Vision of Language," 168–90.

Investigations. Which is to say that, as it stands, it is the first instance of philosophical emptiness. Of course, there is nothing, in general, problematic about asking for the meaning of the word "five." But the interlocutor's question is empty for two reasons. First, unlike "But how does he know where and how he is to look up the word 'red' and what he is to do with the word 'five'," this question has, in the context presented, no natural occasion. There is nothing in the example of the use of language in *PI* §1 that motivates this question from within the plane of the ordinary or everyday.[16] And, second, as Wittgenstein works to show throughout *Philosophical Investigations*, a remark or question only derives its sense from the circumstances of its natural employment. Accordingly, because it lacks, as it stands, any relation to circumstances of natural employment, this question is not simply idle, but empty. It is empty because it is idle.

This emergence of emptiness in *PI* §1 constitutes a rupture or break. It redirects attention. However, while it can seem otherwise, it does not direct attention toward anything. For in the place of an object of attention there is emptiness. The interlocutor's question creates the illusion that, because attention is redirected, it must be redirected toward something, and, indeed, toward something of pressing importance. This redirection of attention toward emptiness while creating the illusion that it is directed toward something is, I think, one central mark of the philosophical or metaphysical for Wittgenstein. And it is precisely this, I suggest, that eclipses the aspects of things that are most important for us.

To say that, for Wittgenstein, philosophical or metaphysical emptiness blocks the aspects of things that are most important may not be especially surprising. But that is not quite what I am suggesting. Rather, I am suggesting that the emergence of philosophical emptiness, that rupture of attention and its redirection toward a nothing that seems to be a something, is motivated. It is a manifestation of the recurrent human drive to repudiate the ordinary. So, blocking our

---

[16] Given my emphasis on the peculiarity of this example, one may wonder whether there are sufficient grounds for judging what might be a meaningful question within these circumstances. I am taking it that, for all its oddity, it preserves enough of a sense of an ordinary situation for us to make such judgments, and the fact that we can is suggested by Wittgenstein's allowing the first two questions – even while not answering them – and dismissing this last one.

appreciation of the most important aspects of things is not merely an unfortunate consequence of philosophical emptiness; it is its purpose. Accordingly, it is not philosophical emptiness itself that blocks my appreciation of the aspects of things that are most important. It is I, as I stand, who do so. I do so recurrently, and I do so precisely through turning away from them and toward philosophical emptiness.[17]

4.

What I have been suggesting is sketchy, and I do not take myself to have *shown* any of it. However, on the basis of these considerations I want to return to the "therapeutic" reading and to what I regard as its important limitations. Crary claims that "standard" interpretations of Wittgenstein's later work *"utterly fail to capture its therapeutic character."*[18] While I would not quite say the same of the "therapeutic" reading, I do want to claim that it fails to capture essential aspects of the therapeutic character of Wittgenstein's later work and of what it must undertake.

Philosophical Investigations offers several images of the goal of therapy or of therapeutic success. There is the idea, in *PI* §133, of arriving at (a perhaps fleeting) peace (*Ruhe*) from the torment of philosophical questions and demands, a torment depicted in, for example, the feeling that we have to "repair a torn spider's web with our fingers" (*PI* §106). There is the idea, implicit in *PI* §115, of arriving at (again, a perhaps fleeting) liberation from our wish to be held captive (by language).[19] And there is the idea of overcoming a kind of paralysis and being able to take steps (with words or thoughts) in *PI* §107. What is involved in the process leading to these, perhaps momentary, achievements?

---

[17] I trust it is clear that this is not a personal confession but a remark about what Wittgenstein shows to be human. It may be less clear that I am alluding to a remark of Cavell's in which he says that "It is I, as I stand, who opposes such examination of details in philosophy." See Cavell, *The Claim of Reason*, 21.

[18] *The New Wittgenstein*, 3. The emphasis is Crary's.

[19] This is not how *PI* §115 is generally read. I have argued for this reading in my "Captivating Pictures and Liberating Language: Freedom as the Achievement of Speech in Wittgenstein's *Philosophical Investigations*," *Philosophical Topics* 27 (1999): 255–85.

Clearly, the details of the process will differ in individual cases; we have to find, in each case, what Wittgenstein calls "the liberating word" (*PO* 165). However, we can sketch the general, structural moments of the therapeutic process.

The "therapeutic" reading, as formulated by Crary, has hold of *one* moment in this process: the moment of the process in which one is led to realize that one's words are empty and that no meaningful rendering of them will express what one wishes to say because there is, finally, *nothing* (meaningful) that one wishes to say. One's sense that one has something meaningful to say is shown to be "merely illusory."[20]

Crary does not say how or why coming to realize this is therapeutic. However, I think we can say on her behalf that she understands the empty voice of philosophy to be produced by the wish to occupy, or the illusion of actually occupying, an external point of view on our language. She claims that Wittgenstein traces "the sources of our philosophical confusions to our tendency, in the midst of philosophizing, to think that we need to survey language from an external point of view," and that he "sees our difficulty as one of coming to recognize that the idea of such a point of view creates the *illusion* of understanding the sentences we want to utter in philosophy."[21] Accordingly, coming to recognize that our words are empty and that we have been under the illusion of meaning something is at the same time overcoming the wish for an external standpoint and recognizing that "the demand for reflective understanding that drives us to philosophize will be met, not by explanations of our lives with language which thus seem to proceed from outside, but rather by explanations grounded in the ordinary circumstances of those lives."[22] For Crary, this process produces therapeutic peace by showing us where we may actually find the reflective satisfaction we had sought in the emptiness of philosophy. The empty voice of philosophy is silenced in coming to recognize the true home of its satisfaction.

---

[20] I am adapting Crary's remark that some voices in *Philosophical Investigations* "endeavor to show us ... that our sense that we understand what we want to say in our efforts to philosophize is merely illusory" (*The New Wittgenstein*, 7).

[21] Ibid., 1, 6.

[22] Ibid., 8.

I will return to the issue of silencing the voice of philosophy shortly. Immediately, however, I want to make two points.

First, the idea that there is a single source of philosophical emptiness – thinking, "in the midst of philosophizing, ... that we need to survey language from an external point of view" – not only expresses a much more academic and narrowly intellectual conception of philosophy than is found in *Philosophical Investigations*, but misses the variety, specificity, psychological accuracy, and human depth of the sources of emptiness that Wittgenstein reveals. (Indeed, in its apparent clarity and comprehensiveness, such a view may divert attention from the very sources of emptiness Wittgenstein is at such pains to depict.) Further, while it cannot be denied that there is a distinct type of activity called being "in the midst of philosophizing," Wittgenstein is not primarily concerned with those who understand themselves to be involved in this recognizably distinct type of activity. His focus, rather, is on what becomes of ordinary individuals when they are led by circumstances – which need not be at all dramatic or "philosophical" – to stop to think and to undertake to express themselves about some ordinary matter. His focus, that is, is not on moments in which we explicitly understand ourselves to be stepping back from our ordinary lives, but on the emergence of philosophical emptiness precisely in the course of those lives. And one of his central discoveries, as Stanley Cavell was the first to emphasize, is that "we may at any time ... be speaking without knowing what our words mean, what their meaning anything depends upon, speaking, as it were, in emptiness."[23] We may at any time, that is, and without realizing it, be in the midst of philosophizing – not as a special activity, but as ordinary, recurrent, human emptiness.

But second, the sole moment of the therapeutic process recognized by the "therapeutic" reading is not, in itself, especially therapeutic. Clearly, showing the empty voice of philosophy the true home of its satisfaction is very important. But alone it is not especially therapeutic because two crucial questions are left unrecognized and unaddressed. First, allowing for now that the source of emptiness is the desire for an

---

[23] Cavell, "Notes and Afterthoughts on the Opening of Wittgenstein's *Investigations*," *Philosophical Passages: Wittgenstein, Emerson, Austin, Derrida* (Oxford: Blackwell, 1995), 133.

external standpoint, why does one desire it? Second, how could one have been speaking in emptiness, wanting to say something meaningless, without realizing it? It is, after all, essential to Wittgenstein's manner of proceeding (and to "ordinary language" procedures generally) that speakers of their native language are competent to recognize when expressions, in particular circumstances, make sense, fit, or are at home (*PI* §116), and when not. Apart from reliance upon this competency his procedures cannot so much as get off the ground much less carry any power of conviction.[24] So some account of the recurrent failure of this competency must be forthcoming, and none is offered by the "therapeutic" reading. Accordingly, if the whole of Wittgensteinian therapy is that offered by the "therapeutic" reading, it leaves me a mystery to myself. If I have been relieved of the torment of trying to mean emptiness, I am left even more tormented by the mystery of why I would have done so and how I could have failed to notice.[25]

I meant my discussion of *PI* §1 to show that the emergence of philosophical emptiness is motivated – and, in that case, motivated most centrally by the desire to divert attention from an abyss of contingency in the face of our life with language and the myriad conditions on and for that life. I wanted to suggest that we do not merely fail to notice philosophical emptiness, but that we turn to it, embrace it, while under the illusion that we are turning to something quite important. (It is not quite, then, that our competency to distinguish sense from nonsense recurrently fails. It is that we recurrently refuse this competency.)

It is a central part of Wittgenstein's ambition in *Philosophical Investigations* to reveal not only *that* we recurrently turn toward emptiness, but concretely and specifically *why* we do so. He wants to bring to light and depict in as compelling a manner as he is able the various human drives, cravings, anxieties, fantasies, perversions, wishes, and

---

[24] Cavell emphasized this vital point as early as "Must We Mean What We Say?" and "The Availability of Wittgenstein's Later Philosophy," both of which are in *Must We Mean What We Say?*

[25] As said, Crary's "therapeutic" reading neither recognizes nor addresses these questions. However, her implicit response to both seems to amount to the claim that we are "in the midst of philosophizing." But this is no explanation. It simply renames exactly what needs to be explained.

the like that lie behind and are manifest in the turn to philosophical emptiness. Surely part of why he wants to do so is that he seeks to understand and depict at least some of the complexities of our human nature as currently constituted. (This is not a merely intellectual interest in a type of philosophical anthropology. A man as tormented as Wittgenstein must also have been seeking to better understand himself.) However, it is even more important that Wittgenstein bring to light the aspects of our nature manifest in the emergence of philosophical emptiness because they are exactly what must be treated in genuine Wittgensteinian therapy. His therapy, that is, cannot merely treat symptomatic emptiness. It must treat the aspects of human nature that recurrently produce this emptiness.

Accordingly, while Wittgenstein does want to calm the restless and tormented voice of philosophical emptiness, he *must* also provoke it, call it forth. He must do this, in part, because it is his only means of discovering and investigating the aspects of human nature requiring his treatment. But he must also provoke the voice of philosophical emptiness because it is in and through that voice being called forth from each of us, in the encounter with Wittgenstein's text, that we discover ourselves to harbor the drives, cravings, anxieties, and the like that its emergence reveals. It is only in and through the voice of emptiness being called forth from us that we recognize our need for Wittgenstein's therapy and that it can begin to work upon us.[26]

At this point, I can perhaps express my sense of the limitations of the "therapeutic" reading this way: what it presents as Wittgenstein's therapy starts too late and ends too early. That is, it does not provide an account, or a satisfactory account, of the emergence of philosophical emptiness in quite specific aspects of human nature, and it does not address how Wittgenstein's work undertakes to treat those aspects of human nature. Another way to put my sense of the limitations of the "therapeutic" reading is this: it does not recognize, and therefore

---

[26] One might ask: "If Wittgenstein's therapy consists in revealing and treating human drives, cravings, etc., why do we need him? Hasn't Freud, most notably, already developed a method for doing so?" I am suggesting, but clearly cannot argue here, that Wittgenstein's work shows Freud's to be incomplete. It shows that there are specific (forms of) human drives, cravings, etc., related to, but distinct from, those revealed by Freud, that are only revealed in the emergence of philosophical emptiness, and that only such methods as Wittgenstein's can reveal and treat.

does not illuminate, the depth of Wittgenstein's therapeutic ambition. It regards his therapeutic mbition as directed solely toward revealing and dissolving moments of narrowly philosophical emptiness. However, as I have emphasized from the outset, Wittgenstein works to show that narrowly philosophical moments of emptiness express aspects of our human nature. His therapeutic ambition, then, consists in nothing less than repeated, specific efforts to reveal our nature to us and, even if only for moments, to transform it. It consists in repeated, specific efforts to afford us moments of peace from, or within, our riven and self-tormenting nature. And it is these efforts that give his text its deep moral urgency.

It is perhaps our skepticism about the viability of such a project (even more than the regrettable, and too familiar, academic penchant for imagining that the thinkers we admire share only our same academic concerns and ambitions) that leads us to underestimate Wittgenstein's ambition. Who can seriously believe that this writing, or any writing, could transform human nature? I am suggesting that Wittgenstein believed exactly this. He frequently doubted the extent of his success in crafting such writing.[27] (How could he not?) But these doubts themselves testify to his belief that his writing could be, and should be, deeply transformative. Detailing specifically how, in individual instances, his writing works to achieve its extraordinary ambitions would constitute, in my view, a genuinely therapeutic reading.[28]

---

[27] "It is not impossible," he memorably writes toward the end of the Preface to *Philosophical Investigations*, "that it should fall to the lot of this work, in its poverty and in the darkness of this time, to bring light into one brain or another – but, of course, it is not likely" (*PI* x).

[28] Earlier versions of parts of this essay were presented as part of a panel, "A Double Take on Wittgenstein's Aspect-Seeing Remarks," held at the annual meeting of the American Society for Aesthetics in 2001, and at a seminar on *Philosophical Investigations*, sponsored by the Center for Research on Culture and Literature at Johns Hopkins University in 2000. I would like to thank the participants at these events for their questions, comments, and provocations. I would also like to thank David Cerbone, Kelly Jolley, Victor J. Krebs, and Edward Minar for comments on earlier drafts of this essay. Finally, I owe special thanks to William Day (not only for comments, but for the invitation to participate in the Aesthetics Society panel, without which the essay would not exist) and Martin Stone (the co-leader of the Hopkins seminar and in conversation with whom many of the ideas in sections 3 and 4 of this essay were first developed).

IV.2 Seeing Connections

14

Overviews

What Are They of and What Are They For?

Frank Cioffi

1. AN OVERVIEW OF OVERVIEWS

My interest in Wittgenstein's notion of problems which can be solved by "putting into order what we already know without adding anything," i.e., by overviews, is not merely exegetical. I address the notion of the nature and point of overviews because of its resonance. When I first encountered Wittgenstein's contrast between perplexities that require empirical explanation and those which could not be so relieved, but would only yield to a "perspicuous view," I felt like Moliere's M. Jourdain at his first encounter with the concept of prose and his realization that he had been talking it all his life. Wittgenstein's remarks, and their exemplification in his comments on Frazer's *Golden Bough*, alerted me to the extent of our indebtedness to those who, in the words of Orwell's tribute to James Joyce, "open[ed] up a new world not by revealing what is strange, but by revealing what is familiar."[1]

When I consider the overviews which I have frequented and striven to create, they seem to fall into two broad categories: the heuristic-explanatory and the self-clarificatory. Wittgenstein's remarks on magic and ritual sacrifice fall into the same two categories. When he reminds us, in connection with effigy-burning, that we kiss pictures of our loved ones, he is contributing to an heuristic-explanatory

---

[1] George Orwell, "Inside the Whale," in *A Collection of Essays* (New York: Houghton Mifflin Harcourt, 1970), 212–13 .

overview; when he tells us that, in responding to the Beltane fire festivals, it is not their genesis from a practice in which men were really
burned which is the source of our uneasiness, but something intrinsic
to the festivals themselves, he is clarifying our impression of the festivals by laying out rival determinants – cognitive and physiognomic.

Wittgenstein's counsel to seek overviews has a negative and a positive side. The negative is comparatively straightforward and com-
prises what Brian Clack refers to as the "prohibition on explanation."[2]
Wittgenstein contends that there are perplexities which, though they
may appear hermeneutic, are misaddressed when further information is sought to resolve them. His positive thesis is that the appropriate method of dealing with these perplexities is by the construction
of overviews.[3]

Though the notion of an overview is most often raised in connection with philosophical problems, I shall focus on the kind of questions
in connection with which Wittgenstein first introduced it, questions
which were apparently empirical, such as explaining magical rites in
general and human sacrifice in particular. This was in 1930 in the
"Remarks on Frazer's *Golden Bough*," where one of the most pertinent
texts is: "One must only correctly piece together what one *knows*, without adding anything, and the satisfaction being sought through the
explanation follows of itself" (*PO* 121).

In the entry on overviews in his *Wittgenstein Dictionary*, Hans-Johann
Glock says of these "forms of understanding," in which "one can shed
light on a diverse multitude of phenomena without discovering anything new," that "Wittgenstein thought of this methodological idea as
a world-view competing with the scientistic one."[4] There is one respect
in which this misrepresents Wittgenstein's position. Wittgenstein is not
opposing merely scientific enquiry but empirical enquiry of any kind,
including historical narrative. The antithesis to the overview is not science but information – that is, anything not immanent to the phenomena which it is proposed to illuminate. Whereas some commentators

---

[2] Brian Clack, *Wittgenstein, Frazer and Religion* (New York: Palgrave, 1998), 79–93.
[3] Wittgenstein once wrote (MS 219.8): "What is disastrous in the scientific way of
   thinking (which today rules the whole world) is that it wants to respond to every
   discomfort by giving an explanation." (Gordon Baker called my attention to this
   remark.)
[4] Hans-Johann Glock, *A Wittgenstein Dictionary* (Oxford: Blackwell, 1996), 279.

have seen Wittgenstein's "putting into order what we already know" as a heuristic device in the service of an ultimately explanatory consummation, there is an alternative rationale: this "putting into order" is not propaedeutic to some ulterior, explanatory aim, but is produced to assuage an autonomous (if intermittent) craving for synoptic presentation. But it must be acknowledged that not everyone will experience this craving, and so the coercive tone adopted by some of those who share Wittgenstein's epistemic priorities is inappropriate. Sometimes the most that can be said is that there is an alternative direction of interest; and it is in reminding us of this that the value of Wittgenstein's remarks lies. It is only if we bear this distinction in mind that we can absolve Wittgenstein of the charge that, in his dealings with ritual, he has fallen into the fallacy of assuming that, when we have found a mode of making sense of a practice, we will also have understood what it meant to its practitioners. What warrants his proscription on explanation is not its irrelevance to the task of accounting for the enigmatic behavior which initially aroused our interest, but, rather, in the fact that explanatory problematicality does not exhaust the kinds of problematicality that their behavior may possess for us. There is also what we might call "explanation-unassuageable" problematicality.

There is an expression of this explanation-unassuageable problematicality in the discussion of overviews by Gordon Baker and Peter Hacker in their commentary on *Philosophical Investigations*, where they say that the method of overviews is particularly apposite "when we wish to fathom our own reactions [of] awe and horror."[5] But a comprehensive overview of types of problematicality must include not only those which can be relieved by understanding our response to the phenomena, rather than by explanation of the phenomena themselves, but also those which may not be relievable by knowledge of any kind.

2. THE HEURISTIC RATIONALE FOR OVERVIEWS

The kind of overview which is pertinent will thus depend on the character of the perplexity to be assuaged. If a practice is enigmatic – as some have found the burning of effigies to be – then the perplexity

---

[5] G. P. Baker and P. M. S. Hacker, *Wittgenstein: Understanding and Meaning* (Oxford: Blackwell, 1980), 303.

is hermeneutic, and what we want perspicuously laid out are the different possible reasons which might move people to behave in this perplexing manner. It is widely held – and not just by Frazer – that burning effigies occupies the same instrumental role in the culture of many exotic peoples that burning enemies or malefactors once occupied in ours. Wittgenstein thinks that, once we have reminded ourselves that we kiss the pictures of loved ones without any expectation of conferring ulterior benefit on them, we will no longer find Frazer's instrumental account compelling. We will have deprived burning effigies of its opacity without the invocation of misconceived notions of what it can effect. (Though Wittgenstein would have done better to invoke the fact that we too burn effigies non-instrumentally – Guy Fawkes, for example – since kissing the picture of loved ones, unlike effigy-burning, is private and not communal, and it is not performed at predetermined intervals but spontaneously.) But what Wittgenstein's analogy nevertheless demonstrates is that we engage in non-instrumental, expressive transaction with images. The real problem Wittgenstein sets us is how he could think that, having reminded us of this, we now understood the rationale of the ritual practice of mankind, without the necessity for further enquiry.

There is a rude riddle which asks: "Why does a dog lick its balls?" I have long thought the solution ("Because it can") both obscurantist and penetrating. Obscurantist, because of its peremptory foreclosure of the possibility of an empirically informative answer to the question. Penetrating, because of its recognition that not all problems require further information for their resolution, but may yield to a change of the view from which we regard them. Wittgenstein on more than one occasion attempts to foreclose empirical inquiry in a manner akin to the solution to the riddle of the balls-licking dog. In one of the lectures on aesthetics and psychology he asks of a specimen of bizarre behavior, "Why do we do this sort of thing?" and replies, "This is the sort of thing we do do" (*LC* 25). In the remarks on Frazer, he deplores attempts at explanation of ritual sacrifice and contents himself with pronouncing, "Human life is like that" – just as the solution to the balls-licking riddle might have run, "Canine life is like that."

There are questions with respect to which further empirical enquiries are irrelevant, but why exotic people burn effigies is not such a question. One such question is why, when reading of pretense burnings like those of Beltane, we may be assailed with feelings of horror.[6] Whether, as Wittgenstein maintains, it is something about the Beltane ritual itself, rather than our conviction as to its origin in human sacrifice, that explains our horror may well depend on "evidence" which is "non-hypothetical, psychological" (*PO* 147). But this is not a question about the ritualists, but about our relation to Frazer's account of their doings. It is a self-clarificatory question, not an hermeneutic one. Similarly with the burning of effigies in general: the question of why they do it must be distinguished from the question of what are our resources for understanding why they do it, or why it makes the impression it does. The latter two questions may be served by an overview but not the former, unless the service is of the heuristic kind of bringing the practice within the scope of our intelligibility-conferring devices.

There is a further objection to an overview of our transactions with images which, like Wittgenstein's, confines itself to those, like kissing the picture of a loved one, which are purely expressive: It falsifies the degree of our inwardness with transactions with images which embody occult instrumental beliefs. Wittgenstein asks rhetorically, apropos of Frazer's cognitive account of magic, whether Saint Augustine was in error when on every page of the *Confessions* he called on God. Perhaps not; but this does not preclude others calling on God and being deeply disappointed when He does not answer. I have argued that a synoptic array of the role of images in our ritual life could not resolve the question of why **exotic** people burn effigies, since it will include both our inclination to non-instrumental transactions with images, like kissing the picture of loved ones, and instrumental ones, like praying for help before the statues of sacred personages.

Let us remind ourselves of the kind of problem which Frazer addresses:

In one district the victim was put to death by slow fire. A low stage was formed, sloping on either side like a roof; upon it they laid the victim, his limbs bound round with cords to confine his struggle. Fires were then lighted and hot brands applied to make him roll up and down the slopes of the stage as long as possible; for the more tears he shed the more abundant would be the supply of rain.[7]

---

[6] Ibid., 304.

[7] James George Frazer, *The Golden Bough*, abridged ed. (London: Macmillan, 1967), 573.

Wittgenstein finds Frazer's instrumental homeopathic rationale for practices like this – that it was for the sake of insuring a good crop – ludicrous. With what, then, are we to replace it? Tears for the sake of tears, screams for the sake of screams? "Life is terrible; let us do something terrible to express this"?

Wittgenstein's non-instrumental, symbolic account of why victims were sacrificed may well be veridical, and Frazer's non-symbolic, instrumental account mistaken, but can it be correct to insist that a symbolic-expressive rationale is so transparent that it doesn't need explaining? And that Frazer's proffering an instrumental one instead shows how lacking he was in spirituality? Colleagues who find the relation between "the life of the spirit"[8] and burning men alive so natural as to be immediately intelligible make me nervous.[9]

I think I have said enough about the function of overviews in those cases where the satisfaction sought is that of dissipating the opacity of enigmatic practices.

3. OVERVIEWS FOR THE SAKE OF OVERVIEWS: THE SYNOPTIC SENSIBILITY

I use the term "synoptic sensibility" to refer to the satisfaction taken in overviews, irrespective of any contribution they might make to the explanation of the phenomena of which they afford a perspicuous view. One advantage of this notion is that it enables us to understand better the nature of disputes as to the merits of putatively explanatory texts.

It is obvious that the heuristic rationale does not exhaust the appeal of overviews for Wittgenstein. He would not think the effort

---

[8] P. M. S. Hacker, "Developmental Hypotheses and Perspicuous Representations: Wittgenstein on Frazer's *Golden Bough*," *Wittgenstein: Connections and Controversies* (Oxford: Oxford University Press, 2001), 93.

[9] This is the kind of thing I mean: Wittgenstein once remarked to Drury that he hoped the story was true that Ivan the Terrible blinded the architect who created St. Basil to prevent it having any rivals. Drury was horrified by this sentiment. Rhees argues in mitigation that on another occasion Wittgenstein had added, "What a *wonderful* way of showing his admiration!", and that this addendum puts Wittgenstein's remark in a different light. "'What a *wonderful* way of showing his admiration!' is akin to what he might have said of certain forms of human sacrifice as a gesture of deepest reverence. If we had said 'But it's horrible!' he'd have said this showed we didn't know what was taking place" (*RW* 224).

at an explanatory overview unrewarded, if it left us no wiser as to the motives for the opaque practices which instigated it, but nevertheless provided us with a clearer grasp of the nature of the understanding for which we sought. What he says in another connection has application here: unlike the scientist he desires clarity for its own sake (*CV* 7). When Wittgenstein deplored the explanatory pretensions which he found in Darwin's book on the expression of emotions in men, and in Freud's dealings with "psychical facts" (*PO* 107), but nevertheless commended their talent for introducing order into the matters with which they dealt, he was evincing his distinctive proclivity for overviews.

In the case of ritual practices, the satisfaction in question was an enhanced grasp of the devices at our disposal for dissipating their opacity, even if this left them, in the end, no less opaque to our understanding. When we set out to resolve an hermeneutic puzzle, a rival enterprise sometimes presents itself – that of articulating more fully our apparatus of understanding – and this may even come to involve us in a dilemma as to whether this synoptic enterprise should take precedence over the narrowly explanatory justification for the overview. I can, for example, become so absorbed in the question as to which explanatory principles I am inward with, and which are opaque to me, as to lose interest in the initial question as to the meaning of a particular ritual practice. This is what I think happened to those commentators on the Nemi priesthood who expressed enthusiasm for Wittgenstein's synoptic procedure but were no more able to solve the problem of the meaning of the Nemi rite of succession than was Frazer. What they were really expressing appreciation for was their enhanced clarity as to the enterprise of explaining ritual practices, though they may have confusedly thought that they had been given a non-empirical method of resolving hermeneutic issues.[10]

But though it was a source of great satisfaction to me, when I felt myself able to lay out our explanatory resources for dealing with magic and ritual in a synoptic format, how could I defend myself against the charge that I was deriving from a footling taxonomic exercise a satisfaction which only successful explanation should have occasioned?

---

[10] See Frank Cioffi, *Wittgenstein on Freud and Frazer* (Cambridge: Cambridge University Press, 1998), 259–62.

Though the case of ritual is well adapted to illustrate how the value of an *Übersicht* (overview) can be quite independent of any contribution it makes to the explanatory problem which instigated it, it does not follow that we are not sometimes wrong to prioritize synoptic exercises over investigative enquiries. Isn't it more important to know how the Aztecs got to the point of ritually slaughtering thousands in the course of a morning, than to have our explanatory paradigms with respect to such practices synoptically arrayed? Not, it seems, for everyone.

The satisfaction taken in overviews irrespective of their explanatory value seems to be the manifestation of a distinctive synoptic sensibility which can seem perverse not only to those who do not share it but even, on occasion, to those who do. Can these judgments be more than just personal? Consider a notorious instance of explanatory perplexity – the problem posed by the thirty-eight witnesses of a murderous attack on a young woman who failed either themselves to intervene or even to notify the appropriate authorities. This episode inspired a series of experiments which explored three possible reasons why the onlookers did not intervene: (1) fear for their own safety; (2) fear of embarrassment if they had misconstrued the situation (social inhibition); (3) awareness that there were many other witnesses and consequent conviction that someone else would intervene (diffusion of responsibility). The general upshot of the experiments was that diffusion of responsibility proved to be a potent motive for non-intervention. Imagine someone who placed a higher value on the overview of the alternative motives for non-intervention than on the experimental evidence as to which was most likely. This could strike even those with an appetite for overviews as prioritizing synopticality over explanation to an excessive degree. What kind of disagreement is this?

There are also cases where, though the rationale is explicitly explanatory, the discourse itself seems actively to invite frequentation for the synoptic satisfactions it affords rather than for its explanatory potential. It sometimes happens that we come to feel that what was offered as a "putting into order" in the service of a social-scientific agenda performed a distinct and even antagonistic function: the satisfaction of an autonomous craving for synoptic views of social practices and predicaments. Suggestive evidence for the existence of a powerful appetite for overviews, irrespective of any explanatory value they might have, is provided by the widespread appreciation of Erving Goffman's exercises in interactional taxonomy.[11]

In his review of a collection of Goffman's essays, a fellow social scientist, Fred Strodtbeck, takes him to task for just those synopsizing features of his discourse in which so many take satisfaction.[12] Strodtbeck treats as a representative example of Goffman's procedure his naming and brief characterization of the varieties of "face" – "the positive social value a person claims for himself in social encounters." Among types of "face" Goffman names "pride," "honor," "dignity," "tact," "savoir faire," "diplomacy," "discretion," etc., each of which is neatly characterized and exemplified. This is Strodtbeck's comment: "If this naming is meant to be taken as a serious scientific enterprise ... it should not be." Why not? Because, Strodtbeck objects, Goffman offers no suggestions, in his dealings with presentational predicaments, as to which of the synoptically arrayed stratagems will be deployed when "face" is threatened. What is the moral of the common indifference to this obvious objection to Goffman's "microanalyses" of social encounters?

The case for a synoptic, non-explanatory rationale for Goffman's dealings with presentational phenomena is even stronger than in the case of Wittgenstein's dealings with ritual; for in the cases of ritual, there is a hermeneutic puzzle to be resolved, for example, why were effigies burned? No comparable issue is addressed by Goffman; thus Strodtbeck's complaint.

Despite the novelty of much of the material contained in his citations, what Goffman is really putting into order is not the discoveries of sociological research into the interaction order, but the obscurely familiar, though rarely explicitly formulated, principles which govern social encounters. One commentator on Goffman speaks of his "labyrinth of insights into the implicit half-sensed meaning of

[11] Erving Goffman, "The Interaction Order," *American Sociological Review* (February 1983): 1–17; see Cioffi, "The Propaedeutic Delusion," *History of the Human Sciences* 13:1 (2000), 109–23, and Cioffi, "Stating the Obvious," *Erving Goffman*, 4 vols., Masters in Modern Social Thought Series, ed. Gary Alan Fine and Gregory W. H. Smith (London: Sage Publications, 2000), Part Four: Methods.

[12] Fred L. Strodtbeck, review of *Interaction Ritual: Essays on Face-to-Face Behavior*, by Erving Goffman, *The American Journal of Sociology* 76, no. 1 (1970): 177–79.

daily encounters." This "labyrinth of insights" is not the product of empirical research, and yet it is eminently eligible for synoptic arrangement.

For example, in *Stigma*,[13] Goffman calls attention to an arresting situation. Consider that if someone has a deformity as evident as a hare-lip, though he must learn to deal with any embarrassment it might occasion, he is relieved of the quandary as to whether to announce it; whereas if he has a criminal record, or a racial or religious or sexual identity other than is assumed, and which might disconcert those with whom he associates, he must decide whether to disclose it and when. Delay entails the risk of premature exposure, which will add duplicity to whatever penalty attaches to the stigma itself. On the other hand, an untimely and inopportune revelation may result in shock or embarrassment so intense as to destroy the relation it was intended to preserve.

What kind of knowledge is it to know that these two contrasting predicaments exist? Must the point of Goffman's introduction of terms to designate them ("managing tension" and "controlling information") be that he is laying the foundations for an advance in social theory? Can it be a coincidence that the discourse in which Goffman engages in this and kindred enterprises found such enthusiastic appreciation among people with a meager interest in advances in social theory?

If we employ a Meno stratagem but, instead of asking about the properties of squares, ask about the presentational principles governing the behavior of people in social situations, I suspect the result of the exercise would be a realization of how independent of the literature of his discipline are the classifications and distinctions which Goffman proliferates. What Goffman's presentational principles and categories really put into order is "what we already know," that is, "the implicit half-sensed meaning of daily encounters." But does the fact that we already know why – indeed cannot help but know why – people would be reluctant to acknowledge their secret deviance from a norm, while at the same time fearing being exposed as deceitful should they fail to reveal it, constitute a decisive argument against a proto-scientific, non-contemplative rationale for a taxonomy of presentational stratagems? It could be argued that the value

[13] Goffman, *Stigma* (Englewood Cliffs, New Jersey: Prentice Hall, 1963).

of such a taxonomy consists not in the gratification occasioned by Olympian synoptic views of our social travails, but in its enhancing the accessibility of what we already know – just as the fact that we prefer the conventional, alphabetically arranged telephone book to an alphabetically scrambled one, though it contains no more information than the scrambled one, does not impugn an epistemic rationale for our preference.[14] But I do not think that the satisfaction we take in Goffmanian overviews is to be accounted for in such pragmatic terms. I postpone discussion of who "we" are.

4 . OVERVIEWS IN THE INTEREST OF SELF-CLARIFICATION

In addition to heuristic, explanation-seeking overviews, there are self-clarifying ones, and Wittgenstein thinks the former sometimes mask the latter. The aim of a self-clarificatory overview is to achieve a clearer realization of what it is that constrains the course of our thoughts on certain matters and confers on our recurrent ruminations their distinctive character.

What Wittgenstein's remarks on human sacrifice offer, besides hermeneutic speculation as to its rationale, is a schematic overview of the "crush of thoughts" it incites. This gives us an alternative aim to that of explanation. But Wittgenstein goes further and deplores and proscribes the search for explanation. Consider the observation Hacker and Baker make in their chapter on *Übersicht*.[15] They take Wittgenstein to be maintaining that what "is most deeply perplexing and disturbing" about human sacrifice is not to be "resolved" by empirical enquiry. Avishai Margalit agrees but holds the abjuration of empirical enquiry to be obfuscatory, rather than illuminating. He says that what Wittgenstein "offers as an alternative [to explanation] seems extremely odd. Instead of asking ... what meaning it has for them, Wittgenstein asks what impression the ritual has on us, the observers, and what its significance is with respect to our own tendencies."[16] What is at issue here? I think that when the

---

[14] Cioffi, "The Propaedeutic Delusion," 117–18.
[15] Baker and Hacker, *Wittgenstein: Understanding and Meaning*, 305.
[16] Avishai Margalit, "Sense and Sensibility: Wittgenstein on the 'Golden Bough'," *Iyyun: The Jerusalem Philosophical Quarterly* 41 (1992): 303.

confusion as to the limits on the hermeneutic value of overviews has been dispelled, what it comes down to is a difference between those who place a greater value on determining why the ritual makes the impression that it does, than on why it was done, and those who do not.

In Moore's notes on Wittgenstein's lectures in 1930–33, Wittgenstein compares the problem posed by exotic practices to one which also arises in the case of works of art – that of clarifying the impression that they make. And most of his remarks on ritual are addressed to this enterprise rather than that of fathoming the motives of the ritualists. For example, we are told that, though we may think that it is the account of the origin of the fire festival in rites in which men were really burned that makes the festival sinister, we are mistaken, and this is due rather to features of the festivals themselves, such as the demeanor of the participants, and to our preexisting conceptions of man and his past. We are also told that learning of rituals of human sacrifice is like being shocked at hearing a normally mild man speak severely, and that the use of a cake for drawing lots makes a particularly striking impression on us and is analogous to betrayal through a kiss. We are told that it is not just the suffering of the victim that impresses us but the fact that the suffering is deliberately inflicted. Finally, and this is the most general of his self-clarificatory claims, we are assured that, confronted by accounts of ritual sacrifice, what we want is not explanation but something else – an understanding of the source of our disquietude, or perhaps "peace," where these can be distinguished.

That Wittgenstein has abandoned hermeneutic issues for self-clarificatory ones is made clear by the nature of his objection to speculation about origins. The reason for his injunction to confine ourselves to what we already know is that the sinister, terrible, tragic impression made by the festivals arises before we have formed any conviction as to their derivation from an ancient practice of human sacrifice. But an additional assumption is required if we are to forgo further empirical enquiry on these grounds: the assumption that the source of the disturbance that accounts of human sacrifice induce matters more to us than the explanation of the practice.

5. WHAT IS SINISTER ABOUT HUMAN SACRIFICE?

Rush Rhees asks why we are "moved to say" that Frazer's accounts of ritual sacrifice are "deep and terrible."[17] Baker and Hacker say that the method of overview is particularly apposite when we wish to "fathom our own reactions of awe and horror."[18] But what of the case where several competing accusatives of this awe and horror figure in the overview? Brian Clack develops the suggestion that it is the incongruity between the festal character of the occasion and the gruesomeness of the events it suggests, such as the burning of a man, which carries the main burden of our impression. He thinks the centrality Wittgenstein imputes to incongruous features like the use of a cake for choosing the victim supports this construction: "The idea of a festivity in which death habitually results and often through pure chance (the drawing of lots) may graphically (or subconsciously) remind us of the contingencies of our own existence or even of the nature of human life itself."[19] It could be countered that Wittgenstein's emphasis on the ritual aspects of human sacrifice as the source of our response to what is "dreadful," "terrible," "tragic," etc., in Frazer's account smacks too much of "a backwards-looking Clever Elsie" (*PO* 145). Why worry about something so rare and remote as ritual torture and murder?

Suppose we came across an account of the burning of a man in which the rationale was to entertain the onlookers (as in Huizinga's story of the people of Mons purchasing a brigand "for the pleasure of seeing him quartered").[20] There would then be no ritual dimension and thus no "queer pointlessness." Would this not nevertheless be as disquieting as a ritual burning? Suppose we believed that, whereas at Beltane they only pretend to burn men for the fun of it, their forbears really burned men not just ritually but for the fun of it: would this make it less "striking," "impressive," or "dreadful"? Would it have forfeited its "depth" or problematicality? Clack, who has done as much as anyone to take us beyond the merely celebratory in his account

[17] Rush Rhees, "Introduction to 'Remarks on Frazer's *Golden Bough*'," *The Human World* 3 (May 1971): 26.
[18] Baker and Hacker, *Wittgenstein: Understanding and Meaning*, 304.
[19] Clack, *Wittgenstein, Frazer and Religion*, 147.
[20] Johan Huizinga, *The Waning of The Middle Ages* (London: Penguin, 1968), 22–23.

of Wittgenstein's views, is nevertheless over-indulgent on this matter. Clack asks us to consider two forms of cannibalism, one occurring in times of severe hardship and one not. He says that the first would strike us as tragic but not sinister, whereas in the case of the ritual variety, "in which the most appalling of sufferings is heaped upon the poor victim," who may be obliged to construct the oven in which he is to be roasted or made to watch as his severed limbs are devoured before him by the company, "it is the 'queer pointlessness' of the act which creates the sinister impression."[21] But does the "queer pointlessness" exhaust the source of our horror at this scene? If we subtract the "queer pointlessness," it would be deprived of the puzzling aspect which engages Wittgenstein, but is there not a residual problematicality? And could this not lie in the demonism of man and the world rather than just the ritual commemoration of that demonism? It may be asked how, in suggesting this, I am to know I am not importing my own wimpish sensibilities on to material alien to them. I will know if you – collectively – tell me so. But the "you" who will tell me so is anonymous. It is the "mysterious, kind reader" described by Karel Capek as someone who "as soon as you receive a letter from him is not the person you are writing for" because "this is not anyone you know but the personification of all the people you don't know."[22] It is the suffrage of "all the people you don't know" which will decide whether "the feelings and thoughts" – and epistemic preferences – imputed to them are really theirs. Of course, the indeterminacy of this identification affords opportunities for evasiveness and recalcitrance; but this can't be helped. (However, even were I to withdraw the implication of generality from my utterance it need not, therefore, have been deprived of its point and its function.)

6. OVERVIEWS AS A RESPONSE TO AMBIVALENCE, INCONSTANCY, AND ABSENCE OF CLOSURE

A prime candidate for synoptic arrangement are those "feelings and thoughts" which seem to strive for some kind of resolution but which repeatedly fail to achieve it. These, though they may be private, are

[21] Clack, *Wittgenstein, Frazer and Religion*, 145.
[22] Karel Capek, *Intimate Things* (London: Allen and Unwin, 1935), 127.

often not just personal, and we are constantly recognizing signs of their existence in others. What is it about certain topics which incites so many of us to seek and take satisfaction in non-heuristic, self-clarificatory overviews? I think that what these topics have in common is the failure of repeated recurrence to them to produce closure – an attitude or decision in which we can rest.

Social life with its recurrent hopes and disappointments is one of the areas with respect to which an absence of closure is often felt. It appears to possess an intrinsic problematicality. Like sexual life, social life has something peculiarly importunate about it, but also something which causes us to question its prerogatives. The pursuit of status or popularity, like the pursuit of carnal gratification, is one as to which we are ambivalent. A reminder that I am a potential object of interest or indifference, admiration or contempt, may incite in me a desire for a detached contemplation of this predicament, and so any discourse which both stimulates and assuages this need for detached contemplation, even though its ostensible rationale is explanatory, will have a value independent of its explanatory inadequacies. If we begin with a topic of concern to us, such as the hazards of interactional existence, "the pursuit of reputation in the eyes of others," and the remedies for "humiliation and expressive failure" – to draw on items in Rom Harré's agenda for ethogenic science[23] – we can often watch the epistemic bifurcation of our reflections into, on the one hand, explanatory perplexities as to which advances in empirical knowledge might well enlighten us, and on the other, a vague desire for a clearer view of the possibilities which shape our social existence and give it its texture.

7. WHY OVERVIEWS MAY FAIL TO BRING "PEACE"

What often presents itself as theorizing propaedeutic to some empirical, explanatory consummation is in large part an attempt to meet a different need: a craving for adequate articulation of a subliminally apprehended thought-crush. However, with respect to certain topics, this is just a stage to the recognition of a deeper problem: why we cannot long rest in the attitudes we take up toward the phenomenon in question. The *Übersicht* allows us to hold, in one view, the conflicting

[23] Rom Harré, *Social Being* (Oxford: Blackwell, 1979).

demands that obstruct resolution and, it may be, reconciles us to their intractability.

It is not a coincidence that so many topics which are raised in an explanatory context, or with an explanatory rationale, turn out to be not only explanation-unassuageable but even overview-unassuageable, due to a profound ambivalence toward the topic addressed. The demonism of man, as exemplified in the sacrificial practices recorded by Frazer, and the hazards of interactional existence, are both characterized by incessant rumination whose failure to achieve closure instigates attempts at an overview. But even when we substitute for an array of possible explanations an array of possible sources of problematicality or disquietude, the overview may not, as we hoped, put a term to our brooding, but may just make our ambivalence and tergiversation less surprising.

What the overview achieves in such cases is not the attainment of an attitude in which we can rest, but only a surveyable grasp which makes our ambivalence and indecision comprehensible and reconciles us to a state of permanent irresolution – "getting used to not getting used to it." There is an irony here, in that the reason why we abandoned explanation in the first place was that it did not minister to the need which incited the search for it, and now it seems that not even the synoptic view which was sought in place of explanation need do so.

I have argued that social life, which appears to possess an intrinsic problematicality, is among the topics that seem to demand the ordering of our feelings and thoughts in a more perspicuous mode than the ordinary process of reflection affords. The peculiar importunacy of "the pursuit of reputation in the eyes of others" led one social theorist to remark hyperbolically that it was "the overriding preoccupation of human life."[24] But along with its importunacy goes a profound ambivalence. A striking expression of this is provided by the self-reproaches of Tolstoy's Prince Andrei in *War and Peace*:

I want glory, want to be famous and beloved. … It's the only thing I care for, the only thing I live for. Yes, the only thing! … Death, wounds, the loss of my family – nothing holds any terrors for me. And precious and dear as many people are to me – father, sister, wife – those I cherish most – yet dreadful and

[24] Ibid., 3.

unnatural as it seems, I would exchange them all immediately for a moment of glory, of triumph. ...[25]

The upshot of certain contemplative dealings with social existence is an enhanced awareness of fundamental conflicts among our desires. (Emerson: "Solitude is impracticable, and society fatal.")[26] Alongside our conventional aspirations to distinction are reminders of how often we long to be free of them, of how much we envy the condition of one of Charles Spencelayh's old codgers contentedly pottering about among his memorabilia, or of Geppeto or the Tailor of Gloucester at their workbenches amidst the products of solitary craftsmanship. But not for long. The final outcome of an overview of interactional existence may be an insight into the ineradicability of concupiscence, something we find expressed succinctly in the story of the hermit in Johnson's *Rasselas* who, when he tired of his cave and turned with avidity to the great world beyond it, provoked the comment that he might "in a few years, go back to his retreat, and, perhaps, if shame did not restrain, or death intercept him, return once more from his retreat into the world."[27]

Both Prince Andrei's shame as to the intensity of his craving for glory and the visions and revisions of Johnson's hermit strike me as having what Husserl called "thereness for others." Who has not dreamt of a sequestered monastic existence in some remote Tibetan fastness (but with central heating and an indulgent attitude toward masturbation)? Or failing this, life as a station master on a small West Country branch line with only one track. Regressive? Yes. Idiosyncratic? Doubtful. But it need not matter how large is the "we" to whom a schematic overview of social life, which exposes the intractability of our longings, trepidation, and ambivalence, is familiar and welcome, as long as it reaches some who recognize and embrace it. One of Joyce's Dubliners has an archetypal response to an episode of adolescent humiliation: "I saw myself as a creature driven and derided by vanity; and my eyes burned

[25] Leo Tolstoy, *War and Peace*, trans. Rosemary Edmonds (London: Penguin, 1982), 306.

[26] Ralph Waldo Emerson, "Society and Solitude," *Emerson's Complete Works*, 12 vols. (Boston: Houghton, Mifflin, 1883), 7:20.

[27] Samuel Johnson, *The History of Rasselas, Prince of Abissinia* (1759) (London: Penguin, 1976), 87.

with anguish and anger."[28] Who has not felt himself similarly "driven
and derided"? It is those for whom this question is rhetorical who are
best placed for appreciating the point of a non-propaedeutic, non-
heuristic, autonomous overview of social existence.

8. THE EPISTEMIC FALLACY

So there are problems which though they incite us to the creation of
overviews are not resolvable by them. Problematicality need take neither the form, "What would move people to behave in such bizarre
ways?", nor even, "What in the turmoil of my feelings and thoughts is
the major source of the impression made by this behavior?" What began
as an explanatory problematicality may in the end prove, not just explanation-unassuageable, but not even assuageable by an understanding
of why we are troubled by the spectacle. An epistemic problematicality masks a deeper, less tractable problematicality: an irresolvable conflict among diverse perspectives or different routes to "peace." When
we have grasped that the problem posed by the terrible things that
are done is not exhausted either in an understanding of why they are
done, or as to what in their doing most perturbs us, there is still the fact
that terrible things are done. This enduring and pervasive feature of
human life is one we strive to be reconciled to, but it is doubtful how
this reconciliation is furthered by advances in understanding.

The epistemic fallacy consists in the mechanical pursuit of further
knowledge, where this is not what is really called for. The explanatory
version of the epistemic fallacy runs: For every opaque state of affairs
there is another, unknown state of affairs, discovery of which would
relieve it of its opacity. But there is also a non-explanatory kind of
epistemism. In his book on Simone Weil, Peter Winch says that the
bewilderment provoked by the Nazi death camps "is not one to be
removed by any sort of explanation." So far so good. Winch is rejecting explanatory epistemism. But Winch goes on to argue that when
we complain that we "do not understand how people could behave
in such a way," the use of the word "understand" is "important" and
"irreplaceable."[29] I think that the word "understand," far from being

[28] James Joyce, "Araby," in *Dubliners* (New York: Penguin, 1976), 35.
[29] Peter Winch, *Simone Weil: "The Just Balance"* (Cambridge: Cambridge University
Press, 1989), 155.

irreplaceable, is the very word we ought to avoid. There may be nothing to be understood, only something to be reconciled to – though it is understandable why it should sometimes appear otherwise. Mosca in Stendhal's *Charterhouse of Parma* illustrates how this confusion can come about: "When I think I am using my reason, I am not reasoning at all. I am simply turning round and round to find a less painful position."[30] C. S. Lewis seems to have experienced a similar revelation when he concluded that his attempts to make sense of his bereavement were "the senseless writhings of a man who won't accept the fact that there is nothing we can do with suffering except to suffer it."[31]

We may concur with Winch that there is something problematic about holocaust stories, which isn't the sort of problematicality to be dissipated by any advances in empirical understanding, without concluding that what will relieve them of their problematicality is further understanding, though of a non-empirical kind. The residual problematicality may be of a non-epistemic kind which no mode of knowledge will relieve. The *volatility* of aspects presented to us may be the problem, rather than just their imperfectly apprehended diversity. And so self-clarification still leaves us with a problem. There may be no further understanding to be achieved, but only decisions to be resolved on, truths to be reconciled to.

What does someone disabled by grief come to know or understand when he finally resumes his responsibilities to the living? Can his ameliorated condition be said to consist in his having learned something? We can always insist that when a shoe stops pinching, the foot has learned something. But to what end? The illusion that there is a question to be answered may arise through our tendency to epistemize all our dilemmas: disguising indecision and vacillation or intractable ambivalence as ignorance.

9. THE RELEVANT COMMUNITY AS ARBITER: HOW IS IT IDENTIFIED?

Suppose it were maintained that a self-clarificatory overview of human sacrifice, which did not contain reflections on the demonism of man

---

[30] Stendhal, *The Charterhouse of Parma* (Harmondsworth, U.K.: Penguin, 1958), 150.
[31] C. S. Lewis, *A Grief Observed* (London: Faber and Faber, 1961), 59.

and the world, but confined itself only to our response to the ritual expression of these, would be untrue to the feelings and thoughts provoked by the phenomenon. How could this judgement be justified to anyone inclined to contradict it? When it is said that we are not really seeking explanations for human sacrifice but something else – *viz.*, the source of the impression of "depth" – the "we" referred to is unspecified, though some of Wittgenstein's other judgements are so intuitively correct that this escapes notice; for example, that "we" feel differently toward inflicted and uninflicted suffering. But when it is said that what "is most deeply perplexing and disturbing" about human sacrifice "is not to be resolved [by empirical enquiry] although it is easy to be fooled into thinking it is,"[32] a view is being advanced which has been vigorously disputed. There are many who find nothing more deeply disturbing about human sacrifice than the question why it was practiced. This doesn't mean that Baker and Hacker are mistaken, but only that there are implicit but unacknowledged limitations of scope on those to whom the Baker/Hacker thesis refers. (Every Wittgensteinian should have regular exchanges with someone who subscribes to *The Scientific American* and participates in its ethos.)

The philosopher/sociologist Georg Simmel attempted to discriminate the genre of assertion which is meant to be taken neither as claiming universality, nor as merely autobiographical and personal, when he characterized its presuppositions as "deep-rooted and not easily described by traditional concepts."

Simmel thought that such judgements address "something in man beyond his individual subjectivity," but also beyond "the logically objective thinking which is universally convincing."[33] Simmel was calling attention to a kind of judgment which is both familiar and yet not often theorized about or explicitly formulated. This sets us the task of determining the mode of validation appropriate to these judgements which neither express a "particular real individuality," nor "represent an objectivity beyond men and their lives," yet nevertheless lay claim to some kind of veridicality.

---

[32] Baker and Hacker, *Wittgenstein: Understanding and Meaning*, 305.
[33] Georg Simmel, "The Nature of Philosophy," *Essays on Sociology, Philosophy and Aesthetics*, ed. Kurt Wolff (New York: Harper Torchbooks, 1965), 296.

The problem posed by rejection of the pertinence of empirical enquiry to the resolution of certain perplexities, once it is recognized that they are not conceptual, and so pertain not to the coherence of our discursive practices but to our epistemic priorities, is that of deciding whose epistemic priorities are at issue. Just who is it for whom not vulgar explanation, but "the concept of a perspicuous representation is of fundamental significance" (*PI* §122; cf. *PO* 133)? How can we claim to speak for all pertinent others, when there are those with as plausible a claim to representativeness who would not agree that their epistemic priorities have been correctly formulated?

It is a general feature of our situation that often we simply do not know how representative we may be. At times what we took diffidently for idiosyncrasies turn out to be widely shared; but just as often what we thought was, if not universal, at least general enough to be true of anyone likely to read our words, proves opaque or eccentric to many more than we suspected. It may be an essential feature of this kind of communication that we are uncertain as to just who is being addressed. Yet there are judgments of this kind about whose truth we have no doubt. We are sure that Wittgenstein's statement that lilac is a "reddish-whitish-blue" (*RC* §126) will meet with general agreement, but that Kandinski's "orange is red brought closer to humanity by yellow"[34] will not. And though it is clear that the claim that Janáček's music is related to the rhythms of the Czech language does not entail a general "thereness for others," but only thereness for relevant others, *viz.*, speakers of Czech, it is not clear who the relevant others are who are entitled to a say as to whether "Bach's music is more like language than Mozart's or Haydn's" (*CV* 34).

Is there anything as coercive in the case of epistemic priorities, as the agreement of speakers of Czech in the case of Janáček's music? Sometimes.[35] But this need not matter. In an essay on James Joyce, his biographer, Richard Ellmann, remarks that it was Joyce's ambition to "give dignity to the common life we all share." He went on to quote from a letter expressing Joyce's conviction that, when he "lowered a bucket" into his "soul-well," the water he drew was Ibsen's and

---

[34] Wassily Kandinski, *Concerning the Spiritual in Art and Painting in Particular* (New York: George Wittenborn, 1912), 63.

[35] See Cioffi, *Freud and the Question of Pseudoscience* (Chicago: Open Court, 1998), 285–86.

Shelley's and Renan's as well as his own.[36] That Joyce's boast was to some degree justified is suggested by Orwell's tribute:

Joyce dared ... to expose the imbecilities of the inner mind and in doing so discovered an America which was under everybody's nose. Here is a world of stuff which you supposed to be of its nature incommunicable and somebody has managed to communicate it. The effect is to break down, at least momentarily, the solitude in which the human being lives.[37]

Should it have mattered to Orwell that there might be many who did not share his sense of community in revelation?

10. SUMMARY AND CONCLUSION

The questions with which I began were: What are overviews for, and what are they overviews of? My answer was that, where the problems are hermeneutic, what is being put in order are our intelligibility-conferring devices, and their point is either to facilitate resolution of the hermeneutic puzzles which incite them, or to provide the intrinsic satisfaction proper to surveys for those susceptible to such satisfaction. Where the problem is one of uncertainty or dispute as to what determines the character of our impression, it is the feelings and thoughts provoked by the phenomena which are to be put in order, so that their conflicting claims to account for the impression can be weighed. There is also non-epistemic problematicality, where what is laid out for us are the competing perspectives on matters which trouble us. None of these perspectives may satisfy us for long, and we may be condemned to perpetual oscillation between them.

I denied that an overview can resolve an hermeneutic problem and claimed that, even where an ostensibly heuristic rationale of our intelligibility-conferring paradigms fails to relieve the opacity which instigated it, there is, for many, an intrinsic satisfaction in such exercises. I argued for the existence of an intransitive, overview-relishing sensibility, and suggested that Wittgenstein's appreciative remarks on Darwin's "Expression of the Emotions" and Freud's joke book evince

---

[36] Richard Ellmann, *Four Dubliners: Wilde, Yeats, Joyce, and Beckett* (London: Hamish Hamilton, 1987), 76.
[37] George Orwell, "Inside the Whale," *Selected Essays* (London: Penguin, 1957), 12.

such a sensibility. I instanced social life as a topic whose ambivalence generates a particularly importunate need for overviews, and cited some ostensibly explanatory texts which are more plausibly construed as overview-gratifying than as genuinely explanatory.

But what kind of assertions are these? I suggested that whoever prioritizes synopticality over explanation need not assume his representative status in some intuitively identified group. The value of the judgement that what is most deeply perplexing and disturbing about human sacrifice is not to be resolved by empirical enquiry need not depend on the unanimity of the community addressed. There is an alternative way of taking such judgements. We can treat them as addressed to anonymous others in the hope that among these are some who will recognize, in the disparagement of the perspicuity-conferring or tranquilizing powers of explanation, a penetrating account of their real desires with respect to matters which trouble them. For example, it is not to be expected that everyone would sympathize with a response to the holocaust which gave enlightenment as to our feelings and thoughts priority over the discovery of more narrative detail or deeper historical comprehension. It is enough if, among those presented with such an overview of their feelings and thoughts, there were some who were brought to realize that their pursuit of further information was misplaced, and who responded to a discourse which eschewed explanation, in favor of a perspicuous view of the sources of their disturbance, with the appreciative admission, "That's what I really wanted."

15

On Being Surprised

Wittgenstein on Aspect-Perception, Logic, and Mathematics

Juliet Floyd

Wittgenstein's remarks invoking aspect-perception mirror his overall development as a philosopher. While I do not want overly to geneticize the philosophical terrain connected with aspect-perception, I do think it worth emphasizing that the duck-rabbit of the *Philosophical Investigations* is only one kind of example of aspect-perception, and that some of the most vivid, natural, and compelling uses of the idea of seeing aspects, interpreting one system in another, or being struck by a new aspect of a diagram, word, or sentence – as well as the earliest, most frequent, and systematic appearances of these themes in his philosophy – occur in Wittgenstein's discussions of mathematics and logic.

After a few remarks about the constructive nature of Wittgenstein's preoccupation with pictures (Section 1), I consider the earliest passage in his writing invoking puzzle-pictures (Section 2), then consider *PI* §§523–25 in relation to his earliest thoughts (Section 3), and finally look at how his uses of aspect-perception bridge the evolution in his thought from earlier to later (Section 4).

1.

In his writings on logic and mathematics, Wittgenstein points recurrently toward cases of seeing aspects anew, not to maintain that mathematical objectivity is based upon intuition in anything like Kant's sense, but instead to transform Kantian ideas about how mathematics and logic structure our forms of perception and understanding.

Like Kant, Wittgenstein hoped to reorient the notion of "discovery" as it plays a role in discussions of logic, mathematics, and philosophy, critiquing the idea that the mathematician or philosopher uncovers surprising novel facts and objects. Unlike Kant, Wittgenstein replaces this with the idea that the mathematician allows us to "see the value of a mathematical train of thought in its bringing to light something that surprises us" (*RFM* I, Appendix II, §1).[1] Wittgenstein therefore points toward the importance of active arrangement of concepts and symbols, open-ended self-discovery, pleasure, and absorbed intuitive preoccupation with diagrams and symbols as ineradicable features of our philosophical, logical, and mathematical activities. And his ambition, from early on, was to replace the Kantian idea that the universality, objectivity, and necessity of mathematics is rooted in our *a priori* forms of sensation, with the idea that the role of mathematics, like that of logic and of philosophy, is to allow us to expand, rearrange, and interpret our expressive and representational powers.

There is nothing objectionable *per se*, on Wittgenstein's view, with relying on pictures, diagrams, and other visible symbolic and representational structures. Use of these properly informs our uses of language in the everyday – including, obviously and ineradicably, what we say and do in mathematics and logic. If a child or a teacher cannot produce, recognize, and become captivated by polygons and animal pictures that are "open to view" (not hidden or ambiguous, not so messy as to be hard to recognize, and so on), then there are questions about whether, and in what sense, she will be able to command concepts in the ways we do. If a person lacks the ability to take pleasure in the game of spotting pictures hidden in puzzle-pictures, or in playing the game I Spy (in which shared words are sought for what we together can see) then she may not be able to go on in language in ways our culture demands. Nothing Wittgenstein writes is intended to contradict or express skepticism about *this*.[2]

---

[1] For an excellent discussion of Wittgenstein's Appendix on the surprising in mathematics in *RFM*, see Felix Mühlholzer, "Wittgenstein and Surprises in Mathematics," in *Wittgenstein und die Zukunft der Philosophie: Eine Neubewertung nach 50 Jahren, Proceedings of the 24th International Wittgenstein Symposium* (Vienna: öbv & hpt, 2002), 306–15.

[2] Compare Gordon Baker, *Wittgenstein's Method: Neglected Aspects*, ed. Katherine Morris (Oxford: Blackwell, 2004).

My view is that, in grammaticalizing our talk of the intuitive, Wittgenstein was proposing even in his early philosophy a new kind of criticism directed at our paths of interest when we discuss mathematics in philosophy. He was proceeding on the assumption that there are ways of speaking about experiences, interests, and activities within logic and mathematics – about what we *see* and *do* in them – that are part of the ordinary and everyday and that, therefore, may be repudiated, misapplied, and misunderstood when we philosophize.

His recurrent interest in aspect-perception in logic and mathematics is thus not metaphysical phenomenology, in which the existence of a certain kind of intentional object is at stake,[3] nor is it an uncritical obsession with freezing language as it is. He aims to do justice, instead, to ordinary experiences in mathematics and logic. This amounts to a philosophical alternative, both to formalism (which attaches no significance to the ways in which the patterns in symbol systems shape the ways we see extra-mathematical situations or ourselves), and to Frege's and Russell's ways of arguing against formalism (*WWK* 150ff.). Wittgenstein's focus on our immediate, unvarnished responses to proofs, equations, and diagrams – on our puzzlement, surprise, frustration, and pleasure – was designed to work through this expressive "raw material" in face of the idea that it might be made wholly irrelevant to debates about meaning in mathematics.[4] It is the idea that what we say about immediate mathematical experience *has* no cognitive or grammatical significance, but *merely* sensory or

[3] In what sense there are phenomenological strands in Wittgenstein's thinking is much debated. A useful range of essays includes Jean-Philippe Narboux, *Dimensions et Paradigms, Wittgenstein et le problème de l'abstraction* (Paris: Vrin Mathesis, forthcoming); Mathieu Marion, "Phenomenological Language: Thoughts and Operations in the *Tractatus*" and Jaakko Hintikka, "Reply to Marion," both in Randall E. Auxier and Lewis Edwin Hahn, eds., *The Philosophy of Jaakko Hintikka*, Library of Living Philosophers, vol. 30 (Chicago and La Salle: Open Court, 2006), 413–36; Wolfgang Kienzler, *Wittgensteins wende zu seiner Spätphilosophie 1930–1932* (Frankfurth am Main: Surhkamp Verlag, 1997); and Dagfinn Føllesdaal, "Ultimate Justification in Husserl and Wittgenstein," in Maria E. Reicher and Johann C. Marek, eds., *Experience and Analysis* (Vienna: öbv & hpt, 2005), 127–42.

[4] On what the mathematician throws off as "raw material" for philosophy, see *PI* §254; as we see from MS 124, page 35, the original version of this remark was directed at G. H. Hardy's *Apology of a Mathematician*, which I look at briefly below (see *CM*). Compare also Steven Gerrard's analogy between the quotation from Augustine at *PI* §1 and Hardy's remarks about mathematics in "Wittgenstein's Philosophies of Mathematics," *Synthese* 87, no. 1: 1991, 125–42.

aesthetic or psychological significance, that forms the target of much of his best writing on aspect-perception and mathematics. Aspect-perception is a way he has of calling attention to what interests us, to our voicing of what we take to be important (*RFM* III, §47).[5]

It remains a question whether, in the end, Wittgenstein's talk of what we see *in* a notation or proof or system of equations was intended by him to be merely transitional talk, prose to be worked through and replaced, ideally, by other, less perceptual sounding poetry. My sense, in attempting to make sense of the intersection of his remarks on mathematics and on aspect-perception, is that the answer is, "No".

2.

The first mention in Wittgenstein's writings of puzzle-pictures and the seeing of situations occurs in his wartime notebooks (8–9 November 1914):

What can be confirmed by experiment, in propositions about probability, cannot possibly be mathematics.

Probability propositions are abstracts [or "extracts," *Auszüge*] of scientific laws.

They are generalizations and express an incomplete knowledge of those laws.

If, e.g., I take black and white balls out of an urn I cannot say before taking one out whether I shall get a white or a black ball, since I am not well enough acquainted with the natural laws for that, but *all the same I do know* that if there are equally many black and white balls there, the numbers of black balls that are drawn will approach the number of white ones if the drawing is continued; I do know the natural laws as accurately as *this*.

Now what I know in probability statements are certain general properties of ungeneralized propositions of natural science, such as, e.g., their symmetry in certain respects, and asymmetry in others, etc.

Puzzle pictures and the seeing of situations. (*NB* 27–28)

The passage meditates on the distinction between probability as a purely logical notion unfolded in a system of calculations,

5 On the issue of value and importance being central to aspect-perception I am indebted to Judith Genova's *Wittgenstein: A Way of Seeing* (New York: Routledge, 1995), to Stephen Mulhall's *On Being in the World: Wittgenstein and Heidegger on Seeing Aspects* (New York: Routledge, 1990), and to the other essays in this volume.

and probability applied to situations of everyday life. The technical details of Wittgenstein's effort to reduce probability to logical terms need not detain us here; they are by contemporary standards unsatisfactory because of their tie to his truth-functional conception of the logic of propositions.[6] What is of interest here instead is that by 1914 he already regarded the distinction between calculation and experiment – a distinction invoked and explored in every period of his writing about mathematics – not as a distinction between two disjoint domains of fact or necessity (e.g., *a priori* and *a posteriori*), but instead on analogy with parts of a puzzle-picture, a picture in which the name of the game is to spot one or more pictures or scenes in another.

Wittgenstein imagines a complete list or representation of all the balls in the urn, black and white, perhaps ordered by their names (lexicographically) – a numbering or a list of elementary propositions representing possible events of drawing from the urn (imagine, analogously, a representation of all the pairs of faces of two different die, presented in a sequence of pictures, diagramming possibilities for throwing them once). In any such (finite)[7] presentation of the total space of possible draws, we can see, "internally" to the presentation given by the list, that there are as many black balls as white

---

[6] For discussions that go into further detail, see G. H. von Wright, "Wittgenstein on Probability," in his *Wittgenstein* (Minneapolis: University of Minnesota Press, 1983); Brian McGuinness, "Probability," chapter 18 of his *Approaches to Wittgenstein: Collected Papers* (New York: Routledge, 2002), and M. C. Galavotti, *Philosophical Introduction to Probability* (Stanford: CSLI, 2005), chapter 6.5. I hope what I say in this essay might slightly assuage the sense of inarticulateness and unclarity Galavotti finds in Wittgenstein's discussion of the relation between *a priori* and *a posteriori* elements in probability, but there are nonetheless difficulties that Wittgenstein never did come to terms with (probability is practically not mentioned in *RFM*). Wittgenstein discussed probability frequently through about 1934; one may look at *PR* 289ff., *WWK* 93ff., and *BT* 98ff. (§33) for some relevant passages.

[7] Wittgenstein's remarks on aspect-perception have seemed to most (including himself) to fit the finite case most naturally. The issues surrounding the wider question whether he was committed, in principle, to a denial of the infinite are complex and I cannot go into them here; see, however, my "Wittgenstein on Philosophy of Logic and Mathematics" in Stewart Shapiro, ed., *The Oxford Handbook of Philosophy of Mathematics and Logic* (Oxford: Oxford University Press, 2005), 75–128 for an accessible and brief survey of the theme, as well as my "Critical Study of Mathieu Marion, *Wittgenstein, Finitism, and the Philosophy of Mathematics*," *Philosophia Mathematica* 10, no. 1 (2002): 67–88.

ones. Situations are available for probabilistic modeling – that is, are subject to being seen in terms of the generalized calculus of probabilities – insofar as we compare and discern these internal ("logical," "grammatical") features of their arrangement (its "symmetries" and "asymmetries"). Finding these is, Wittgenstein suggests, like finding (how to see) a rabbit or a ship hidden within a larger picture or perceived scene. We can, for example, count, order, and rank the probabilities associated with choosing ten black balls in a row (or rolling two sixes with the die six times out of ten) by looking at the list and counting elements of the representation. Here we apply arithmetic *intramathematically*, within our application of probability to the "extract" of propositions.

It is important that we can draw out the "internal" features of the list (can count and calculate specific probabilities of cases) without actually drawing any balls or throwing the die. In fact, as Wittgenstein remarks, no matter how many draws from the urn we might try out empirically, these could never provide empirical confirmation of our probability calculations ("by experiment"). Probability is applicable to actual draws from the urn, but only insofar as we suppose that no intervening empirical biases or unknown factors, no interruptions of what we now take to be the physical and psychological laws governing draws from the urn, are relevant – insofar, that is, as we view our representation of the possibilities as an "extract" of a form of description that we apply to reality, *as if* it gives us a complete and correct description of our world.

So much must be counted as an ordinary understanding of probability. When I draw from the urn in any particular case, knowledge of the probabilities does not answer the question, "Is *this* draw going to produce a white or black ball?" Knowledge of probability does not have the function of speaking to this, as Peirce noted long ago.[8] Probability does not apply to any particular case individually, but only to a case conceived of within a represented system or domain of alternative (contrasting) possibilities, however they may be conceived and interpreted theoretically (in terms of draws in the long run, conditional probabilities, truth-functions, and so on). As

---

[8] Charles Sanders Peirce, "On the Doctrine of Chances, With Later Reflections," in *Philosophical Writings of Peirce*, ed. Justus Buchler (New York: Dover, 1955), 157–73.

the *Tractatus* says, "In itself, a proposition is neither probable nor improbable" (*TLP* 5.153).

Like Peirce before him, Wittgenstein is emphasizing that there are no unconditional facts or objects of probability (cf. *TLP* 5.1511: "There is no special object peculiar to probability propositions"). Wittgenstein's image of seeing probability in an extract of propositions relieves us of the need to say that probabilities are really out there in nature, apart from us, or even that they are merely "conventionally" or "imaginatively" applied to situations.[9] Probabilities are neither facts nor fictions. Empirical applications of the calculus of probability are instead parasitic on our taking ourselves to have represented a world of events accurately and completely enough, and on our ability to draw out (write down, symbolize, arrange) our representations concisely enough, that we can spot symmetries and asymmetries within *them* (and apply mathematics, in turn, to them and with them). To apply probability we are obliged to regard our powers of representation as successful but conditional in application, as open to further articulation and arrangement. Again: In answer to a question about what will happen on a particular draw from the urn on a particular occasion, probability says, "Don't ask me."[10]

None of this implies that I might not be overwhelmingly and vitally interested in the question of whether on the first pick I should get a black ball or a white one. (Peirce imagined a kidnapped man whose life would turn on the pick of one card, red or black). But if I am interested in *this* (and no other outcome) then the relevance of probability disappears from view. Under the aspect of the calculus of probability (as I might put it), whatever the particular outcome

---

9 As Brian McGuinness writes, "there is no *tendency* in things, no tendency, say, to fall out a certain way in 57.8 percent of all cases on average" ("Probability," *Approaches to Wittgenstein*, 210). Avner Baz stresses that seeing aspects is not the same as perceiving, that it need involve no representation, that is, does not concern "external world talk" and involves "a step beyond grammar" ("What's the Point of Seeing Aspects?" *Philosophical Investigations* 23, no. 2 [2000]: 97–121; cf. 120). On the importance of human gesture and body, alongside mental or intellectual construction, to aspect-perception, see Victor J. Krebs, "The Subtle Body of Language and the Lost Sense of Philosophy," also in *Philosophical Investigations* 23, no. 2 (2000): 147–155.

10 See Charles Sanders Peirce, "Philosophy and the Conduct of Life," in *Reasoning and the Logic of Things*, ed. Kenneth Laine Ketner (Cambridge: Harvard University Press, 1992), 111.

of a particular draw from the urn, as long as I take my action to fall within the domain of possibilities represented I cannot really *be* surprised. Thus, picking from the urn of 100 balls, half white, half black, I might be very surprised to pull out 10 white balls in a row, having not expected such a turn of events. Reflecting on what I know of probabilities, that surprise might vanish in the thought that I should *not*, perhaps, have been surprised. But suppose I draw a *red* ball. This outcome would surprise me; at this point the system of situations connected with the urn would change. (I might look in the urn, alter my description, or look for the culprit who put in the red ball when I was not looking.) And I would be something other than surprised or interested – I would be stupefied or astonished or amazed – if the 100 balls suddenly disappeared for no apparent reason (compare *PI* §§80, 141–42; *OC* §§133–34).

Seeing an action in terms of a space of possibility, like seeing aspects generally, does not imply or require, in and of itself, that there is another way of seeing or regarding it.[11] But mathematics and philosophy shape, and are shaped by, our contingently given ways of looking at and experiencing events, actions and experiences. They involve *forms* or *arrangements* of facts, ways of intuiting (*Anschauungsarte*) the particular (*RFM* III, §12). As Wittgenstein often emphasizes in his later writings, mathematics shows us that the limits of empiricism lie "not in [*a priori*] assumptions guaranteed, but in the ways in which we make comparisons and in which we act" (*RFM* VII, §21).

The making of comparisons, the game of seeing one thing as like or in another, can be refused. *Can* I be surprised that in a draw of 25 balls from the box of 100 that are half white, half black, I get 13 white and 12 black ones? What if I am? What if I say, "But isn't it amazing, this confirmation in the empirical sphere of my draws of that *a priori* law"? Wittgenstein's remarks in his notebook are directed against the notion that a direct answer to this question will help one make sense of probability. To think so is to subscribe to a fantasy that my experience and the totality of relevant necessities can meet one another on unconditionally given ground, apart from my acceptance of a particular form of representation. The notions of possibility and necessity

[11] Compare Baz, "What's the Point of Seeing Aspects?" 114, note 17.

are *contrastive*, finding their place within multi-dimensional modes of representation. Probability can change the aspect under which we regard a particular experience only because we already regard that experience as an element *in* a structured order of possible experiences, that is to say, as a form, something displaying possible structure (in the early Wittgenstein's way of phrasing it).

What if I nevertheless insisted that I *did* find it, the very fact of the thisness of *this* draw from the urn – this draw itself, and not its consequences for my life – intrinsically surprising? This should be compared with Wittgenstein's remark to Engelmann about being in a state in which one *cannot get over* the existence of a fact.[12] What I may need here is a new way of looking at things, a way that allows me to change the quality of my attachment to this particular fact, word, or description, to see that what may be as interesting or important as the way things have gone here, now, is their place in a wider train of thought or experience or action to which I might also become attached. Such new articulations allow me to appreciate something anew, something I missed in my original way of seeing things, just as I might miss a figure hidden in a puzzle-picture. (This is not to deny that the original way of looking at things is just as much there, perhaps available still for my focus.)

It follows that our ways of regarding situations *as* probable, improbable, possible, or necessary are not themselves perceptions or single facts, but instead reflect our acceptance and experience of domains of possibilities that we have ourselves articulated and understood. We see one system of experience *in* another when we employ the calculus of probability. "Seeing-in" implies that there is nothing intrinsically necessary that requires us to apply a concept to a particular situation, and that we therefore bear some responsibility for the application of a structure (here, a mathematical one) to the interpretation of experience. We may have good psychological, emotional, ethical, or philosophical reasons for feeling that probability's way of seeing a situation does not speak to our lives or interests at all. The grammar of what to say then is, so far as the calculus of probability goes, open. This is where philosophy may step in.

---

[12] See Paul Engelmann, *Letters from Ludwig Wittgenstein: With a Memoir* (Oxford: Blackwell, 1967), 33–34 (Wittgenstein to Engelmann, 21 June 1920).

3.

The probability example shows one way in which Wittgenstein concerned himself with the human drive toward the symbolical, including in it the drive, familiar enough in mathematics, logic, and philosophy, *not* to engage only in descriptions of particular facts (assertions true and false), but instead to seek and find perspectives from which the specific content of what is true or false can take a back seat to our absorption in aspects we can draw from (find or see in) a scheme of interpretation or arrangement. I am stressing here that such finding – which may involve the discovery of emptiness or irrelevance, the vanishing of our interest (in, e.g., the calculus of probability, or in the outcome of *this* pick) – is itself constructive, sometimes pleasurable, and characteristic of certain kinds of significance we find and create in our lives.

Shifting attachment to, and surrender of, a particular kind of situation or word are involved in the aspect examples Wittgenstein explores in Part II, Section 11 of the *Investigations*. Memorableness, vividness, and ease of perception characterize these examples in comparison with the more detailed investigations of proof pictures, notations, diagrams, and formulae in his writings on mathematics, those writings that he set aside from the last two major drafts of the *Investigations*.[13] But it was the open-ended, familiar experiences of multi-dimensional interweaving in the examples from mathematics and logic, pure and applied, that brought Wittgenstein himself face to face with the idea that these experiences are part and parcel of our open-ended experience of, in, and with language.

The double cross (*PI* 207c) is an example for which no particular concept seems necessary to invoke the experience of change in the figure. Tracing the figure may help. Seeing it in terms of perspective, foreground versus background, may help or hinder seeing its doubleness, for two crosses may be experienced as something *in* the one figure. The duck-rabbit figure (*PI* 194b), also exhibiting a bivalent contrast in what we can see in it, calls forth, by contrast, a pair

---

[13] On the composition of *PI*, see G. H. von Wright, "On the Origin and Composition of *Philosophical Investigations*," *Wittgenstein*, 111–36; compare P. M. S. Hacker, Preface to *Wittgenstein: Mind and Will* (Oxford: Oxford University Press, 1996), xiv–xviii.

of mutually exclusive concepts of animals. This goes along with the fact that we cannot see both sides *in* the figure at once, one *in* the other – although, if both duck and rabbit are spotted, their appearance to the viewer may be varied at will, by desire, instantaneously, partly because it is easy to hold both concepts in mind (if not in sight) at once.

Our experience of these figures seems complete even if complex, bivalent or trivalent. In other cases of aspect-perception there is a more open-ended range of significance: What is to be discerned is not an object or fact or concept, but a world, a human being, an expression or gesture, a total field of significance. The distinction between object and world is an old one in Wittgenstein; in his wartime notebooks he contrasted seeing the stove before him as just one object among many and seeing it as an open-ended world, his life for the moment, beside which everything else is by contrast "colorless" (*NB* 83 [8 October 1916]). So we might contrast the picture-face (*PI* 194c), seen as a schematic picture of a particular emotion (happiness, sadness, surprise), with the kind of absorption involved in seeing a world of possibilities: children playing with dolls or hearing fairy tales, seeing my friend smiling down on me from the wall, and so on. More open-ended yet is a case like a figure of a triangle (*PI* 200c): Here the variety of possible contexts into which the figure may be imagined fitting is even wider (a blueprint, a paradigm for a child, a decorative motif, an illustration in a textbook, a diagram in a geometrical proof …), so that what seems to engage us is less the representation itself than the words and activities with which we surround it.

Each of these cases of aspect-perception replaces an idea of accuracy (isomorphic depiction) with an idea of interest and relevance; the contrast drawn is between the perception of a field of possibility or significance for the applications of concepts, and an application of a concept. What holds these cases together is a sense that seeing necessity or possibility requires us *not* to imagine that we have seen *all* possibilities – that, as Kant put it, the modality of judgments "contributes nothing to the content of the judgment … but concerns only the value of the copula in relation to thought in general."[14]

---

[14] Immanuel Kant, *Critique of Pure Reason*, trans. Norman Kemp Smith (London: Macmillan, 1929), A74/B100.

Remarks 522–24 of the *Investigations* comment on variety in picturing:

If we compare a proposition to a picture, we must think whether we are comparing it to a portrait (a historical representation) or to a genre-picture. And both comparisons have point.

When I look at a genre-picture, it "tells" me something, even though I don't believe (imagine) for a moment that the people I see in it really exist, or that there have really been people in that situation. But suppose I ask: "*What* does it tell me, then?"

I should like to say "What the picture tells me is itself." That is, its telling me something consists in its own structure, in *its* own lines and colors. (What would it mean to say "What this musical theme tells me is itself"?)

Don't regard it as obvious, but as a remarkable fact [*merkwürdiges Faktum*], that pictures and fictitious narratives give us pleasure, occupy our minds.

("Don't regard it as obvious [*als selbstverständlich*]" means: wonder over it [*Wundere dich darüber*], as you do some things which disturb you. Then what is problematic in the latter will disappear, by your accepting this fact as you do the other.).

((The transition from patent nonsense to something which is disguised nonsense.))[15]

These remarks invoke the concepts of the interesting, the pleasurable, and the remarkable in asking us to allow ourselves to be struck by the complexity in our uses of pictures in everyday settings. The closing line of *PI* §524, a parenthetical reversal of the earlier §464 ("My aim is: to teach you to pass from a piece of disguised nonsense to something that is patent nonsense"), raises the prospect of a certain pattern in Wittgenstein's understanding of his philosophical methods, a back and forth movement from latent to patent nonsense. The idea that nonsense may require attractive articulation to be seen aright alludes, I take it, to his own development: The interlocutor's patently odd remark at *PI* §523 ("I should like to say 'What the picture tells me is itself'") is implicitly contrasted with the latently nonsensical remark at *TLP* 2.1: "We make to ourselves pictures of facts."[16] From the point of view of the *Investigations* this latter remark, perfectly grammatical and even jejunely true, was misplaced, forced into

---

[15] I have slightly altered Anscombe's translation of this remark, deleting her use of the verb "surprising." My reasons for doing so will become clearer in what follows.

[16] Trans. C. K. Ogden.

a setting in which it occurred wrongly punctuated, inviting the non-sensical idea that all our ways of picturing rest, ultimately, upon our ability to represent facts truly or falsely.[17] But illustrations of poems and fairy tales, diagrams in textbooks of engineering and mathematics, also form "a complicated amalgam of ... words and pictures" (*BT* 69 (§22)) no less important to us. There was an overarching confusion at work in the *Tractatus* between the isomorphic character of portraits of states of affairs and the more complexly saturated modeling involved in diagrams and illustrations.[18] We have seen from scrutiny of his note-book remark on probability that even the early Wittgenstein struggled to emphasize much beyond fact-depiction in his discussions of math-ematics, untangling such confusions. But as the probability example also shows, his early view was explicated in terms of a vision of "ungen-eralized" elementary sentences, a collection of pictured facts treated as ultimate.

The *Investigations*' repeated revisiting of the fictional and the imaginative questions this idea of primary versus secondary forms of sense (cf. *PI* §232, II.xi), asking us to release philosophy from its ancient task of ranking the literal depiction of objects and truths above the fancies of poetry and fiction. It is striking that in *PI* §525 Wittgenstein explicitly ties the notion of wonder, philosophy's classic prompt since the time of Plato and Aristotle, to the idea of surren-dering a disturbance or disquieted puzzlement about the possibil-ity of picturing. In raising the prospect of such a "disappearance" of disquiet, aside from voicing his ambition to speak of philosophy in its ancient sense, Wittgenstein alludes to *PI* §133, in which it is remarked (evidently paradoxically, given the unending stream of questions with which the reader of the *Investigations* is confronted) that "the philosophical problems should *completely* disappear," and that "the real discovery is the one that makes me capable of stopping doing philosophy when I want to.—The one that gives philosophy peace, so that it is no longer tormented by questions which bring *itself* in question." While some have rejected this remark as trivializing of philosophy, as too "quietist," it should be noted that Wittgenstein is

[17] Here I concur with Hacker's discussion of these remarks in *Wittgenstein: Mind and Will*.
[18] Jean-Philippe Narboux, "Diagramme, Dimensions et Synopsis," *Théorie, Littérature, Enseignement* 22 (Saint-Denis: Presses Universitaires de Vincennes, 2005): 115–41.

here suggesting how philosophy might be *defended*, protected from exposure to questions about its ultimate worth. The idea that philosophy's origins lie in our capacity for wonder over phenomena that surprise or puzzle or frighten us, that its end lies in a certain tranquility and satisfaction uniquely its own, and that it is an art of ordering the imagination, proceeding from surprise to wonder to admiration by drawing unforeseen connections (especially among phenomena that appear at first to be familiar and uninteresting), is a quite traditional one, familiar from Plato through Nietzsche.[19] Adam Smith, in his "History of Astronomy," explicitly articulates such a view:

When something quite new and singular is presented, we feel ourselves incapable of [referring to some known species or class of things]. ... Imagination and memory exert themselves to no purpose, and in vain look around all their classes of ideas in order to find one under which it may be arranged. ... It is this fluctuation and vain recollection, together with the emotion or movement of the spirits that they excite, which constitute the sentiment properly called *Wonder*. ... What sort of a thing can that be? What is that like? are the questions which, upon such an occasion, we are all naturally disposed to ask. ... Upon the clear discovery of a connecting chain of intermediate events [Wonder] vanishes altogether. ...

Philosophy is the science of the connecting principles of nature ... [and] endeavours to introduce order into this chaos of jarring and discordant appearances, to allay this tumult of the imagination, and to restore it, when it surveys the great revolutions of the universe, to that tone of tranquility and composure, which is both most agreeable in itself, and most suitable to its nature. Philosophy, therefore, may be regarded as one of those arts which address themselves to the imagination. ...[20]

What is new in Wittgenstein is less his vision of the aims and purposes of philosophy than a post-Kantian, post-Fregean, post-Russellian preoccupation with releasing the imagination from its domination, in the empiricist tradition, by too unimaginative a conception of how words and ideas associate with one another.

---

[19] For Wittgenstein and Nietzsche, see Gordon C. F. Bearn, *Waking to Wonder: Wittgenstein's Existential Investigations* (Albany, N.Y.: State University of New York Press, 1997).

[20] Adam Smith, "The History of Astronomy," *Essays Philosophical and Literary*, (London: Ward, Lock & Co., 1880), 330–31, 333–34, 336.

4.

In the (ordinary) sentence "There are three plums on the table," the *Tractatus* asks us to see the word "three" not as just another name, concept, or adjectival word, but instead as a representational aspect, a space of form located within a larger picture (here, the sentence expressing a proposition, true or false). This may be seen in the idiosyncratic rewriting of the sentence that the *Tractatus* proposes, in which a separable grammatical term for the number three vanishes: $(\exists x,y,z)(Px \ \& \ Py \ \& \ Pz)$.[21] What Frege or Russell would have treated as an identity assertion about the concept "plum" (*viz.*, that the number of objects falling under it is identical with the number three), Wittgenstein asks us to see *in* our depiction of the situation, like a part of a puzzle-picture. Three is part of (the grammar of) how we view this sentence as a picture of reality, an "internal" feature of our thought to be drawn out; we can count the variables to see this. This does not mean that Wittgenstein held a substitutional view of quantification on which numerals, as opposed to objects, are what we quantify over when we do mathematics; he is not siding with the formalists. Instead, the vanishing of the term "three" from his rewriting of the sentence asks us to see number words as an aspect of (a way of using) a symbolism. Such aspects are themselves subject to further, different forms of articulation. The *Tractatus* goes on to concoct specific terms for each number, placing these within an open-ended series of forms: 0, 1+1, 1+1+1, 1+1+1+1 ... (*TLP* 6.02). This is not a "meta" form, standing outside the standpoint of the original space; instead, the point is to see the number three *in* it, and so to do something new with "3."

Strange though it may sound to say so, Wittgenstein's conception offered him a way of recovering (rearranging, making sense of) some of the everyday ways of speaking about mathematics with which he

---

[21] One must interpret the variables "x," "y," and "z" here as referring to distinct objects, and not in the way we are used to from ordinary first-order logic; Wittgenstein assumes that identity has been eliminated by the device of taking different names to refer to different objects. For more detail, see my "Number and Ascriptions of Number in Wittgenstein's *Tractatus*," in Juliet Floyd and Sanford Shieh, eds., *Future Pasts: Perspectives on the Analytic Tradition in Twentieth Century Philosophy* (Oxford: Oxford University Press, 2001), 145–92.

was familiar from his days as an engineer. One is the idea that logic and mathematics consist essentially of calculations; another is the idea that it is what we can discern in the signs themselves, as we calculate with them, that contains their essential interest and importance (*TLP* 6.21, 6.2331). One may find nearly the same words about mathematics in, for example, Whitehead's *An Introduction to Mathematics*, a work Wittgenstein knew:

In mathematics, granted that we are giving any serious attention to mathematical ideas, the symbolism is invariably an immense simplification. It is not only of practical use, but is of great interest. For it represents an analysis of the ideas of the subject and an almost pictorial representation of their relations to each other. If any one doubts the utility of symbols, let him write out in full, without any symbol whatever, the whole meaning of the following equations which represent some of the fundamental laws of algebra:

(1) $x + y = y + x$
(2) $(x + y) + z = x + (y + z)$
(3) $x \times y = y \times x$
(4) $(x \times y) \times z = x \times (y \times z)$
(5) $x \times (y + x) = (x \times y) + (x \times z)$. ...

By the aid of symbolism, we can make transitions in reasoning almost mechanically by the eye, which otherwise would call into play the higher faculties of the brain.

It is a profoundly erroneous truism, repeated by all copy-books and by eminent people when they are making speeches, that we should cultivate the habit of thinking of what we are doing. The precise opposite is the case. Civilization advances by extending the number of important operations which we can perform without thinking about them.

One very important property for symbolism to possess is that it should be concise, so as to be visible at one glance of the eye and to be rapidly written. Now we cannot place symbols more concisely together than by placing them in immediate juxtaposition. In a good symbolism, therefore, the juxtaposition of important symbols should have an important meaning. This is one of the merits of the Arabic notation for numbers.[22]

Compare with this what Wittgenstein writes about equations in the *Tractatus*:

---

[22] Alfred North Whitehead, *An Introduction to Mathematics* (New York: H. Holt, 1911), 60. My "Number and Ascriptions of Number in Wittgenstein's *Tractatus*" discusses in more detail the issue of Wittgenstein, formalism, and Whitehead.

If two expressions are combined by means of the sign of equality, that means that they can be substituted for one another. But it must be manifest in the two expressions themselves whether this is the case or not. ...

Frege says that the two expressions have the same meaning but different senses.

But the essential point about an equation is that it is not necessary in order to show that the two expressions connected by the sign of equality have the same meaning, since this can be seen [learned, *ersehen lässt*] from the two expressions themselves.

And the possibility of proving the propositions of mathematics means simply that their correctness is seen [understood, *einzusehen ist*] without our having to compare what they express with the facts as regards correctness. ...

An equation only marks the point of view from which I consider the two expressions: it marks from the point of view of their equivalence in meaning. (*TLP* 6.23–6.2323)[23]

For Frege, an equation is a logical identity, true or false, in which sameness of reference (*Bedeutung*) is said to hold between two names. The informativeness of an equation resides, Frege also holds, in the contrasting, complex senses (*Sinne*) of the numerical terms involved, not in their references. The numerals are proper names insofar as Frege was wont to emphasize that each number is, in and of itself, unique, having its own identity and unique set of properties. In the *Tractatus* and ever after, Wittgenstein explicitly rejects Frege's conception of equations as logical identities; with this he rejects Frege's sense/reference distinction and his account of what it is to understand the specific content of a mathematical truth. As in the probability case, Wittgenstein assumes that what is of interest *within* arithmetic and algebra is not that we reach this *particular* number or form at the end of a calculation, but instead *how* we reach it and what we do *having* reached it, i.e., through which comparisons, substitutions, and arithmetical calculations we go on to see and apply it. Truth, at least if it is conceived of in terms of a "comparison with reality," has no primary role in the *doing* of mathematics or logic, on Wittgenstein's view. Instead, "a number is what it does";[24] its primary significance and interest for

---

[23] I've altered slightly the Pears and McGuinness translation in the last two paragraphs (6.2321–6.2323), inspired in part by Ogden's.

[24] Timothy Gowers, *Mathematics: A Very Short Introduction* (Oxford: Oxford University Press, 2002), 18.

us lie in the characteristic "internal" features of the expressions we draw out, uncovering the multiple standpoints from which we are able to view, arrange, see, and manipulate terms within the process of calculating. Here – as in logic and philosophy – punctuation, syncopation, arrangement of notation, simile, and emphasis in expression are everything: "Process and result are equivalent" (*TLP* 6.1261; cf. *NB* 42 [24 April 1915], *RFM* I, §§80–84). Logical and mathematical operation signs are "punctuations" (cf. *TLP* 5.4611), that is, what they articulate are not special objects, but ways of arranging what we feel the need to write and say. These expressions include the parentheses, brackets, circlings, underlinings, index-marks, and other surrounding signs that we use in logic and mathematics to help us to see. These expressions of emphasis and alteration of emphasis are not, as Frege might have held, inessential because they express the origin of our thoughts (cf. *BT* 277); instead, they show us what thinking in such cases *is*.

Though Wittgenstein's thought evolved, these ideas never left him; instead they were rearranged, repunctuated, seen anew, in hundreds of examples that he explored, some from fairly advanced mathematics, some from the most elementary mathematics. We can see the very same lines of thought addressed in the opening remark of *Remarks on the Foundations of Mathematics*. Suppose we ask, as Wittgenstein does: Are there two variables at work in

$$y = (x^2 + z)^2 - z(2x^2 + z)?$$

Well, obviously, Yes. Just *look at* the expression. (We see "x" and "z" before our eyes.)

But we can see the question *differently* if we work the equation out (i.e., calculate with it). Rewriting (expanding the notation) we get first

$$(x^2 + z)(x^2 + z) - z(2x^2 + z)$$

And then

$$x^4 + zx^2 + zx^2 + z^2 - 2zx^2 - z^2.$$

By adding and canceling, we see that this is equivalent to x^4. We see how the algebraic formulae express the concept of x raised to a fourth power. In compacting our signs, we enlarge (can make more general) our point of view. We also see that the answer to the original question really is now (was?), "No". For there are not two variables essentially at work in the original equation.

This may be a surprise for those who have not yet seen the variable "z" vanish. But the vanishing – and hence the *mathematical* surprise – evinces itself only in the course of working out the equation. Once it is worked out, we *see* both equations *in a new way*. The seeing or coming to see in a new way is, in fact, both process and result of the process: the activity of puzzling through to a solution is both the problem and the solution. For without this working out, this *coming to see*, the mathematical interest of the problem, its mathematical content or point, cannot be seen – just as the interest of a puzzle-picture cannot be seen by one unable or unwilling to (try to) see several pictures in it. But with the working out, the interest vanishes from *inside* the problem, shifting it, so to speak, to its outside (*RFM* I, Appendix II, §2), i.e., to the fact that it can be a puzzle at all, though not for the one who knows how to solve it.

It is the same within logic, according to Wittgenstein, from the *Tractatus* onward. Consider a sentence structure of the following form:

$$(p \mathbin{\&} \neg r) \vee (p \mathbin{\&} q \supset r)$$

This looks like a structure that would express a sentence with sense, a picture of reality, assuming that the elementary components of the sentence themselves have sense. But if we rewrite it in the form of a truth-table, as the *Tractatus* says we can, we see it anew. For in this diagram we can see the tautologousness of the original sentence form *in* the final column, which contains only T's; the sentence's apparent sense, its ruling in and ruling out of states of affairs, vanishes. It may surprise us to see, when written out this way, that the sentence yields a tautology. But once we see the sentence written *in* this diagram, we change our way of viewing what we might have regarded as a sentence representing a state of affairs, true or false. We also see *in* the senseless sentence the general form of tautology, a so-called "proposition" of logic.

Now in the *Tractatus*'s notion of what is proper to logic alone we do meet a kind of claim to completeness or maximality with respect to our capacity to see one system in another. I have so far contrasted the idea of a "meta" stance on logic or language with that of the ability to see one system *in* another. But in the *Tractatus*, Wittgenstein claims to have found, in his general form of proposition, a diagram expressing the entire grammatical space of all propositions, a scheme expressing the three words beyond which everything else is just roaring and booming (*viz.*, "So it goes," "*Es verhält sich so*") (*TLP* 4.5, 6).

By way of a single logical operation, operator N, a generalized version of the Sheffer stroke of joint denial, Wittgenstein lays bare what he thinks of as a complete systematization or diagram in which we can *see* the system (the one and only system) of logical operations. But he goes even further, writing that "It is possible … to give at the outset a description of all 'true' logical propositions. Hence there can *never* be surprises in logic" (*TLP* 6.125–26.1251). Wittgenstein is claiming to have found the most concise possible symbolic way of depicting, not merely the essence of the proposition, but the essence of logic itself. All so-called logical propositions are sentences without sense – tautologies or contradictions. In them the portrayal of reality (sense) vanishes. Since on Wittgenstein's view a new proposition is nothing but the coordination of truth values to the whole on the basis of the truth values of the elementary parts, all logically equivalent sentences share the same general form of tautologousness. So in the end there is ultimately only one kind of tautology, only one form of such *Sinnlosigkeit*. It is as if we have reached the limit of our ability to see one system in another, and can see no further, though we see darkly and partially. For only a being like Leibniz's God, capable of seeing an infinite number of calculations at a glance, would be able to see every instance of the one form of tautology for what it really is. For Leibniz's God alone could there *never* be (even apparent) surprises *within* logic.

The general form of proposition is a scheme whose physiognomy is fixed, not open ended, not subject to elaboration of new aspects. Wittgenstein does not take into account, for example, the (later discussed) possibility of a multi-valued logic, or proof methods which do not rely on the law of the excluded middle. Thus in logic even more than in mathematics, there can *never* be surprises – and more than just in the sense in which "process and result are equivalent" within calculations. Wittgenstein's philosophical task, as he understood it in the *Tractatus*, was to examine his own uses of language with an eye toward seeing them *in* the general form of proposition. What he strove for was a perspective that would transcend the limitations of any particular notation or symbolism, while at the same time encompassing, i.e., diagramming, the logical aspect of any possible notation or language. This was a struggle to design a particular notational method (the truth-tables, the a–b notation) that could operationalize – that is to say, fully formalize or mathematize – the intuitive notion of one sentence's following from another *by pure logic alone*, in such a way that the method would be complete (in applying to any and every possible notation), yet unbiased with respect to the particular notation chosen for any language.[25]

By 1929 Wittgenstein had surrendered this aspiration to completeness. Although the notation of truth-tables was all right in its place, it worked for only a fragment or one aspect of language, not the whole: one could not see *in* the general propositional form *the* logic of language. The *Tractatus*'s recursive specifications of the general propositional form and of the grammar of number words were too "nebulous" (*PR* 131 [§109]). As Russell pointed out in his introduction to the *Tractatus*, the mathematics of the higher infinite had not been diagrammed, but only gestured at, in Wittgenstein's remarks on mathematics. As Ramsey emphasized, the method of truth-tables could not help with the more fine-grained needs of mathematical logicians. Ordinary statements of color, measurement, degree, and continuity could not be seen in the method of truth-table diagramming either. And the idea that the needs of natural science, perhaps of cosmology, would be decisive in determining the particular choice of notational system came to seem to Wittgenstein a cop out. It was both too much of a concession to promissory scientism, and too little engaged with the task of seeing aspects of grammar and notation in the small. It also held philosophy hostage to the deliverances of the empirical as it would be understood in physics.

---

[25] For an elaboration of this reading, see my "Wittgenstein and the Inexpressible," in Alice Crary, ed., *Wittgenstein and the Moral Life: Essays in Honor of Cora Diamond* (Cambridge: MIT Press, 2007).

In this, as Wittgenstein explained to Waismann and Schlick, he had unwittingly made of philosophy something "dogmatic":

One fault you can find with a dogmatic account is, first, that it is, as it were, arrogant. But that is not the worst thing about it. There is another mistake, which is much more dangerous and also pervades my whole book, and that is the conception that there are questions the answers to which will be found at a later date. It is held that, although a result is not known, there is a way of finding it. Thus I used to believe, for example, that it is the task of logical analysis to discover the elementary propositions. I wrote, we are unable to specify the form of elementary propositions, and that was quite correct too. It was clear to me that here at any rate there are no hypotheses and that regarding these questions we cannot proceed by assuming from the very beginning, as Carnap does, that the elementary propositions consist of two-place relations, etc. Yet I did think that the elementary propositions could be specified at a later date. Only in recent years have I broken away from that mistake. At the time I wrote in a manuscript of my book (this is not printed in the *Tractatus*), "The answers to philosophical questions must never be surprising." In philosophy you cannot discover anything. I myself, however, had not clearly enough understood this and offended against it.

The wrong conception which I want to object to in this connection is the following, that we can hit upon something that we today cannot yet see, that we can discover something wholly new. That is a mistake. The truth of the matter is that we have already got everything, and we have got it actually present; we need not wait for anything. We make our moves in the realm of the grammar of our ordinary language, and this grammar is already there. Thus we have already got everything and need not wait for the future. (*WWK* 182–83)

Wittgenstein replaced his reliance on the idea of the independence of the elementary propositions, as well as the primacy of the truth-table notation as part of a specification of a complete general form of proposition, with an image of *Satzsysteme*, systems of propositions exhibiting grammatical variety, autonomy, and distinctive internal character or physiognomy. While he continued to emphasize the importance of the calculational aspect of mathematical activity, everywhere we see aspect-perception and the dawning of new ways of seeing systems lifting his account beyond the limits of this way of seeing logic. Like Peirce, he seems to have regarded our ability to shift our way of seeing a given diagram, projecting it into a new dimension, as a mark of what makes human mathematical reasoning distinct from anything codifiable in deductive formal logic alone, or solvable by mechanical means.[26]

In leaving behind part of his perspective, Wittgenstein did not surrender his reliance on aspect-perception; he instead increased and intensified it, precisely so as to retain the underlying idea that in philosophy there are no (deeper than aspectual) surprises (necessities, possibilities). He extended and refined his appeals to the seeing (and failing to see) of one system *in* another, applying them to a wide range of mathematical and logical examples – including the Sheffer Stroke itself (*BT* 477–78). Aspect-perception lay behind not only his idea that proofs by induction in arithmetic are schematic pictures, rather than proofs consisting of sequences of sentences with sense, but also his idea that consistency and impossibility proofs for systems are similarly a matter of embedding one system inside another, as well as his idea that because proofs of elementary sums written out in the prose of *Principia Mathematica* would require us to apply arithmetic to the formalism – counting variables to check the proofs – the claim that Russell's foundation of arithmetic provided a substantial epistemic foundation is like the claim that the painted rock is the foundation of the painted tower (again, an analogy with aspects of pictures; cf. *RFM* VII, §16). This allowed Wittgenstein to retain and deepen his earlier idea that in logic and mathematics there are no surprises – no discovery of facts or of possibilities construed on the model of properties or facts – but instead activities, trains of thought and arrangements of grammar that strike us.

The grammars of different "systems" can cross and so change our ways of looking at each of them. This forms a nascent but significant element in articulating what was to become a crucial theme in Wittgenstein's later philosophy: namely, his critique of the idea that human thought and language is everywhere governed by grammatical rules in the same way, his insistence that the evolution of language, and of mathematics and logic in particular, is both open-ended and *unforeseeable in general*. This makes itself felt in

---

[26] On Peirce's views see Judson C. Webb, "Hintikka on Aristotelean Constructions, Kantian Intuitions, and Peircean Theorems," in Auxier and Hahn, *The Philosophy of Jaakko Hintikka*, 195–301 (cf. 246ff).

the fact that Wittgenstein's discussions of figurative or "secondary" meaning, as Cavell puts it so well in *The Claim of Reason*, takes place in regions where "there is no antecedent agreement on criteria" and that "this is itself a grammatical remark."[27] Surprises are ineradicable in mathematics, in logic, and in philosophy. Part of what it is to command language is to incorporate into it, case by case, the unforeseen and the interesting. That is the beauty and the importance of looking at how to arrange it.[28]

[27] Stanley Cavell, *The Claim of Reason: Wittgenstein, Skepticism, Morality, and Tragedy* (Oxford: Oxford University Press, 1979), 355.
[28] I should like to thank Avner Baz, Robert Bowditch, Robert Briscoe, Akihiro Kanamori, Wolfgang Kienzler, Matthias Kross, Montgomery Link, Felix Mühlhölzer, Jean-Philippe Narboux, Norbert Schappacher, Peter Simons, Hartley Slater, and Anja Weiberg for helpful discussion of the ideas in this essay, as well as William Day and Victor J. Krebs for their patience and unwavering intellectual support in putting together this volume. Some of the ideas presented here received helpful responses from audiences at the Einstein Forum Potsdam, the University of Kent at Canterbury, and the University of Chicago.

16

The Enormous Danger

Gordon C. F. Bearn

One asks oneself "Where is this going to end?" (*PI* 202d)

In the midst of Wittgenstein's discussion of aspect-seeing he warns us of what he calls an enormous danger.

Here we are in enormous danger [*ungeheure Gefahr*] of wanting to make fine distinctions.—It is the same when one tries to define the concept of a material object in terms of "what is really seen".—What we have rather to do is to *accept* the everyday language-game, and to note *false* accounts of the matter *as* false. The primitive language-game which children are taught needs no justification; attempts at justification need to be rejected. (*PI* 200b)

I think Wittgenstein's fear of wanting to make fine distinctions goes to the heart of his philosophy. If he gave in to his desire for fine distinctions, he would no longer be able to stop doing philosophy when he wanted to (*PI* §133). And since the way he brings philosophical investigations to an end is by bringing words back from their metaphysical to their everyday use, it becomes plausible that the enormous danger which grips Wittgenstein in the midst of his discussion of aspect-seeing is the enormous danger of metaphysics (*PI* §116).

Giving in to the desire to make fine distinctions may plausibly be interpreted as permitting yourself to be drawn into the deep disquietudes [*tiefe Beunruhigungen*] from which it was Wittgenstein's goal to release us (*PI* §111). The hope of his philosophizing, throughout his life, was to release us from care and anxiety to peace, to peace and security, *Ruhe und Sicherheit* (*PI* §607).[1]

There is nothing revolutionary about these goals. Even when philosophers have not, like some Hellenistic philosophers, made *ataraxia* the explicit goal of their work, some form of intellectual and therefore existential peace is the traditional goal of philosophers. In Wittgenstein's case the worries he sought to calm were worries about how to describe, or about what words to use to describe, the human world. In 1937, thinking back over his early work with Russell, Wittgenstein wrote:

> In the course of our conversations Russell would often exclaim: "Logic's hell!"—And this *perfectly* expresses the feeling we had when we were thinking about the problems of logic; that is to say, their immense difficulty, their hard and *slippery* texture. ... But that is the difficulty Socrates gets into in trying to give the definition of a concept. Again and again a use of the word emerges that seems not to be compatible with the concept that other uses have led us to form. We say: but that *isn't* how it is!—it *is* like that though!—and all we can do is keep repeating these antitheses. (*CV* 30b)

This is a linguistic problem, and I will criticize Wittgenstein below for his exclusive concern with linguistic expression. But it is important to note that while this is first of all a linguistic problem, it is not the *merely* linguistic problem that it seems to some of Wittgenstein's detractors, because language itself is not merely linguistic. Thinking about our lives and the troubles of our lives – thinking about hatred, disappointment, jealousy, betrayal – depends for its power on our knowing what, for example, betrayal is, what to call and what not to call "betrayal." The problems of philosophy are "deep disquietudes; their roots are as deep in us as the forms of our language and their significance is as great as the importance of our language" (*PI* §111).

But now there is something puzzling about the enormous danger. For if Wittgenstein is concerned to release us from deep disquietudes by attending to what we would say, why is he so afraid of the tendency to make fine distinctions? You might have thought that when you were

---

[1] I discuss the distinction between certainty (*Gewissheit*) and security (*Sicherheit*) in Wittgenstein's mature philosophy, including the text known as *On Certainty*, in Gordon C. F. Bearn, "Wittgenstein and the Uncanny," *Soundings* 76:1 (1993), 29–58.

pulled this way and that – " 'But this isn't *seeing*!'—'But this is seeing!' "
(*PI* 203c) – that fine distinctions would be just what you needed, fine
distinctions that you could use to capture the precise sense in which
a given case was or was not seeing. But for Wittgenstein, the quest for
fine distinctions is not the answer; it is rather the enormous danger
itself. What is the danger? Well, what is he trying to do?

The enormous danger surfaces in various places in the *Investigations*,
but the passage I cited occurs when Wittgenstein is trying to describe
the difference between two uses of the word "see" (*PI* 193a). In one
use what I see is a fairly standard object. Suppose it is a grandmother's
face. In the other use, what I see is a similarity between a toddling
little grandson and the grandmother's face. In the second case, while
the grandmother's face has not changed, I may suddenly see the little
boy *in* her face. In the first use of seeing, in order to see something
different I must be looking at a different object; but in the second use
of seeing, what I see (the likeness) is novel, though the object of sight
(the grandmother) is unchanged. The enormous danger looms just
when Wittgenstein is trying to understand this second use of seeing,
which he calls "noticing an aspect" (*PI* 193c).

Let's see how it presents itself. When we express the fact that we
have noticed a change in aspect – for example, noticing the family
resemblance between the grandson and the grandmother – we seem
to be doing two things: First, we are expressing the fact that we are
seeing something new – "*Now* I see the resemblance!" – but at the
same time, by continuing to look at the same grandmotherly face,
we show that what we are looking at has *not* changed. So what kind
of seeing is this which, without getting near hallucination, seems to
offer a change in visual perception without a change in the perceptual object? And now I can feel the need to make fine distinctions.
The enormous danger looms.

Suppose we didn't notice the danger; suppose we did try to capture
the way it felt to notice an aspect. In the case of the family resemblance, what we noticed might be that we could see the geography of
the grandson's face *in* the geography of the grandmother's face. But
what is that like? Is it as if the faces were merged together into one
face? Not quite, for I would not normally see one new combined face;
rather, what I see is a new aspect of the grandmother's face, almost as if
I were seeing both faces together, one on top of the other. But, again,

it is not really like that. What is it really like? Here we will be inclined to make finer and finer distinctions to capture the precise modality of seeing which characterizes noticing a family resemblance.

Change cases. Suppose the case were the now famous figure reproduced in Jastrow which Wittgenstein calls the duck-rabbit.[2] The figure can be seen as a duck and again as a rabbit. The puzzling use of seeing that Wittgenstein is struggling with is the way we can see something different – duck or rabbit – when quite obviously the object seen, the figure from Jastrow, has not changed at all. Again, pretend that we do not notice the enormous danger, and imagine trying to describe the difference between seeing the duck in the figure from Jastrow and seeing the rabbit. In this case we might find ourselves describing something like the trajectory in space of *what we see*. As a duck, the figure's momentum carries it to the left, whereas when I see it as a rabbit, its momentum carries it to the right. But not really. The figure has no momentum. What I am trying to describe, I am, once again, failing to describe. We could try again, but there is little reason to hope that we will ever hit upon a precise, perfect description of what it is like to see the figure one way rather than another. That is the point of Wittgenstein's pained, "'Where is this going to end?'" (*PI* 202d). And that is why there is an enormous danger of wanting to make fine distinctions. You think making fine distinctions will be able to bring your disquietude to an end, but if you start making fine distinctions, you may never come to an end of it.

In another part of the *Investigations*, Wittgenstein describes the enormous danger as a dead end. He is worrying the question of how sentences manage to represent when he comments:

Here it is easy to get into that dead-end in philosophy, where one believes that the difficulty of the task consists in our having to describe phenomena that are hard to get hold of, the present experience that slips quickly by, or something of the kind. Where we find ordinary language too crude, and it looks as if we were having to do, not with the phenomena of every-day, but with ones that "easily elude us, and, in their coming to be and passing away,

---

[2] Thanks to Don Campbell for the gift on December 4, 1987 of his copy of Joseph Jastrow, *Fact and Fable in Psychology* (Boston and New York: Houghton Mifflin, 1900). The illustration appears on page 295 with the caption: "Do you see a duck or a rabbit, or either?" (From *Harpers Weekly*, originally in *Fliegende Blätter*.)

produce those others as an average effect." (Augustine: Manifestissima et usitatissima sunt, et eadem rusus nimis latent, et nova est inventio eorum.) (*PI* §436)

There is a tangle here because it is not clear whether Wittgenstein is worried that his investigations will come to a dead end, or whether they will never be able to end. I take seriously Wittgenstein's interest in bringing philosophical anxiety peace, by learning how to bring philosophical investigations to an end (*PI* §133). And it is important to recognize that this end is not one final apocalyptic end; it is rather, as Cavell puts it, that each investigation comes "to an end somewhere, each in its time, place by place."[3] But in that sense of an ending, it remains true that the point of Wittgenstein's writing is to be able to bring our philosophical investigations to an end: "The difficulty here is: to stop" (*Z* §314). The enormous danger is that once you start looking for fine distinctions there will be no end of it. Ordinary language is on this account simply too crude to make the fine distinctions which would satisfy us, which would be able to bring our worries to an end. And so if we gave in to the desire to make fine distinctions, philosophy would never end. No security. No peace.

Wittgenstein's solution? Just say, "No": "The strange thing about philosophical disquietude [*Beunruhigungen*] and its resolution might seem to be that it is like the suffering of an ascetic who stood raising a heavy ball, amid groans, and whom someone released by telling him: 'Drop it'" (*PO* 175). The solution to the enormous danger is to "*accept* the everyday language-game, and to note *false* accounts of the matter *as* false" (*PI* 200b). So how do we describe, in everyday language, that kind of seeing which Wittgenstein calls noticing an aspect, for example, an aspect of the figure from Jastrow? Here is his answer: "'You can think now of *this*, now of *this*, as you look at it, can regard it now as *this*, now as *this*, and then you will see it now *this* way, now *this*'.—*What* way? There *is* no further qualification" (*PI* 200d, punctuation altered). You will see it in different ways depending upon what you are thinking of. The desire to *describe* the different seeings of the same object is simply to be resisted. Don't give in. Resist the temptation. Think about the grandson's face as you look at the

---

[3] Stanley Cavell, "The Division of Talent," *Critical Inquiry* 11 (June 1985): 531.

grandmother, and you will (probably) see the family resemblance. That's it. That's all. Stop. It's a matter of will. Don't give in to the desire to make fine distinctions.

But why? Why should we *not* give in to that desire? In yet another place where Wittgenstein considers the enormous danger, the answer comes more plainly into view. He is once again worrying the question of how sentences can represent the world, and he remarks:

> Here it is difficult as it were to keep our heads up,—to see that we must stick to the subjects of our every-day thinking, and not go astray and imagine that we have to describe extreme subtleties, which in turn we are after all quite unable to describe with the means at our disposal. We feel as if we had to repair a torn spider's web with our fingers. (*PI* §106)

The vigor of the final figure is so powerful that until recently I didn't realize what was going on here. We can't repair the spider's web with our fingers, so stop trying. But the spider's web still needs fixing. So what Wittgenstein is asking us to do is not to notice that the spider's web is torn, or to notice that it is torn but not to want to do anything about it. The important thing for me is that the web is still torn and no amount of Wittgensteinian theatrics can do anything except hide that fact from me.

It begins to sound as though Wittgenstein is simply saying: If you take that demand – for fine distinctions – seriously, you will never find peace and security; so stop. Just stop. But who ever told us that we would be able to answer every question we can ask? Who ever thought that *the riddle* does not exist (*TLP* 6.5)? It would be nice if there were a metaphysical proof against unanswerable questions, but it begins to look as if Wittgenstein is making the very unanswerability of a question into a sign that the question cannot be seriously meant. In Lyotard's terms, this is to make differends *impossible* by reducing what is real to what can be meaningfully given to this or that subject.[4]

If this proves correct, then we will have to adjust our response to a famous moment toward the end of Wittgenstein's discussion of

---

[4] Jean-François Lyotard, *The Differend: Phrases in Dispute*, trans. Georges Van Den Abbeele (Minneapolis: University of Minnesota Press, 1988), §3. This is the kind of reduction that my colleague Michael Mendelson thinks of as incestuous, the refusal to conjugate with anyone outside the family.

aspect-seeing. I am thinking of the place where he addresses himself to security (*Sicherheit*), which Anscombe translates as "certainty."
The passage comes in the midst of a discussion of different kinds of
certainty. " 'But, if you are *certain* [*sicher*], isn't it that you are shutting
your eyes in face of doubt?'—They are shut" (*PI* 224d). If certainty or
security is a product of closing our eyes to doubt, then it would just be
pretend certainty. So it is important that Wittgenstein deny that certainty is simply a matter of closing our eyes to doubt. And this is what
he says. He says that we do not actively close our eyes to doubt. Rather,
we can think ourselves into a position, or be led by Wittgenstein's
theatrical writing into a position, in which we find our eyes naturally
closed to doubt. Thus the involuntary construction of "*Sie sind mir
geschlossen*," "They are shut."

But it is not clear that that interpretation of discovering our eyes
involuntarily shut is consistent with Wittgenstein's discussion of
Jastrow's figure of the duck-rabbit. The insecurity here concerns the
difference between the two kinds of seeing: on the one hand, simply
seeing the figure in Jastrow, and, on the other hand, seeing either
the duck or the rabbit in the figure. The difference between these
two kinds of seeing is just the kind of difference whose insecurity
is the source of philosophical disquietude. Trying to understand
aspect-seeing, we may feel that we have to make very fine distinctions to characterize seeing the figure as a rabbit and differentiating
that seeing from seeing it as a duck. But each fine distinction breeds
another. They breed like duck-rabbits. And now if quieting these worries required an act of will – saying, "No," to the desire to make fine
distinctions – then philosophical security will never be more than
willful ("Drop it").

Can it be? Can it be, as Wittgenstein's detractors (and those of his
defenders inspired by Rorty) always said, that stopping doing philosophy did not depend on discovering grammatical essences but only on
an act of will? Can it be that Wittgenstein's peace is held in place by
gritting our teeth, holding back tears (*PO* 161)? For so long we had
been hoping for more. We were hoping for philosophical peace. And
there is Wittgenstein, giving out earplugs.

Perhaps I have been too quick. I would not be the philosopher I am
were it not for Wittgenstein's writings, and it is of the nature of fast
friends falling out that they can fall out over irrelevancies. Perhaps I

am. Wittgenstein does say, in the very pages I am writing about: "It is possible—and this is important—to say a *great deal* about a fine aesthetic difference" (*PI* 219b). And this, it must be admitted, seems to be in flat contradiction with my leading passage which warns of the "enormous danger of wanting to make fine distinctions" (*PI* 200b). Wittgenstein's text would avoid self-contradiction if the almost endless process he encourages, when the issue is fine aesthetic differences, were a process of sorting linguistic acts, whereas the process he refuses, when the issue is the present experience which slips quickly by, is a process of savoring sensual experience. This distinction between being a wine taster of words and savoring the flavor of wine may not be as sharp as we would like, but it is a distinction with an Austinian pedigree.

In the midst of a well-known discussion of other minds, Austin finds himself thinking about two different ways we might hesitate over a description of a taste or sound or smell or color or feeling.[5] Suppose it is a novel taste. We might, first of all, be hesitant in this way. We might say, " 'I simply don't know what it is: I've never tasted anything remotely like it before. ... No, it's no use: the more I think about it the more confused I get: it's perfectly distinct and perfectly distinctive, quite unique in my experience'."[6] Austin remarks that this pure case of uniqueness "shades off into the more common type of case where I'm not quite certain, or only fairly certain, or practically certain, that it's the taste of, say, laurel."[7] In this more common version of this case we rummage through our linguistic repertoire in an effort to come up with just the right words to describe the novel experience. I suspect that this is the kind of case that Wittgenstein had in mind when he said that it was of course possible to say a great deal about fine aesthetic differences. Here is Wittgenstein once more: "It is possible— and this is important—to say a *great deal* about a fine aesthetic difference.—The first thing you say may, of course, be just: "*This* word fits, *that* doesn't"—or something of the kind. But then you can discuss all the extensive ramifications of the tie-up effected by each of the words. That first judgment is *not* the end of the matter, for it is the

---

[5] J. L. Austin, "Other Minds," *Philosophical Papers*, 3d ed., ed. J. O. Urmson and G. J. Warnock (Oxford: Oxford University Press, 1979), 92.
[6] Ibid.
[7] Ibid.

field [*Feld*] of a word that is decisive" (*PI* 219b). The reason it is possible to say a great deal about a fine aesthetic difference is that the
grammar of any aesthetic distinction will extend over acres of the
linguistic landscape that Wittgenstein's writings criss-cross in every
direction (cf. *PI* Preface). The first judgment is not the end of the
matter because we can pursue the grammar of our aesthetic description into the grammar of other, and still other, concepts.

   This appears to be consistent with what Wittgenstein is reported to
have said in lectures on aesthetics that he delivered in 1938. Swerving
from beauty, he remarked: "Perhaps the most important thing in connection with aesthetics is what may be called aesthetic reactions, e.g.
discontent, disgust, discomfort. The expression of discontent is not
the same as the expression of discomfort. The expression of discontent says: 'Make it higher ... too low! ... do something to this" (*LC*
13). This is related to what Wittgenstein called "clicking." A surprising
number of Wittgenstein's examples in these lectures involve tailors
and suits. And when deciding on the length of trousers or the width
of a lapel, a tailor might say: "Too long ... too long ... too short ...
there! that's right" (see *LC* 7–8). He speaks similarly about the sizes
of doors where, once again, a certain size can click (see *LC* 13). Of
course, nothing really clicks, and Wittgenstein suggests you could say
that the clicking simply was my being satisfied with the length of the
suit or the height of the door (*LC* 19). But this sudden satisfaction
with a size is not unlike the phenomenon where we say "'*This* word fits,
that doesn't'—or something of the kind" (*PI* 219b). But in the case of
doors and trousers that is far from the end of the matter. For we could
relate the size of the door to the role of the building (ceremonial,
domestic, institutional), the role of the spaces the door opens from
and towards, the importance of the typical occupants of the building, the social/political/historical contexts of these issues, and so on.
Similar connections could be made with the roles a suit or its inhabit-
ant will be playing. And so it is clear that we can say a great deal about
a fine aesthetic difference, even when the aesthetic judgment appears
suddenly (oh yes ... that's it ... that's the tempo), because "it is the
field [*Feld*] of a word that is decisive" (*PI* 219b).

   But so far we have only looked at one side of the Austinian distinction I have invoked. There is another way we might be hesitant
about describing a novel taste. It is a difference in where we take the

difficulty of description to lie: whether it is in the words we would employ or in the experience itself.[8] It appears that for Wittgenstein, when the subject is fine aesthetic differences, then it is a matter of which words would be appropriate. Now we turn to the other way of being hesitant about a description of a novel taste, the one which may be the source of what Wittgenstein calls the enormous danger. Here's Austin:

The other case is different, though it very naturally combines itself with the first. Here, what I try to do is to *savor* the current experience, to *peer* at it, to sense it vividly. I'm not sure it *is* the taste of pineapple: isn't there perhaps just *something* about it, a tang, a bite, a lack of bite, a cloying sensation, which isn't *quite* right for pineapple? Isn't there perhaps just a peculiar hint of green, which would rule out mauve and would hardly do for heliotrope? Or perhaps it is faintly odd: I must look more intently, scan it over and over: maybe just possibly there is a suggestion of an unnatural shimmer, so that it doesn't look quite like ordinary water. There is a lack of sharpness in what we actually sense, which is to be cured not, or not merely, by thinking, but by acuter discernment, by sensory discrimination (though it is of course true that thinking of other, and more pronounced, cases in our past experience can and does assist our powers of discrimination).[9]

The passage concludes by recalling us to the task at hand, conceptual description, but it is the savoring itself that draws me in, this savoring sinking into the experience until our powers of conceptual discrimination melt with us into the flavors themselves. Precisely this is the enormous danger: the temptation to describe phenomena that are hard to get hold of, like the present experience that slips quickly by (see *PI* 200b and §436).

Sharing the page with Wittgenstein's observation that we can indeed say a great deal about fine aesthetic differences, is another warning against this enormous danger. Wittgenstein is talking about finding the right word: "At last a word comes: '*That's* it!' *Sometimes* I can say why. This is simply what searching, this is what finding, is like here" (*PI* 218g). Once again the danger looms of describing the experience of a word's coming, and once again Wittgenstein just tells us to

---

[8] These two ways of being hesitant about a description, which Austin introduces in "Other Minds" (1946), are the parents of what in "How to Talk" (1952–53) is called the onus of match. See Austin, *Philosophical Papers*, 141–42.

[9] Austin, "Other Minds," 92–93.

stop. The passage continues: "But doesn't the word that occurs to you somehow 'come' in a special way? Just attend and you'll see!—Careful attention is no use to me. All it could discover would be what is *now* going on in *me*" (*PI* 219a). The enormous danger once again.

I do not think therefore that I have been too quick. There is no inconsistency between Wittgenstein's insistence that we can say a great deal about fine aesthetic differences and his anxiety about succumbing to the temptation to savor his experiences to the point of never being able to stop. Let's return therefore to the enormous danger.

When Wittgenstein names the enormous danger, he remarks almost parenthetically, "the primitive language-game which children are taught needs no justification; attempts at justification need to be rejected" (*PI* 200b). The implication is that the roots of the enormous danger rest in that old epistemological earth: the demand for justification, in particular, the demand for a justification of the difference we want to draw between seeing the figure as a duck and as a rabbit. And Wittgenstein does devote considerable attention to showing that we will not be able to differentiate seeing the duck in the figure and seeing the rabbit in the figure by discovering that there "is really something different there *in me*" (*PI* 202b, my emphasis). It is a natural move. The figure, *out there*, is unchanged, and yet what we see has changed, so it can seem that the only other place to look for a difference which would justify our experience of the difference between seeing the duck and seeing the rabbit will be to look for something different there *in me*. However, these inner objects were already dismissed in the sections of the *Investigations* devoted to the question of whether we can imagine a necessarily private language. And if you follow Wittgenstein in denying that we can imagine this possibility, then the demand for a justification of the difference between seeing a duck and seeing a rabbit can be grounded neither from the outside (the figure in the book doesn't change), nor from the inside (there are no private objects).

But I want to go over some of that material again.

I will hurry things along by relying on Cavell's discussion of these questions in *The Claim of Reason*.[10] Cavell singles out, as something like

[10] Stanley Cavell, *The Claim of Reason: Wittgenstein, Skepticism, Morality, and Tragedy* (Oxford: Oxford University Press, 1979).

the climactic moment in the discussion of privacy, the moment where the writing of "S" in a diary of my private sensations is realized to be, itself, an *expression* of the sensation, and not merely a dehydrated *reference* to the sensation (*PI* §270).[11] Cavell:

I understand Wittgenstein's teaching to be something like this: My references to my pain are exactly my expressions of pain itself; and my words refer to my pain just because, or to the extent, that they are (modified) expressions of it. ... The picture of a *connection* needing to be set up between an experience and the words for it is symbolic of the giving of expression to the experience, giving vent to it. If the expression is broken, the reference itself cannot establish the connection. Then what are my references to another's pain? They are my (more or less) modified responses to it, or to his having had it, or to his anticipations of it; they are responses to another's expressions of (or inability to express) his or her pain.[12]

For Cavell the remark of Wittgenstein's which most obviously asks for his interpretation is this: "For how can I go so far as to try to use language to get between pain and its expression?" (*PI* §245).

The relevance of these considerations for my discussion of the enormous danger is this: if linguistic reference depends on expression, and expression is far more inclusive than everyday language, then what – besides begging the question – justifies Wittgenstein's insistence that in trying to express the difference between seeing the family resemblance and simply seeing the grandmother's face we must, at all costs, "stick to the subjects of our everyday thinking" (*PI* §106)? Again: If expression is more inclusive than everyday linguistic expression, why should we not try to express the differences in question with more than everyday linguistic tools? Wittgenstein might in some sense be right about the enormous danger but still wrong about this larger question. I mean that the enormous danger can be narrowly construed as the enormous danger of trying to make everyday language more precise, more scientific, more icy (*PI* §107). And I can agree that an attempt to make very fine distinctions, the dream of icy cold precision, will not do the trick. But that means to me that (1) the rough ground of everyday language, and (2) the souped-up precision

---

[11] I owe my understanding, such as it is, of Cavell's reading of this passage to the teaching of Norton Batkin.

[12] Cavell, *The Claim of Reason*, 342.

of scientific language, are both unable to express the sensual singularity of what it is like to see the figure as a duck, or to see the family resemblance. But are those our only two options? The result of trying to imagine a private language is not the ascendancy of everyday language. It is the ascendancy of expression. And what is that?

A few years ago I was teaching a course on beauty and sensual experience with a friend, a scene designer from the Department of Theater.[13] One morning, with our class, we were walking barefoot on the sand of a beach volleyball court on our campus. The sand was some of it in the sun and some of it still shaded from the night, so some of it was colder and some warmer, and it was lumpy all over. We were walking around on the sand talking to each other about how the sand felt. And then Drew asked that we express what we were feeling with our feet. All I could think about was broadcasting, for example, the temperature of the sunny warm and clammy cold parts of the volleyball court; I couldn't shake the thought that to express what my feet were feeling of the sand would be something like translating what I felt into semaphore so it would become legible at a distance. This is a picture that goes with the idea of a sensation only *contingently* related to expression. But one of the central meanings of the verb "to express" is to press out, as when milk is expressed from a mother's breast. And this was a clue, a clue that expression might be an *essential* part of sensation, that perhaps there are no unexpressed sensations. And this is of a piece with the ascendancy of expression in Cavell's reading of the *Investigations*' discussion of privacy.

Think of how your sweater feels. It's a knit wool sweater and so it feels wooly. But you know that without even feeling it. When I reach out to it and pick it up off the floor, I notice the thickness of the knit, and holes in the sleeves. But this is still a long way from the feel of the sweater. When I concentrate on how it feels in my hands, I rub it gently between my fingers, the way I sometimes fondle the fingers of those I love. As I concentrate more on the way the sweater feels, my eyes close and I bring the sweater to my face only to find that I am disappearing into the dirt smells in the sweater, suddenly thinking of the dry dirt floor of an old root cellar I can remember lying on.

[13] I owe the stimulus for all my recent thinking about expression and color to this dear friend, Drew Francis.

What I want to emphasize here is that in order to feel the sweater, I have to open myself to it. I have to attend to, reach out to, the sweater. There are touchings, feelings, that are less receptive and those that are more so. Opening a button and feeling the sun on your naked neck. Examining an arm and caressing it. But in order to feel the sweater I have to do something: I have to be ready to receive. And the *way* I get ready to receive the feeling of the sweater has the effect of broadcasting the fact that I am listening to the feel of the sweater. My first reaction to Drew's request that we express what the sand felt like on our bare feet restricted expression to this additional semaphore effect. But expressing is also, and for my purposes more importantly, what brings sensual experience into being. You cannot see what you do not express. The expression may be dehydrated and minimalistic, as for example when all I do is look or point down the hill: there's our dog Islay. But the expression and the sensation can become together richer and more robust.

Return to aspect-seeing. Wittgenstein himself tells us that seeing the Jastrow figure as a rabbit goes with trying to see it as a rabbit (*PI* 206b). Trying to see it as a rabbit is an expression. And as expression, it is opening yourself to the rabbit in the figure much as I opened myself to the smells of the sweater when I closed my eyes and inhaled the past. And there is nothing private about this. What I see in the figure, the rabbit for example, I see *in the figure*, not in some private space behind my eyes. And the feel of the sweater is the feel *of the sweater*. There is nothing private about it, either. It is the sweater and the figure that we are discovering things about. Wittgenstein probably addressed himself to the problem of privacy during these remarks on aspect-seeing because the difference between seeing the figure as a duck and seeing it as a rabbit is a difference which seems not to be a difference in the figure itself. But there is no need to run off to a private object. Nor is there any need to force yourself to stick to the everyday language. We can express our sensual awareness of the world otherwise – sometimes linguistically, sometimes not; it doesn't matter.

This puts us in mind of Bergson. When he addresses himself to the immediate data of consciousness, his constant effort is to draw our attention to the qualitative differences between those of our experiences we think of as differing only in quantity. For instance, we are convinced that each object has more or less one color, and when an object is placed in brighter light, we convince ourselves that what we see is qualitatively the same color; the change, we say, only affects the quantitative intensity of that one color. We compare the change in color of the object to an oboe playing one note louder and louder, instead of to an orchestra with more and more instruments joining or leaving the oboe.[14] This is true even if we begin not with the color of an old sweater but with what we take to be "pure colors of the spectrum":

As the luminous source is brought nearer, violet takes a bluish tinge, green tends to become whitish yellow, and red a brilliant yellow. Inversely, when the light is moved away, ultramarine passes into violet and yellow into green; finally, red, green and violet tend to become whitish yellow. Physicists have remarked these changes for some time [Bergson cites both Rood and Helmholz, and there might be some connection to Wittgenstein's early psychological experiments conducted at Cambridge]; but what is still more remarkable is that the majority of men do not perceive them, unless they pay attention to them or are warned of them. Having made up our mind, once for all, to interpret changes of quality as changes of quantity, we begin by asserting that every object has its own peculiar color, definite and invariable. When the hue of objects tends to become yellow or blue, instead of saying that we see their color change under the influence of increase or diminution of light, we assert that the color remains but that our sensation of luminous intensity increases or diminishes.[15]

In order to see the color of a wall, you have to attend to it, you have to try to see the orange in the shadows. The supposedly pure color was already so many different colors. We would not ordinarily say that the yellow wall is also at the same time green. But don't think! Look! (*PI* §66). Even a white sheet of paper under different illuminations is different shades of white.[16] But you have to pay attention to the sheet of paper, you have to look for the changing shades as you look for the rabbit or the duck or the family resemblance between the grandmother and the grandson. This is what I mean by saying that sensual experience is essentially linked to expression. In order to taste the

[14] Henri Bergson, *Time and Free Will: An Essay on the Immediate Data of Consciousness* (New York: Harper and Row, 1960), 35.

[15] Ibid., 51.

[16] Ibid., 53.

soup you can't just swallow, you have to reach for it, taste it, hold it in your mouth. Savoring is expressing. Savoring is caressing.

Colors and tastes were perhaps an easy case for Bergson, but he demonstrates famously that, even if all you do is make a fist and squeeze gradually harder and harder, you should not describe this in the everyday way as if the pressure on your fingers (one quality) were getting more and more intense. It's not just Wittgenstein who gives us commands that can change our philosophical lives. Here's Bergson: "Try, for example, to clench the fist with increasing force."[17] Sure enough, as you clench tighter and tighter, what you feel is your hand, wrist, arm, shoulder, until what you finally feel is way over on the other side of your body, your other hand shaking.

The qualitative changes of sights, tastes, and feelings are enormous. We can describe many of them, and although sometimes we will get some help from very fine distinctions, these will not always help at all. Consider temperature: "Close attention can easily discover specific differences between the different sensations of heat, as also between the sensations of cold. A more intense heat is really another kind of heat."[18] This is the one that stopped me. Perhaps it was the fact that there are thermometers that made me skeptical of this one. But then, in my shirt sleeves, I stepped outside into the winter air, and there it was, a sharp biting that I almost recognized, but which I had never addressed as a modality of the cold, itself.

Wittgenstein nearly explicitly combats Bergson over the enormous danger of wanting to make fine distinctions. Wittgenstein's example of the kind of phenomenon that ruins the hope of finding the perfect, fine distinction is "the present experience that slips quickly by" (*PI* §436). But this is the very phenomenon which Bergson seeks to draw our attention to: the "succession without distinction" which he calls "pure duration":[19] "Pure duration is the form which the succession of our conscious states assumes when our ego lets itself *live*, when it refrains from separating its present state from its former states ... the notes of a tune, melting, so to speak, into one another."[20] Expressing

[17] Ibid., 24.
[18] Ibid., 47.
[19] Ibid., 100–1.
[20] Ibid., 100.

pure duration takes more than the tools of everyday language; and if, like Wittgenstein, we stuck to the subjects of our everyday thinking, we would never attend to the continuously changing features of our experience. If, like Wittgenstein, you would like philosophical investigations to end, the effort to express the sensual singularity of what it is like to see the duck in the figure from Jastrow, the effort to express the sensual singularity of the feeling of bitter cold, will never help. ("Where is this going to end?") For Wittgenstein, the only move is to stop expressing your sensual experience at a dehydrated, everyday level. You can, by an act of will, stop this, but what you miss is the delight of sensual enjoyment.

John Wisdom once parenthesized, "(If I were asked to answer, in one sentence, the question 'What was Wittgenstein's biggest contribution to philosophy?', I should answer 'His asking of the question "Can one play chess without the queen?".')"[21] This says it all. (The quotation marks say it all.) There is the appearance of sensitivity, for I can imagine being told that of course after you have lost your queen and are proceeding as usual to lose the game, you have definitely not stopped playing chess. But there is at the back of this appearance of sensitivity, the tough, gruff implication that if you started without the queen, you would be playing a game related to chess, but definitely not chess. Period. Everything's in its place. And don't be fooled by psychology. Some people might think that if we were playing checkers with chess pieces, there would be an odd feeling about the game which would be important to describe (Z §448). Don't. Drop it. You will miss the delight of sensual enjoyment, but at least you will not be troubled by questions your everyday language cannot answer. The traditional philosopher's bargain: purchasing peace at the price of excitement. What a bargain.

I want to end by using this discussion of aspect-seeing to reveal a feature of Wittgenstein's philosophical practice, in general, that is open to the same objections. The enormous danger is one of never knowing what to say. The danger is that the world will slip through, or overflow, our (linguistic) representations. The whole point of Wittgenstein's writing is to teach us how to find our way around

21 John Wisdom, "Ludwig Wittgenstein 1934–1937," *Paradox and Discovery* (Oxford: Basil Blackwell, 1965), 88.

the language of our life. "Language is a labyrinth of paths. You approach from *one* side and know your way about; you approach the same place from another side and no longer know your way about" (*PI* §203). The whole point is to master the labyrinth, to get out. The problem is that we can find ourselves in situations where our language seems unable to control or to represent the world, and we have to reclaim our "*mastery* of this language," to reclaim the representational powers of language (*PI* §20). Language has gotten away from us, it seems to have a life of its own, and we have to exercise our mastery in order to bring it back in line: peace and security achieved through mastery. Our words slide dangerously between the metaphysical and the everyday, and to achieve peace, Wittgenstein tells us, we must "bring words back from their metaphysical to their everyday use" (*PI* §116). And it is possible. Wittgenstein is right. It is possible to achieve peace. But only for a spell. Wittgenstein knows that this peace cannot last for more than that, because he knows that "what dawns here lasts only as long as I am occupied with the object in a particular way" (*PI* 210d).

All of this is well known to Wittgensteinians. They know that peace will not be achieved apocalyptically, once and for all, but rather that each philosophical investigation must be brought to an end, peacefully and momentarily, "each in its time, place by place." But what is rarely interrogated is the metastability of disquietude and quietude, the metastability of the icy smooth and the earthy rough, the metaphysical and the everyday. What I am interested in is what the world must be like for its Wittgensteinian investigation to issue in this metastability. I am interested in another labyrinthine metaphysics, the metaphysics revealed by this metastability. What does the metastability of Wittgenstein's philosophical investigations tell us about the world? We already know the answer.

The traditional metaphysical description of the world, aiming at icy precision, slips slidingly into the everyday description of what we all already know, and back again (*PI* §128). The metastability of philosophical unease and philosophical peace shows that representational simplicity, whether rough or smooth, floats atop an untamed world of barely nameable sensuality. That is the other metaphysics. That is the labyrinth. The point is not to get out by following a frictionless beam of light nor by following rough jute twine; the point is to disappear into a labyrinthine sensuality as near to you as your tongue. Go ahead. Taste it. Put it in your mouth.

As much as I have learned from Wittgenstein, I do not share his conception of the point of philosophy: achieving peace and security. I have different aims: to make our lives beautiful, to achieve intense pleasures by riding the very multiplicity and pointlessness which it was Wittgenstein's aim to overpower. Wittgenstein's work therefore presents itself to me as a problem, the problem of determining philosophy's goal. Should that goal be the achievement of peace, resting momentarily in security and comfort, or should it risk the worst as it aims at the best: riding delirious desires, becoming beautiful. Becoming becoming.

Appendix

A Page Concordance for Unnumbered Remarks *in* Philosophical Investigations

William Day

There have been four editions of *Philosophical Investigations* published by Blackwell.[1] The first and second editions (published in 1953 and 1958, respectively) use identical paginations, the third edition (published in 2001) introduces a new pagination, and the most recent edition (2009) employs still another pagination. Since several remarks in Part I, and all of the remarks in Part II, of the *Investigations* are unnumbered in the first three editions, the difference in pagination creates a problem, to say the least, for anyone wanting to refer to these remarks, as one invariably does in discussions of aspect-seeing.

We have chosen to follow the practice of more than a half-century and use the pagination of the first two editions when referring to unnumbered remarks from the *Investigations*. We have also adopted the convention, employed by Stephen Mulhall and others, of adding a letter to indicate the position of a remark on a given page. Thus,

---

[1] The publication history of the *Investigations* in English translation is complicated: there have been two major publishers (Macmillan and Blackwell), German/English and English-only versions, and multiple reprintings. A further nuisance is that two distinct versions, published more than thirty years apart, both claim to be the third edition. (The first of these simply adds an index to the second edition.) However, if one considers only the revisions to G. E. M. Anscombe's translation, then one can speak of four distinct editions: those of 1953, 1958 (Anscombe's first revision), 2001 (the "50th Anniversary Commemorative Edition" incorporating Anscombe's final revisions), and 2009 (Anscombe's translation revised by P. M. S. Hacker and Joachim Schulte).

"193a" refers to the first remark on page 193, "193b" to the second remark, and so on.[2]

We wanted this volume's citations to be useful, however, independent of which version of the *Investigations* one happens to have at hand, or which edition predominates in the years to come. We considered the practice of citing multiple editions in the body of the text, much as David Stern does in his Cambridge Introduction to the *Investigations*.[3] But Stern in 2004 was working with two distinct paginations, not three, and the fat parentheticals that would result from citing three different editions struck us as unsightly. We settled on my constructing the following page concordance, which promises some additional utility beyond the context of the present volume.

The first section of the concordance lists the unnumbered remarks from Part I of the *Investigations*. These remarks, written on slips that Wittgenstein inserted in the pages of his typescript, appear in the first three editions at the foot of some pages, and in the fourth edition in separate boxes in the body of the text. The remainder of the concordance lists every remark from Part II, which the fourth edition renames *Philosophy of Psychology—A Fragment*. Entries are grouped by the section numbers (i, ii, iii, ... xiv) that appear in all four editions.

The fourth edition of *Philosophical Investigations*[4] improves on the third by including the original page numbers from the first two

---

[2] In the first three editions, individual remarks in Part II of the *Investigations* are set off from one another by an additional line (i.e., a double space). But, since the third edition occasionally adds or subtracts lines between the paragraphs of the earlier editions, and since none of them indicates whether a paragraph starting at the top of a page is a new remark or a continuation of the previous remark, what counts as a separate remark differs among these editions. In preparing the concordance, I have followed, with two exceptions, Hacker and Schulte's counting of the remarks in the fourth edition. (The exceptions are §9 and §205, remarks in which they fuse what appear as two separate remarks in every earlier edition.)

Two further conventions should be mentioned: (1) When one edition counts as a continuation of a remark what another counts as a separate remark, the concordance shows the remark indicator for the former repeated in parentheses. (2) In assigning letters to the remarks in the first three editions, the continuation of a remark onto the next page (whether it begins with a new sentence or not) is always numbered as the first ("a") remark of that new page; thus the "b" remark is always the first remark preceded by a double space.

[3] David G. Stern, *Wittgenstein's* Philosophical Investigations: *An Introduction*, Cambridge Introductions to Key Philosophical Texts (Cambridge: Cambridge University Press, 2004).

[4] Ludwig Wittgenstein, *Philosophical Investigations*, ed. P. M. S. Hacker and Joachim Schulte, trans. G. E. M. Anscombe, P. M. S. Hacker, and Joachim Schulte, rev. 4th

editions, in small verticals, in the body of the text. More significantly, the fourth edition is the first to assign consecutive numbers to the remarks in Part II. These remark numbers appear in the concordance below as "PPF §n," where n is the remark number given in *Philosophy of Psychology—A Fragment*. The numbers make it easy to refer to individual remarks in the later pages of the *Investigations*, including the remarks on aspect-seeing, so long as one sticks with the fourth edition. But, since that edition gives only page numbers for the first two editions – not the more refined numbering convention of page number plus position-indicating letter – cross-references between the fourth and the first two editions (not to mention between these and the third edition) would seem to benefit from a page concordance.

I have not included the German text in the concordance, since our primary aim here is to help readers in locating passages discussed in the chapters above when they turn to the more recent, third and fourth editions. Since each of these later editions includes the German on facing pages, one is able to check the original German once the corresponding English passage is found.

The text from *Philosophical Investigations* in the far left column of the concordance is from the second edition.

First words of remark	First (1953) and Second (1958) Editions	Third (2001) Edition	Fourth (2009) Edition
	PI I		
Imagine a picture representing a boxer in a particular stance.	Bottom of page 11	Bottom of page 9	Box on page 14
Could one define the word "red" by pointing to something that was *not red*?	Bottom of page 14	Bottom of page 12	Box on page 17

ed. (Oxford: Blackwell, 2009). This edition was scheduled for release as the present volume was going to press. A pre-publication, partial, online copy of the revised 4th edition was used in preparing the concordance, which was then checked against the published version during our volume's page proofs stage.

(*cont.*)

First words of remark	First (1953) and Second (1958) Editions	Third (2001) Edition	Fourth (2009) Edition
	PI I		
What is it to *mean* the words "*That* is blue" at one time as a statement about the object....	Bottom of page 18	Bottom of page 16	Box on page 22
Someone says to me: "Shew the children a game."	Bottom of page 33	Bottom of page 28	Box on page 38
Faraday in *The Chemical History of a Candle*: "Water is one individual thing—it never changes."	Bottom of page 46	Bottom of page 39	Box on page 50
Must I *know* whether I understand a word?	Bottom of page 53	Bottom of page 46	Box on page 59
(a) "I believe the right word in this case is....".	Bottom of page 54	Bottom of page 46	Box on page 60
What we have to mention in order to explain the significance, I mean the importance, of a concept, ...	Bottom of page 56	Bottom of page 48	Box on page 62
(a) "Understanding a word": a state.	Bottom of page 59	Bottom of page 50	Box on page 65
The grammar of the expression "a quite particular" (atmosphere).	Bottom of page 66	Bottom of page 56	Box on page 72
(a) "The fact that three negatives yield a negative again	Bottom of page 147	Bottom of page 124	Box on page 155
	PI II.i		
One can imagine	174a	148a	PPF §1
"Grief" describes a	174b	148b	PPF §2
"For a second	174c	148c	PPF §3
But don't you	174d	148d	PPF §4
"I must tell	174e	148e	PPF §5
For think of	174f	148f	PPF §6

First words of remark	First (1953) and Second (1958) Editions	Third (2001) Edition	Fourth (2009) Edition
PI II.ii			
In saying "When	175a	149a	PPF §7
If you were	175b	149b	PPF §8
The words "the	175c	149c	PPF §9
We take a	175d	149d	(PPF §9)
Experiencing a meaning	175e–176a	149e	PPF §10
Can one keep	176b	149f	PPF §11
"The whole scheme	176c	149g	PPF §12
I exclaimed "Now	176d	150a	PPF §13
If a meaning	176e	150b	PPF §14
If I say	176f	150c	PPF §15
When I say	176g	150d	PPF §16
PI II.iii			
What makes my	177a	151a	PPF §17
Suppose, however, that	177b	151b	PPF §18
PI II.iv			
"I believe that	178a	152a	PPF §19
Suppose I say	178b	152b	PPF §20
"I believe that	178c	152c	PPF §21
My attitude towards	178d	152d	PPF §22
Religion teaches that	178e	152e	PPF §23
If the picture	178f	152f	PPF §24
The human body	178g	152g	PPF §25
And how about	178h	152h	PPF §26
PI II.v			
Suppose we were	179a	153a	PPF §27
Then psychology treats	179b	153b	PPF §28
"I noticed that	179c	153c	PPF §29
A doctor asks:	179d	153d	PPF §30
"But then they	179e	153e	PPF §31
I describe a	180a	(153e)	PPF §32

(cont.)

First words of remark	First (1953) and Second (1958) Editions	Third (2001) Edition	Fourth (2009) Edition
PI II.v			
Doesn't a presupposition	180b	154a	PPF §33
It is like	180c	154b	PPF §34
PI II.vi			
Suppose someone said:	181a	155a	PPF §35
How should we	181b	155b	PPF §36
The meaning of	181c	155c	PPF §37
Though—one would	181d	155d	PPF §38
Are you sure	181e–182a	155e	PPF §39
Suppose we found	182b	155f	PPF §40
One misjudges the	182c	156a	PPF §41
Does a person	182d	156b	PPF §42
The if-feeling is	182e	156c	PPF §43
The if-feeling would	182f	156d	PPF §44
But can this	182g	156e	PPF §45
Is it in	182h	156f	PPF §46
We say this	182i	156g	PPF §47
"I sing it	183a	(156g)	PPF §48
The experience is	183b	156h	PPF §49
Thus the atmosphere	183c	156i	PPF §50
Here is a	183d	156j	PPF §51
PI II.vii			
People who on	184a	157a	PPF §52
Does this mean	184b	157b	PPF §53
"The mind seems	184c	157c	PPF §54
The evolution of	184d	157d	PPF §55
PI II.viii			
"My kinaesthetic sensations	185a	158a	PPF §56
"But after all,	185b	158b	PPF §57
It is the	185c	158c	PPF §58

First words of remark	First (1953) and Second (1958) Editions	Third (2001) Edition	Fourth (2009) Edition
PI II.viii			
A sensation *can*	185d	158d	PPF §59
What sense-impression? Well,	185f	158f	PPF §61
What I am	185g	158g	PPF §62
Let us leave	185h–186a	158h	PPF §63
I say "Do	186b	158i	PPF §64
This looks *so*;	186c	159a	PPF §65
Our interest in	186d	159b	PPF §66
PI II.ix			
If you observe	187a	160a	PPF §67
A touch which	187b	160b	PPF §68
When do we	187c	160c	PPF §69
If you trained	187d	160d	PPF §70
If I let	187e	160e	PPF §71
Are the words	187f	160f	PPF §72
I say "I	187g	160g	PPF §73
We can imagine	188a	(160g)	PPF §74
We ask "What	188b	161a	PPF §75
I can find	188c	161b	PPF §76
What is fear?	188d	161c	PPF §77
Could I also	188e	161d	PPF §78
Describing my state	188f	161e	PPF §79
And do I	188g	161f	PPF §80
When it is	189a	(161f)	PPF §81
But here is	189b	161g	PPF §82
A cry is	189c	161h	PPF §83
We surely do	189d	161i	PPF §84
But if "I	189e	161j	PPF §85
PI II.x			
How did we	190a	162a	PPF §86
Moore's paradox can	190b	162b	PPF §87

(cont.)

First words of remark	First (1953) and Second (1958) Editions	Third (2001) Edition	Fourth (2009) Edition
	PI II.x		
So it *looks*	190c	162c	PPF §88
Similarly: the statement	190d	162d	PPF §89
"At bottom, when	190e	162e	PPF §90
One can mistrust	190f	162f	PPF §91
If there were	190g	162g	PPF §92
Don't look at	190h	162h	PPF §93
The language-game of	190i–191a	162i	PPF §94
Suppose I were	191b	162j–163a	PPF §95
"I believe …." throws	191c	163b	PPF §96
If, however, "I	191d	163c	PPF §97
Imagine a language	191e	163d	PPF §98
I say of	191f	163e	PPF §99
"One feels conviction	191g	163f	PPF §100
"Here it *looks*	191h	163g	PPF §101
This is how	191i–192a	163h	PPF §102
My own relation	192b	163i	PPF §103
If I listened	192c	163j	PPF §104
"Judging from what	192d	164a	PPF §105
Even in the	192e	164b	PPF §106
Think of the	192f	164c	PPF §107
Different concepts touch	192g	164d	PPF §108
Consider the misbegotten	192h	164e	PPF §109
Don't regard a	192i	164f	PPF §110
	PI II.xi		
Two uses of	193a	165a	PPF §111
The one man	193b	165b	PPF §112
I contemplate a	193c	165c	PPF §113
Its *causes* are	193d	165d	PPF §114
We are interested	193e	165e	PPF §115
You could imagine	193f	165f	PPF §116
Here perhaps we	193g–194a	165g	PPF §117
I shall call	194b	165h–166a	PPF §118

First words of remark	First (1953) and Second (1958) Editions	Third (2001) Edition	Fourth (2009) Edition
	PI II.xi		
Here it is	194c	166b	PPF §119
I may, then	194d	166c	PPF §120
I should not	194e–195a	166d	PPF §121
It would have	195b	166e	PPF §122
One doesn't "*take*"	195c	166f	PPF §123
If you say	195d	166g	PPF §124
I see two	195e	167a	PPF §125
"I saw it	195f	167b	PPF §126
I should never	195g	167c	PPF §127
I am shewn	195h	167d	PPF §128
The change of	195i	167e	PPF §129
"Now I am	196a	(167e)	PPF §130
I suddenly see	196b	167f	PPF §131
And above all	196c	167g	PPF §132
The concept of	196d	167h	PPF §133
If you put	196e	168a	PPF §134
If I know	196f	168b	PPF §135
And this by	196g	168c	PPF §136
If I saw	196h–197a	168d	PPF §137
I look at	197b	168e	PPF §138
But since it	197c	168f	PPF §139
Hence the flashing	197d	168g	PPF §140
Someone suddenly sees	197e	168h	PPF §141
For might not	197f	168i	PPF §142
I meet someone	197g	169a	PPF §143
Now, when I	197h	169b	PPF §144
The very expression	198a	(169b)	PPF §145
What is the	198b	169c	PPF §146
The concept of	198c	169d	PPF §147
How does one	198d	169e	PPF §148
If someone sees	198e	169f	PPF §149
Hold the drawing	198f	169g–h	PPF §150
The figure (a)	198g	169i	PPF §151
Imagine the duck–rabbit	199a	170a	PPF §152

(cont.)

First words of remark	First (1953) and Second (1958) Editions	Third (2001) Edition	Fourth (2009) Edition
	PI II.xi		
If you search	199b	170b	PPF §153
But you would	199c	170c	PPF §154
There are here	199d	170d	PPF §155
Then is the	199e	170e	PPF §156
Of course we	199f	170f	PPF §157
"What I really	199g	170g	PPF §158
If you ask	199h	170h	PPF §159
The concept of	200a	170i–171a	PPF §160
Here we are	200b	171b	PPF §161
Take as an	200c	171c	PPF §162
"You can think	200d	171d	PPF §163
But how is	200e	171e	PPF §164
When it looks	200f–201a	171f	PPF §165
How would the	201b	171g	PPF §166
A triangle can	201c	171h	PPF §167
Could I say	201d	172a	PPF §168
What does it	201e	172b	PPF §169
Here we are	201f	172c	PPF §170
And *is* it	201g–202a	172d	PPF §171
"And is it	202b	172e	PPF §172
Certain drawings are	202c	172f	PPF §173
And then it	202d	172g	PPF §174
When I see	202e	172h	PPF §175
What does anyone	202f	172i	PPF §176
People often associate	202g	173a	PPF §177
Here it occurs	202h	173b	PPF §178
This figure	203a	(173b)	PPF §179
What does it	203b	173c	PPF §180
"But this isn't	203c	173d	PPF §181
But this is	203d	174a	PPF §182
"The phenomenon is	203e	174b	PPF §183

First words of remark	First (1953) and Second (1958) Editions	Third (2001) Edition	Fourth (2009) Edition
	PI II.xi		
If the picture	203f–204a	174c	PPF §184
The first thing	204b	174d	PPF §185
Someone tells me:	204c	174e	PPF §186
The best description	204d	174f	PPF §187
Do not try	204e	174g	PPF §188
Of course I	204f	174h	PPF §189
"Is it a	204g	174i	PPF §190
Here it is	204h	174j	PPF §191
For when should	204i	174k	PPF §192
"To me it	205a	175a	PPF §193
But can I	205b	175b	PPF §194
You need to	205c	175c	PPF §195
If you see	205d	175d	PPF §196
Perhaps the following	205e	175e	PPF §197
This need not	205f	175f	PPF §198
I say: "We	205g	175g	PPF §199
I might say:	205h	175h	PPF §200
The duck-rabbit. One	205i	175i	PPF §201
(In giving all	206a	(175i)	PPF §202
"Now I see	206b	175j	PPF §203
Do not ask	206c	176a	PPF §204
How does one	206d	176b	PPF §205
Here is a	206e	176c	(PPF §205)
And does the	206f	176d	PPF §206
And if you	206g	176e	PPF §207
If I heard	206h	176f	PPF §208
But the expression	206i	176g	PPF §209
"Fine shades of	207a	(176g)	PPF §210
The aspects of	207b	176h	PPF §211
In this, however,	207c	176i	PPF §212
You must remember	207d	177a	PPF §213
(The temptation to	207e	177b	PPF §214

(cont.)

First words of remark	First (1953) and Second (1958) Editions	Third (2001) Edition	Fourth (2009) Edition
	PI II.xi		
Those two aspects	207f	177c	PPF §215
You only "see	207g	177d	PPF §216
It is possible	207h	177e	PPF §217
The aspects A	208a	177f	PPF §218
I can see	208b	177g	PPF §219
How does one	208c	177h	PPF §221
One *kind* of	208d	177i	PPF §220
In the triangle	208e	178a	PPF §222
But how queer	208f	178b	PPF §223
It is only	209a	(178b)	PPF §224
For how could	209b	178c	PPF §225
Such a concept	209c	178d	PPF §226
The epithet "sad",	209d	178e	PPF §227
Think of this	209e	178f	PPF §228
Think of the	209f	178g	PPF §229
And if I	209g	178h–179a	PPF §230
We react to	209h	179b	PPF §231
One might say	210a	(179b)	PPF §232
If you feel	210b	179c	PPF §233
I can imagine	210c	179d	PPF §234
I should like	210d	179e	PPF §237
The aspect presents	210e	179f	PPF §238
"I observed the	210f	179g	PPF §239
"After the likeness	210g	179h	PPF §240
I should like	210h–211a	179i–180a	PPF §241
Someone tells me:	211b	180b	PPF §242
"Just now I	211c	180c	PPF §243
The likeness makes	211d	180d	PPF §244
Is being struck	211e	180e	PPF §245
('Thinking' and 'inward	211f	180f	PPF §246
The colour of	212a	(180f)	PPF §247
It is almost	212b	180g–181a	PPF §235

First words of remark	First (1953) and Second (1958) Editions	Third (2001) Edition	Fourth (2009) Edition
	PI II.xi		
Imagine a physiological	212c	181b	PPF §236
Do I really	212d	181c	PPF §248
Now it is	212e	181d	PPF §249
Only do not	(212e)	(181d)	PPF §250
We find certain	212f	181e	PPF §251
If you look	213a	(181e)	PPF §252
(It is anything	213b	181f	PPF §253
The concept of	213c	181g	PPF §254
"Imagine this changed	213d	181h	PPF §255
Seeing an aspect	213e	182a	PPF §256
The question now	213f	182b	PPF §257
Ought he to	213g–214a	182c	PPF §258
(Anomalies of *this*	214b	182d	PPF §259
Aspect blindness will	214c	182e	PPF §260
The importance of	214d	182f	PPF §261
In a law-court,	214e	182g	PPF §262
Suppose I had	214f	182h	PPF §263
"When I read	214g	183a	PPF §264
When I pronounce	215a	(183a)	PPF §265
Perhaps it could	215b	183b	PPF §266
But if a	215c	183c	PPF §267
Think here of	215d	183d	PPF §268
"But what is	215e	183e	PPF §269
"I feel as	215f	183f	PPF §270
You can say	215g	184a	PPF §271
If a sensitive	215h–216a	184b	PPF §272
But the question	216b	184c	PPF §273
Given the two	216c	184d	PPF §274
Asked "What do	216d	184e	PPF §275
Here one might	216e	184f	PPF §276
Only if you	216f	184g	PPF §277
The secondary sense	216g	184h	PPF §278
Someone tells me:	216h–217a	184i–185a	PPF §279

(cont.)

First words of remark	First (1953) and Second (1958) Editions	Third (2001) Edition	Fourth (2009) Edition
	PI II.xi		
The intention *with*	217b	185b	PPF §280
'Talking' (whether out	217c	185c	PPF §281
The *interest* of	217d	185d	PPF §282
"At that word	217e	185e	PPF §283
If God had	217f	185f	PPF §284
"Why did you	217g	185g	PPF §285
In saying this	217h	185h	PPF §286
The language-game "I	217i	185i	PPF §287
"I have already	217j–218a	185j	PPF §288
"At these words	218b	185k	PPF §289
"Why did you	218c	186a	PPF §290
Meaning it is	218d	186b	PPF §291
There are important	218e	186c	PPF §292
"Now I know!"	218f	186d	PPF §293
The familiar physiognomy	218g	186e	PPF §294
How do I	218h	186f	PPF §295
But doesn't the	219a	(186f)	PPF §296
It is possible—	219b	186g	PPF §297
"The word is	219c	187a	PPF §298
James, in writing	219d	187b	PPF §299
The words "It's	219e	187c	PPF §300
Silent 'internal' speech	220a	(187c)	PPF §301
The close relationship	220b	187d	PPF §302
"But saying things	220c	187e	PPF §303
"So I don't	220d	187f	PPF §304
One can say	220e	187g–188a	PPF §305
A hypothesis, such	220f	188b	PPF §306
That what someone	220g–221a	188c	PPF §307
"What anyone says	221b	188d	PPF §308
"I know what	221c	188e	PPF §309
"I know…" may	221d	188f	PPF §310
One says "I	221e	188g	PPF §311
It is possible	221f	188h	PPF §312

First words of remark	First (1953) and Second (1958) Editions	Third (2001) Edition	Fourth (2009) Edition
	PI II.xi		
With this is	221g	188i	PPF §313
"A new-born child	221h–222a	188j–189a	PPF §314
I can know	222b	189b	PPF §315
"A man's thinking	222c	189c–d	PPF §316
If I were	222d	189e	PPF §317
Let us assume	222e	189f	PPF §318
The criteria for	222f	189g	PPF §319
(Assuming that dreams	222g–223a	189h	PPF §320
There is a	223b	189i–190a	PPF §321
All this would	223c	190b	PPF §322
"What is *internal*	223d	190c	PPF §323
If I see	223e	190d	PPF §324
We also say	223f	190e	PPF §325
"I cannot know	223g	190f	PPF §326
If a lion	223h	190g	PPF §327
It is possible	223i–224a	190h	PPF §328
Two points, however,	224b	190i	PPF §329
I can be	224c	190j	PPF §330
"But, if you	224d	191a	PPF §331
Am I less	224e	191b	PPF §332
"He alone knows	224f	191c	PPF §333
Let yourself be	224g	191d	PPF §334
We remain unconscious	224h	191e	PPF §335
What is the	224i	191f	PPF §336
There is such	224j	191g	PPF §337
One judges the	225a	191h	PPF §338
We should sometimes	225b	191i	PPF §339
"While you can	225c	192a	PPF §340
There can be	225d	192b	PPF §341
Even then it	225e–226a	192c	PPF §342
But am I	226b	192d	PPF §343
It is no	226c	192e	PPF §344
What has to	226d	192f	PPF §345
Does it make	226e	192g	PPF §346

(cont.)

First words of remark	First (1953) and Second (1958) Editions	Third (2001) Edition	Fourth (2009) Edition
	PI II.xi		
This consideration must,	226f	192h	PPF §347
"But mathematical truth	226g–227a	192i–193a	PPF §348
Of course, in	227b	193b	PPF §349
"We all learn	227c	193c	PPF §350
There is such	227d	193d	PPF §351
There is in	227e	193e	PPF §352
I am sure,	227f	193f	PPF §353
"You're all at	227g	193g	PPF §354
Is there such	227h	193h	PPF §355
What is most	227i	193i	PPF §356
"The genuineness of	228a	194a	PPF §357
It is certainly	228b	194b	PPF §358
The question is:	228c	194c	PPF §359
Imponderable evidence includes	228d	194d	PPF §360
Ask yourself: How	228e	194e	PPF §361
Pretending is, of	228f–229a	194f	PPF §362
A child has	229b	194g	PPF §363
There might actually	229c	194h	PPF §364
	PI II.xii		
If the formation	230a	195a	PPF §365
I am not	230b	195b	PPF §366
Compare a concept	230c	195c	PPF §367
	PI II.xiii		
When I say:	231a	196a	PPF §368
Remembering has no	231b	196b	PPF §369
Would this situation	231c	196c	PPF §370
	PI II.xiv		
The confusion and	232a	197a	PPF §371
An investigation is	232b	197b	PPF §372

List of Works Cited

Affeldt, Steven G. "Captivating Pictures and Liberating Language: Freedom as the Achievement of Speech in Wittgenstein's *Philosophical Investigations*." *Philosophical Topics* 27 (1999): 255–85.

"The Ground of Mutuality: Criteria, Judgment, and Intelligibility in Stephen Mulhall and Stanley Cavell." *European Journal of Philosophy* 6 (April 1998): 1–31.

Aldrich, Virgil C. "An Aspect Theory of Mind." *Philosophy and Phenomenological Research* 26 (March 1966): 313–26.

Philosophy of Art. Englewood Cliffs, N.J.: Prentice-Hall, 1963.

Aristotle. *Physics*. Edited by W. D. Ross. Oxford: Oxford University Press, 1936.

Augustine. *Confessions*. Translated by Albert C. Outler. Translation revised by Mark Vessey. New York: Barnes and Noble, 2007.

Austin, J. L. *How to Do Things with Words*. Edited by J. O. Urmson and Marina Sbisà. 2d ed. Cambridge: Harvard University Press, 1975.

"The Meaning of a Word." In Austin, *Philosophical Papers*, 55–75.

"Other Minds." In Austin, *Philosophical Papers*, 76–116.

"A Plea for Excuses." In Austin, *Philosophical Papers*, 175–204.

Philosophical Papers. Edited by J. O. Urmson and G. J. Warnock. Third Edition. Oxford: Oxford University Press, 1979.

Sense and Sensibilia. Edited by G. J. Warnock. Oxford: Oxford University Press, 1962.

"Truth." In Austin, *Philosophical Papers*, 117–33.

Austin, J. L., and others. "Discussion générale." In *Cahiers de Royaumont, Philosophie No. 4, La Philosophie Analytique*, 330–80. Paris: Editions de Minuit, 1962.

Auxier, Randall E., and Lewis Edwin Hahn, eds. *The Philosophy of Jaakko Hintikka*. Library of Living Philosophers, vol. 30. Chicago: Open Court, 2006.

Baker, Gordon. *Wittgenstein's Method: Neglected Aspects.* Edited by Katherine Morris. Oxford: Blackwell, 2004.

Baker, G.P. and P.M.S. Hacker. *Wittgenstein: Understanding and Meaning.* Oxford: Blackwell, 1980.

Batkin, Norton. "Formalism in Analytic Aesthetics." In *Encyclopedia of Aesthetics,* edited by Michael Kelly, 2:217–21. 4 vols. New York: Oxford University Press, 1998.

Photography and Philosophy. New York: Garland Publishing, 1990.

Baxandall, Michael. *Giotto and the Orators: Humanist Observers of Painting in Italy and the Discovery of Pictorial Composition 1350–1450.* Oxford: Oxford University Press, 1971.

Baz, Avner. "Seeing Aspects and Philosophical Difficulty." In *The Oxford Handbook of Wittgenstein,* edited by Marie McGinn and Oskari Kuusela. Oxford: Oxford University Press, forthcoming.

"What's the Point of Seeing Aspects?" *Philosophical Investigations* 23 (April 2000): 97–121.

Bearn, Gordon C.F. *Waking to Wonder: Wittgenstein's Existential Investigations.* Albany, N.Y.: State University of New York Press, 1997.

"Wittgenstein and the Uncanny." *Soundings* 76, no. 1 (1993): 29–58.

Bergson, Henri. *Time and Free Will: An Essay on the Immediate Data of Consciousness.* New York: Harper and Row, 1960.

Blanchot, Maurice. "Thinking the Apocalypse: A Letter from Maurice Blanchot to Catherine David." *Critical Inquiry* 15 (Winter 1989): 475–80.

Breithaupt, Fritz, Richard Raatzsch, and Bettina Kremberg, eds. *Goethe and Wittgenstein: Seeing the World's Unity in Its Variety.* Wittgenstein Studien, band 5. Frankfurt am Main: Peter Lang, 2002.

Budd, Malcolm. *Wittgenstein's Philosophy of Psychology.* London: Routledge, 1991.

Capek, Karel. *Intimate Things.* London: Allen and Unwin, 1935.

Cavell, Stanley. "Aesthetic Problems of Modern Philosophy." In Cavell, *Must We Mean What We Say?,* 86–96.

"Austin at Criticism." In Cavell, *Must We Mean What We Say?,* 97–114.

"The Availability of Wittgenstein's Later Philosophy." In Cavell, *Must We Mean What We Say?,* 44–72.

"The Avoidance of Love: A Reading of *King Lear.*" In Cavell, *Must We Mean What We Say?,* 267–353.

The Claim of Reason: Wittgenstein, Skepticism, Morality, and Tragedy. Oxford: Oxford University Press, 1979.

"Companionable Thinking." In Crary, *Wittgenstein and the Moral Life,* 281–98.

"Declining Decline: Wittgenstein as a Philosopher of Culture." In *This New Yet Unapproachable America: Lectures after Emerson after Wittgenstein,* 29–75.

"The Division of Talent." *Critical Inquiry* 11 (June 1985): 519–38.

In Quest of the Ordinary: Lines of Skepticism and Romanticism. Chicago: University of Chicago Press, 1988.

"The *Investigations*' Everyday Aesthetics of Itself." In *The Cavell Reader*, 369–89. Edited by Stephen Mulhall. Oxford: Blackwell, 1996.

"Knowing and Acknowledging." In Cavell, *Must We Mean What We Say?*, 238–66.

"Music Discomposed." In Cavell, *Must We Mean What We Say?*, 180–212.

Must We Mean What We Say? A Book of Essays. Cambridge: Cambridge University Press, 1969.

"Notes and Afterthoughts on the Opening of Wittgenstein's *Investigations*." In *Philosophical Passages: Wittgenstein, Emerson, Austin, Derrida*, 125–86. The Bucknell Lectures in Literary Theory, vol. 12. Oxford: Blackwell, 1995.

Pursuits of Happiness: The Hollywood Comedy of Remarriage. Cambridge: Harvard University Press, 1981.

"Something Out of the Ordinary." In *Philosophy the Day After Tomorrow*, 7–27. Cambridge: Harvard University Press, 2005.

This New Yet Unapproachable America: Lectures after Emerson after Wittgenstein. Albuquerque, N.M.: Living Batch Press, 1989.

"The Wittgensteinian Event." In Crary and Shieh, *Reading Cavell*, 8–25.

Cavell, Stanley, Cora Diamond, John McDowell, Ian Hacking, and Cary Wolfe. *Philosophy and Animal Life.* New York: Columbia University Press, 2008.

Churchland, Paul M. *Matter and Consciousness.* Revised ed. Cambridge: MIT Press, 1988.

Cioffi, Frank. *Freud and the Question of Pseudoscience.* Chicago: Open Court, 1998.

"The Propaedeutic Delusion." *History of the Human Sciences* 13, no. 1 (2000): 109–23.

"Stating the Obvious." In *Erving Goffman*, edited by Gary Alan Fine and Gregory W. H. Smith, Part Four: Methods. 4 vols. Masters in Modern Social Thought Series. London: Sage Publications, 2000.

Wittgenstein on Freud and Frazer. Cambridge: Cambridge University Press, 1998.

Clack, Brian. *Wittgenstein, Frazer and Religion.* New York: Palgrave, 1998.

Coetzee, J. M. *Elizabeth Costello.* New York: Viking, 2003.

The Lives of Animals. Edited by Amy Gutmann. Princeton: Princeton University Press, 1999.

Coleridge, Samuel Taylor. *The Statesman's Manual*, 437–8. Edited by W. G. T. Shedd. New York, 1875. Quoted in Angus Fletcher, *Allegory: The Theory of a Symbolic Mode* (Ithaca, N.Y.: Cornell University Press, 1964), 16 n. 29.

Collingwood, R. G. *The Principles of Art.* Oxford: Clarendon Press, 1938.

Conradi, Peter J. *Iris Murdoch: A Life.* New York: W. W. Norton, 2001.

Crary, Alice, ed. *Wittgenstein and the Moral Life: Essays in Honor of Cora Diamond.* Cambridge: MIT Press, 2007.

Crary, Alice, and Rupert Read, eds. *The New Wittgenstein.* London: Routledge, 2000.

Crary, Alice, and Sanford Shieh, eds. *Reading Cavell.* London: Routledge, 2006.

Davidson, Donald. "The Emergence of Thought." In Davidson, *Subjective, Intersubjective, Objective*, 123–34.

"The Second Person." In Davidson, *Subjective, Intersubjective, Objective*, 107–21.

Subjective, Intersubjective, Objective. Oxford: Clarendon Press, 2001.

Day, William. "The Aesthetic Dimension of Wittgenstein's Later Writings." Unpublished manuscript.

"Knowing as Instancing: Jazz Improvisation and Moral Perfectionism." *The Journal of Aesthetics and Art Criticism* 58 (Spring 2000): 99–111.

Dennett, Daniel C. "Can Machines Think?" In *Brainchildren: Essays on Designing Minds*, 3–29. Cambridge: MIT Press, 1998.

Consciousness Explained. Boston: Little, Brown, and Company, 1991.

Descartes, René. *Meditations on First Philosophy: In Which the Existence of God and the Distinction of the Soul from the Body Are Demonstrated*. Translated by Donald A. Cress. 3d ed. Indianapolis: Hackett, 1993.

Diamond, Cora. "The Hardness of the Soft: Wittgenstein's Early Thought About Skepticism." In *Skepticism in Context*, edited by James Conant and Andrea Kern. London: Routledge, forthcoming.

The Realistic Spirit: Wittgenstein, Philosophy, and the Mind. Cambridge: MIT Press, 1991.

"Rules: Looking in the Right Place." In *Wittgenstein: Attention to Particulars*, edited by D. Z. Phillips and Peter Winch, 12–34. London: Macmillan, 1989.

Dreyfus, Hubert L., and Harrison Hall, eds. *Husserl, Intentionality, and Cognitive Science*. Cambridge: MIT Press, 1982.

Drury, M. O'C. "Conversations with Wittgenstein." In Rhees, *Recollections of Wittgenstein*, 97–171.

"Some Notes on Conversations with Wittgenstein." In Rhees, *Recollections of Wittgenstein*, 76–96.

The Danger of Words and Writings on Wittgenstein. Bristol: Thoemmes Press, 1996.

Eldridge, Richard. *Leading a Human Life: Wittgenstein, Intentionality, and Romanticism*. Chicago: University of Chicago Press, 1997.

Ellmann, Richard. *Four Dubliners: Wilde, Yeats, Joyce, and Beckett*. London: Hamish Hamilton, 1987.

Emerson, Ralph Waldo. "Society and Solitude." In *Emerson's Complete Works*, 7: 9–20. 12 vols. Boston: Houghton Mifflin, 1883.

Engelmann, Paul. *Letters from Ludwig Wittgenstein: With a Memoir*. Oxford: Blackwell, 1967.

Floyd, Juliet. "Critical Study of Mathieu Marion, Wittgenstein, Finitism, and the Philosophy of Mathematics." *Philosophia Mathematica* 10, no. 1 (2002): 67–88.

"Number and Ascriptions of Number in Wittgenstein's *Tractatus*." In *Future Pasts: Perspectives on the Analytic Tradition in Twentieth Century Philosophy*, edited by Juliet Floyd and Sanford Shieh, 145–91. Oxford: Oxford University Press, 2001.

"Wittgenstein and the Inexpressible." In Crary, *Wittgenstein and the Moral Life*, 177–234.

"Wittgenstein on Philosophy of Logic and Mathematics." In *The Oxford Handbook of Philosophy of Mathematics and Logic*, edited by Stewart Shapiro, 75–128. Oxford: Oxford University Press, 2005.

Føllesdaal, Dagfinn. "Husserl's Notion of Noema." *Journal of Philosophy* 66 (1969): 680–87.

"Ultimate Justification in Husserl and Wittgenstein." In *Experience and Analysis*, edited by Maria E. Reicher and Johann C. Marek, 127–42. Vienna: öbv & hpt, 2005.

Fodor, Jerry A. *The Language of Thought*. New York: Thomas Y. Crowell, 1975.

Frazer, James George. *The Golden Bough*. Abridged edition. London: Macmillan, 1967.

Freadman, Richard. *Threads of Life*. Chicago: University of Chicago Press, 2001.

Frege, Gottlob. "On *Sinn* and *Bedeutung*." In *The Frege Reader*, 151–71. Edited by Michael Beaney. Oxford: Blackwell, 1997.

Galavotti, M. C. *Philosophical Introduction to Probability*. Stanford: CSLI, 2005.

Genova, Judith. *Wittgenstein: A Way of Seeing*. New York: Routledge, 1995.

Gerrard, Steven. "Wittgenstein's Philosophies of Mathematics." *Synthese* 87, no. 1 (1991): 125–42.

Gibson, John, and Wolfgang Huemer, eds. *The Literary Wittgenstein*. New York: Routledge, 2004.

Glock, Hans-Johann, ed. *Wittgenstein: A Critical Reader*. Oxford: Blackwell, 2001.

A Wittgenstein Dictionary. Oxford: Blackwell, 1996.

Goffman, Erving. "The Interaction Order." *American Sociological Review* 48, no. 1 (February 1983): 1–17.

Stigma. Englewood Cliffs, N. J.: Prentice Hall, 1963.

Goldfarb, Warren. "I Want You to Bring Me a Slab: Remarks on the Opening Sections of the *Philosophical Investigations*." *Synthese* 56 (1983): 265–82.

Gould, Timothy. *Hearing Things: Voice and Method in the Writing of Stanley Cavell*. Chicago: University of Chicago Press, 1998.

Gowers, Timothy. *Mathematics: A Very Short Introduction*. Oxford: Oxford University Press, 2002.

Hacker, P.M.S. "Developmental Hypotheses and Perspicuous Representations: Wittgenstein on Frazer's *Golden Bough*." In *Wittgenstein: Connections and Controversies*, 74–97. Oxford: Oxford University Press, 2001.

Wittgenstein: Mind and Will. Oxford: Oxford University Press, 1996.

Hagberg, Garry L. *Art As Language: Wittgenstein, Meaning, and Aesthetic Theory*. Ithaca, N.Y.: Cornell University Press, 1995.

"Autobiographical Consciousness: Wittgenstein, Private Experience, and the 'Inner Picture'." In Gibson and Huemer, *The Literary Wittgenstein*, 228–50.

"Davidson, Self-Knowledge, and Autobiographical Writing." *Philosophy and Literature* 26:2 (October 2002): 354–68.

Meaning and Interpretation: Wittgenstein, Henry James, and Literary Knowledge. Ithaca, N.Y.: Cornell University Press, 1994.

"The Mind Shown: Wittgenstein, Goethe, and the Question of Person Perception." In *Goethe and Wittgenstein: Seeing the World's Unity in Its Variety,* edited by Fritz Breithaupt, Richard Raatzsch, and Bettina Kremberg, 111–26. Wittgenstein Studien, band 5. Frankfurt am Main: Peter Lang, 2002.

"On Philosophy as Therapy: Wittgenstein, Cavell, and Autobiographical Writing." *Philosophy and Literature* 27:1 (April 2003): 196–210.

"Rightness Reconsidered: Krausz, Wittgenstein, and the Question of Interpretive Understanding." In *Interpretation and Its Objects: Studies in the Philosophy of Michael Krausz,* edited by Andreea Deciu Ritivoi, 25–37. Amsterdam: Rodopi, 2003.

"The Self, Reflected: Wittgenstein, Cavell, and the Autobiographical Situation." In *Ordinary Language Criticism: Literary Thinking after Cavell after Wittgenstein,* edited by Kenneth Dauber and Walter Jost, 171–98. Evanston: Northwestern University Press, 2003.

"The Self, Speaking: Wittgenstein, Introspective Utterances, and the Arts of Self-Representation." *Revue Internationale de Philosophie,* no. 219 (2002): 9–47.

"The Self, Thinking: Wittgenstein, Augustine, and the Autobiographical Situation." In Lewis, *Wittgenstein, Aesthetics and Philosophy,* 215–33.

"Wittgenstein and the Question of True Self-Interpretation." In *Is There a Single Right Interpretation?,* edited by Michael Krausz, 381–406. University Park, Pa.: Pennsylvania State University Press, 2002.

Hardy, G. H. *Apology of a Mathematician.* Cambridge: Cambridge University Press, 1990.

Harré, Rom. *Social Being.* Oxford: Blackwell, 1979.

Heidegger, Martin. *Being and Time.* Translated by John Macquarrie and Edward Robinson. New York: Harper & Row, 1962.

What is Called Thinking? Translated by J. Glenn Gray. New York: Harper, 1968.

Hintikka, Jaakko. "Reply to Marion." In Auxier and Hahn, *The Philosophy of Jaakko Hintikka,* 431–36.

Huizinga, Johan. *The Waning of The Middle Ages.* London: Penguin, 1968.

Husserl, Edmund. *Logical Investigations.* Vol. 1. Translated by J.N. Findlay. London: Routledge, 1970.

Jastrow, Joseph. *Fact and Fable in Psychology.* Boston and New York: Houghton Mifflin, 1900.

Johnson, Samuel. *The History of Rasselas, Prince of Abissinia* (1759). London: Penguin, 1976.

Johnston, Paul. *Wittgenstein: Rethinking the Inner.* London: Routledge, 1993.

Joyce, James. "Araby." In *Dubliners.* New York: Penguin, 1976.

Kandinski, Wassily. *Concerning the Spiritual in Art and Painting in Particular.* New York: George Wittenborn, 1912.

Kant, Immanuel. *Critique of Pure Reason.* Translated by Norman Kemp Smith. London: Macmillan, 1929.

Critique of Judgment. Translated by J. H. Bernard. New York: Hafner Press, 1951.

Kienzler, Wolfgang. *Wittgensteins wende zu seiner Spätphilosophie 1930–1932.* Frankfurt am Main: Surhkamp Verlag, 1997.

Klagge, James C., ed. *Wittgenstein: Biography and Philosophy.* Cambridge: Cambridge University Press, 2001.

Krebs, Victor J. "Against Idolatry and Toward Psychology: A Review of Ray Monk's *Ludwig Wittgenstein: The Duty of Genius.*" *The San Francisco Jung Institute Library Journal* 12, no. 3 (1993): 21–39.

Del alma y el arte: Reflexiones en torno a la cultura, la imagen y la memoria. Caracas: Editorial Arte, 1997.

"'Around the Axis of our Real Need': On the Ethical Point of Wittgenstein's Philosophy." *European Journal of Philosophy* 9, no. 3 (December 2001): 344–74.

"'Descending into Primaeval Chaos': Philosophy, the Body, and the Pygmalionic Impulse." In *Mythos and Logos: How to Regain the Love of Wisdom,* edited by Albert A. Anderson, Steven V. Hicks, and Lech Witowski, 141–60. Amsterdam and New York: Rodopi, 2004.

"The Subtle Body of Language and the Lost Sense of Philosophy." *Philosophical Investigations* 23, no. 2 (April 2000): 147–55.

Kripke, Saul. *Wittgenstein on Rules and Private Language: An Elementary Exposition.* Cambridge: Harvard University Press, 1982.

Kuhn, Thomas S. *The Road Since Structure: Philosophical Essays, 1970 – 1993, with an Autobiographical Interview.* Edited by James Conant and John Haugeland. Chicago: University of Chicago Press, 2000.

Lessing, Gotthold Ephraim. *Laocoön: An Essay on the Limits of Painting and Poetry.* Translated by Edward Allen McCormick. Baltimore: Johns Hopkins University Press, 1962, 1984.

Lewis, C. S. *A Grief Observed.* London: Faber and Faber, 1961.

Lewis, Peter B., ed. *Wittgenstein, Aesthetics and Philosophy.* Aldershot: Ashgate, 2004.

Lyotard, Jean-François. *The Differend: Phrases in Dispute.* Translated by Georges Van Den Abbeele. Minneapolis: University of Minnesota Press, 1988.

Margalit, Avishai. "Sense and Sensibility: Wittgenstein on the 'Golden Bough'." *Iyyun: The Jerusalem Philosophical Quarterly* 41 (1992): 301–18.

Marion, Mathieu. "Phenomenological Language: Thoughts and Operations in the *Tractatus.*" In Auxier and Hahn, *The Philosophy of Jaakko Hintikka,* 413–31.

McDowell, John. *Mind and World.* Cambridge: Harvard University Press, 1994.

McGinn, Colin. "Can We Solve the Mind-Body Problem?" *Mind* 98 (July 1989): 349–66.

McGinn, Marie. *Wittgenstein and the Philosophical Investigations.* London: Routledge, 1997.

McGuinness, Brian. *Approaches to Wittgenstein: Collected Papers.* London: Routledge, 2002.

" 'The Lion Speaks, and We Don't Understand': Wittgenstein after 100 Years." In McGuinness, *Approaches to Wittgenstein*, 3–9.

"Probability." In McGuinness, *Approaches to Wittgenstein*, 201–14.

Merleau-Ponty, Maurice. *Phenomenology of Perception.* New York: Routledge, 1999.

Minar, Edward. "Feeling at Home in Language (What Makes Reading *Philosophical Investigations* Possible?)." *Synthese* 102 (March 1995): 413–52.

Monk, Ray. *Ludwig Wittgenstein: The Duty of Genius.* New York: Free Press, 1990.

Moran, Richard. *Authority and Estrangement: An Essay on Self-Knowledge.* Princeton: Princeton University Press, 2001.

Moyal-Sharrock, Danièle, ed. *The Third Wittgenstein: The Post-*Investigations *Works.* Aldershot: Ashgate, 2004.

Mühlholzer, Felix. "Wittgenstein and Surprises in Mathematics." In *Wittgenstein und die Zukunft der Philosophie: Eine Neubewertung nach 50 Jahren.* Proceedings of the 24th International Wittgenstein Symposium. Vienna: öbv & hpt, 2002.

Mulhall, Stephen. *Inheritance and Originality.* Oxford: Clarendon Press, 2001.

On Being in the World: Wittgenstein and Heidegger on Seeing Aspects. London: Routledge, 1990.

"Seeing Aspects." In Glock, *Wittgenstein: A Critical Reader*, 246–67.

Nabokov, Vladimir. *Speak, Memory: An Autobiography Revisited.* New York: Vintage, 1989. Originally published as *Conclusive Evidence.* New York: Harper, 1951.

Nagel, Thomas. "What Is It Like to Be a Bat?" *Philosophical Review* 83 (October 1974): 435–50.

Narboux, Jean-Philippe. "Diagramme, Dimensions et Synopsis." In *Théorie, Littérature, Enseignement* 22. Saint-Denis: Presses Universitaires de Vincennes, 2005: 115–41.

Dimensions et Paradigms, Wittgenstein et le problème de l'abstraction. Paris: Vrin Mathesis, forthcoming.

Nietzsche, Friedrich. "On Truth and Lying in a Non-Moral Sense." In *The Birth of Tragedy and Other Writings*, 139–53. Edited by Raymond Geuss and Ronald Speirs. Cambridge: Cambridge University Press, 1999.

Ogden, C. K. and I. A. Richards. *The Meaning of Meaning.* San Diego: Harcourt Brace Jovanovich, 1989.

Orwell, George. "Inside the Whale." In *A Collection of Essays*, 210–52. New York: Houghton Mifflin Harcourt, 1970.

Pascal, Blaise. *Pensées. Œuvres complètes.* Edited by Jacques Chevalier. Paris: Gallimard, 1954.

Pascal, Fania. "Wittgenstein: A Personal Memoir." In Rhees, *Recollections of Wittgenstein*, 12–49.

Peirce, Charles Sanders. "On the Doctrine of Chances, With Later Reflections." In *Philosophical Writings of Peirce*, 157–73. Edited by Justus Buchler. New York: Dover, 1955.

"Philosophy and the Conduct of Life." In *Reasoning and the Logic of Things*, 105–22. Edited by Kenneth Laine Ketner. Cambridge: Harvard University Press, 1992.

Pippin, Robert B. *Idealism as Modernism*. Cambridge: Cambridge University Press, 1997.

Putnam, Hilary. "Sense, Nonsense, and the Senses: An Inquiry into the Powers of the Human Mind." In Putnam, *The Threefold Cord*, 3–70.

The Threefold Cord: Mind, Body, and World. New York: Columbia University Press, 1999.

Quine, W. V. "Five Milestones of Empiricism." In *Theories and Things*, 67–72. Cambridge: Harvard University Press, 1981.

Rhees, Rush. "Introduction to 'Remarks on Frazer's *Golden Bough*'." *The Human World* 3 (May 1971): 28–41.

"Postscript." In Rhees, ed. *Recollections of Wittgenstein*, 172–209.

" 'Seeing' and 'Thinking'." In Rhees, *Wittgenstein's On Certainty*, 16–26.

Wittgenstein and the Possibility of Discourse. Cambridge: Cambridge University Press, 1998.

"Wittgenstein's Builders." In *Discussions of Wittgenstein*, 71–84. Bristol: Thoemmes Press, 1970.

Wittgenstein's On Certainty: There – Like Our Life. Edited by D. Z. Phillips. Oxford: Blackwell, 2003.

ed. *Recollections of Wittgenstein*. Oxford: Oxford University Press, 1984.

Rorty, Richard. *Contingency, Irony, and Solidarity*. Cambridge: Cambridge University Press, 1989.

Philosophy and the Mirror of Nature. Princeton: Princeton University Press, 1979.

Rousseau, Jean-Jacques. "On the Origin of Languages." In *Jean-Jacques Rousseau and Johann Gottfried Herder: On the Origin of Language*, 5–83. Translated by John H. Moran and Alexander Gode. Chicago: University of Chicago Press, 1966.

Sass, Louis A. *The Paradoxes of Delusion: Wittgenstein, Schreber, and the Schizophrenic Mind*. Ithaca, N.Y.: Cornell University Press, 1994.

Schulte, Joachim. *Experience and Expression: Wittgenstein's Philosophy of Psychology*. Translated by Joachim Schulte. Oxford: Oxford University Press, 1993.

Simmel, Georg. "The Nature of Philosophy." In Georg Simmel et al., *Essays on Sociology, Philosophy and Aesthetics*, 283–308. Edited by Kurt H. Wolff. New York: Harper Torchbooks, 1965.

Smart, J. J. C. "Materialism." *Essays Metaphysical and Moral: Selected Philosophical Papers*, 203–14. Oxford: Blackwell, 1987.

Smith, Adam. "The History of Astronomy." In *Essays Philosophical and Literary*, 342–85. London: Ward, Lock & Co., 1880.

Stendhal. *The Charterhouse of Parma*. Harmondsworth, U.K.: Penguin, 1958.

Stern, David G. *Wittgenstein on Mind and Language*. Oxford: Oxford University Press, 1995.

—. *Wittgenstein's* Philosophical Investigations: *An Introduction*. Cambridge Introductions to Key Philosophical Texts. Cambridge: Cambridge University Press, 2004.

Strawson, P. F. *The Bounds of Sense: An Essay on Kant's* Critique of Pure Reason. London: Methuen, 1966.

Strodtbeck, Fred L. "Review of Interaction Ritual: Essays on Face-to-Face Behavior, by Erving Goffman." The *American Journal of Sociology* 76, no. 1 (1970): 177–79.

Tolstoy, Leo. *War and Peace*. Translated by Rosemary Edmonds. London: Penguin, 1982.

Tomasello, Michael. *The Cultural Origins of Human Cognition*. Cambridge: Harvard University Press, 1999.

Travis, Charles. "Taking Thought." *Mind* 109 (2000): 533–57.

Webb, Judson C. "Hintikka on Aristotelian Constructions, Kantian Intuitions, and Peircean Theorems." In Auxier and Hahn, *The Philosophy of Jaakko Hintikka*, 195–302.

Whitehead, Alfred North. *An Introduction to Mathematics*. New York: H. Holt, 1911.

Winch, Peter. *Simone Weil: "The Just Balance."* Cambridge: Cambridge University Press, 1989.

Wisdom, John. "Ludwig Wittgenstein 1934–1937." In *Paradox and Discovery*, 87–9. Oxford: Basil Blackwell, 1965.

Wittgenstein, Ludwig. *The Big Typescript: TS 213*. Edited and translated by C. Grant Luckhardt and Maximilian A. E. Aue. Oxford: Blackwell, 2005.

—. *The Blue and Brown Books*. New York: Harper, 1958.

—. *Briefwechsel: Mit B. Russell, G. E. Moore, J. M. Keynes, F. P. Ramsey, W. Eccles, P. Engelmann und L. von Ficker*. Edited by Monika Seekircher, Brian McGuinness, Anton Unterkircher, Allan Janik and Walter Methlagl. CD-ROM. Innsbrucker elektronische Ausgabe, 2004.

—. *The Collected Manuscripts of Ludwig Wittgenstein on Facsimile CD-ROM*. Oxford: Oxford University Press, 2000.

—. *Culture and Value*. Edited by G. H. von Wright. Translated by Peter Winch. Oxford: Blackwell, 1980.

—. *Culture and Value: Revised Edition*. Edited by G. H. von Wright. Revised edition of the text by Alois Pichler. Translated by Peter Winch. Oxford: Blackwell, 1998.

—. *Denkbewegungen: Tagebücher 1930–1932, 1936–1937*. Edited by Ilse Somavilla. Innsbruck, Austria: Haymon Verlag, 1997.

—. *Last Writings on the Philosophy of Psychology*. Vol. 1, *Preliminary Studies for Part II of* Philosophical Investigations. Edited by G. H. Von Wright and Heikki Nyman. Translated by C. G. Luckhardt and Maximilian A. E. Aue. Oxford: Blackwell, 1982.

—. *Last Writings on the Philosophy of Psychology*. Vol. 2, *The Inner and the Outer, 1949–1951*. Edited by G. H. von Wright and Heikki Nyman. Translated by C. G. Luckhardt and Maximilian A. E. Aue. Oxford: Blackwell, 1992.

Lectures and Conversations on Aesthetics, Psychology and Religious Belief.
Berkeley and Los Angeles: University of California Press, 1972.

Notebooks 1914–1916. Edited by G. H. von Wright and G. E. M. Anscombe.
Translated by G. E. M. Anscombe. 2d ed. Chicago: University of Chicago
Press, 1979.

On Certainty. Edited by G. E. M. Anscombe and G. H. von Wright. Translated
by Denis Paul and G. E. M. Anscombe. New York: Harper, 1969.

Philosophical Grammar. Edited by Rush Rhees. Translated by Anthony
Kenny. Berkeley and Los Angeles: University of California Press, 1974.

Philosophical Investigations. Edited by G. E .M. Anscombe and Rush Rhees.
Translated by G. E. M. Anscombe. 2d ed. Oxford: Blackwell, 1958.

Philosophical Investigations. Edited by G. E .M. Anscombe and Rush
Rhees. Revised English translation by G. E. M. Anscombe. 3d ed.
Oxford: Blackwell, 2001.

Philosophical Investigations. Edited by P. M. S. Hacker and Joachim Schulte.
Translated by G. E. M. Anscombe, P. M. S. Hacker, and Joachim Schulte.
Rev. 4th ed. Oxford: Blackwell, 2009.

Philosophical Occasions: 1912–1951. Edited by James Klagge and Alfred
Nordmann. Indianapolis: Hackett, 1993.

Philosophical Remarks. Edited by Rush Rhees. Translated by Raymond
Hargreaves and Roger White. Chicago: University of Chicago Press,
1975.

Remarks on Colour. Edited by G. E. M. Anscombe. Translated by Linda L.
McAlister and Margarete Schättle. Berkeley and Los Angeles: University
of California Press, 1978.

Remarks on the Foundations of Mathematics. Edited by G. H. von Wright,
R. Rhees, and G. E. M. Anscombe. Translated by G. E. M. Anscombe.
Revised ed. Oxford: Blackwell, 1978.

Remarks on the Philosophy of Psychology. Vol. 1. Edited by G. E. M. Anscombe
and G. H. von Wright. Translated by G. E. M. Anscombe.
Oxford: Blackwell, 1980.

Remarks on the Philosophy of Psychology. Vol. 2. Edited by G. H. von Wright
and Heikki Nyman. Translated by C. G. Luckhardt and M. A. E. Aue.
Oxford: Blackwell, 1980.

Tractatus Logico-Philosophicus. Translated by D. F. Pears and B. F.
McGuinness. Atlantic Highlands, N.J.: Humanities Press, 1961.

Wittgenstein and the Vienna Circle: Conversations Recorded by Friedrich Waismann.
Edited by Brian McGuinness. Translated by Joachim Schulte and Brian
McGuinness. Oxford: Blackwell, 1979.

*Wittgenstein's Lectures, Cambridge, 1930–1932: From the Notes of John King and
Desmond Lee.* Edited by Desmond Lee. Oxford: Blackwell, 1980.

*Wittgenstein's Lectures, Cambridge, 1932–1935: From the Notes of Alice Ambrose
and Margaret Macdonald.* Edited by Alice Ambrose. Oxford: Blackwell,
1979.

Wittgenstein's Lectures on the Foundations of Mathematics, Cambridge, 1939.
Edited by Cora Diamond. Ithaca, N.Y.: Cornell University Press, 1976;
Chicago: University of Chicago Press, 1989.

Zettel. Edited by G. E. M. Anscombe and G. H. von Wright. Translated by
    G. E. M. Anscombe. Oxford: Blackwell, 1967.

Wollheim, Richard. *Art and Its Objects: An Introduction to Aesthetics.* New
    York: Harper & Row, 1968.

    On Formalism and its Kinds. Barcelona: Fundació Antoni Tàpies, 1995.

    Painting as an Art. Princeton: Princeton University Press, 1987.

    The Thread of Life. Cambridge: Harvard University Press, 1984.

Wright, G. H. von. "The Troubled History of Part II of the *Investigations.*"
    Grazer Philosophische Studien 42 (1992): 181–92.

    Wittgenstein. Minneapolis: University of Minnesota Press, 1983.

Index

acceptance: of forms of life, 177; of
   language-games, 158, 235, 338,
   341; of the world, 79
aesthetic: differences, 345–48;
   idea, 29–30. *See also* judgment,
   critical or aesthetic
aesthetics, 3–4, 8–9, 11–12, 294,
   310 n, 317
agreement: about what we should
   say when, 12, 51; in form of life,
   200; in judgments, 16, 36, 185,
   198, 200, 202; in language, 12,
   51, 184–85
Affeldt, Steven G., 9, 17–18
Alberti, Leone Battista, 29
Aldrich, Virgil, 8
allegory, 11–12, 72–80, 85, 92, 94,
   97–98
analogy, 12, 25, 27, 37, 65, 79, 105,
   108, 110, 118–19, 136, 155, 294,
   316 n, 318, 336
animals: 13, 34, 81–82, 83 n,
   92, 96–97, 159, 163, 324;
   difference from humans, 216;
   picture-, 262; treatment of, 82,
   84, 87
Anscombe, Elizabeth, 100, 280 n,
   325 n, 344
Aristotle, 107, 162, 167 n, 326
arithmetic, 95, 217, 319, 330,
   336

art: interest in 25 n, 28–29,
   38; responses to, 25 n, 39,
   65, 327; works of, 8–9, 30 n.
   See also aesthetic; aesthetics; critic
   (of art)
aspect-blind, the: abilities of
   76–77, 205, 207, 210, 213, 219;
   community of, 207,
   220; possibility of, 186,
   205–6, 214
aspect-blindness: and language,
   15–16, 185, 213; and
   philosophical ideals, 205; and
   pictures, 66; condition of,
   67–68, 75, 186, 206–7, 219, 275;
   indifference to the appalling
   as, 84
aspect-dawning: experience
   of, 228, 241, 246, 256,
   258, 261, 264, 266; grammar
   of, 246, 247 n, 259; paradox
   of, 17, 230, 237, 239, 243,
   248 n, 265, 267; philosophical
   significance of, 17, 185,
   248, 250. *See also* aspect-
   perception; aspect-seeing
aspect-perception, 13, 19, 109,
   116–19, 130, 157, 228 n, 259,
   314, 316–17, 318 n, 320 n,
   324, 335–37. *See also*
   aspect-dawning; aspect-seeing

aspect-seeing: and discursive
consciousness, 171, 179; and
imagining, 130, 219; and
language 172, 213; and noticing
similarities, 63, 193; and our
relation to pictures, 184, 246;
subject to will, 208, 219; versus
continuous seeing 208, 210, 212,
241. *See also* aspect-dawning;
aspect-perception
aspect-seeing remarks: bearing on
aesthetics, 9, 12; importance to
understanding Wittgenstein, 4,
6 n, 7–9, 11, 14–16, 18, 23 n,
270; reception of, 8–11
aspects: and appearances, 31, 57;
and pictures, 17, 34, 65–66, 70,
76, 79, 109, 127, 130, 177, 184–85,
241 n, 258, 264, 275, 336; desire
for, 215–19; of organization, 196;
of things, 9, 11–12, 17, 49, 56,
70, 74, 178, 209, 266, 271–74,
277–78, 281–83
attachment to (our) words, 10, 13,
15, 56–57, 60–62, 84–88, 129,
133–35, 138, 172, 177, 184, 188,
193, 195, 208, 271
Augustine, 10, 103 n, 163, 211,
214–15, 218, 221, 279–81, 295,
316 n
Austin, J. L., 12, 40, 42–55, 60, 70,
85, 90, 123 n, 213, 285, 345–47
autism, 177
automata, 146, 219

Baker, Gordon, 166, 292 n, 293,
301, 303, 310, 315 n
Batkin, Norton, 12, 349 n
Baxandall, Michael, 29
Baz, Avner, 17, 123 n, 249–57,
260–62, 264–66, 276 n, 320 n,
321 n
Bearn, Gordon C. F., 3, 19, 327 n
Bedeutung, 41–42, 48, 330
behaviorism, 115, 117, 145, 147, 151
belief, 25 n, 43, 46, 121, 150,
152–53, 155–56, 288, 295

Bergson, Henri, 351–53
bewilderment, philosophical, 242,
256, 264–66, 308
body, the: 83, 88, 145 n, 154–60,
189 n, 320 n; and awareness, 156,
353; and gestures, 13, 88, 139,
320; and the soul, 66, 73, 145,
154, 156; internal states of, 133,
147, 155–57; wounded (*Elizabeth
Costello*), 83. *See also* meaning and
the body
brain, the: and the soul, 154; states
of, 146–51, 153
Budd, Malcolm, 61 n
builders, the (of *PI* §2), 204–5, 207,
210, 213–14

Capek, Karel, 304
causal explanations, 166, 258
Cavell, Stanley, 2, 8–10, 12–13,
28 n, 33 n, 36 n, 44, 52, 62,
63 n, 64 n, 65–66, 71–75, 80,
103 n, 115 n, 121 n, 123 n, 125,
126 n, 129, 130 n, 132 n, 134,
138, 145, 159, 165 n, 170 n,
199 n, 200–202, 212 n, 214 n,
215, 218 n, 227, 250, 273 n,
274 n, 275, 281 n, 283 n,
285, 286 n, 337, 342, 348–50
Cerbone, David R., 14–15
children: abilities of, 169,
177; behavior of, 146, 172;
development of, 168, 210–12,
217–18
Churchland, Paul M., 155 n, 156
Cioffi, Frank, 3, 18, 121 n
Clack, Brian, 292, 303–5
Coetzee, J. M., 13, 81–82, 83 n,
88–90
cognitive science 41 n, 166
Collingwood, R. G., 169 n, 175 n
color-blindness, 67, 204
Conant, James, 54 n, 55 n, 137 n
concentration camps, 88, 97
consciousness, 1, 18, 33 n, 77, 90,
127, 132, 144, 159, 272, 351;
discursive, 15, 162–63, 165–66,

171, 177, 179; in the face of
another, 145, 155
continuous seeing, 75, 174, 209–10,
212, 229, 241 n, 257, 261–62,
264–65
Crary, Alice, 83 n, 268–69, 283–84,
334 n
criteria: elicitation of 123 n, 234;
shared, 95, 240
critic (of art), 9, 37, 38 n, 39, 183

Darwin, Charles, 297, 312
Davidson, Arnold, 88
Davidson, Donald, 169 n
Day, William, 16, 113 n, 118 n,
127 n, 133 n
Dennett, Daniel C., 144 n, 145–46,
152, 158–59
depiction(s): fact-, 326; isomorphic,
324; non-geometric, 77; of
an object, 326; of molecular
structure, 153; of philosophical
emptiness, 281; of the human
interior, 156; seeing in, 328;
treating in terms of what they
depict, 265
depth: of human sacrifice, 303,
310; of the everyday, 120–21, 126;
psychological, 270, 285, 288
Descartes, René, 86, 135, 154
description: accompanying a
picture, 31, 44, 165, 171–72,
240; geometric, 76; hesitancy
over a, 229, 243, 346–47; of
one's past experience, 56,
108, 112, 115, 119, 123, 136,
210, 319, 322; of what is seen, 23,
27, 28 n, 63, 111 n, 113, 157, 223,
240, 341; philosophy as, 10, 59,
114 n, 274, 355
Dewey, John, 86
diagram(s), 326; chemical, 152–54;
in a geometrical proof, 315–16,
324; Müller-Lyer, 47; of general
form of proposition, 314–15, 318,
323, 333; truth table as, 332, 334

Diamond, Cora, 13, 55, 58, 90,
96–98, 137 n, 187 n, 334
double-cross, the, 209, 248 n, 275,
278
drawing (an object, figure, etc.), 24,
32–33, 38–39, 63, 106, 113, 127,
172, 222, 231 n, 239–43, 245–46,
247 n, 263, 275
dreams, as motivation for
skepticism, 50, 154
Drury, M. O'C., 10–11, 124, 128,
223, 296 n
dual-aspect figure, 230, 238, 243
duck-rabbit, the: 24, 26 n, 30, 32,
34, 116, 207, 222, 254, 262, 314,
323, 341, 343; as illustrating the
concept of aspect-seeing, 63,
66–68, 97, 207, 233, 236 n,
241 n, 254, 262; inability to
see the duck in, 66–68; report of
one's perception of, 26, 34, 128

effigy-burning, 294, 303
Eldridge, Richard 3 n, 15
eliminative materialism, 144,
155 n
Elizabeth Costello (Coetzee), 13, 81,
82 n, 83–84, 89
Ellman, Richard, 311, 312 n
Emerson, Ralph Waldo, 87, 213 n,
215 n, 307
empirical enquiry, 292, 294, 301–2,
310–12
empiricism, 19, 43, 46, 115, 117, 311
Engelmann, Paul, 322
epistemic fallacy, 308–9
essence: 14, 78, 165 n, 179; "is
expressed by grammar," 92–93,
134, 344; of a thing, 11, 70,
95, 163; of logic, 333; of the
Holocaust, 72–75, 88–90
experience, interest in one's, 71–72,
215–16, 218, 220–21, 224
expressiveness, human: 14–15,
71–72, 74–77, 79–80, 132;
fear of, 77

fire festival, Beltane, 292, 294–95, 303

Floyd, Juliet, 19, 137 n

Fodor, Jerry, 166

Føllesdaal, Dagfinn, 166

food factories, 81, 83–84, 88, 90, 97

form(s) of life, 7, 10, 59–60, 65, 96, 150, 176–77, 189–90, 197, 200, 202, 208, 212, 216, 264, 266, 272, 276–77. *See also* acceptance of forms of life; agreement in form of life; pattern(s) of life

formalism, 28–30, 316, 319 n, 336

Francis, Drew, 433

Frazer, James George, 120–22, 124, 128, 292 n, 294–95, 297, 303 n, 304 n, 306

Frege, Gottlob, 7, 40–43, 48–49, 54, 316, 328, 330–31

Freud, Sigmund, 209, 287 n, 297

Galavotti, M. C., 318 n

Genova, Judith, 62 n, 114 n, 317 n

Glock, Hans-Johann, 110 n, 228 n, 253 n, 292

Goethe, Johann Wolfgang von, 3, 135, 194

Goffman, Erving, 299–300

Goldfarb, Warren, 214 n

Gould, Timothy, 12, 113 n, 255 n, 273 n

grammar: and criteria, 95–96, 337; of aspect-seeing, 11, 17, 209–10; rules of, 259–60, 336

Hacker, Peter, 166, 293, 301, 303, 310, 323 n, 326 n, 357 n, 358 n

Hagberg, Garry L., 3, 13

hallucination, 48–49, 207, 209, 239, 340

Heidegger, Martin, 63 n, 78, 86, 88–91, 97, 231 n, 273

Hintikka, Jaakko, 316 n, 336 n

Huizinga, Johan, 303

Hume, David, 24, 103

Husserl, Edmund, 41 n, 42, 316 n

identity: 30 n, 300, 328, 330; logical, 328, 330; pictorial, 213, 238–39, 243, 261–62

illusion: 53, 282, 286; of meaning something, 284; perceptual, 47, 49–50, 53, 309

image(s) (*Vorstellung*): and noticing aspects, 54, 128; and the visual impression, 109–10, 128, 130; dream-, 207; mirror, 54; of an object, 44; retinal, 47–48; transactions with, 294–95; versus picture, 128–29, 132

imagination: 15, 81, 215, 327; in Kant, 29, 30 n, 31, 36; required for aspect-seeing, 69, 89, 111, 117, 172, 174, 219

imagining: 7, 68, 107, 143, 147, 149, 151, 185, 197, 210–11, 232, 259, 276; subject to the will, 208, 219

imponderable evidence, 127, 137, 177

inner, (the): experience, 33, 121, 123, 131, 135–36, 190, 231; life, 152–53; object or picture, 7, 12, 27–28, 103 n, 188, 192, 348; processes, 136–37, 175, 210. *See also* interior; inward thing

interior, 153, 155–56, 160–61. *See also* inner, (the); inward thing

internal relation: 14, 166, 195, 251, 260; in the dawning of an aspect, 111–12, 115, 117–19, 178, 184, 193, 199, 255

internalization of a linguistic symbol, 170

interpretation(s): kinds of, 40, 48, 73, 200, 283; of illustrations, pictures, etc., 23–26, 31, 192, 262; of the critic, 37; seeing as not, 54, 58, 174, 199; self-, 108, 109 n, 112, 118 n, 250–51

intrinsic properties, 105, 108

inward thing, 157. *See also* inner, (the); interior

Jastrow, Joseph, 24, 341–42, 344, 351, 354
Jolley, Kelly, 279 n
Joyce, James, 291, 307, 308 n, 311–12
judgment, critical or aesthetic, 9, 24, 25 n, 35–36, 37, 39, 76, 200–202, 345–46; logic of, 310
justification: 138, 271, 297; conceptual, 107, 173; demand for, 223; of primitive language-games, 158, 338, 348

Kandinski, Wassily, 311
Kant, Immanuel, 2, 24, 29–31, 35–37, 38 n, 51–52, 60. *See also* universal voice
Krebs, Victor J., 5 n, 14, 320 n
Kripke, Saul, 5, 166, 200
Kuhn, Thomas S., 54

language: and logic, 16, 187–88; differences and resemblances within, 50–52; hypothetical, 56–57; learning or growing into, 15–16, 131, 167, 208, 210–18; on holiday, 59–60; phenomenological, 57, 316 n; systematicity of, 95; Wittgenstein's conception of, 10, 211. *See also* agreement in language; language-game(s); ordinary language (philosophy); private language
language-game(s): 3, 27 n, 34, 66, 68–69, 72–74, 78, 92, 107, 112, 114, 129, 132, 134, 158, 160, 184–85, 189, 193, 207, 214, 217, 231 n, 232, 235, 259, 338, 342, 348; accepting the everyday, 27 n, 158, 235, 338, 342
Laugier, Sandra, 12, 85, 131 n
Leibniz's God, 333
Lessing, Gotthold Ephraim, 38 n
Lewis, C. S., 309
linguistic phenomenology, 12, 40, 51–52, 55, 58

linguistic symbols, 170–71
logic: 70, 86, 164–65, 187–89, 339; problems of, 339; surprises in, 333. *See also* language and logic; mathematics and logic
looking: 34, 38, 110, 221 n, 340; scientific way of, 122; versus seeing, 45, 58
Lyotard, Jean-François, 343

machine: 126; age of the, 90; and consciousness, 145–46
magic, 47, 96, 291–92, 295, 297
manifest form, 28–29
Margalit, Avishai, 301
Marion, Mathieu, 316 n
materialism/materialist(s): 14, 143–47, 151, 157, 161, 163, 179; eliminative, 155–56. *See also* mysterian(s)
mathematics: and aspect-perception, 314, 316–17, 318 n, 324, 335–36; and logic, 19, 314–19, 323, 328–37; and surprise, 315–16, 321, 327, 332, 336–37; examples in, 323, 331, 336; meaning in, 316, 329–30; necessity of, 315, 318, 321–22, 324
McDowell, John, 40, 49–50, 53–54
McGinn, Colin, 144
McGinn, Marie, 185 n
McGuinness, Brian F., 119 n, 318 n, 320 n
meaning: and the body, 83, 88, 129–34; and use, 15, 58–60, 69, 72–73, 85, 91–92, 94–95, 164, 176, 186, 189–93, 198, 200, 212–13, 234–35, 258–60, 272, 279–82, 338–39, 355; experiencing the, 7 n, 61, 63, 70–72, 85, 87, 128, 133–34, 166, 172, 176–77, 185–86, 192–95, 198, 212, 230 n, 280 n; pictorial, 37–39; picture theory of, 5, 163. *See also* Bedeutung
meaning-blindness, 14–16, 184, 186, 191–95, 197, 205 n, 219 n, 258

melody, 112–14, 177, 276
memory, 104, 108 n, 118 n, 129–30, 134, 327
Meno's paradox, 221
mental: categories, 146; defective(ness), 194, 197; state(s), 36 n, 146–47, 169, 195
Merleau-Ponty, Maurice, 14, 61, 131–33, 244 n
metaphor(ical), 30 n, 64–65, 72, 93, 105, 137, 152, 178, 184, 216–17, 259. *See also* secondary sense (of a word)
metaphysics: 12, 63, 69–70, 86; danger of, 338, 355; impulse to, 69
Minar, Edward, 15–16, 133 n
mind(s): 14–15, 74, 86, 106, 111, 122, 124, 135, 144–45, 155, 157, 185, 197; other, 8, 345; philosophy of, 14, 144–46; state of, 215, 223
miracle, seeing the world as a, 120–22, 137
modern(ity): 138; post-, 108
Monk, Ray, 2–3, 220
Moore, G. E., 302
moral: blindness, 97; imperative, 104 n, 116; perfectionism, 215 n; urgency (of Wittgenstein's text), 270, 288
Moran, Richard, 135
Mühlholzer, Felix, 315 n, 337 n
Mulhall, Stephen, 3, 8, 17, 62–66, 75–79, 110 n, 185 n, 205 n, 208–9, 212, 219 n, 227–32, 235–48, 273 n, 317 n, 357
Murdoch, Iris, 14, 101–2, 104–6, 109–12, 114–19
music: 25 n, 65, 111, 114, 176, 221, 224, 276, 311, 325; its importance to Wittgenstein, 10–11, 223–24. *See also* melody; understanding a theme in music
musical ear, lack of a, 67, 186, 205
mysterian(s), 14, 144–45. *See also* materialism/materialist(s)

mysterious, the, 271, 280 n
myth(ological): 64 n, 65, 73, 159, 259; of the Cave, 91; of the Given, 40, 49–50, 58, 60

Nagel, Thomas, 144
name(s): 7, 43, 70, 92–93, 186, 194, 196, 209, 211, 328, 330; proper, 43, 330; simple, 163–64
Narboux, Jean-Philippe, 316 n, 326 n, 337 n
narrative: 84, 109, 119, 195, 292, 313, 325; construction(ism), 103–5, 108; self, 103; thread, 106, 115, 118
natural reactions, 272, 276–77
natural history (of the human), 95, 98, 150, 218, 264, 281
neural activity, events, etc., 148, 151, 163, 174
Nietzsche, Friedrich, 3, 86, 89, 91, 216–19, 221, 327
nonsense, 18, 44, 55–56, 156, 222 n, 269, 273, 286, 325
number(s): 7, 95–96, 196, 279, 317–18, 328, 330, 333–34; Arabic notation for, 329; table of, 93–94; words, 328, 334

object(s): material, 45, 158, 338; of sight, 17, 23, 63, 71, 112, 131, 184–85, 188, 193, 231, 251, 254–56, 340
Ogden, C. K., 41–42, 52, 325 n, 330 n
ordinary language (philosophy), 40, 42, 45–46, 56, 66, 85, 91, 286, 335, 341–42
Orwell, George, 291, 312
overview (*Übersicht*): 18–19, 118, 119 n, 291–93, 295–99, 301–9, 312–13; appetite for, 298–99; heuristic or explanatory, 291, 293, 295–97, 301, 312; self-clarificatory, 291, 301–2, 309; synoptic, 293, 295, 296–301, 304, 306

pain (expression of; image of; picture of; etc.), 74, 86, 92, 129–31, 149, 156, 349

painting(s): act of, 37–39; and photographs, 24 n, 25 n, 33 n, 35; form in (or of), 28–31

past, the: re-thinking of, 102, 104 n, 110–11, 115–19; unfrozen view of, 102, 104–5, 109, 111, 115, 119

peace (*Ruhe*), philosophical, 18–19, 65, 69, 79, 165 n, 228, 283–84, 288, 302, 305–8, 326, 339, 342–44, 354–56

Peirce, Charles Sanders, 319–20, 335–36

perception: and projection, 105–6, 109, 111–12, 115; cognitivism about, 50; object of, 46–48; theories of, 40, 45, 47–48, 60. *See also* seeing; visual experience

perplexity, 293, 298

perspicuous: (over)view, 65, 118, 291, 296, 313; (re)presentation, 18, 67, 121, 124, 134, 183–85, 232, 311. *See also* overview

philosophy: Wittgenstein's conception of, 3, 9, 271, 285; empty voice of, 284–85

photograph(s). *See* paintings and photographs

physiognomy: 15, 71–72, 193, 260, 333, 335; of a word, 10, 71, 86, 133, 134 n, 187, 193. *See also* expressiveness, human; meaning

picture (*Bild*): 5–6, 17, 19, 24–28, 31–35, 65–66, 70–73, 76, 79, 84, 101–7, 116–19, 122, 127, 129–30, 132, 145 n, 152–56, 159–60, 163–64, 174–77, 184, 195, 205, 219, 222 n, 229–30, 233–34, 236–41, 243, 245–46, 247 n, 255, 258, 261–66, 275–76, 291, 294–95, 314–15, 318–19, 323–26, 328, 332, 336; -duck, 238, 245, 265; -face, 26, 239–40, 262, 324;

-object, 24, 238–39, 242, 245, 257–58, 262, 264–65; puzzle-, 27, 217, 258, 314–15, 317–18, 322, 328, 332, 336; -rabbit, 26, 34, 233, 238, 245, 255, 262, 264–65

Pippin, Robert, 178 n

Plato, 91, 93, 162, 326–27

private: experience, 126, 136; language, 3, 5, 75, 185, 348, 350; object, 111 n, 185, 188, 348, 351; rule(s), 192, 199, 201

proposition(s): 42, 55–57, 70, 123–27, 163–64, 188, 272, 280 n, 317–20, 325, 328, 330, 332–35; elementary, 318, 335; empirical 35 n, 126

propositional attitude(s), 165–66, 223

psychological states, 147–49, 151

psychology: 12, 24–25, 28, 61–62, 145–46, 148–49, 266, 354; folk, 156–57; Gestalt, 61, 110 n

Putnam, Hilary, 42, 43 n, 45, 47 n, 48, 50, 53–54

Quine, W. V., 43, 46, 86

realism, 44–45, 49, 51, 55, 85

reference. *See* Bedeutung

regarding-as, 32, 208, 229, 232, 243–45, 248, 257, 263,265, 321–22

Ramsey, F. P., 334

Rhees, Rush, 11 n, 16, 128 n, 187–92, 194, 205 n, 214 n, 215, 221 n, 223 n, 296 n, 303

Richards, I. A., 41, 52

Rorty, Richard, 105 n, 108 n, 166, 344

Rousseau, Jean-Jacques, 212 n

rule(s): 15, 54, 58–59, 68, 184, 198–201, 216, 223, 259–60; -following, 4, 18, 199, 259, 271. *See also* private rule(s)

Russell, Bertrand, 41–42, 44, 55, 57, 86, 316, 327–28, 334, 336, 339

Sass, Louis A., 3
Schulte, Joachim, 205 n, 219 n,
    357 n, 358 n
secondary sense (of a word), 61, 64,
    218, 258–59
seeing: and thinking, 61, 106, 174,
    204, 221 n, 233; genuine, 13–14,
    106–8; (in)direct, 44–45, 49,
    58. *See also* perception; visual
    experience
self-knowledge, 8–9, 13, 101,
    116, 221
sensation: 77, 116, 130–31, 147, 149,
    156, 162, 173, 278 n, 315, 347,
    349–53; expression of (the), 131,
    349; modified concept of, 173
sense-data, 45, 51, 56, 60, 185, 188
sensory awareness, 165, 168, 171–72,
    174, 175 n
Simmel, Georg, 310
Sinn, 41–42, 48–49, 52, 330
skepticism: 50, 52, 55, 75–77, 101–2,
    112, 114, 119, 147, 274 n, 288;
    Cartesian, 47; truth of, 75, 77
Smart, J. J. C., 146–54
Smith, Adam, 327
soul(s): 3, 14, 28 n, 38 n, 126, 128,
    132, 145, 152–56, 158–59, 161–62,
    198, 311; belief that others have,
    14, 74, 79, 143, 145, 152–53,
    155; best picture of, 66, 73,
    154–56
Stern, David, 55, 58, 60, 358
Strodtbeck, Fred, 299
symbolic representations (theory),
    163, 171
synoptic: sensibility, 296, 298;
    view, 298, 301, 306

technique, mastery of a, 15, 35 n,
    164, 175–76, 196, 217
Thoreau, Henry David, 77, 97–98,
    215 n
Tilghman, B. R., 61 n
Tolstoy, Leo, 306–7
Tomasello, Michael, 167–72

tone of voice, 33, 122, 195, 276
Travis, Charles, 49

uncanny, the, 132, 146, 209
understanding: a sentence, 176,
    224; a theme in music, 176
universal voice, 38 n, 200
universals, 93, 269, 271

visual experience, 23–27, 36, 105,
    109 n, 111 n, 113, 116–17, 135,
    172–74, 185. *See also* perception;
    seeing
visual impression, 12, 27–29, 31,
    109–11, 128, 130, 173, 255
voice: metaphysical, 281; tone of, 33,
    122, 195, 276; universal,
    38 n, 200. *See also* philosophy,
    empty voice of

Waismann, Friedrich, 56–57, 335
Whitehead, Alfred North, 329
Winch, Peter, 187 n, 308–9
Wisdom, John, 52, 354
Wittgenstein, Ludwig: *Blue & Brown
    Books,* 95, 179, 187–92, 194,
    205 n, 214 n, 241 n; *Big
    Typescript,* 318 n, 326, 331, 336;
    Collected Manuscripts, 316 n;
    Culture & Value, 2, 5, 59, 91–92,
    120–21, 124, 132–33, 217, 297,
    311, 339; *Last Writings in the
    Philosophy of Psychology,* 4, 56,
    126–28, 129 n, 131, 143, 152, 160,
    222 n; *Lectures & Conversations on
    Aesthetics & etc.,* 25, 132, 217, 294,
    346; *Notebooks,* 55, 317, 324, 331;
    On Certainty, 5, 183, 187–88, 321,
    339 n; *Philosophical Investigations*
    (characterizations of), 5–7,
    9–11, 12, 16–18, 28 n, 62, 69,
    85–86, 187–88, 220–24, 251–52,
    271–73, 283–88; *Philosophical
    Occasions,* 121–26, 132, 138, 284,
    292, 295, 297, 303, 311, 342,
    344; *Philosophical Remarks,* 55,

57, 318 n, 334; *Remarks on Colour*, 5, 204, 222 n, 311; *Remarks on the Foundations of Mathematics*, 5, 185, 315, 317, 318 n, 321, 331–32, 336; *Remarks on the Philosophy of Psychology*, 4, 59, 131, 139, 145, 151, 158–60, 186, 190, 193–98, 217, 219, 236–37, 244, 246; *Tractatus Logico-Philosophicus*, 5–6, 42, 59–60, 120, 137, 163–64, 235, 320, 325–26, 328–35, 343; *Wittgenstein and the Vienna Circle*, 56–57, 316, 318 n, 335; *Zettel*, 4, 156–57, 217, 342, 354
Wittgenstein's writing: method of, 2–3, 5–7, 10–11, 16, 18, 55, 68–71,

114 n, 120–21, 123 n, 125, 128, 134, 184, 191, 204, 212–13, 223, 249, 252, 259–60, 264, 268, 270–71, 287 n, 292–93, 297, 303, 325, 334; reception of, 1–4, 9; style of, 17, 220–22; therapeutic aims of, 11, 16–18, 60, 62, 66–67, 75, 223, 227, 237, 268–70, 283–88; "therapeutic" reading of, 17–18, 268–70, 283–88
Wollheim, Richard, 8, 28–29, 37–38, 61 n, 106 n
wonder, 122, 245, 266, 325–27
Wright, G. H. von, 252 n, 318 n, 323 n